Grateful Ned

The Life Story of
Edward Heriot Shenton

by

E. H. "Ned" Shenton

Foreword by

Amie Shenton McGraham

Komatik Press
Cambridge and St. John's

Grateful Ned
The Life Story of Edward Heriot Shenton

Published in the United States of America in 2018 by
Komatik Press
95 Jackson St.
Cambridge, MA. 02140

Book design by Rex Passion

ISBN: 978-0-9987113-4-8

Library of Congress Control Number:

For Amie McGraham,

My lovely daughter, who got me started on this mission back in 2004 and has done a great job of inspiring me and editing all of it.

Contents

Foreword

by Amie Shenton McGraham

My father is an explorer. For much of his life, he explored the secrets of the sea, as described in the first book he wrote, fittingly titled *Exploring the Ocean Depths*. His adventurous career in oceanography took our family from Boston to the gulf shores of Texas; then Miami, San Diego and finally, a return to the Maine island where he and my mother had first met.

I grew up on that island, attended the tiny three-room schoolhouse, joined the Campfire Girls and romped through the five acres of woods that was our backyard. Together, my father and I built a treehouse in the apple orchard behind the house.

We were the odd family from "away:" two intellectuals and their only child. My mother, a talented graphic artist, freelanced from home and my father, a marine scientist, had previously worked with Jacques Cousteau and traveled the globe. My parents divorced when I was eleven and I began a twenty-five year spiral into alcoholism--a life of half measures and wanderlust, unfulfilled careers and relationships. Sobriety has brought me on a long journey of self-exploration, much like the soul quest my father has written about in this memoir.

Childhood memories were hazy and entire decades blurred, so I asked my father to help me piece things together, to tell me his story. We decided it would be a team writing project. I bought us each a workbook on writing a family history, complete with prompts, exercises and sample timelines. We planned writing workshops during our upcoming vacation to Alaska to celebrate his seventy-fifth birthday.

But like most things, my father chose to do it his way and the memoir workbook grew dusty on the shelf. "I decided to start on my own," he writes. "I chose to tell my tale on the ubiquitous yellow legal pad." Dozens of legal pads later, he painstakingly transcribed his near-illegible penmanship, writing what would become his third book.

His life is an endless adventure from the depths of the sea to the vast world beyond. He's explored the nation, piloting our family across the country in our 1957 Mercedes Benz, and he's seen the world through the lens of the windshield of a Greyhound bus. He's traveled on ships and trains and airplanes to Europe and Scotland, South Africa and South America, Mexico and most recently, on the Trans-Canadian railway through each of that country's provinces.

Yet, as I read his story, I find that in his perpetual pursuit to live a unique life, we are one. Similar passions flow through our veins like the blood that links us as father and daughter. We share a desire for travel and road trips. A mutual delight in telling stories. A passion for writing. An insatiable thirst for reading. The conscious choice to take the road less traveled.

And even now, well into his eighties and living contentedly on an island off the coast of Maine, through its brutal nine-month winters and long summer days filled with sailing and ice cream sundaes, my father continues to explore. As he delves further into his past, he enters a new world of self-discovery, sharing it with us through the portal of this book. Today, his business cards brand him "EXPLOR-ER." His sight may grow dim, and his energy level wane, but my father will never stop exploring.

And for this, I am grateful.

Preface

I have a story to tell. It is a story of my growing up in the1930s and 1940s as an only child in rural Pennsylvania with parents who were both artists and writers. We lived in the country on a rented farm, an apartment house, and finally in our own farm, Sugarbridge. My friends lived in the town several miles away where I went to school. I learned to entertain myself around the farm's eighty acres with lots of animals, a dog and cat. As an only child I was never a lonely kid. Later on I went away to boarding school. My parents didn't expect me to follow their writer/artist careers. By the time I had gone away to college I was on my way to following exciting scientific opportunities. This is that story with its many twists and unexpected turns, living in many different places, and lots of interesting jobs. Over the course of nearly sixty years I've had dozens of jobs ranging from printer's apprentice, college professor, ice core driller, senior engineer, and marine scientist. Married thrice with an extended family of five children, I've lived in coastal locations throughout the nation. During these years I managed to travel to, visit, or pass through some thirty countries. I was inspired years ago to tell my story by my daughter, Amie, also an only child, who wanted to know more about her family. So let me begin.

Prelude

Beginnings
A Little Bit about the Family

My birth certificate says that I was born on July 7, 1932. My mother always said, it was a mistake, "You were born on July fifth, I mean, I should know," she said to me years later, "It was a Saturday and they just didn't record it until Monday." This has never really bothered me; what's wrong with having two birthdays?

My father Ed changed Edward Shenton Jr. and inserted Heriot in pencil.

But recently I went to a perpetual calendar, now available on the Internet, just to see if this tale was true. July fifth 1932 fell on a Tuesday. So much for that theory. I still celebrate the fifth in spite of my driver's license saying the seventh. Furthermore, my birth certificate says Edward Shenton Jr. and then someone has crossed out the "Jr." and written in Heriot in pencil. It's actually my father's writing. Things certainly appeared to be informal in 1932. Heriot is my middle name.

Heriot was also my mother's middle name and a family name that began as Heryt in Scotland around 1214. Later, George Heriot had founded a boys' preparatory school in Edinburgh in 1623 which was called Heriot's Hospital; it still exists as a primary and secondary school for boys and girls. His descendant, Roger Heriot, landed in Charleston, South Carolina in 1787. His brother, George Heriot, my great, great, great uncle, became the Postmaster General of Canada and in 1807 wrote and published *Heriot's Travels Through the Canadas*, with beautiful hand colored drawings that he made. (I have a copy presented to my mother in 1905 by her grandfather,

2

Thomas Adiel Sherwood). George Heriot died in Charleston in 1861. The other side of my mother's family was that of Sherwood. The first of the Sherwoods, Thomas, 48, and his wife, 47, and four children left Ipswich, England in April 21st of 1634 on the ship Francis with 76 passengers for Boston. A year later they moved to Wethersfield, Connecticut. The family had at one time a small stake in Sherwood's Forest. I have a beautiful nail-carved chest from the 16th century brought over by the Sherwood family. Adiel Sherwood, a descendant of Thomas, wound up in Milledgeville, Georgia, where in 1824 he married Emma Heriot from Charleston, South Carolina. They and five children eventually migrated to St. Louis, Missouri.

My mother, Barbara Heriot Webster, was born in Webster Groves about ten miles west of St. Louis, on April 5, 1900. She grew up in a large home, named "Oakwood," with some amount of land, buildings, and numerous servants as was the custom. At this time the town was barely a crossroad with a population of 394 and quite rural. Actually when I looked it up I found the town was first settled in 1804 and incorporated in 1896. According to this article it was named for Daniel Webster, a distant relative according to letters written by my grandfather, George B. Webster. Webster Groves is now a town with a population of 23,000. Barbara went to a private school called Mary Institute in St. Louis from 1908 until her graduation in 1918. I have very little information about her childhood except for two unfinished memoirs written in the last years of her life. She also reflects years later on her memories of the wonderful kitchen there with all its smells of food.

My mother, Barbara, age three, her mother Pansy Sherwood Webster, and her brother John, age one.

3

In *A St. Louis Childhood* she relates her memory of her mother telling her that she was a premature baby. Pansy Webster relates, "I stepped off the trolley too soon. The next day you were born… you were a seven-month child with no finger nails and no eyelashes."

She had a brother, John, two years younger. In 1918, Barbara came east to attend Wellesley College and became a member of the class of 1922. Already attending the college was Gladys Taber, class of 1920, later to become a well-known author of books and magazine columns on country life and dogs and a very good lifetime friend of my mother. Years later she and Barbara met through their publisher, both writing books, and articles about country life. They had never met at Wellesley.

In 1920 Barbara decided she wanted to be an artist and left Wellesley and transferred to the Pennsylvania Academy of Fine Arts in Philadelphia. Here she studied to be a painter and in 1923 won two Cresson European Traveling Scholarships which paid for her to study and travel in Europe. Her passport photograph shows a young girl of twenty-three off to paint and draw at the Kunstgewerbeschule in Vienna, an arts and crafts school. It was here that she met and fell in love with a charming Viennese gentleman named Hans Hatwagner. I'll always remember my surprise years later while she and I were driving from our home in West Chester, Pennsylvania to obtain our passports – I was twenty-one – when she said in a nonchalant way, "I guess I should tell you, since it will probably come up, I've been married before." She and Hans had been married while she was in Vienna.

I guess there was no reason for her to have mentioned it before, and, in fact we even visited Hans later that summer. The marriage was short lived as her father interceded and had an annulment arranged. She was still quite young, impetuous, and easily persuaded. In many ways she retained those qualities for most of her life – a kind of a youthful attractiveness. She returned to the Academy and continued painting and looking for a job. She had met my father, Ed Shenton, at the Academy before going to Europe. Now, in 1927, he was an editor at Macrae-Smith Co.

I never knew my grandfather, George Barry Webster, my mother's father. He died in 1933 shortly after I was born. There are ample records in the form of letters from him to my mother, grandmother, and Uncle John toward the end of his life when he had moved to Los Angeles. My grandmother, Pansy Mary Sherwood, was born in 1875, one of seven children; Adiel, Emma Catherine, Brella, Henry Young, Thomas Andrew, and Roderick McKenzie. Her parents were Thomas Adiel and Mary Ellen Young Sherwood of Long Beach, California. Judge Sherwood had been Chief Justice of the Missouri Supreme Court for thirty years. Pansy had spent most of her time in St. Louis at the family home there in Webster Groves. I gathered from letters that she and my grandfather must have been separated but not divorced. She moved to Philadelphia while George had relocated his practice of law in Los Angeles.

Pansy lived with her son, John, and his wife Georgia Mae inPhiladelphia, an old, narrow row house on an equally narrow street. I remember Uncle John as a quiet, soft spoken man who was tall and slender, always with a slight smile. John was a sports reporter for the *Philadelphia Inquirer* and worked nights so I rarely saw him when I would visit. Aunt Mae was a very warm, vivacious woman with a memorable broad smile. I remembered her during World Wa II where she was a Sargent in the WACs (Women's Army Corps) where she worked as a reporter. She gave me an autographed copy of *The Sad Sack* by Sgt. George Baker who wrote and drew the famous cartoons about army life. Somewhere I have a picture of her uniform. John and Mae had a daughter, Dorothy, who I believe may have been adopted. She and her husband Paul Schirmer (recently deceased in 2004) had a son, Billy, whom I never tracked down.

My earliest memory of my grandmother, "Gigi," which is what I called her, was of a wispy, granny with glasses and long hair done up in a knot. standing all of five foot two. Uncle John called her "Muddy" or "Mutty" as she spoke German. I have pictures of her toting a rifle. She also left my father and me a .22 caliber, long barrel target pistol. I understood she was a good shot.

Other early memories of Gigi were when she took me for several days to Stone Harbor, New Jersey, where we stayed in a hotel going to the beach every day. She was about 65 but as it is with young folks my memory of her was that she was an aged, shriveled little woman. As time went on she came briefly to live with my mother but they had many arguments and finally my mother put her in a nursing home in West Chester where she threw bed pans at nurses, smoked against all regulations, finally died at 97. I recall her best moment was when she was still living with John and Mae in their Bucks county farm house. They had remodeled an old farm house similar in ways to the one I was to grow up outside of Doylestown. One of its fascinating features was a spiral staircase to the second floor. The stairs were extremely narrow, like wedges of cheese and at the bottom there was a door. Both John and Mae were at work for the day when Gigi, then about 88 years old, fell head first down winding stairway. There she was stuck, head wedged between the last step and the closed door. Here she stayed badly bleeding for eight hours, upside down. As the story goes she passed out for a while, then regaining consciousness after several hours managed to push herself back up. When she was found by John she was perfectly OK; no bones broken. Tough lady. She was by all rights, tough as nails. Women from the "west" were tough. My mother, Barbara Webster, writes in her book, *Color of the Country*, in the last chapter: "for I'll live no doubt, like all of my family, to an outrageously advanced old age." Unfortunately she didn't.

On the other side of the family, my great-grandfather, H.A. Shenton, was born at Burton-on-Trent, England in 1844 and, at age eight, was brought to America by his uncle, Frank. I found one reference that records showed that he was adopted. In 1862 at age seventeen, he enlisted with Company C, 128th Pennsylvania Regiment,

The Shenton family in Pottstown, Pennsylvania including my father Ed, his brother Don, and my Aunt Betty.

Union Army, was later wounded that year at Antietam, taken prisoner at Cancellorsville in 1863, and finally escaped during the retreat of the Army of the Potomac. Following the Civil War, he learned the trade of marble cutting and sculpturing and in 1872 moved to Pottstown to start a stone cutting business. In 1877 he entered the National Guard and eventually became a Lieutenant Colonel in 1894. In 1898 he served in the Spanish-American War. Col. Shenton lived until he was fifty-nine. His children were Harry E., my grandfather born 1873, Emma, William, George C., Charley A., Albert H., Elsie Marguerite, and Thomas. My grandfather, Harry E, married Jeanette Benner Thomas on November 7, 1894 in Pottstown, Pennsylvania.

My father was born Harry Edward Shenton, Jr. in Pottstown on November 29, 1895. At age fourteen he dropped the Harry, a name he disliked and became just plain Edward, with no middle name. His younger brother, Donald was born in 1897.

I never knew Uncle Don but I have several pictures of him in his World War I Army uniform when he and my father had joined the 103rd Engineers, 28th Division of the American Expeditionary Force (AEF) in 1917. Donald was tragically killed in 1919, nine days after the armistice by a land mine he and four other army bomb squad members were trying to disarm. Aunt Betty, whose full name was Rose Elizabeth, died in 1939 when I was seven. She had one son, Jack Sixsmith, whom I saw occasionally in my youth.

Jack was well over six feet tall with big thick glasses. During World War II, Jack went to MIT on a program called the "V12." an accelerated technical training program. The last I ever saw of Jack was when he arrived in uniform at our farm in 1946 to claim my grandmother's 1939 Ford coupe she had left to him. Jack went on to work as an engineer for Du Pont in Wilmington, Delaware and I lost track of him. Recently I learned he had retired to Florida where he died in 2002 before I could find him.

My father's family moved from Pottstown to nearby Coatesville, Pennsylvania in 1896 according to a town census book of 1897. This account showed that Harry E. Shenton, his wife Jeannette, and my father resided at Chestnut St. Presumably Don and Betty weren't born yet. My grandfather was listed as a stone cutter at the Shenton Marble Works which he had started in 1896. During my father's life he never mentioned anything about stone cutting or what his father did. Other aunts and uncles of his remained in Pottstown.

Shortly after Coatesville, the family moved to West Philadelphia. In the 1920 census, Harry is now listed as the President of the Water Meter Co. At about age fifteen, Ed contracted rheumatic fever which kept him out of school and at home for nearly two years. Daily his father carried him out to a chair on the sun porch where he spent his time reading many books. His favorite subjects were French and English medieval battles with knights in armor and costume. Then later his other love was fast racing cars. Here he began to seriously teach himself to draw and to write. There are lots of drawings from this period among his collections.

When he was able to return to school he entered West Philadelphia High for Boys in 1912, which had opened in November. It was also the first year of the school's literary magazine. *The Western.* An article of Ed's appeared in Volume 1 and the following year he became the magazine's editor. When he graduated in 1916, he was class president, second highest ranking student, class poet, and coxswain on the eight-oared crew of West Philly. That was the year they beat the Princeton Freshmen team. At this time he was tewnty years old, two years behind his classmates and graduating a year after his younger brother, Don. The interesting thing about this is that he never mentioned anything of these accomplishments to me. It was some years after his death that I pieced together all these facts from copies of *The Western* that I discovered among his belongings. It made me feel tremendously proud but at the same time a bit sad he never told me of his school days when I was growing up.

But before my father met my mother, he had a brief first marriage to Louise Caldwell also an art student at the Academy of Fine Arts. I don't know the date of his marriage, but she appears on his passport when they traveled to Europe in 1922. The only person I was able to find who ever knew her was a fellow student at the Academy, Evelyn Spence, who told me in 1979 that my father's marriage to Louise had not been a happy one. He wrote a long poem dedicated to Louise called "Castles in Spain." After all this time I doubt if I'll ever know more unless perhaps there's references in some of his novels or short stories that I've missed. I do remember Evelyn Spence, who helped put together the memorial art show for my parents in 1979, telling of her recollection of Louise. Evelyn was also a student at the Academy. One day at lunch Ed had asked Barbara Webster, also a student, if he could share part of her sandwich. Louise, then his wife, overhearing this, indignantly spoke up asking what was wrong with the lunch she had already made for him? Was he looking for sympathy or a way out? Ed and Barbara went their separate ways to study in Europe. I describe more about Barbara and her studies in Vienna in the booklet, *Barbara Webster Shenton* (2013).

There is one final Louise Caldwell fact I uncovered a few years ago. In looking for drawings and books by my father I came across an internet article for a Christmas card by Edward Shenton held by a Massachusetts book dealer for $50. I bought it sight unseen. It was a card designed and drawn by my father from him and Louise showing them on a rocking horse with both their names, but no date.

In the late 1920s, Ed and Barbara met again as Barbara was looking for work on her return from Europe. She dropped in at Macrae-Smith on Ludlow Street in Philadelphia where Ed was an editor. His second novel, *The Lean Twilight* (1928), needed a book jacket illustration, so my mother was given the job. It was a scene of sailboats, the central theme of the story. I only noticed several years ago, long after they had both passed away, that she had illustrated the jacket. There in the lower right hand corner were the small initials BW. They were married on March 30, 1930. Her first book, *Nick, Nack, Nob, and Nibble*, which she wrote and illustrated, was published by Macrae-Smith that same year. This was the beginning of the writer/illustrator team that lasted nearly fifty years.

Chapter One

Waynesboro to Westtown
1932 –1940

I was born in a hospital in Philadelphia. Up until this time my parents had been living in Beachwood on the northern coast of New Jersey. Now, shortly after I was born they moved to a very small house near Paoli, Pennsylvania. The house was part of an estate called "Waynesboro" and was the gatehouse to the farm that originally had belonged to General "Mad" Anthony Wayne of the Revolutionary War. Wayne had fought at Valley Forge under Washington and had earned the name "Mad" for his fiery temper.

The Great Depression held the country in its grip. Franklin Roosevelt was running for the first time for the Democrats against Herbert Hoover, and would soon be elected President. There were riots in Dearborn, Michigan instigated by the Communist Party or "Reds." Amelia Earhart became the first woman to fly across the Atlantic Ocean in thirteen hours, half the time it took Charles Lindberg, with only twenty dollars and a bottle of tomato juice. Lindberg Jr, nineteen months old, was kidnapped. And a Russian fanatic assassinated the President of France. The Emperor Hirohito of Japan, at his thirty-first birthday party, was nearly killed by a Korean radical, while the Japanese army marched into Manchuria without declaring war. What time to be born!

My parents rented the gate house to the "Mad" Anthony Wayne estate in Paoli, Pennsylvania in 1932.

We lived in this tiny house for my first two years. There are many pictures from this period, some of me naked sunning in a crib in the back yard or being held by my mother at age six months.

Of course, I don't remember this. But I do remember riding on a sled sitting upright between my father's legs as we coasted down a hill across the road from the house. In my memory I see the hill as fairly steep. Years later when I went past that house and hill it was only a gentle slope at best.

My father at this point had begun concentrating on his drawing for *Scribner's Magazine* where he produced thirty or forty small drawings, as well as the magazine cover, each month. At the same time he had been writing several articles and still working several days a week as Vice President of Macrae-Smith Publishing Company in Philadelphia. Sometime in 1934-35, we moved from the Waynesboro estate to another rented house, this one was called Bonticu Farm and was located on Yellow Springs Road about three miles north of Paoli. The area was in what was known as the Great Valley, not far from Valley Forge where General Washington had his headquarters during the Revolution. I was not aware of the meaning or significance of the name Bonticu until I received an email from an old childhood chum, Craig Ten-Broeck. He mentions the name may have been from a ship but then says the story is probably not true. I have memories of Craig as well as pictures when we were three or four of us sitting on our side porch. I haven't seen him since then but his story is posted under Bonticu Farm. It was his father who built the house at Bonticu Farm in 1920. Maybe when I go on my final "walk about" I'll visit him if he's still with us.

Patch, a Sealyham terrier, and me at age five at Bonticu.

11

It was solid farm house built of stone with a barn and outbuildings at the end of a long dirt lane, as only the main roads were paved in those parts. Here on the farm I had my constant companion, "Patch," a small Sealyham terrier.

I never recall missing or regretting not having a brother or sister. I learned early on to entertain myself. The tenant farmer who lived down the lane and worked the fields around us would let me sit on his lap and "try" to steer while he drove the enormous iron wheeled Fordson tractor. It was long before the days of power steering and of course at age four, I couldn't begin to really hold the wheel. It may have been the beginning of love of driving and vehicles. The big iron cleats on the wheels made a horrible grating noise over rock ledges as we slowly lumbered on toward the fields.

One fleeting memory I have, was my father playing songs for me with his flute. The only one I remember is "*Bye-bye Blackbird*," and I don't know whatever happened to the flute. I have a vague idea that he was in a stripped jersey and had on black cap. And then there was another musical instrument that I have no memory of but there is a photo of me holding an accordion in my lap. I would guess dad played that too.

One of my pleasant memories from the farm was walking by myself down the lane to visit Mrs. Grundy, the farmer's wife, who often served a mid-morning tea and cookies. I vaguely recall the kitchen and a warm wood cookstove with background music from a radio. She was a large, jolly woman always in a bright colored house dress. She would dance with me to the music or that's what my mother wrote in her wonderfully biographic book *The Color of the Country* in which she described in detail my visits. I do remember the kitchen but not the dancing or Mrs. Grundy's fat bare arms. My mother says in the book that I didn't tell her of these visits until some years later. I was good at keeping secrets to myself as we shall see in later days.

In that book I was called "T" and all the names were fictionalized as my mother hadn't quite gotten ready to write in the open so to speak. Although I was Edward at birth, my mother used "Toby" for my nickname. Toby I guess had been one of her favorite names. It may have been her Anglophile leaning. My name for her was "Mimi," it went along with "Gigi," which what I called my grandmother. I remained "Toby" until I was eight when I objected to the name sounding too young for me. So I chose Ned since it was different from my father who was Ed.

The farm house at Bonticu in my memory seemed quite old although it really wasn't. The construction was of fieldstone with stucco over it as was the custom in that part of Pennsylvania. There was an entrance on the west side with a porch that we used as well as one on the rear porch.

12

We moved to Bonticu Farm in 1935. That's me in the snowsuit.

The front also had what may have been a formal entrance at one time, with trees or bushes and a walk. We entered into the kitchen; behind it was a room my father used as his studio. I well remember one winter about 1937, Bob Murphy, a good friend and a senior editor for the *Saturday Evening Post*, needed my father to draw a scene for a fox hunting short story, titled "Gone Away," he had written for the magazine.

In it there was to be a section of post and rail fence. It was a bitterly cold winter and dad wasn't feeling like sitting outside to draw it. To get it just right he went out and found some fence rails and posts and set the whole works up on the back porch where he could look out at it from inside and stay warm. He had usually worked from photos or memory, but this was different. The drawing became a two-page spread and the fence and the running fox on one foot looked convincingly real. The original drawing later became a cherished hanging piece in our house and until some twenty years later it disappeared.

At Bonticu there was a living room and across the hall a dining room. All I can recall about the living room is that here one Christmas my parents had the proverbial struggle with setting up my first electric train set. Neither of them were good at mechanical or electrical things and I believe they had to call for help from the local store owner where they had bought it. As I remember the story the salesman or maybe the owner came out to our house to help on Christmas Eve. This was, happily, my introduction to trains and I was of course overjoyed and never heard the story of whatever problem it was until years later. My room was above the kitchen, gotten to by a back stairway. It was here that my father or mother would tell me the wonderfully contrived bedtime stories. The most memorable of these was a character of my father's making called Johnny Brown Bear.

Dad built a section of fence on the back porch as a model. The drawing was for Saturday Evening Post.

Out back of the house there was a grape arbor which during the summer supported a thick growth of vines. Here also nicely entwined would appear a large black snake perhaps six feet in length who sunned himself each afternoon. My father became fascinated by the snake and in later years I remember him holding smaller snakes so they would coil gently around his bare arm. I think this closeness helped him to draw snakes that populated his book illustrations over the years. I recall the several in *The Yearling* and *Cross Creek*. The fields back of the house were mowed, probably for hay as this was a working farm. They sloped gently up to some woods. My parents would ski down this slope in winter and in the summer we would all three walk to the woods where an old stony road wound down into a valley. I never knew where this road went. It always seemed to be getting dark at the point we neared an abandoned house and had to turn back. A trail that ran along the ridge was called the "Horseshoe Trail" and extended for 140 miles. I always wanted to go back there to see if this memory was really so. Of course, it's probably all built into tract homes now.

In these years before regular school I went to a kindergarten called the Leopard School which I recall was in Berwyn. I started when I was four years old. Somewhere there's a picture of me and some classmates outside at a table, perhaps at milk and cookies time. I remember very little else. Two of the girls there that I liked were named "A" and "B" and many years later I met them again at a dancing class at the Merion Cricket Club on the "Mainline." They were taller than me and I had no interest in them or even in saying hello. The name "Mainline" had become synonymous with social region west of Philadelphia, home to a wealthy set. It had originally referred to the Pennsylvania Railroad line that ran as far as to Paoli. The train I was to ride on in later years was the "Paoli Local."

During these early years at Bonticu, sometime when I was four or five, I managed to fall off my tricycle and break my left wrist. It was no big event, except that while the break was setting in a cast. About two weeks later I succeeded in breaking it a second time. The attending doctor must have noted that the bone was all wrong in that it protruded (and still does) but left it this way and just told me to exercise it; and I did. This was the time I was learning to write and I suddenly became left handed at writing and drawing, but right handed at everything else. Many years later I switched back to being right handed in writing. My other accident at Bonticu happened one day as I was playing with some large cast iron gears I had found out behind the barn. They were extremely heavy but I tried to move them to build some neat, new machine and strained myself. This resulted in a hernia which was a nuisance and meant I had to wear a truss. This was a source of some embarrassment for me for a number of years. I finally had it repaired in the mid '80s and again in 1999. This was the beginning of my accident-prone days.

As an only child in the country I had few playmates nearby and had to amuse myself around the farm. I did have several friends a bit further away. One lived up a dirt road through the fields about a half mile away, Craig TenBroeck. He and another friend, Geordy Di Coursey were my pals at the time and often they came over to visit. Also at this time I had a really close friend, Stacy Wood, who lived ten miles away in Malvern, about ten miles away. We had been "chums" since we were three.

My "chum" Stacy Wood and me with our Teddy bears on the Jersey shore about 1936.

His full name was Stacy Bud Campion Wood Jr. Although I really don't remember doing anything with him before age six or seven, Stacy is the only one of the early friends who came back into my life later on although, through him I did have contact with Craig by e-mail in 2006.

My grandmother, Pansy whom I called "Gigi."

Part of each summer was spent with my maternal grandmother, "Gigi," Pansy Sherwood Webster. She would take me for a week or so to the "shore." We went to Stone Harbor, New Jersey near Avalon where we had a hotel room.

At age three or four I became able to survive in the surf although occasionally got banged around by a wave. I didn't really learn to swim until I was seven or eight.

I also spent time with my father's parents, Pop and Granny Shenton who had a summer cottage in Ocean Grove, New Jersey. Most of my memories of Ocean Grove come later when I was entering my teens. I knew him as Pop which I guess was what my father called him but I really have few if any distinct memories of him; only the pictures in my father's family album. Pop was portly, to use a nineteenth century term, and bald with fringes of hair on the side.

He had a prominent belly like many of his contemporaries. When I stayed for several weeks in the summer with them my several memories are of sitting with Pop and Granny at the table covered with oil cloth by the kitchen window for meals. On Sundays it was going to church in the enormous outdoor tented amphitheater that seated thousands for several hours. This experience neither excited me nor turned me off and I don't suppose I went that many times. There was some connection here with the very popular events called Chatauquas that started as a part of the Methodist church. Members of the family, that is, Thomases, Taylors, and Shentons had some connection with Chatauqua, New York. But the thing I remember most about Pop was on Saturday evenings he would invite me to ride with him in his 1939 Ford coupe, black of course, as we sedately drove over the bridge to Asbury Park to a special parking lot for people from Ocean Grove to leave their cars. Ocean Grove was founded as a religious community so cars were banned all day on Sunday. Actually it was quite nice because we could walk anywhere without looking out for cars and there was no noise. Perhaps, it was a glimpse of the city of the future. The streets of Ocean Grove became totally empty and quiet and everyone walked to church.

"Pop" Shenton and Granny, Ocean Grove, about 1937.

While on the subject of Harry E. Shenton, my grandfather, several other things should be included. While he was listed as a stonecutter, my father called him an inventor. As the story goes he was working on the invention or perfection of the air brake but of course this device was, in fact, invented by George Westinghouse around 1869, several years before my grandfather was born. I've always wanted to know if there was any truth to the story. The other story my father loved to tell was that my grandfather was a good craftsman and at some time had set out to build a bench for my grandmother for the front porch. He spent considerable time and made a beautiful bench in his work shop in the cellar only to realize to his dismay that it was too large to go out through the stairway. My father laughed and said,"

I wish you could have seen the look on his face at that moment, he almost had an apoplectic fit."

My grandfather had a series of strokes or as they were called "shocks" in the summer of 1939 while he was at the Ocean Grove cottage. My mother and I joined my father who had been with him for a week or so. I remember going upstairs in the cottage where it was hot and stuffy and seeing Pop inside a plastic oxygen tent looking grey and ashen and almost dead. It was the first time I had seen someone that close to death. I think he died the next day. I would hardly say that I had known my grandfather very well. Just these few summer memories until I was seven. My grandfather never showed any affection like holding me or hugging me, but maybe that's the way people were then. Of course, now I wish I knew more about him and especially his father, Colonel Shenton, who had come directly from Wales.

Granny Shenton went on living at the shore and I visited every summer for a week or two. She was a small, cheery woman with eyes that always twinkled. In keeping with the times she wore lots of rouge on her otherwise pale cheeks. She was, I would say, the ultimate granny. And while she only lived blocks from the ocean she never took me swimming as did my other grandmother had. At best we went for a walk on the boardwalk.

Sometime around 1937 or 1938 my family began going to a lake in the mountains near Laporte in northeastern Pennsylvania. Looking at a map I see Lake Mokoma and near it Lake View Rd. not far from Route 220. We would drive through coal mining towns with coal blackened rundown houses and names like Tamaqua somewhere near Wilkes-Barre and finally through Eagles Mere. Tamaqua is known as the gateway to the Poconos and was the third town in the country with electricity in 1885. The first was Mt. Carmel, Pennsylvania in 1883.

Our rented cottage overlooked Lake Mokoma. I think we heard about this spot through Bob Murphy our friend and *Saturday Evening Post* editor. He and his wife Isabel had come here earlier and had the next cottage. I vaguely remember both our families sitting in the back of our two houses out of sight of the road sun bathing in the nude. As I learned later my mother and her women friends were great fans of nude sun bathing. I learned much later in 2010 from his son, Shane Murphy, that Isabel had died of leukemia and Bob had remarried. The lake had a few houses right on the water and many boat houses. I met a young man or more likely an older boy, who had a motor boat and would take us riding in his beautiful wooden Chris Craft on the lake. His name was Jim and I have a picture of him with us at a place called the Haystacks which had a series of waterfalls flowing through from small pools, I would guess it was glacial in origin. You can see I'm enjoying the cold spring water in the picture.

And now we come to my first boat. During the summer of 1938 at Laporte my father bought a kayak from a mail order ad in a magazine. The boat which was about twelve feet long and was made by the Meade Glider Company was in kit form using aircraft construction methods of light aluminum frames and wood stringers about 3/4"by 3/4". Dad set up the building shop on the front porch of our cottage. The kayak had a plywood sole and wood frame coaming and the whole framework was covered in light fabric just like a glider. I helped but I'm not sure just how much at the age of six. The fabric was doped to seal and tighten the skin and then we painted it a bright green and white. My father named it the *Fast Frog* for obvious reasons. I have lots of pictures of it at Sugarbridge. I kept it for many years and finally sold it while I was living in Annapolis on Market Street around 1968.

So at the age of six I was set on my course of boats and the sea. You see, my father had grown up around the ocean and had sailed along the Jersey coast as a youth. But I guess he was always too busy or didn't have the money to own a boat. He wanted me to have this experience and got me started early. I found a photo probably taken around 1930 of a cabin cruiser and of my mother standing in the forward hatch. I guess this was in Beachwood, New Jersey. My dad never mentioned it.

Petey Edmiston and me in the kayak dad built for me, 1943.

Actually, my first boating experience occurred at about age four when we rented a row boat from a place by the New Jersey marshes probably around Secaucus. That afternoon my dad made a makeshift sail out of a beach blanket supported by an oar and we ran along before the wind winding through the tall marsh grass and maze of channels.

We returned to our Laporte summer lake retreat for several years until the war began and gas rationing stopped us all from driving anywhere. Driving had been one of our evening entertainments in those days before television became the all-powerful magnet. We would drive the back roads, which were still mostly dirt, at dusk looking for deer or other wildlife in this mountainous terrain of northeastern Pennsylvania. One late afternoon my dog, Patch, had a run in with some of this wildlife in the form of a porcupine; unfortunately he tried to bite it. The inside of his mouth was full of barbed quills and he was clearly in agony. After some unsuccessful attempts to remove the quills my father decided to find a veterinarian. Thus we raced over the same dirt roads to Eagles Mere, maybe thirty miles away. I was terrified at my father's high speed driving and that somehow we wouldn't make it in time. Thankfully, Patch was fine after the vet expertly pulled the quills out; Patch lived for several years more.

Sometime in 1938 my parents decided to leave Bonticu Farm and we moved ten or twelve miles away to Westtown. I think they were beginning to look for a place of their own to buy as well as a good school for me. In the interim we moved into a boarding apartment called the Westtown Farmhouse. It was a large square two-story stone building with eight or ten apartments surrounded by fields, a large barn, and most important to me, lots of animals. We took our meals along with other residents in a common dinning room. In this sense it was really like a hotel.

Two of the residents that we got to know were both artists and writers as were my parents. One was a woman named Laura Benet (1884-1979) who wrote children's books as well as poetry. The only book I recall was called *The Hidden Valley* which I read some time later. She was a pleasant, quiet person with long hair. She was always very interested in talking to me. I recall her brother visiting and staying awhile. He looked much older and quite stooped over and wore glasses; actually she was twelve years older. I remember shaking his hand with him and answering some questions. It was some time later that I was told this was Steven Vincent Benet already famous for his long prose poems which I read years later in school. I particularly remember *John Brown's Body*, perhaps his most well known and *The Devil and Daniel Webster*. Laura's other brother was William Rose Benet, editor of the *Saturday Review of Literature*.

The other resident artist, also a woman, was Nancy Cox-McCormack Cushman, a portrait painter and as I found out many years later a somewhat famous sculptor. I only knew her as "Miss Nancy." She made a small portrait of me using a photo that had cut out lace and me as an angel with wings. Nancy had already made busts of Mussolini, Ezra Pound and Mahatma Gandhi from life perhaps in the 1930s. Through the marvels of the Internet in 2003 or so I was contacted by a

Toby Shenton in a portrait by Nancy Cushman at Westtown Farm House, 1938.

librarian, Nancy Weyant, at Smith College who told me this story because she was doing a biography of Nancy Cushman. She sent me a wonderful collection of my mother's handwritten letters to Nancy over the years up to 1954. Miss Nancy also painted a miniature of me at age six which I still have in an oval frame; it's a good likeness of me. The Farmhouse turned out to be an artist's and writer's haven.

In September of 1938, I was enrolled in the first grade of the elementary branch of the Westtown School, the Lane School about a half-mile walk from the Farmhouse. I have a few memories of the Lane School. The only teacher I remember was Teacher Faith; it was the custom of this Quaker school to call the teachers by their first name. I have several report cards from this time up through the second grade. As was the practice, the report is quite detailed and typewritten.

Several things happened to me. Not too long after my broken wrist at Bonticu there was an incident in which I, then still called Toby, was swinging boldly from bars or whatever we hung from, some sort of a jungle gym gadget on the school playground, when I slipped and fell on my head. This was the first of many such events in which I did damage to myself and resulted in a mild concussion. I don't want to say that I was accident prone as maybe these sorts of incidents are normal for kids. And then later, while we were at West-town, I wound up in the school infirmary with one or more of the childhood ills; measles, whooping cough, mumps, or one of those. During these years, Stacy Wood visited me. My father made a sketch of him sitting in bed in the Westtown infirmary where we both spent time with our childhood infirmities.

Although Westtown School was a Quaker school I didn' take part in things to do with the Quaker religion, although my parents and I went to a Quaker wedding once. It must have been for a friend of theirs or maybe one of my teachers. We sat in a meeting house and at the end we all trouped outside where it had begun to rain. I made some sort of remark that it was a perfect "wetting." It was the sort of pun that was typical of my father.

I often walked to school. I remember vividly one winter when we woke up to a heavy blizzard and maybe the car was snowed in but my father walked with me across the field in what seemed like knee-deep snow to the Lane School. This was before schools were cancelled for too much snow, rain, or whatever and definitely before school buses. Most kids did walk to school for distances of a mile or so.

The farm at Westtown held a real fascination for a six year old. I would explore and play around the barn and being very small I could slip into stalls with cows. I had no fear of them. My mother told the story of me supposedly eating bull food or trying to. I don't recall it. One day, when I had been given a brand new pair of corduroy knickers and I was wearing them for the first time I went on my usual rounds in the barn. I was walking on the top of a narrow stone wall. On one side was a large pit with manure and associated liquid. Of course, I proceeded to lose my balance and fell about six or eight feet into it. Somehow, I managed to struggle out and with a profusion of tears, retreated to the house. My mother was not at all pleased but I don't remember being scolded. But then my parents rarely scolded me and neverused any physical force. I'm proud to say I was never spanked.

Every evening after dinner my parents and I and others would gather in a small sitting room that had a large cabinet radio with a fabric covered grill and listen to the world news. The announcer was Gabriel Heater or maybe Lowell Thomas. As the looming clouds of World War II approached in 1939 and 1940, the adults were understandably gravely concerned. I was too young to care about what was going on Europe. But I do remember the daily episodes of "I Love a Mystery" just before I had to go to bed. The story featured three soldiers of fortune, Jack, Doc, and Reggie. The theme song was from *Valse Triste* and anytime I hear it played I think of those evenings.

Among my parents good friends in Westtown were the Goldsmiths. When I first recall meeting them they were building a large, new spacious house east of the school on a treeless bare lot. I was out there one day watching the lot being graded when suddenly the bull dozer doing the grading tipped over on a steep hill. The driver leaped off just in time to avoid being seriously hurt. I had a fascination with trucks, tractors, and heavy equipment.

Clifford Goldsmith was a quite successful playwright for radio or rather he wrote radio scripts. (We were ten years away from commercial television.) His most notable claim to fame was the creation of a popular show called *Henry Aldrich* which aired every week. We all listened to each weekly episode. The show involved the tales of Henry and his high school classmate Homer and their girlfriends Kathleen and Agnes. Clifford's wife Kay had two young high school boys Pat and Pete White from a previous marriage. The boys were perfect material for many of Henry's weekly antics. Clifford was always looking for new situations for his show. Several years later when I was about ten or eleven years old I gave him a story from my own school experience. Clifford loved it and soon had Henry suffer the embarrassment of a split in the seam of his pants. But luckily he is saved by girl friend, Agnes, who deftly used a football needle to sew up his pants. I don't remember how it happened to me but it was fun to have sold my first story. Clifford was one of the top radio script writers in the 1940s and according to *Time Magazine* earned $3000 per week for his shows, a rather large sum for those days

As a reward Clifford took me to the local sporting goods store in West Chester and said "You can have anything you want." I wish you could have seen the expression on my face at that moment! I was overwhelmed, but went immediately for a baseball glove that cost all of $25, a big amount in those days. The glove was signed by Pee Wee Reese who played for the Brooklyn Dodgers. It was very professional looking with lots of padding except in the pocket. All my schoolmates envied it and I kept it for many years after I quit playing baseball. Clifford was always including familiar locations in his Henry Aldrich shows with all the kids meeting at De Haven's Drug Store at the soda fountain. My friend Stacy Wood recently reminded me "I don't recall why, but yesterday DeHaven's drugstore, *Henry Aldrich*, and your godparent Clifford Goldsmith came to mind. I remember when you and I would go in for a soda after a Saturday movie matinee which may have been, a *Don Winslow of the Navy* short."

Some years later when I was fifteen, Clifford and Kaye officially became my god parents when I was baptized into the Episcopal Church in West Chester. About this time their whole family moved to Tucson, Arizona because Barclay, the youngest son suffered from severe asthma and the dry Southwest was much better for him. Barclay went on to become the founder and producer of Borderlands Theater in Tucson to carry on his father's tradition. My father visited the Goldsmiths out there in 1949 while he was on a business trip to find potential authors for his company, Macrae-Smith Publishing Company. It was here that he was interviewed on a local radio station. I have a copy of this short conversation. It's the only record of his voice that I have.

My other godparent, who lived nearby in the town of Cheney, was Claude Rains, a well established actor from the English stage who had come over here in the mid- thirties and began a distinguished career in Hollywood movies. He was best known for his starring role in *Casablanca*. There must have been some sort of small group of actors, writers, and artists that hung out in Westtown. Claude was a good friend of my parents and sometime around 1940 he and his wife Frances and their daughter, Jennifer all moved away to a large working farm not far from Coatesville about twenty miles west. It was there that I got to know Claude much better as I was growing up.

My last memory of the Farmhouse was the sad death of my dog, Patch, who at the time was probably not more than five years old. He had been a close friend since the early days at Bonticu and is well described in my mother's book *Color of the Country* although there he was given the name "Puddy." In that book my mother hadn't quite become totally confident about writing non-fiction, so all the characters were given different names. Maybe it had something to do with those times in publishing and not using real names. Patch was always making his rounds and managed, we think, to find some rat poison in the barn. He was the first pet of mine to come to an untimely death but I don't remember feeling particularly upset.

Not long after, we too, moved from the Farmhouse and Westtown. One of the big events of my early life during this period was the trip to New York to see the 1939 World's Fair, held in Flushing Meadow in Queens. I went with my parents probably in the late summer or fall. The scene we saw from afar was the logo of the Fair, the Trylon and Perisphere that shone in a beautiful futuristic white. There were a large number of new technologies unveiled at the Fair, which was open at nearly the same time that Hitler was marching through parts of Europe. The world was about to plunge us all into total conflict.

On the opening day President Franklin Delano Roosevelt addressed the crowds by television which was being pioneered by RCA and a real first, while Dr. Albert Einstein dramatically threw the switch that would turn on the fair's lighting system. None of this was of the slightest interest to me. I'm sure we rode the General Motors Futurama but I have no recollection. It seems to have been the most memorable of all the exhibits where a sprawling scene of America pictured in 1960 is laid out beneath the fairgoers who ride seated in high backed chairs as if on an airplane. Below them are super highways with remotely controlled cars, bridges, and cities all what we now have. Upon exiting Futurama spectators received a button stating "I have seen the future."

Perhaps the most exciting event I recalled was the parachute jump. My mother and I were seated in a type of gondola car for two, something like a Ferris wheel, tightly belted in as we were hoisted about 200 feet in the air. At the top our parachute opened above our heads as we looked out over the sprawling fairgrounds beneath us and we floated effortlessly back to earth. Of course, we were moored by a set of guide wires that assured we wouldn't drift away in the breeze. It was a real thrill and probably the only time I'll ever make a parachute jump.

Then the other point of fascination for me was the model train exhibit held in an enormous auditorium where the spectators sat in a balcony above the train layouts. My experience with model trains was limited to the small oval of Lionel "O" gauge trains received for Christmas. Over several years my father and I had added a crossing and a couple of manually operated switches. In front of my amazed eyes was the most complex and real life looking maze of tracks, grades, switches, cars, and engines beyond counting, all moving in different directions through hills, mountains with tunnels, and towns. In the center of this layout, that was perhaps fifty-feet long were four or five men controlling each one of the many trains. During our fair visit I went back to the train hall several times by myself, totally enchanted. I've thought many times since then of becoming a model train buff but somehow I never have had the space or the commitment. A few years after I met Ellie, we went to a couple of model train shows and even bought a several "HO" scale engines and cars. They still sit on a shelf at the Peaks Island house gathering dust, waiting patiently for action.

The final memory I have from the World's Fair is visiting the various pavilions represented by countries from around the world. For some forgotten reason I was attracted to the Finnish exhibit. Perhaps this was the beginning of my love of northern climes. I came away with a souvenir of a hunting knife with a silver tipped leather case. I cherished it for many years and often wonder what became of it.

To put the '39 World's Fair in a broader perspective I found that it had a number of firsts:

- First television broadcast of a speech by an American president
- First public use of fluorescent lighting
- First Kodachrome transparencies/color home movies
- First 3D film viewed through Polaroid glasses
- First use of nylon
- First use of Lucite
- First use of Plexiglas
-

Although there have been several World fairs since 1939, I feel this one was the high point of World's Fairs at a time when so much technology was coming on the scene. With all the world strife and conflict rampant now it is inconceivable that we could envision another such event.

Chapter Two

Growing up at Sugarbridge
1940-1946

During the spring of 1940, my parents had been actively looking for a suitable place of their own in the general vicinity. Reluctantly, I would be dragged along on long rides through the country with their favorite realtor, a man by the name of Lanier Jordan. The search bore fruit finally and on July 5 we made the grand move to a ninety-acre farm about three miles west of West Chester.

We move into our new home, Sugarbridge, on my eighth birthday July 5, 1940.

I was excited. I was eight years old and it was my birthday. They gave me a present of a shiny new Columbia eighteen-inch bicycle with a horn and a light on the handlebars. I didn't know which was more exciting, the new bike or the new house. Actually the house was quite old, probably built around 1745 although I don't think it was ever accurately dated.

It was small by today's standards, with two rooms and a kitchen down and two rooms and a bath upstairs. Like most houses of that period, it was made of fieldstone covered with mortar and whitewashed outside. There was a spring house, a stream with a small pool, and a large barn in rather poor repair. The pool was shallow, partly filled with silt. We drained it and had someone scoop out the silt so we could swim in it. I put my kayak, the *Fast Frog*, in a few times as well as a small toy submarine that became prophetic of my future. There were other buildings — a chicken coop and an outhouse up the hill behind the house hidden respectfully by some bushes. My parents had bought the farm, including the ninety acres, for $8,200 which was probably an average price for the times but unbelievable now.

Soon after our arrival, I was racing down the dirt lane on my new bike and hit a stone and skidded, landing on the side of my face. It was another of many such incidents to follow in which I did physical damage to myself. I was what some call accident prone or, more aptly, just plain careless.

As Vice President of Macrae Smith Publishing in Philadelphia, and teaching at The Pennsylvania Academy of Fine Arts, my father was doing quite well during this time. He also had a teaching appointment at the School of Industrial Arts. Although I never had any idea of the amount of money he earned, his pen and ink drawings for the first edition of *The Yearling* by Marjorie Rawlings as well the many books and magazines had made him well known. Although I don't distinctly remember it, a few years earlier he had used me to model for the boy lying down by the water wheel in Chapter One in that book. I may also have modeled for the now-famous book jacket. As I grew up, he called on me to be the model for many of his drawings over the years that I lived at home.

When we moved in that July of 1940, the front of the house had a large and rather ugly dormer addition of two rooms over the front porch. And it was here that I slept that first summer. It was most peculiar because the floor sloped almost with the pitch of the roof giving a strange sensation, like one of those rooms in the circus or carnival.

My father recounts in his book, *The Rib and Adam*, how I was attacked one night by fleas, much to the amusement of his many readers. I have totally forgotten this scene, although over the years of country living, I was surely bitten by bees, wasps, ticks, and most unpleasantly, chiggers, those microscopic sized red bugs that live in the grass. And mentioning bees brings to mind later that summer in the west wall of the room adjacent to mine we discovered there was a major beehive inside the wall with an active colony. In our ignorance of country matters, we had called an exterminator to remove the hive and spoiled hundreds of pounds of good honey. Later local beekeepers scolded us for failing to notify them for they would gladly rescued the bees. This was just the beginning of lessons to be learned about becoming real country dwellers.

There's a picture of my mother and me posing in front of the rather large ancient bell hung between two posts. It probably measured two feet across and was quite rusty and certainly very heavy. That first summer I recall my mother was excited by the new experience of our own farm. She wanted to hear the sound of the bell and, I, a typical eight-year-old, was only too pleased to ring it loudly. It had such a beautiful clear tone. But to our surprise and dismay, in just several minutes cars and farm trucks began rushing up the dirt lane to our house. It turned out to be the local fire and distress alarm. Anyone who remembers seeing the film *Witness*, about a Pennsylvania Dutch farm under attack will understand how effective the bell can be.

We were most embarrassed and thanked our neighbors for their speedy response. This was how we met several of them from their nearby farms. One of the men was Walter Connor from over the hill behind us. Tall and lanky with a lined, weather-beaten face and bib overalls, he could have stepped right out of a photo from the depression. He ran a dairy farm where we went for years to buy our milk, butter, and eggs every week. Some years later, after I had left West Chester, I found a strange coincidence in the fact that the Connors were cousins of ours. On learning this my mother, in her characteristic snobby way, was not at all impressed and I'm sure had no intention of pursuing the relationship.

My mother and me by the farm bell at Sugarbridge shortly after moving in.

After the demise of my first dog, Patch, while at Westtown, my parents decided we all should enjoy another dog. Why they chose a Great Dane I have no idea but we soon after moving became owners of a Great Dane of merle pattern, a mottled gray color. She was quite small as Danes go these days. My father named her Draga whom my father said was the Queen of the Danes. I later discovered Draga was, in fact, Queen of Serbia. My Draga became my sole companion around the farm and a sort of surrogate mother. She didn't come with the usual AKC thoroughbred papers which made no difference to us. However, a few years later when we had her bred, it did matter.

She had an enormous litter of thirteen pups, a near record, although two were stillborn. We used the now abandoned chicken coop as dog pen. We managed to sell all the pups but at a greatly reduced price because of no papers. She looked less like Danes we know today because her ears weren't cropped to a point. She and I used to have wrestling matches on the lawn. Danes have short life spans, usually six to eight years. Sadly, hers was less; she died of some sort of bone cancer.

Our Great Dane, Draga, with her 13 pups about 1942.

Dux of Sugarbridge, or Duke our next Dane about 1950.

By this time I was attending boarding school but my mother now wanted another Dane and Duke came into our lives.

His full name was Dux of Sugarbridge. He also became the subject of writings of both parents in my mother's books and my father's short stories, one of which, "My Dog is a Gold Mine" was published in 1955 in the *Saturday Evening Post*.

Sugarbridge was somewhere between a working farm and a "gentleman's" farm. We began with chickens, possibly because there was a chicken house just up the hill behind our house. I remember a lean-to building with two rooms and a fenced-in yard. It had been neatly whitewashed. The chicken period was short lived. While at first it was fun to have an almost unlimited supply of eggs, the care, feeding, and cleaning up for somewhat stupid birds was not my idea of fun.

After chickens, we started with one pig -- which I learned years later when I had my own farm was not nearly as productive as having two pigs who then compete in their typically hoggish ways to see which one can eat the most. We named our piglet Albert, only to discover soon after that we had made a gender error. She then became Albertina. In this, my first experience with pigs, I realized how intelligent pigs were. And how much they appeared to communicate with humans in what we called pig talk. As the age-old farm saga goes, Albertina met her fate that fall, providing our small family with an enormous supply of ham, bacon, sausage, and of course, scrapple, the famous Philadelphia breakfast treat made of leftover scraps, usually fried in thin slices.

Our first horse, Pet, with me astride about 1944.

The missing animal in this menagerie was the horse which would complete my mother's dream farm. I was around eleven years old when we found a mare named Pet, albeit not very horse-like of a name.

I had begun taking riding lesson from Dorothy Montgomery, a local friend. Pet had been in an accident that damaged her neck and she could only raise her head about halfway up. But she was still fun to ride and very gentle. All three of us rode all around the countryside. Besides lessons I rode frequently at Stacy Wood's farm, Rock Bottom, in Malvern just west of Paoli.

I rode Colonel a western pony-horse who was very spirited. I still picture one time Stacy taking off rapidly into a field on his horse, when Colonel bolted after them, taking me by surprise and I wound up flying off his back and landing ker-thump on the ground, the only time I remember falling off a horse.

Dad, Duke, Delaware and my mother about 1952.

The perfect companion to Duke was my mother's second horse, Chief, who came to her at age fifteen. He replaced Pet, whom we had sold.

His full name was Delaware Chief, a full bred Morgan, standing only fifteen hands in height, small by standard hunters' seventeen hands. Morgans were known as compact, muscular horses about sixty inches high; they were good for harness racing, military use, and pleasure riding. Even at middle age Chief was spirited and loved a good long ride with either my mother or father; occasionally I rode him. However, I was at the age where I was fast becoming more involved with cars than horses.

We were one of the first families to move in from the more urban areas and also among the first to become what was later called "gentlemen farmers," those not depending on the farm for a livelihood. In our case we rented out the land to a local farmer. That fall of 1940 my parents voted for Mr. Roosevelt in the national election at the local township, East Bradford. I remember later how they described the looks they got because they were the only Democrats in the whole township.

Soon after moving into the farm my parents realized that it needed a name. Looking around at local historic landmarks they came on Sugars Bridge. It had a nice sound to it and so the farm became known as Sugarbridge. Actually, the name came from a bridge about a mile away that crossed the famed Brandywine River. It was correctly called Sugars Bridge and it had been a covered bridge at some earlier time. It had been named for William Sugar in 1850.

I vaguely recall my father painting the name "Sugarbridge Farm" on our 1940 Plymouth "woody" station wagon. The car was later repainted an ugly tan, almost an olive drab later to cover the stained wood. We hung a Sugarbridge sign in front of the barn where our lane joined Valley Creek Road. That sign remained there for the three decades my parents lived at the farm. Our lane had no name although the house was referred to as the old Jefferies place. A few years after my parents left the farm in 1968, the township named the road "Shenton Road." I recall my father once mentioning that there was "Shenton Way" in Singapore. It turns out this was a major street named after Sir Shenton Thomas (1879-1962), governor of Singapore and the Straits from 1934 to 1942. He was famous for his decision to remain in Singapore during the Japanese occupation even though it meant three years in a Japanese prison. Shenton Way is now known as Singapore's Wall Street. I have no information whether Sir Shenton is a relative as Shenton is a common British name. Thomas also is family name.

It was sometime around this time that I got the idea I could become an entrepreneur. Maybe it was my father who suggested it. I began harvesting watercress from the stream in little bunches and selling them for something like a dime to a small grocer in West Chester. My mother was sure to see that all proceeds went to the local Red Cross.

In the fall of 1940, we to had deal with the beginning of my school. Because we lived outside the West Chester school district, I was expected to attend the local elementary grade school in East Bradford Township. It was about a mile away from us and I suppose perfectly good but it was the traditional one-room schoolhouse for all grades from first to sixth. My parents, with their urban background, weren't ready for me to try it. I don't remember any discussion — and was not consulted — I just wound up going to the High Street School in West Chester to enter the third grade.

The school was a large, two story brick building on High Street the principal north-south route through the town. I was probably the only "country kid" there. I don't recall any particular anxiety over starting a new school and making new friends but there must have been some knowing how timid I was as an only child. Nor do I remember any teacher's names, but I can still see the face of one, actually she may have been Miss James. She was white haired, small, and had large thick glasses. I don't think there were any male teachers then only spinster, maiden types. Years later I bumped into her on the street and she recognized me.

The schoolrooms were dimly lit, dark-walled with worn, dark wooden floors. The classes also were not memorable. I vividly recall one of the girls named Delsey Sharrett with pretty pigtails and a girl from Australia named Jill for Gillian. I had a crush on Delsey and one winter on Valentine's Day, I had put together a homemade valentine for her which was not signed, as was the custom. My card had said something about a heart but I had misspelled it so it said "heat." The teacher read them all and I was most embarrassed and scrunched down in my seat.

The best part of school was on the playground where we played marbles in the dirt. There were various marble games ranging from the traditional circle drawn in the dirt to the drop bomb type which I'm sure was inspired by the war. I had a large bag and we were always trading marbles but no money was involved.

Billy Chambers, me, Petey Edmiston at the High Street School, 3rd grade, 1942.

The only picture I have from this time is of several of my friends: Billy Chambers, Petey Edmiston, and John Linden. We were standing along a low wall each with a toy car or truck. While Billy became one of my better friends for a number of years, Petey, whose full name was Rodman Wannamaker Edmiston III, was probably my best friend during these years. I would spend weekends at his family's farm south of West Chester. They had a large and comfortable house much more elegant than mine with lots of land and a barn.

Petey was a bold, confident kid whom I admired. He had not one but two cars he was allowed to drive on farm property. One was an electric "buck-board," a sort of 40s go cart. The other was a Crosley, a miniature car first sold in 1939 with a two cylinder gas engine and convertible top. Crosley also made refrigerators and radios. Petey and I were about nine or ten at this time. We would drive the car on dirt tracks or up and down the driveway.

Petey's father, Rodman, was a big hunter and he taught us to shoot a .22 rifle and his 4-10 shotgun. I think Rod was some sort of salesman of insurance or the like. And a sort of character whom I enjoyed probably because he was quite different from my father, telling endless jokes. Petey and I had a secret hideaway cabin across a field from his house where we would go and read comic books. On one occasion, we made pretend cigarettes out of newspaper and almost choked trying to smoke them.

It was here that Petey told me in great confidence, "You know that your father is not really your father!" I was, of course quite shocked but pretended not believe it. I never found out any more, or whether it was just a joke. I'm sure I must have worried over this for a while. When we were about thirteen or so, Rod died quite suddenly. Like many men in those days, he was a heavy drinker. He was also the first parent of any of my friends to die. He and my father had been friends but I never thought of them as especially close.

It wasn't until after my father died many years later that I came across one of the West Philly High magazines, *The Western*, where I found that Rod Edmiston had been a classmate of my father in the class of 1917. He had been in the Navy and wrote an article on his experiences at sea during "The Great War." I thought it strange that my father had never mentioned Rod at WPHS. But then, I found there were lots events my father never spoke about. I should have asked more questions like a good interviewer would.

When his dad died, Petey, his mother, and older sister Patsy, moved away to Mountchanin, Delaware to live in the gatehouse on the DuPont estate. They were related to the Carpenters; Bobbie Carpenter at that time owned the Philadelphia Phillies, our hometown baseball team. I visited Petey once and we went to watch an illegal cockfight in a barn where everyone was betting on this "sport" which was a bloody battle to the death. It was the last I ever saw my friend Petey. As with what seems like so many of my old chums, Petey shuffled off this mortal coil in March of 2010. His obituary says he attended University if Miami, joined the Navy, then spent the rest of his life working his way up at DelMarVa Power Co. I can't say how many times I set out to track him down, but never did.

One of my memories from the third or fourth grade was one afternoon when school was out, sitting on the steel pipe railing out in front waiting for my mother to pick me up. One of the schoolkids approached me and suddenly shoved me backwards and I fell over. I don't know what made him do it. Maybe I was one of those kids that was always picked on because I was small and somewhat timid.

I ended up fighting a much bigger guy. It turned out to be a sort of wrestling match on the sidewalk with other kids standing around. I finally got a stranglehold on him while observers hollered that it was unfair. But he gave up and I had begun on my way to becoming a wrestler which came about a few years later when I went to the Haverford School.

Another memory during this period was that of the Pearl Harbor bombing. I was visiting my friend Stacy Wood for the weekend. He and I were lying on the floor in his living room. We were reading the Sunday paper, perhaps the "funnies" when an announcement came over the large cabinet radio. I was nine years old and Stacy, eight. I'm not sure we realized how important this day was.

Stacy's father, Campion, must have been in the Naval Reserve because he immediately went off into active duty. At age forty-six, my father was too old to go in the service and I'm not sure if he even wanted to. But he did become a Civil Defense warden which meant he wore a special CD arm band during air raid drills and made sure that people's lights were shaded by blackout curtains. And one of the other special things was we had a "C" sticker on our 1940 Plymouth wagon that allowed us to buy extra rations of gas. My mother became a driver of Red Cross vans for some official duties like taking soldiers on leave to the local USO (United Service Organization). I often try to picture my mother, who actually was not a good driver, wheeling some hulking truck or bus along full of GIs. She wore a grey Red Cross uniform.

I never knew whether the air raid blackout drill made much sense but maybe there was a possibility of an attack. It certainly was important along the Atlantic seacoast where German submarines prowled. We were part of the "home front" and doing our part in the war effort. There was food rationing and with it stamps and coupons for meat, sugar, butter, and other scarce items. On the farm we didn't suffer because we raised all our own pork, lamb, ducks, and chickens for eggs only.

Our neighbor across Valley Creek, Jack Brennan, raised beef cattle and sold us some so we hardly were in want. Jack was a gentleman farmer on the side. His company made specialized machine tools for the war industry. I can remember him telling us of his experiences in dealing with the Russians, our allies. My parents and I had always thought of the Russians as fine patriotic men just as we saw their pictures on a favorite record album of the Red Cossack Army singers. Jack, with first hand experience, related how difficult it was to negotiate with the Russians. Of course, he was all too right as we all found out a few years later. But at that time we loved the Russians and Red Army singers.

Starting in the fifth grade, when I was ten years old, I went to the Auditorium School on the north side of town. I was never altogether sure why my parents moved me from High Street School. At Auditorium, the classrooms were attached to a large and quite new auditorium for the high school across the street. Our rooms were also new and very light and sunny, with lots of windows. It was a great improvement over the dark and dingy High Street School.

The year was 1942 and the country was at war. My father was working on a book about airplanes which he both wrote and produced the drawings for, entitled *The New Alphabet of Aviation* and published by Macrae Smith. He had started as an editor at the publishing house in 1926 and had recently become vice president. He later went on to write several other books about planes and tanks and all the equipment of war. The books were for the juvenile reader. I was an enthusiastic fan of these as they came out.

At school we had War Bond drives that started with a minimum of a $25 bond that we could buy for $18.75 and then would be worth $25 at maturity, in about five years or so. Most of the kids would buy war stamps which we pasted into books, similar to the green stamps concept. Each Friday we were instructed to bring in our contributions for the bond drives and there was a competition between classes. My father was doing very well in his career, writing and editing, as well as teaching in those days so he would give me a check to buy a bond each week. I was always the winner when I brought in a check for a $500 or $1,000 bond. I was proud, of course, but a little embarrassed at being the "rich kid." Wealth never became me.

When we visited back and forth, Stacy Wood and I often talked about the war and battles and planes and such partly because his dad was out there somewhere in the Pacific. And as kids then we "hated" the Japs and the Germans but I never remember any bad feelings toward the Italians. There were plenty of Italians in our school but almost no Germans and certainly no Japanese. There was a German family named Bergdoll, who lived a few miles away from our farm in a very elegant estate high on a hill looking down over the valley.

The Bergdoll children went to my school at one point and were older than I. The father was from a well-known Philadelphia family who owned a brewery, and have been a relative of Grover Bergdoll, the famous aviator and draft dodger. Interestingly, one of my father's childhood illustrations, circa 1911, was of a race car driven by a Bergdoll, perhaps the same family.

At some time in the early years of World War II, the Bergdoll family suddenly disappeared. I often speculated that they were taken away to an internment camp. Their whole estate was abandoned and a few years later I remember going over to their house with some of my West Chester friends and poking through rooms full of their belongings, books, and old stock certificates. We wondered where they were taken or maybe they simply just left. Yet, somehow I doubt that they left of their free will; there was too much furniture and personal belongings left behind. Later I've found that some 11,000 German-Americans were interred during the war but nothing like the 120,000 or more Japanese.

During this time my father was turning out lots of books and drawings of war planes. And I, as most young boys, loved to build model planes crafted with sticks and paper. I also liked the line of detailed solid models, too. I started this hobby when I was still living in Westtown. I remember so well my father helping me to build a model submarine from a kit. At age seven, I was more an observer as he did most of the assembly and got me started.

One of my favorite kits was a Swedish fighter with a two foot wingspan with an olive drab color. It might have been a Saab since they were the only Swedish aircraft maker. It was long before their first car, which came out in 1947. I made a number of sketches of war planes as I emulated my father, but even then I had no aspiration to be an artist. I felt that my father was so good that I could never hope to be an artist like him.

Sometime during this period, my parents and I witnessed a dramatic air disaster. On a hazy, gray morning, we were standing out in the yard when we heard a strange, high pitched whine somewhere overhead but we couldn't see anything. Then in a moment we saw faintly what looked like a bomber coming out of a layer of clouds. It was a B-25 spinning out of control like a leaf falling to earth, appearing as tiny as one of my models. Down, down it fell just like a movie scene of a plane being shot down.

We watched with horror as it disappeared behind a hill toward the east. Excitedly we jumped in the old Plymouth station wagon and drove over the back roads north of West Chester to where we could see a plume of black smoke rising. Although we were near to it we never saw the actual wrecked plane. I did manage to retrieve a small piece of twisted aluminum with torn rivet holes. I proudly showed my souvenir to all the kids at school the next day. But due to wartime security there was never any news account of the crash. A story circulated later that the people living close to the crash site had heard the plane just before impact with men frantically beating on doors trying to get out. This was the closest I got to the war.

In the early years at Sugarbridge I enjoyed the freedom to roam up the steep hillside behind the house. At that time it was completely cleared. I remember Pierce running his horse drawn mowing machine across it and almost tipping over, or so it seemed. At the top was a huge beech tree with its wonderful smooth gray bark probably some two hundred years old. Beyond was scrubbrush and then fields planted in corn by our neighbor, Ralph, whom we allowed use of the land for farming. There were some patches of woods mostly on the boundaries of the property and we frequently went walking along the old woods paths. At the bottom of the hill just behind the house was an ancient, large gum tree with a long stout branch reaching down almost to the ground. To my delight my father built a tree house near the trunk. It was only a platform made of an old door but it was a perfect place to climb to and hide from the world, the traditional kids' fort. Later we moved the same concept to the weather safety of the barn.

Our barn, in those days, was in moderately good repair although we only used a small part of it. Our farmer friend across the road rented much of it for hay storage as well as renting the fields for growing corn. My father and I put up a sort of house in the rafters above the area where we kept the car. Actually it was really just a platform with a ladder up to it, a treehouse of sorts.

Here, I had an enormous cache of comic books and on rainy days I and one or the other of my friends, Petey or Stacy, would hide away in our fort, safe above the floor, like the tree dwelling aborigines from the comic books we read. I don't remember the specific comic books it was likely before the violent ones came out. My mother barely tolerated my comic book habit. I truly missed out on reading the traditional literature read by young boys because instead I had a seemingly endless supply of what were called juvenile books. These were books that my father illustrated but few of my classmates had any interest in them. There was a whole series I especially liked by Stephen Meader about the historic adventures of young boys exploring the new west in the 1800s to modern times and episodes with German submarines off the Jersey coast.

In T-Model Tommy *by Stephen Meader, my father drew some of his finest and most detailed drawings all about an aging truck and a young man's adventures in starting a businessx*

My father illustrated all of these books and they resided on the shelves in his studio. One of them, *T-Model Tommy* from 1938, stands above the rest for beautiful, fine line drawings. Although I was too young at the time, I realized many years later these drawings may have been among his best because of the very detailed light and dark lines of pen and ink and the "Shenton Shadow" that was his trademark. The story was about a young man and his model T Ford and various run-ins he had with the other truck drivers. The truck scenes were very real. The action took place in the coal mining country of northeastern Pennsylvania, the very route we drove going to our summer cottage in Laporte.

I certainly wasn't aware as I was growing up that my father was then an important illustrator or in any way famous and I'm sure he wasn't either. But now as I write it's very evident that he was. So you might think that growing up an only child with two parents who were both artists and writers some of it would rub off on me, or maybe like N.C. Wyeth, my father would want to home school me as Wyeth did his son Andrew. The closest I came to this was when I was in my early teens and my father sent me to a series of Saturday classes in Philadelphia at the School of Industrial Arts, now the Museum School. I went with my friend, Murdoch Simon-Davis for only one season. I really didn't enjoy it or feel that I showed any promise as a young artist. I never knew if my father was disappointed that I didn't follow him in some way. He seemed pleased that I wanted to do what I wanted. I don't remember ever having a conversation or discussion on my future or what I might try as a career. But it was clear that I was not going to follow in the footsteps of my father as an illustrator.

I first met Murdoch one evening at the movies, at the Warner Theater, in West Chester, sometime in 1942, a few years after moving there. He was sitting in a large, overstuffed easy chair in the lobby and someone I knew introduced us. He went to the "Dem" school or demonstration school, a part of the West Chester State Teacher's College. I found out soon enough that he had reputation of being one of the troublemakers and a wise guy. His mother was divorced and I'm sure she had difficulty managing him. I guess Murdoch wished he had a father and was always getting into trouble. But he and I became very good friends and I would spend overnights at his house or he at mine.

A while later his mother, Virginia, married a mild mannered architect named Albert Davis. Murdoch wasn't all that happy about his new stepfather or to suddenly having his name changed to Davis. Albert had little control over him and he became all the more rebellious and up to tricks and devilment. He showed me how to break windows in an abandoned warehouse and to run like hell down the railroad tracks behind his house hoping no one was chasing us. Of course, he and I had great fun at times like Halloween when kids still did real tricks. When we were a little older, Murdoch decided to make a rocket using a toilet paper roll and a lot of gunpowder we got out of .22 caliber bullets from my rifle. With some sort of wick, we lit the "rocket" off on the windowsill in his room. There was an enormous whoosh of smoke and noise as our rocket ignited and flew out the window. Alas, some of it caught the curtains on fire. His mother was not at all amused. For me, a timid, only child country boy, Murdoch's antics were thrilling.

The last of my close friends from this period was Billy Chambers from the High Street School gang, one of the kids in the picture with toy trucks on the wall. Billy could have stepped out of a 40s movie like *The Dead End Kids* with a round smiling face, curly hair, and a bit on the tough side. He was a scrapper often getting into fights. I sometimes wonder, why did I seem to fall in with this kind of friend rather than the opposite sort of an intellect? Billy, like Murdoch was raised by a single mother. He lived quite far out in the country in what I believe was a rented house, something not ordinary in those days. We would visit back and forth. He liked to visit our farm and my parents sympathized with his need for a family. The most memorable of these visits was the fire.

One afternoon while Billy was down at the barn, perhaps feeding animals, he came running excitedly to the house shouting, "The barn's on fire!" My father immediately called the fire department which was about four miles away in West Chester. Billy and I ran to the barn which was a good hundred yards from the house, grabbed buckets by the horse trough, and ran up to the loft. Luckily we didn't have livestock at this time.

The flames were about to reach the roof. My father had arrived and somehow we all managed to douse the fire at the last critical moment. At this point the fire truck roared up the lane. Whew! It was a close call as they soaked the barn pumping water from our pond. We were grateful to Billy for having alerted us. However, sometime later my parents suspected that maybe Billy had set the fire since there was nothing that could have started it like green hay or such. Not too long after this we heard that Billy was sent to a school for orphans and delinquents, The Church Farm School, on Route 30 near Malvern. I vaguely remember going there to visit him. Many years later my mother told me she discovered that Billy had become a successful tailor with a prospering business for the horsy crowd with a shop on High Street not too far from our old school. I never saw him again but always meant to look him up. Billy, a custom tailor of West Chester and Oxford, Pennsylvania, died in 2003, another of my old gang of friends slipping away.

The invasion of Normandy on June 6, 1944, occurred right around this time period. I wrote the date beneath the front porch of the house in pencil where it remained for many years. As the war began to wind down that year, I had to move across the street from the Auditorium School to the seventh grade in the Junior High in the time before what is now middle school. This was a big change because we had home rooms and went to different classes. At that time also the Junior High was in the same building as the Senior High before it was destroyed by fire in 1947 and moved outside of town.

Two teachers stand out in my memory. Mr. Urick was both my home room teacher and, more importantly, he was my science teacher. He made science interesting. He was tall with graying hair that spiked upward, glasses, tie and a tweed jacket. It was the wild looking hair and his dry wit that made him the perfect "mad" scientist. Mr. Urich gave me push in the right direction on my way toward things scientific; I regret I never went back to see him in later years. My other favorite teacher was Mrs. Edwards, our art teacher. I made lots of drawings and why not? I was the son of an artist although I'm sure I was no better that some of the other kids. My favorite subjects were airplanes and cars. Mrs. Edwards was a stimulating art teacher and I thought that I might be a budding artist at that point.

The previous summers I had gone to Camp Lenape near home and Camp Appoquinimink in Middletown, Delaware, neither of which I particularly liked. But it turned out that the summer of 1945 was my last year to go to camp. I had been recruited by our High School Principal, "Pop" Henderson, to come to Camp Wyanoke outside of Wolfeboro, New Hampshire. He promised me that this camp would be much better than my previous ones.

John Halstead and I were the only boys from West Chester. All the boys from the local area met at Philadelphia's 30th St station one summer afternoon under the careful watch of "Pop" a tall, skinny, balding, and very likable person who I believe had been a counsellor at Wyanoke for many years. We took the overnight train and, as predicted, the camp turned to be a wonderful experience. There were about six or eight boys in our tent.

Camp Wyanoke, Wolfeboro, New Hampshire. "Pop" Henderson, principal at West Chester High School, 1945.

41

We wore uniforms of dark blue wool shorts and matching shirts. My clothes and belongings arrived the same day we did in a large steamer trunk that had been my parents' for trips by boat. It was the kind the stood up on end and with drawers and a space to hang clothes. Its faint and perpetual musty odor of moth balls never failed to remind me of camp even years later.

That summer I was thirteen years old. It was my first time in New England and I really enjoyed the crisp, clear mornings that we rarely got in Pennsylvania. Camp life was all controlled by bugle calls and posted schedules for activities for each hour of the day. The best activities were the rifle range and swimming and boating. We marched on the drill field nearly every day which was not fun. Several days a week we had shooting practice on a rifle range. I became a good shot and made marksman first class using a Mossberg .22 rifle, also used for US Navy training. Looking back it all sounds pretty military. I guess it was too, because we were still at war that summer. We had to swim 300 yards which I barely managed as I struggled behind an attending rowboat on Lake Winnipesauke. I also learned to live with my camp mates in close quarters. There was Chris White, Harold Strickler, Bill Barrett, and John Halstead among others.

Suddenly the outside world intruded in to our idyllic setting. It was August 6 and we suddenly received the news that the war was over with Japan's surrender. I don't recall any mention of Hiroshima but that news came in later days. My parents came to pick me up soon after.

In the fall of 1945, I entered the seventh grade and in October my parents took me out of school so I could travel with them to Virginia for the best part of a month. I took along schoolwork to do. I had to write a report on my travels that somehow related to my history class. My father had an assignment to produce a set of drawings for a book in the *Rivers of America* series, a very distinguished publication that started in 1937 and ran until 1970 with some sixty-five books in all published by Farr and Rinehart. Entitled *The James*, the book was written by Blair Niles who had written an extensive history of the James River.

We arrived in Virginia in early October as fall was in full color with its lingering warmth. We stayed at various inns filled with southern history; the most memorable was Williamsburg. The town that is now the most important tourist destination in Virginia was then under construction since it was nearly all new with only few old buildings left. There had been other truly historic towns that were candidates for this project, namely Newburyport and Annapolis. But both were dropped in favor of Williamsburg which was much easier to recreate.

This entre Colonial Williamsburg project was funded by John D. Rockefeller and other private funds had rejected the two "real" locations in favor of creating a town where there had been no infrastructure. I spent a lot of time watching the building and taking photos while my father sketched plantations along the James. When I returned to school I gave my report on my travels for history class. Although I probably looked through the book on the James, I never read it.

There was one other teacher that bears mention, Mark Muth, a tall, heavyset man with a firm authoritative manner. He taught shop which consisted of woodwork one semester and metal the other. The next year we had at least one class in mechanical drawing. These subjects, I gather, are no longer offered in most public schools and certainly not in the private school I went to later. In those days we boys took a shop course while the girls dug into Home Economics.

In wood shop I became handy with a wood lathe although not all my classmates were allowed to use one. We had all been required to make an obligatory broom holder. Mine was hardly a thing of beauty. I had painted it a horrible shade of green and given to my mother who dutifully used it. We also made a door knocker and a sugar scoop. But my big project was to turn a walnut nut bowl on the lathe. First I had to glue two pieces together and then gradually shape it using various tools. The hard part was carefully cutting out the inside to get a graceful shape with a thin wall without chipping or gouging. Then last, it was sanded and polished. Actually, I think my mother was pleased with this gift. I still have that bowl.

In metal shop we made tin sugar scoops which were soldered together. In retrospect, I must say that I have greatly benefited throughout my life from these "manual arts" courses. I suspect that many of my friends and colleagues would have also benefited from learning how to be handy with tools and machines.

Mr. Muth's daughter, Peggy, who was in my class took a liking to me. She was solidly built like her father with a nice smile and several inches taller than I. At thirteen, she became my first girlfriend. We "dated," that is, we went to parties, held hands, and I especially remember dances at the "Y." I remember being smothered by Peggy as we danced; she towered over me. Somehow I was not put off by her height but I was teased about it by classmates in my shop classes. I used to visit her at her home just on the corner of High Street and Rosedale Avenue right across from West Chester State Teachers College which has now been elevated to a University. We were carefully chaperoned as we sat in the living room. Our brief romance lasted for that year, after which I never saw her or kept up. It was the first of many "puppy loves."

The next summer that I met my second cousin, Nancy Murphey, while was staying with my grandmother in Ocean Grove, New Jersey. We were both around thirteen or fourteen years old. The Murpheys had either a rented cottage or one of the tent platforms. Nancy's father, Ken, was a librarian somewhere in the state. My parents never had much to do with our relatives.

I found Nancy very attractive. She was dirty blond, a smart dresser, and wore white and tan saddle shoes. She was probably a year older than I was. We would go out together in the evening to the amusements at Asbury Park or to a movie. I remember seeing Van Johnson and June Allyson in one of their typical romantic musical films, *Two Girls and a Sailor*. Most memorable was our ride on the Ferris wheel one night and I got up the nerve to put my arm around her, but that was the extent of it. I don't think I ever would have gone on the ride by myself so this was real fun. But I found myself becoming quite enamored of her although she hadn't the slightest interest in me. And of course, we were cousins. I never saw or heard of her after that summer.

Some years later I found a copy of a large family reunion flyer held in 1951. I think my parents attended. Listed were all the names of these cousins whom I never kept up with. The most memorable is a second cousin, George "Lefty" James, somehow related to the Murpheys. He was a famous football coach from 1947-1960 at Cornell. I met him once in Ocean Grove at my grandparents' home. Looking back as an only child I now wish I had had more contact with all these relatives.

Perhaps the most colorful of my relatives was my great Aunt Catherine, one of Pansy Sherwood Webster's many sisters. She was my Italian connection amid all the other English, Scottish, Welsh ones. Aunt Catherine had studied voice in Rome and was on her way to becoming an opera singer when she met and married Nicola Montani. After her marriage to him she became very Italian, trading Catherine for Carina and speaking Italian much of the time.

Great aunt Carina Sherwood Montani, voice and opera teacher.

44

She and Nicola lived in an older brick row house in Rittenhouse Square, an upscale part of Philadelphia. Going to visit as a child, I was always excited to enter the four storied house and have Aunt Carina greet us in her long gown with her hair wound up in a tall pile on her head. She was I remember an imposing figure always welcoming me with "botcha, bitcha, bio," a fond kiss on both cheeks.

Uncle Nicola was a slight man, who dressed in typical European elegance: dark suit, vest, watch chain, with a warm smile. He spoke English but with a heavy accent. Together they ran St. Gregory's Guild, where he wrote liturgical music for the Catholic Church and Carina gave voice lessons. A composer, conductor, accomplished musician, Nicola specialized in Gregorian chant. He was born in Utica, New York in 1880, but spent most of his life in Philadelphia, part of a very talented family. He is best known for the St. Gregory Guild Hymnal, 1920, which is still in print. He died in 1949.

My parents and I visited Nicola and Carina for Thanksgiving in the early 1940s. They had servants and the kitchen located in the cellar with a working dumbwaiter that ran up the third floor dining room. My real thrill was to ask one of the servants to give me a ride all scrunched up in the dumbwaiter. As I think about it, this may have been the beginning of my liking of small dark enclosed places which later became small submarines.

The other thing memorable about Aunt Carina's house was the very steep stairways lined with framed photographs of relatives and important people, something I recreated in several of my homes, most recently at Peaks Island.

My last memory of the Montanis was going to the funeral of Uncle Nicola which was sometime toward the end of 1949. There's a wonderful picture taken of me standing beside my parents in front of the Rittenhouse Square town house, my hand tucked in my tweed jacket a bit like Napoleon. Aunt Carina continued running her music school and the St. Gregory's Guild until her death which must have been around early 1960. She was ninety-one.

Many years later in the mid 1990s, I was working in a home in Newton, Massachusetts where the owners were deeply involved in church music. It was such a pleasure to find out they were quite familiar with the name of Nicola. Uncle Nicola enjoyed taking us to dinner at a most grand and elegant Italian restaurant, Palumbo's, on 6th St in Philadelphia. Here he was most respectfully treated by the owners where we were always shown to a special private backroom and served a many-coursed dinner in true Italian style with no tomatoes. It had all the flavor of a *Sopranos* style dinner. I suspect the restaurant had mafia connections.

While reflecting on various uncles and aunts, I should mention my favorite uncle, John "Jack" Thomas, actually a great uncle from the Pottstown relatives and brother of my grandmother Jennie. He returns to the story later on when I go out

45

Great uncle J .C., Jack Thomas, co-founder of Continental Oil Company.

west during college. Uncle Jack didn't come to visit often but when he did he always had something for me. Usually it was a crisp five dollar bill, a serious gift in the 1940s. It was probably meant to buy a model airplane or such.

I have pictures of Jack as a young surveyor somewhere out in the wild west, a small but dashing guy alongside the other men. He and his wife Eleanor headed west on a motorcycle in the 1920s to strike it rich. At some point they decided to stay a while and moved into a sort of dugout cave in a river bank. I don't know how he made it into the oil business but he did and later became an important part of the startup of Continental Oil. The plate presented to him, probably on retirement, is inscribed with his name, along with a picture of an early style oil derrick. This plate sits in a place of honor in a corner cupboard at my Peaks Island home.

Daniel Webster is another famous relative, about whom I know very little. He had three children but none lived to continue the male descendant line. Pansy Webster, my grandmother, left me a number of books and pictures of Daniel. The connection may have been through Stephen Webster, whose picture is among them, although it is hard to track down. I have heard Steven was my great grandfather and owned the farm where my mother later grew up.

Uncle Jack Thomas, co-founder of Continental Oil Company received this plate upon his retirement for service from 1928-48.

While in my early teens, I started taking piano lessons along with my father who, although he could play, felt he needed some improvement. We usually went at the same time to Miriam Brinton, a friend of my parents. I didn't really enjoy the piano. Perhaps I was too old as I was about to be bitten by the car bug, and horses, and girls. I stuck it out for a year or so, but long enough to meet an about-to-be-famous American composer.

At the end of our lesson year we had a recital with all the students performing. We were visited by Samuel Barber, who had been a West Chester youth and friend of Mrs. Brinton. He politely listened to each of us play our pieces. He became best known for his *Adagio for Strings* first played by the NBC Orchestra conducted by Arturo Toscanini in 1936 when he was only twenty-eight years old. He later was considered the most celebrated composer of the twentieth century. At the time, I knew nothing of him or his music for that matter.

I continued to enjoy my time at the "shore" in Ocean Grove, mostly at the amusements in Asbury Park. I became a pretty good player of skee-ball, spending much of my allowance there and getting a fair number of free games. But more fun were the bumper cars and occasional rides in the small two-person motor boats.

Many times I would find myself the only little kid in with bunch of big guys in the bumper cars who got great kicks out hitting me very hard from behind and even standing up to give extra weight to the crash. There was a wonderful merry-go-round in one of the halls that I rode many times but never got the brass ring, always cheap steel. When I went back to Ocean Grove many years later around 1990, the merry-go-round was the only remaining part of all the park. It stood in a separate building and had been beautifully restored in a sort of glass palace. The rest had all succumbed in the riots of the '60s and the fires which destroyed everything else.

Most of my time was spent at the beach. I had little love for sand and sitting in the sun as anyone who knows me is aware, but I was a water child and loved the surf. Whenever I had the 25-cent-an-hour fee I would rent an inflatable rubber raft or really a mattress, a sort of predecessor to surf boards, and float occasionally catching a ride on a big wave. I never met any other kids there on the beach but I never recall feeling lonely either. In the next block to us in Ocean Grove was a row or two of wooden tent platforms where people came every summer and set up their tents for vacation. Both my great Aunt Eleanor and Aunt Mary had these summer homes so we would visit when they came.

My return to Ocean Grove in 1990 was like many of those to one's childhood haunts; it might have been better if I hadn't gone. The Ocean Grove of my memories was, of course, long gone. The changes of those fifty or sixty years had been drastic. People's summer vacations weren't the same and I don't know what happened to the religious community. St. Elmo, the rambling, three story hotel where my father had stayed on occasion, was gone, as were all the tent platforms and the Ocean Avenue cottage that Pop and Granny lived in. The main street felt abandoned and forlorn. I went into a coffee shop and it was full of old, down and out looking bums. Just recently friends have told me that Ocean Grove has now become the place to buy shore front property and it is making a miraculous comeback. It was an important part of my childhood.

In the summer of 1946 my father decided to charter a sailboat for a cruise for the three of us. David Scott, one of my father's students from the Academy of Fine Arts, offered to charter to us his father's 46-foot schooner, *Heron*, for two weeks. We drove to Essex, Connecticut in our aging 1940 Plymouth station wagon sometime in June where David met us with *Heron*. We spent the first night up the Connecticut River at Hamburg Cove, a favorite spot for cruising boats. The cove was well protected from the river and, as I recall, totally undeveloped with only a few houses up the slopes to the water. The area now it has a yacht club with upwards of forty moorings and all the upscale conveniences.

David Scott and me aboard the schooner, Heron *in Nantucket 1946.*

Heron was typical of the older yacht style. She was designed by B.B. Crownin-shield, who also designed two Americas' Cup contenders. She was built in Chelsea, Massachusetts in 1911, and was forty-six feet overall with a low freeboard and only nine feet on the beam. She drew six feet with no guard rails which is now a standard for safety. Of course from this period she was gaff rigged, heavy canvas sails, dead eyes for standing rigging; nothing modern like turnbuckles. Also she was steered by a tiller which caused my poor mother no end of grief as she was trying to steer a compass course.

We headed for Nantucket Island where my godparents Cliff and Kaye Gold-smith had a grand summer cottage on the beach. David was a very competent skip-per although he was just nineteen. I think he had also gotten his airplane pilot's license by this time. I'm sure I looked up to him. I had little to no sailing experience but caught on quickly to the sailing routine.

I have a group of photos taken by my father which bring back the pleasant memories of our time. We spent several days at Nantucket visiting Cliff and Kaye. At this time Nantucket was still undiscovered and charming in its original way. Big money and New Yorkers hadn't made it there yet.

This was my introduction to Joanne Scott who was called "Jib" then. She sum-mered on the island with her parents and was the girlfriend of Pat White, Kaye Goldsmith's son from a previous marriage. I remember him and his older brother

Pete from our days in Westtown, both tall good looking college men. And as I mentioned earlier, David with his many moonlight sails won out over Pat and later married Joanne.

On the return voyage we stopped in Woods Hole. With the war recently over I believe it wasn't possible to buy meat so we bought a large chunk of freshly caught swordfish. We headed through Quicks Hole, a narrow passage with strong currents sometimes reaching five knots. Once through, we headed for Hadley Harbor in Naushon Island, a private island long used by cruising folk. I remember coming back here over many years and it has never changed. Naushon is still owned by the Forbes family who prohibit any one coming ashore. John Forbes Kerry, former US Secretary of State, is part of the family. We had our wonderful dinner of swordfish and watched the faint lights come on in the several cottages powered by small generators. Several of the Forbes family still summer there and according to the 2000 census it has a population of thrty.

Joanne Scott on board The Heron *at Nantucket 1946.*

And so ended my first experience in cruising on sailboats. It was a great introduction to sailing which has continued most of my life. David Scott went on to finish at the Academy to become an accomplished illustrator. He joined the Air Force, flew P-51s in Korea, and raised a family. Our paths crossed again in 1962 in Annapolis.

After one of these summer vacations, when we returned to Sugarbridge, we realized something had happened in our absence. This 200-year old house never expected thieves or the need for a security system. There were no locks of the modern kind but instead the door handle, normally pushed down to activate the lock, was turned counter-clockwise and we took the very large key with us. As usual, upon return we would simply wind the handle back on. This time, however, as we stepped into the dining room we immediately felt something was missing and suddenly realized the two part original drawing of the fox and the wonderful section of fence my father had done in 1939 for the *Post* was gone! How fitting the story's title "Gone Away" was! Nothing else was missing; someone had clearly wanted that particular drawing. It was the only time we were ever robbed and remains a mystery to this day.

Chapter Three

I Leave Home
The Haverford School Years
1946-1950

In the fall of 1946, when I was fourteen, my parents delivered me to my new school, The Haverford School in Haverford about twenty-five miles from Sugarbridge Farm. They had decided it was time for me to go to a private boarding school instead of the ninth grade in the West Chester public school. Several of my friends from West Chester were already attending Haverford, including Gibby Cornwell, his brother Danny, and Tommy Parke, a cousin. Many of the girls in our group went to Main Line girls schools.

Haverford was predominately a day school of 600 boys, with a small boarding department of about thirty-five boys. Most of the boarders came from long distance locations like Caracas, Venezuela, El Salvador, Green Bay, Wisconsin, and Indiana. My roommate that first year was Conrad Weinrich from Narbeth, Pennsylvania. He was in Second Form, a scrawny red haired kid with a decidedly German accent. We tolerated each other but hardly became friends.

I was only twenty-five miles from home but it seemed much more. Some weekends I would go home but mostly, I stayed on campus. We all lived in an old, three-story building called The Oakes. A large part of what had been the dorm had been destroyed by a fire and was not usable. We were all in one wing with two upper floors of rooms. My West Chester friends were day students which meant they rode the train from Paoli and were picked up by their parents. As a boarder, I definitely felt elite.

First of all, there was the formality of having our own dining room for dinner instead of the cafeteria where all the day students ate. Then we had to dress for dinner in black suits instead of the customary sport jacket and tie normally worn at prep schools. (Most masters wouldn't even allow a sweater under the jacket). Each of us boys took turns in waiting on tables. I had the good fortune to be assigned to Dr. Wilson's table in the corner as you entered the dining room. Most of the boys dreaded Dr. Wilson's table but somehow I enjoyed it.

"Buck" Wilson, as he was known, had been Haverford's Headmaster in the 1930s and was retired since the early '40s and just lived in the Oakes. He was a tall, ram-rod straight man, balding with white hair, and wore wire-rimmed glasses, with a gold watch chain dangling from his dark suit. He had a nineteenth century elegance and was definitely from the "old School." A North Carolinian, his accent was intriguing as he told wonderful stories of the past at the school.

Hudson Covert, another Oakes teacher and head of our dorm, was quite a contrast with Dr. Wilson, I remember Mr. Covert in his tweed jacket with suede elbow patches, balding, and always with a tan and a smile. He taught French, which I did not take, so I never had him in class; he was a bit more of one of the boys. He certainly befriended me when I first arrived, probably looking a little lost.

Charlie Dethier, master of the third floor in the Oakes dormitory 1946-48.

On the third floor of the Oakes dorm there were five rooms with two boys each. In the room across the hall from mine was Charlie Dethier (pronounced De-chair) the floor master who taught in the lower school. Charlie turned out to be one of the most important people in my future. In many ways the dorm life was a more meaningful part of my four years of Haverford than school itself. It was here that I learned the value of regular study, probably only because every evening after dinner we had a two hour or so study hall. It was held in Physics/Chemistry classroom on the lower floor of the dorm and usually run by Henry "Hank" Cleaves, who taught English in the upper school.

Hank came from Bar Harbor and his was my first introduction to a real Maine accent. He was certainly at the far end of the spectrum from Buck Wilson as he slouched, half sitting on a desk. If we were quiet and good he would sometimes tell us about life in Bar Harbor. In the fall of 1947 he was especially anxious to get news of the great Bar Harbor fire which nearly destroyed most of the fine old estate houses in that town. That fall was probably the worst fire damage throughout all of Maine due to the extreme drought. Hank's wife Rachel also taught English in the lower school. They had an apartment in the dorm. By the time I got to college I had no trouble getting my homework done each night because of the forced study hall habit and Hank Cleaves.

There were two things we boys were forced to do monthly as boarding students. We had to attend the dances held at the Merion Cricket Club. I had already had a bit of this in West Chester but I really wasn't comfortable as we all sat on one side of the room in our tuxes staring awkwardly at the fancy dressed girls on the other side. It was not fun. I recall meeting up with one of the twin sisters I'd gone to kindergarten with at the Leopard School, either A or B. We had nothing much to say. She was much taller than me.

The other monthly event was much more to my liking. Again dressed up, all of us trooped into the Philadelphia Orchestra's evening concert under the expert direction of Eugene Ormandy. It was a real treat and the beginning of my love of classical music and a live orchestra.

Haverford School was started about 1884 and was located across the road from Haverford College which as far as I knew was not connected in any way. The curriculum was based on that of the Boston Latin School with four courses each semester. A predominantly waspish school, Haverford also required that a history of religion course be taught each year so I took courses in the Old Testament and New Testament. I'm not sure what this meant to the few boys who were Jewish. The only Jew I recall was David Harrison, whom I saw again at our fifty-fifth reunion.

Our other two courses of religion were fairly interesting. Headmaster Dr. Leslie R. Severinghaus taught the course on comparative world religions. He had spent many years in the East with missionaries and later married Emmavail Luce, sister of Henry Luce, who co-founded *Time Magazine*. Emmavail was a student at Wellesley and graduated in 1922, the same class as my mother, but they weren't acquainted. We called him Mr. instead of Dr. as he had several honorary doctorate titles. He began teaching English in Beijing, China where his parents were missionaries. Mr. Severinghaus had acquired the nickname at Haverford of "Buddha" from his long time teaching various courses on Eastern religion. Many years later I ran into him while we both lived in Miami, a bit older but still the tall impressive man I had remembered.

Our other courses were four years of English, two of Latin, two of Spanish, several histories of which American was the best and Algebra 1 & 2, Geometry, and Trigonometry, which I never got to. Perhaps it would have been better if I had started Haverford in seventh grade or First Form, as our grades were known. By starting in Third Form I was already behind a whole year in math. So after a year of introductory algebra, I was given a test to see if I could jump ahead to Algebra 2. I failed the test with a 42 but some well-meaning teacher decided it would okay to skip algebra I. Later, I found out that he had made a terrible decision. If only I could have found this person and wrung his neck! I found myself hopelessly lost in second year algebra and was faced with summer school.

In spite of my failure, my math teacher, Dr. Harold Garner, stands out as one of the more memorable teachers. Known as "Pop" Garner, he was likely in his sixties but to us he seemed ancient. He was slightly balding, gray-white hair, glasses: your typical geezer of a teacher. I remember him in very rumpled, light blue seersucker suit. He was a real disciplinarian and put up with no nonsense or horseplay. But this was just what the guys loved, to taunt him while his back was turned while at the board. If anyone whispered or created a disturbance he somehow always knew who the culprits were and have them march up to the front of the room.

Here he had his favorite narrow stick, a part of the desk pencil rack, which he deftly slipped out from the desk. He might have as many as three or four of us. Each, in turn, had to lift his jacket, bend over and receive a smart, stinging whack on the behind. This punishment was being "Garnerized"; no one was spared. It happened to me more than once and it really hurt. Of course, we all deserved it and never thought of complaining. Things were different in private school although I doubt this behavior and discipline would occur today. Mr. Garner was a good math teacher even though I didn't do well.

Pop" Garner, algebra teacher for Three and Four Form; he was a real disciplinarian.

While on the subject of favorite teachers, my other favorite was Mr. Herman Shaw. We always addressed him as "Colonel" and he taught American History. He came from South Carolina but I don't know in what war, if any, he earned the title Colonel. He, like Mr. Garner, was in in his sixties, had a white mustache, wore a tweed jacket, and spoke with that South Carolinian accent. The year I had him was either 1948 or 49 and while he taught mostly from the history textbook by Muzzey and came from the south, he was clearly bothered by the racial problems that were growing in our country. (It would be many years before an African-American would attend Haverford). Looking back he was able to see the difficulties that the south was to experience. He said to us one day with a slight twinkle in his eye, " The solution to the problem of the Negro in America will be that sometime in the future all of us will have slightly darker skin color and a little bit of wavy hair." I've thought of his statement over the years and always concluded it was a pretty amazing one for such a gentleman from the old South to make.

Colonel Shaw from South Carolina taught us American history.

I received one more lesson from Colonel Shaw. He used to give short quizzes in his history class, usually five questions. I happened to be in his room after school for make-up test. Somehow, I switched one test with another; in fact, I cheated. And he caught me. This was long before the practice of cheating had become so prevalent. He gave me a stern lecture but had no intention of reporting my action. I was thoroughly chastised and never attempted to cheat again.

Another memorable Haverford tradition was the morning assembly. Each day before classes began we would all gather in a large room on the third floor for brief prayer and announcements. It was here that we had our study hall, home room desks, and Fifth Form speaking presentations. Every boy was required to present a public speech before the entire school for five minutes. I can't recall what my subject was or what sort of grade I received, but I was definitely nervous about it. It turned out this was good training for presenting papers later in my career.

When I had left West Chester public school at the end of the eighth grade to start at Haverford I met a new group of kids my age from the north end of town. Some continued going to the local schools but most went to the private schools along the Main Line. It wasn't until I began to commute to Haverford, however, that I got to know this gang who daily went back and forth. The girls included "Cissi" (Anne Emlen) Graham, her younger sister, Wawa (Marie Louise), "Jerry" (Marjory) Parke, Nancy Smith, and Betsy Barnes. While I had brief crushes on these girls, Cissi became my "steady" for the best part of those last two years at Haverford.

Being sixteen years old was also the coming of age and being able to drive. It meant a large amount of freedom and having girls in my car. I remember many sessions where all of us guys and girls would gather in the spacious kitchen at the home of Cissi and Wawa. Their mother, Mala Graham, had re-married Frank Keene, a wealthy older gentleman who at that time was quite ill. We would all congregate in this large, cold, dark kitchen while the parents were upstairs in the living room. The house was built all of stone and was rumored to have been a castle imported from France. Next to the kitchen was a three-car garage where Cissi and I would sneak away from the gang and neck in one the Keene's fancy leather-seated convertibles in the garage.

Anne Emlen Graham, "Cissi" to us, with Duke at Sugarbridge 1950
in my Haverford "H" jacket.

Cissi was short and athletic, about five foot four, with dark hair. She had a flair for drawing and loved art. She used to come to visit my father at Sugarbridge and watch him draw, learning tips from him. She and I rode the train to school that one year I commuted.

I remember the day Cissi broke my nose. We were at a friend's house and she was sitting on my lap. Suddenly she threw her back as a wasp or bee flew toward her and her head smashed my nose. I had already broken it wrestling, and rebroke it later in a Jeep accident at Exton. Somewhere along the line a doctor told me I had a deviated septum. My mother, ever the anglophile, would often reproach me, saying: "You had such a straight English nose without any bumps on it!"

The next time I caught up with Cissi was in 1991, while visiting Jerry Parke Kinkead in Wayne, Pennsylvania, who had arranged a West Chester gang reunion. There had been a major reunion earlier that summer but I missed it because I was working in Greenland. I hadn't seen any of my high school colleagues for nearly forty-five years. Shockingly, the girls Jerry, Cissi, Wawa, and Nancy all looked just the way I remember their mothers looking.

Cissi had aged a bit, as had we all, with gray hair. She was divorced from her husband, Nick Minich, a minister, and had several grown children, one of whom was a television newscaster on one of the Portland stations. She worked at an art store in Philadelphia and was painting odd but most interesting renderings that were on exhibit at various galleries. She told me she had a plan to earn enough money to buy a house at Days Landing, just north of Bath, Maine on the Kennebec.

Ellie and I went to see her exhibit at Bowdoin College sometime in the '90s. Her work was filled with lots of nudes, sexual genitalia, antiwar statements, and dark, foreboding images. It was somewhat disturbing but certainly in keeping with how I knew her and so unlike her free-spirited sister Wawa, an art guide at the N.C. Wyeth house at the Brandywine Museum, whom I saw several years ago. Cissi and I exchanged Christmas cards and postcard notes for a few years. I don't think she ever escaped from her workday job to the dream house in Maine. I still get announcement cards from her telling of her various art shows in Maine and Pennsylvania.

When I went to the West Chester schools I never got involved in sports. Actually, unless you were an outstanding athlete the only option was to take "gym" which meant getting into white shorts, shirt, and sneakers and playing basketball or some other indoor exercise. I hated it. But when I arrived a private school I found there were so many different sports and teams that it became fun. In the fall there was soccer or football so I chose football. Teams started at seventy pounds in the lower school and worked all the way up to 135 pounds before becoming Junior Varsity and Varsity. I was placed on the 105-pound team and played tackle or guard. Later on I made it to the 120-pound team, where we played other schools. Of course we wore all the protective equipment under the gold and maroon uniforms. The difference was here my parents had to pay to buy my equipment. which was not cheap.

Neil Buckley, wrestling coach, with the best high school record of 500 wins over his long career.

For winter sports I was recruited for the wrestling team in my Third Form year by Neil Buckley, second floor master in the Oakes. Mr. Buckley was just starting at Haverford after returning from Japan after the war where he had been an MP. He was a tall, well-built pleasant man, probably in his mid-twenties and hailed from Methuen, Massachusetts. He, like most of the teachers in a boarding school, was required to coach a sport. Since he had known jujitsu it was perfect match for him to take on the job as wrestling coach.

The wrestling team had started the previous year and some of the boys knew a bit of the sport but Mr. Buckley set out to teach us all. I started at the 103-pound class. That first year we lost more matches than we won although we did have several pretty good kids like Dickie and Buster Dillon, Bill Buckley (no relation to the coach) and Red Roland, who, at heavyweight and over 200 pounds, was undefeated.

Neil Buckley took his coaching job seriously and made us work hard. We had to run twenty laps every day around the track, even in bad weather. And then we did the usual sit ups, push ups, and neck bridging. I never became a very good wrestler or made first team. But the coach used me in later years if we didn't have a man at a particular weight to keep from forfeiting. In other words, I was a sacrificial player. If I could keep from getting pinned which was a five-point loss, the team would only lose three points. When we once went to St. Andrews School in Delaware, Neil asked me to wrestle at 165 pounds, even though I weighed barely 130. My only advantage was that I would be faster than my opponent. I got badly tossed around but managed to avoid the dreaded slap on the mat by the ref and we saved two points. I felt pretty proud.

My father was also proud of me as a wrestler but I can only recall that he came to one meet. It was a home meet at the school and I was probably in the 133 pound match. Dad was in the stand watching and as with most all of my matches, I lost, but wasn't pinned. Dad went on to write an article about that day which he titled, "The Son He'd Never Met". It was published in *The Saturday Evening Post* in 1951 dad had published twelve short stories in the *Post*.

I earned two letters, a baby H and a jock H, but the thing I was most proud of was that Neil Buckley went on as coach at Haverford for another forty-plus years and had a record of 646 wins, the national record for high school wrestling. I saw him several times on returning to reunions and he looked amazingly young and fit. He died in 1994 at age seventy-eight. Haverford honored him by building a new section of the gym just for wrestling and naming it for him.

During the summer of 1947, when I was fifteen, I got my first job. I had always been given plenty of chores to do around the farm, mainly caring for the farm animals, for which I received an allowance. Now, through friends of my parents, I was offered a chance to work at the *Archive*, a weekly newspaper published in the neighboring town of Downingtown. The owners, Bob and Jane McIlvane, were journalists who had bought this paper and its somewhat antiquated printing press and associated machines. I was given job of "printer's apprentice" and I took the print or hot "lead" as it came off the Linotype machine along with photo cuts and helped set up ads. All the type was backwards and it took me a while to learn how to read backwards. Each ad was set up, locked in place with spacers, carefully leveled out with a block and hammer, and after "pulling" a proof, made up for a whole page. It wasn't hard work but a bit boring for a fifteen-year-old boy. Although I only worked part time, even in those days the $10 per week wasn't enough to keep my interest. I lasted about a month. In retrospect I realize that I was lucky to have had this experience of learning about typesetting with the Linotype process which totally disappeared in the 1960s. Offset printing was giving way to electronic publishing and ultimately led to computers and the internet.

Jane McIlvane had published a book about the *Archive* called *It Happens Every Thursday* which was the day the paper came out. Bob had good political connections and a few years later became an advance man for the Eisenhower campaign in 1952. They came frequently to our Sugarbridge parties along with Claude and Frances Rains, and Harry Rosen, a sculptor who about this time made the "Head of Ned" when I was about fourteen. I sat patiently many hours in his studio for this work, of which he made two copies. Later on, Bob and Jane moved to the Washington area where Jane became involved in writing another book about the Antarctic. She wrote an "as told to" book about her neighbor in Virginia, Jenny Darlington, who in 1947 with Finn Ronne's wife, Jackie, who were the first women to go to the Antarctic. *My Antarctic Honeymoon* was published in 1957. In 2007 at the Explorers Club Annual dinner, Julie Palais, my stepdaughter, introduced me to Jackie Ronne and her daughter Karen Ronne Tupek. Together, they presented the Finn Ronne award. Strange how everything is connected.

It was equally interesting that through Jane's connection with the Antarctic, I had met up with Bob and Jane in Washington when I had finished my Master's degree in 1957 and was looking for a way to do polar research as part of the International Geophysical Year (IGY). I recall having lunch with them at a fancy hotel where they introduced me to Paul Siple, famous for his trip to the South Pole with Byrd. He later wrote *A Boy Scout with Byrd* in the 1930s. But, as I came to later learn, the old adage of "it's who you know" didn't work for me.

Also at that luncheon I met Joseph Alsop who, together with his brother, Stewart, were among the most distinguished journalists in Washington. I confess that I really was not that aware of either of them at the time. Jane had good horse riding connections where she rode with Jack Kennedy in Virginia just before his rise to fame. Her photo of him is good for a laugh. So, in a way my short job as a printer in 1947 came close to getting me into to doing the polar work that I later wound up with in the 1990s.

Jane McIllvane, editor of Downingtown Archive *with Sen Jack Kennedy as riding partners in Virginia about 1952.*

During this time, we had an occasional visitor to the farm, Hans Kindler, who had been a long time friend of my mother. Hans was from Holland, was a well known cellist, and founder of the National Symphony in Washington. He started out with The Philadelphia Orchestra in 1927. When he visited, my mother and he went on long walks through the woods in deep conversation. Occasionally I would go along. I recall him as being tall and quiet. When I was fifteen, we drove to DC to hear him conduct the National Symphony where we sat up front as special guests. Hans died in 1949. I still have a couple of his best known 78 rpm records.

During the summer of 1947, my family and I decided to try our hands at cruising again after the previous summer aboard David Scott's *Heron*. This time we chose to go aboard an unusual vessel skippered by Captain Pete Culler. He became better known as R.D. Culler and was later famous for over one hundred designs of small boats. Pete had fallen in love with the *Spray*, a thirty-five-foot yawl on which, in 1895 Joshua Slocum had been the first person to singlehandedly circumnavigate around the world. Culler had begun construction of his replica in 1929 in Oxford, Maryland. Slocum had found a derelict boat in Mattapoisett, Massachusetts and rebuilt her for his world voyage. Culler tried to reproduce this shallow draft, oyster-type vessel with the expert help of Alonzo Conley, a master builder. Culler's *Spray* was as plain as the original with no varnish or brass or other typical yacht trim, just a plain, simple work boat.

My parents and I met Pete and his wife, Toni, in Newport, Rhode Island to begin our charter. We were shown our quarters in the main cabin. At the time I was totally unaware of the history and fame of Slocum and his world encircling feat, although I suspect my father knew of it. The cabin was well decorated with photos and books about Slocum which helped fill in the background. Slocum's own book, *Sailing Alone Around the World* is a classic of the first degree, and one I read soon after.

We headed for Nantucket again, although at a somewhat slower pace. *Spray* was solid and very heavy, making it a slow sailor even in higher winds. I remember sitting at the wheel which had many spokes and steering on my watch. Pete and Toni were in the aft cabin which gave us a bit of privacy, not easy on a thirty-five-foot boat. Each morning Pete would be up early washing down the paint of the house and deck with buckets of salt water; most yachts were washed with fresh water to keep the salt off. There was no main engine but the dinghy had a small motor for maneuvering in harbor. I have several pictures of Pete with his well known, long-billed cap, pipe in mouth, and his worn, black and red checked wool shirt. He was short on words like many New Englanders, but possessed a great sense of humor.

Capt RD "Pete" Culler and his Wife, Toni about to board Spray, *Newport, RI, 1947.*

Soon after departing Newport as we entered the Cape Cod Canal, I was seized with an attack of appendicitis late at night. I was just fifteen at the time. My parents were most concerned, as were the s. We pulled into a dock about halfway through the canal and called a taxi that took me and my parents to the emergency room of the Cape Cod Hospital in Hyannis. I don't recall being in any great pain, just uncomfortable. It was about one in the morning. The young doctor on duty poked around a bit, then decided to pack the suspect area with ice. By morning the inflammation had subsided and I was

Spray, *35-foot replica of Joshua Slocum's ketch that circumnavigated the world in 1896.*

discharged. We continued our voyage to Nantucket. My appendix supposedly atrophied and never bothered me again. Years later I read in an article on Pete Culler and found that he and Toni sold their beloved ship in 1951. Although there are many replicas of Slocum's *Spray*, I always believed that Pete Culler's was the closest to the original. Around 1990, I became friends with a Window Quilt customer named Joel Slocum who lived in Wellesley and was a direct descendant of Joshua. Although Joel wasn't a sailor he had many photos of the original *Spray* and knew much about Joshua's mysterious disappearance. After his return from his remarkable three year voyage in 1898, he left again in 1909 but was never heard from again. My brief two week cruise with Pete and Toni Culler was a most memorable sailing experience for a young novice sailor.

When I was in my mid-teens I recall going to visit my godfather, Claude Rains, at his farm called Stock Grange about ten miles from Sugarbridge. The farm spread over six hundred acres of beautiful rolling Pennsylvania countryside. It was a working farm with steers and fields of hay and crops. The hired man, Charles, took care of it while Claude made movies and lots of money. He and Frances, his fourth wife, spent as much time as possible there and had an amazing collection of antiques. He would invite me to spend weekends there and swim in the large farm pool which my friend Stacy claimed had leeches in it. A few years later while on one of these weekend jaunts Claude celebrated my twenty-first birthday with British tradition: he gave me his personal knife, a stainless steel pocket model by Eliot-Pernet. In return it was custom for me to give him a penny, which I did. I still have the knife

My Godfather, Claude Rains, at his Farm Stock Grange Coatesville, Pennsylvania , 1952.

Claude Rains in Casablanca, *his best known movie, 1942.*

somewhere. I also recall sometime in the late '40s sitting out on his terrace with his English nephew, Dirk Bogarde, who was just starting out on his acting career. He later went on to become Sir Dirk with quite a distinguished movie life with some seventy movies and TV productions.

The farm was sold in 1957. Their only daughter, Jennifer, changed her name to Jessica, as there was already a Jennifer Rains in films. After attending Bennington she continued on in the film business, producing a marvelous biography of her father in 2008. I visited Claude once in the 60s when he had married for the sixth time. He died in 1967 at seventy-eight at his home in New Hampshire. He left a remarkable legacy of more than a hundred movies and plays. He was nominated twice for an Oscar but never won. I always felt proud that he had been a special friend and my godfather.

In my later years at Haverford I went to wild weekend parties. Often, the parents or chaperones who should have been there were absent, and rowdy brawls resulted because there was always plenty of booze. I still felt like an outsider. Perhaps this was so partly because I was by nature small and quiet and my classmates were all tall and loud. So, sometime in my Sixth Form year I convinced my father to let me have a party at Sugarbridge for all my Haverford guys and their girls. To my surprise a great number of my class of about sixty boys drove the thirty miles and much to my parents displeasure it turned out to be a mistake.

I may have been foolish enough to promise them that there were would be no drinking or such, but of course there was. Actually, my father had gotten a keg of beer. As you might expect the kids got a little drunk and slightly out of hand. My father tried his best to keep order and amazingly everyone survived the return trip to their far away homes. These days it is surely considered criminal to serve minors alcohol. The things my parents went through for their only son! Finally, I had achieved fame for all the wrong reasons and was remembered for a great party. Several of the "big men on campus" wrote their thanks and memories of "that party" in my Haverford yearbook. Looking back on that party I wish I had been remembered for brains or even brawn, not merely for a party.

Haverford School was a good experience and I owe a lot to the school for the learning side and the growing up side. I often wonder how I would have done if instead I had stayed at West Chester in the High School, both academically and socially. Quite a few of my buddies and girls from there went away to private school, although most of them came back to live nearby. And I wound up at Haverford with a D+ average, in the lower fifth of my class. Clearly I wasn't into trying to get good grades. I'm sure my parents deplored my grades but they never demanded or punished me about them; there was far less pressure than today's kids are subjected to. Part of my low standing was that the academic level was considerably beyond that of the public schools I'd been attending. This was certainly true in math.

Although I never took classes from Charlie Dethier, the master of the third floor in the Oakes, I was fascinated with his brilliance. He truly had what was called a "photographic memory." I remember watching him scan diagonally across down one side of a page and up the other in a few seconds and then tell you the complete contents of what he had read. He was especially good at math and was aware of the difficulties I had encountered. Charlie had mentioned that during the summer he ran the yacht club in Blue Hill, Maine. So when it came time for summer school, as seemed inevitable, he asked if I would be able to go to Maine for the summer where his cousin Bernie would tutor me so I could pass Algebra 2. Of course, I leaped at the chance since Mr. Cleaves had repeatedly described the beauty of his home state. The summer of 1949 was a turning point for me. My father drove me to Blue Hill in our 1949 Plymouth. The town and harbor were situated at the foot of Blue Hill, a steep hill about 940 feet high. On top was a fire tower and from its sixty foot height you could see for miles and miles along up and down the coast. I think Charlie had told us to try a family boarding house run by the Partridge family. The Partridge House was right in the village across from the town hall which also doubled as the local movie theater at night. I rented a room there on the third floor with a shared bathroom. The price was $7 a week, a bargain even in 1949.

Every morning at about ten thirty, Bernie Dethier would arrive and we had an hour's tutoring session in the living room. His repetitive drills did the job and put a better foundation under me. Even so, math never became my strong suit. But sailing did. Charlie Dethier's summer job during his vacation was running the Kolligewidgewok Yacht Club, the local Indian name for Blue Hill. The clubhouse was newly built just after the war on a point in the inner harbor on the north end of Blue Hill Bay. This and the Country Club were the centers of activity for all of us young summer people. It was here at the Yacht Club that I met my lifelong friend, Berto Nevin.

For the record, his full name was Ethelbert Nevin II and he hailed from Darien, Connecticut. Berto's family had a large summer cottage near Blue Hill Falls, several miles south of the village, with a commanding view over the bay. As I got to know the family, I learned that Berto's grandfather, Ethelbert, was a major American composer best known for his piano songs of the late nineteenth century. Among these *Mighty Lak' a Rose* and *The Rosary* were the most familiar. Most of the family members played the piano.

Berto's father, Paul, worked for Sparkman and Stephens in New York, a firm famous for some of the best sailboat designs of all time. Needless to say sailing was in a major part of the family's life. Although I had had experience sailing as a passenger on some larger boats my introduction to sailing with Berto was in his 21-foot sloop, a "J" class, one of several racing classes in Blue Hill, and incidentally design No 1 by Olin Stephens when he was about twenty-three years old. Stephens turned out to be one of the most successful designers of the twentieth century.

Shortly after meeting Berto he took me for a short sail in his boat. We were running before the wind off Long Island in the bay in a fresh breeze. He very boldly handed me the tiller and said something to the effect, "you're sailing the boat." Although I'd spent time on bigger boats with a paid skipper, I really wasn't very knowledgeable. Berto, on the other hand, had been sailing probably from age five or six, like most of the summer kids there. Without realizing what I was doing, I let the boat fall off course and suddenly with no warning the mainsail boom came crashing across the stern — a scary all standing gibe. Later I would learn there were plenty of warning signs. I was never sure whether Berto wasn't paying attention or that he wanted me to learn from this mistake.

Such a maneuver puts a lot strain on the mast and rigging. I later recall seeing photos of boats being dismasted by such dumb tricks. Berto calmly remarked that this was a no-no and not a good move. From that time on I've always been keenly aware of the "accidental gibe" and its brother, the "goose wing gibe" where the boom cocks up at an angle catching on the back stay and potentially carrying it away leaving the mast unsupported. It was a heck of an introduction to sailing. I spent much of that first summer crewing for Berto with races every Wednesday and Saturday. All I can remember of our races was one where the tiller of *Ranger* broke, leaving us just a bare stub attached to the rudder post. Somehow between us we managed to finish the race. Berto and I had fun at racing while there were others who had already become serious and determined competitors...shades of the world to come!

Ethelbert "Berto" Nevin, Blue Hill, Maine, 1950, A LifetimeFriend.

There were two "older" young men who assisted Charlie Dethier at the yacht club, Chet Harrington and George Wales. Both were going into their junior year at Colby College in Waterville, Maine. So during the summer Chet and George made sure that I was aware of the many outstanding points in favor of Colby and tried their best to recruit me. Unlike today, where there is such early preparation for college, I hadn't given much thought to where I wanted to go to college the following year. I filed their suggestion for future reference, but I had my sights set on other more prestigious colleges. Luckily, the seed was planted and had it not been for Chet's strong recommendation for Colby, I doubt that I would have attended.

That summer of 1949 the year before college I went through a typical summer romance in Blue Hill. I had just turned seventeen. I fell for one of the gals in our group named Deedee Tate. Her real name was Diane; she was a good sailor, golfer, and tennis player. She was cute, a bit of a tomboy, and really she was quite shy. Deedee was small, very athletic, with short brown hair and twinkly blue eyes. The Tates came from Westport, Connecticut and were in some way related to the Rockefellers. They had a beautiful, elegant compound of a house with outbuildings, and dock on the water about halfway between the town and the Falls. Deedee drove around in her new Pontiac station wagon. I was enchanted by her but I doubt she felt the same way about me. We went on group dates and movie dates.

On one occasion, we double dated with Berto. It was a perfect Maine evening with a moon on the water. We were in the back seat of Berto's 1941 Ford convertible. While Deedee was a good kisser, she was a bit uneasy about boys. Our romance was short lived but still one of those memorable teen loves. It was through Deedee, however, that I met her school roommate, "Yassu," an exotic gal who was visiting from Russia. Being Russian, she had five names but now all I can remember is Arianna Yassukovich. She was tall, slender, darkhaired and lots of fun — the sort of person you could imagine becoming a model these days. Murt Davis and I drove to visit her on Long Island, in my father's illegally borrowed car. It was hardly a serious affair but it helped me get to know a variety of girls. I never saw or heard of Deedee again until quite recently when Berto mentioned that she had died. I wish that I had been able to see her again in later life.

By the end of August, 1949, my tutoring was complete and my father drove all the way from West Chester to pick me up at the Partridge House, tanned, happy, and most important, a young man hooked on sailing and on Maine. And incidentally, I passed my math test on return to Haverford, so I was able to graduate, thanks to Bernie. I vaguely remember taking some sort of SAT that fall but have no memory of the score. My grades were certainly below average, so I had no chance at the colleges where I applied, Swarthmore and Stanford. Why on earth I had a notion to apply to these I don't recall. They were hardly realistic choices with my Cs and Ds.

All I can remember is arriving with my parents at Colby in Waterville, Maine in late April of 1950. We had a tour of the campus and met George Nickerson, Dean of Men. The campus back then was bare and windswept with only a handful of small sapling trees; construction was still going on. Colby then was a long way from the hallowed halls of ivy. I decided to apply even at this late date.

As I was finishing up my last days at Haverford late that May or maybe even early June, to my surprise I received an acceptance letter. Needless to say I was excited about getting into college and felt really good about it. It was sometime later that fall I learned the real story. It turned out the Admissions Department, in its infinite wisdom, had decided to take an extra thirty men in anticipation of the looming conflict on the horizon in Korea, a place few of us had heard anything about. I knew nothing about the fact that on June 25, Communist North Korean troops had crossed the 38th Parallel and invaded South Korea.

Supposedly, the college officials thought there might be some of the freshmen dropping out to join up — the whole patriotic feeling was still strong from after the last war. Going to war at age eighteen was hardly anything I had ever thought of. So I got in on a fluke. At least two of the guys on our floor did drop out at the end of their first year and joined the Army, one of them came back to graduate several years later, the other disappeared. This "Forgotten War" lasted for thirty-seven months of fighting in which 53,000 Americans died and 103,000 were wounded. It was also the first conflict in which the United Nations sanctioned such intervention, the beginning of many of our country's bad decisions.

The summer of 1950, after graduation from Haverford, I returned to Blue Hill pleased that I would be going to Waterville in the fall and going to a Maine college.

Berto had invited to me to stay with him for the summer at his Blue Hill house. A great deal of my attraction to Blue Hill began that summer as I was taken into the Nevin family. I ate meals with them and Berto and I shared adjoining screened sleeping porches on the second floor. Known as "Airly Beacon," this wonderful turn-of-the century Maine cottage had a grand front porch looking over the whole of Blue Hill Bay. Every morning Berto and I sat on the front porch and had a leisurely breakfast, basking in the warmth of the early morning sun, and the cool from the nearby ocean. Later, we would be joined by his mother, Jennie, who was in her late fifties and now a widow as his father, Paul, had died the summer before.

*Jane Nevin in her classic 1947 MG TC; she would lean out the low
cut door to strike a match for her cigarette.*

I really never knew Paul Nevin at all. I had met him briefly that summer before he became ill. The summer before, Berto and I visited his dad in New York. We had flown out of Trenton which was and still is called Bar Harbor Airport although it's about six miles or so before you reach Bar Harbor. It stands out in my memory because this was my first time to fly in any kind of an airplane. I was thrilled in taking my first flight.

The aircraft was a DC-3, the backbone and workhorse of so many start-up airlines. The airline, Northeast, is now long gone. Later, I flew on DC-3s for many years in various countries. It was a less happy time to visit Paul Nevin in the hospital. I think he died soon after.

Jennie Nevin was an attractive woman and so warm toward me. I really did feel like one of the family. Berto had two older sisters. The younger one, Jane, had the Nevin family look of their grandfather, Ethelbert, with the long, narrow face, dark hair and complexion, and an irreverent, off-the-wall sense of humor. Her language was as unladylike as I'd ever heard and filled with expletives. She was famous around

Blue Hill for her familiar 1947 MG TC, with the big wire wheels and clamshell fenders now worth a mint and a half — well, at least $50,000. She was famous also for leaning out over the road to strike a match to light her cigarette, a trick that could only be done from the low-cut door of the MG. Jane that summer became my idol and favorite character. Even though she was about five years older than me we bonded over literature like the favorite that summer, J.D. Salinger's *Catcher in the Rye* and Ray Bradbury's *Martian Chronicles*.

The Nevin family gathered on the front porch of the "Airly Beacon" cottage in Blue Hill, 1949 Jenney, Jane, Paul, and Berto Nevin.

In subsequent years we wrote each other; she was at Barnard while I was at Colby. Somewhere, in an obscure file I have preserved at least one of her memorable letters. Jane and I once paddled her canoe from the house all the way to the yacht club around midnight, then we paddled back in the fading moonlight and finally in total darkness avoiding rocks and ledges. She also had a beautiful boat, an Atlantic class, a thirty-one-foot racing sloop of which there were half a dozen or so in Blue Hill. Her father was instrumental in getting this class of boats introduced to Maine

Although I didn't realize it at the time, those two Blue Hill summers became the foundation on which I would build a large part of my subsequent life. How lucky I was to have been led to Maine by a math deficiency!

Chapter Four

I Leave Home for Good
The Colby Years 1950-1954

In late August of 1950, right after a mild hurricane with gusts up to 85 mph, I realized it was time to head home briefly to West Chester to pack for college. Then sometime in early September, I returned on the fabled Bar Harbor Express. The age of the overnight train was drawing to a close and this was one of the last runs of this train. I boarded the train in Philadelphia at 30th St station late in the afternoon. The station, a bit like Grand Central, had enormous high ceilings and equally tall windows; the afternoon light slanted through and made long rays in the poorly lit space. It has changed very little in the last fifty years.

I was shown to an upper berth in the sleeping car by the porter. As soon as I had stowed my gear I went back to the Club car with ample comfortable seats, tables, and a steward ready to take orders. I ordered a drink and that's how I met a most interesting person. I sat toward the rear of the car and talked to this new acquaintance. After a while as we were nearing New York and having shared various experiences and some talk of Maine and such, he leaned forward and asked if I could do him a favor. Of course, I responded. He said he had an elderly mother who lived in Blue Hill and since I was going there, asked if I would be kind enough to carry a package to her? Later that evening as I was in my berth he came by and handed me two cartons of eggs tied together. Can you imagine someone trying such a thing now? Me, the trusting kid from the country, thought nothing of it and certainly didn't even consider taking a peek in the package.

I arrived the next morning in Ellsworth, took a taxicab to Blue Hill and on the way down to the Falls and Berto's house, asked the driver to stop at a small, old house just before the country club. I knocked on the door, met the woman, and told her of my trip the evening before. She thanked me but made no comment. I'll never know what was in the package; was it eggs or something else? It's always been a question to ponder.

I spent a week at Airly Beacon before heading to Colby and was lucky to get a ride from Blue Hill to Waterville. Patty LeVecque, a long time summer person, was a returning junior at Colby and had offered me a ride. She and her brother Freddy both went to Colby, but, unlike Chet and George, I never remember them trying to recruit me for the college. Patty was small, quite attractive, with reddish blond hair.

She had a brand new Hudson convertible, sporty and low slung. It truly lived up to the advertising slogan of "you have to step down to get in."

We arrived on Mayflower Hill, top down, car loaded with Patty's clothes piled high on the backseat and swooped around the corner of Averill Hall in the late afternoon with a great fanfare. A group of freshmen was standing around at the entrance to the quadrangle as she screeched to a halt. I felt very self-conscious and at the same time pretty important to be arriving like this. I saw Patty from time to time that first year in History class, but we were hardly close friends.

Patty and Freddy had found themselves extremely wealthy a few years earlier when their parents both died in an airplane accident. The LeVecques were from Columbus, Ohio where there was a building named for them. There was some connection with the atomic bomb and their father; his beautiful Chris-Craft motorboat was named the *Manhattan P*. Patty went on to marry Dave Heiliner, also a summer person, and settled in Blue Hill at least in summers and maybe some winters. I think both Patty and Freddy are no longer with us.

I was off to a good start at college. Earlier that summer I had received a letter from Colby, the usual sort of freshman indoctrination with college announcements. It said my roommate was named Derek Tatlock and he was from Pittsford, New York.

Derek Tatlock was my freshman roommate in Averill Hall, 1950-51.

73

When I had read the name Tatlock, a movie name came to mind, *Miss Tatlock's Millions*. Although it carried images of great wealth, Derek, or "Tat," as was his nickname, turned out to be about as average in wealth as the all rest of us. He was, on the other hand, a good choice as a roommate. I have no idea how roommates were selected but he was an outdoor type — a skier, hiker, and an enthusiast for geology. We both took the freshman geology course, one of the largest in attendance partly because it had the reputation of being a "gut" course. It may have been some of Tat's influence that eventually made me choose geology for a major later on.

He was a most personable guy with a broad smile, blond hair, and a bit shorter than me, about five foot seven with an upstate New York accent. Interestingly, Derek, who somewhere along the way we dropped the "Tat," is still one of my better friends. Our room was on the third floor in Averill Hall, a brand new dormitory and we were the first class to live in it. It was absolutely sterile, no art, no interior decoration at all, no common room, just institutional, pale green painted walls of cinderblock.

There were two men to each room. On the end rooms of each floor there were two small sleeping rooms and a large study/living space in the center. For each floor there was a proctor, a senior, who made sure everything was under control. At the outset, there was no drinking allowed in the dorms or, for that matter, anywhere on campus. Of course, some illegal drinking did go on. Our proctor was Charlie Tobin from Everett, Massachusetts, Tobin being a good New England Irish name. Chet Harrington and George Wales, my Blue Hill recruiters, were also dorm proctors in Johnson Hall, the other freshman dorm.

There were about 275 freshmen men and women with most of the students from New England and more than half from Massachusetts and Maine. Although we had a few foreign students I don't recall any being on our floor. There were only nine foreign students, a far cry from today's enrollment from over seventy countries. Our class had two African American men and one woman, Anna Thomas from Tallahassee. Our class may have been the first for persons of color. Both men were on sports scholarships, although I didn't know it that at the time. Neither Gene Floyd from Oyster Bay, New York a three-letter outstanding player, nor Alpheus Trumpeter, a track star, graduated. I never knew Gene very well. There was an incident during freshman year where the barber in Waterville refused to cut his hair. Colby students boycotted the barber. I saw Gene at several reunions later on and we compared notes on our lives since Colby. In the recent list of departed classmates, I see he died in 2013 after working most of his life for the city of Oyster Bay.

A few of the men had been to prep schools but the majority were from public high schools. This, I found, meant that I had a head start on many of the students by having had forced study halls and heavy loads of homework. Did this mean I would wind up with better grades? It should have, but I found I could get by easily

74

with less work. Had I had the sense to work harder I know I would have done much better. Unfortunately, getting good grades was not a goal for me. And, thinking about it now, I'm not sure I had ever set any goals for myself.

Since possession and use of alcohol on the campus was illegal, but certainly occurred. Therefore, most of our drinking was done downtown in Waterville about two miles away. The most memorable spot for Colby students was Onie's Bar, a tavern where all the first year students went to socialize. The state liquor laws stated that customers had to be seated to be served. And what was served was beer only; hard liquor was only sold at hotels, which meant, according to Maine law, there had to be six rooms for rent. Some of these "hotels" existed solely for the purpose of meeting the rule and I doubt that they ever rented rooms. So at Onie's we sat while waiting for the waitress named Alice to take our orders. She was a plump, dark-haired woman I would have guessed to be Greek or maybe Armenian and very jolly.

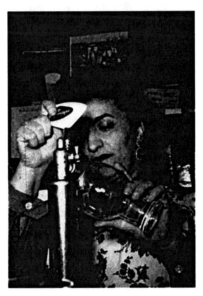

Alice at Oney's Bar in Waterville. We had to be seated to be served and couldn't walk around with our beers.

As young eighteen-year-olds, we also faced the recent change in Maine law that said you had to be twenty-one to be served alcoholic beverages. Many of my class-mates easily passed for twenty-one. I certainly didn't. Somehow, my mentor and friend, Chet Harrington, now a lofty senior and also a star football player, offered to "modify" my newly obtained draft card. With a few bold pen strokes, Chet suddenly made me twenty-one years old. Since he had completed the forgery I could honestly say I hadn't tampered with it.

That fall of 1950, a group of us boys decided to go to Boston instead of to our homes for Thanksgiving. Two things I recall from that weekend: the Yale-Harvard game and going to Loch Ober's. On Saturday, the day of the game, an enormous number of students and curious bystanders had gathered in Harvard Square just milling about. In this crowd I recognized an old friend from Haverford School, Paul Dabney, a fellow member of the wrestling team, who attended Dartmouth. As we chatted, standing in the middle of the street with the crowd all about us, we watched a bold, young man rush up behind one of the electric trolley buses and pull down the one of the poles that make contact with the overhead wires. The angry driver had to get out of the bus and re-connect it. By this time the crowd completely filled the street right where Au Bon Pain is now. Traffic was stalled.

We all moved down a side street outside of Jim Cronin's Bar and Restaurant. A lone car was slowly attempting to move up the street toward the Square through the crowd in the street. Finally, it could go no farther. For some reason the crowd began to rock the old '37 Ford from side to side and its two young passengers, a guy and his date. They were trapped and looked terrified. Then, suddenly without warning two strong guys pushed the car over on its side. Things had turned ugly for no reason. We all quickly moved away from the scene not wanting to be any part of it. That picture still so clear in my mind, and I always wondered if those two in the car would tell their grandchildren this story.

We all then went to the game. We made a point of going to downtown Boston to Loch Ober's Restaurant that evening, as we had heard it was famous for good food and drink. It was here that we could take our glasses of beer and then walk around freely from table to table or wherever we wanted, not having to sit in obedience to the laws of the state of Maine. Later that evening, I recall wandering with my classmates from one party to another in Cambridge, drinking too much rum punch and rushing outside in the dark to throw up in the bushes. It was hardly something to be proud of.

What I remember most about going to bars in Maine had to do with the "sit-down-to-be-served" rule. There was, we found, an exception to this rule. There was a tiny, hole-in-the-wall bar on Main Street in Waterville called appropriately, The Stand Up. It was a very narrow sort of alley space between two large buildings where there was really only room to stand along a narrow bar. It was clearly marked, "MEN ONLY." Naturaly, such a rule had to be challenged. Two of our more illustrious freshmen classmates, "The Bear," aka Paul McDermott and his drinking pal, Phil Tocantins dared a sophomore girl, Mary Jane Fitzpatrick into dressing as a man. They then quietly smuggled her in, dressed in heavy, navy pea jacket with her hair tucked up into a golf cap. She passed, had a drink, and of course, was able to boast of her feat.

I had some courses that were memorable probably more for the professor that the course materials. As freshmen we all had to take certain courses like English lit and composition. I was lucky to have a young, recent college graduate not much older than we were. His name was Paul Estaver and he would come into our eight o'clock class, then held in one of the many rooms in the upper floors of Miller Library, looking as though he had slept in his rumpled clothes, a baggy tweed jacket, tie, and moccasins and occasionally unzipped fly. The girls in the class often giggled; he paid no attention, sitting crossed legged on the desk up front like a kid. He made our dull freshman textbook a lot of fun to read. Unfortunately, he didn't return the next year.

Then there was a modern European history course taught by a small, short, dark haired German with a heavy accent. I had wanted to take an American history course but it wasn't available until the next year. I always loved his accent when he talk about "ooou" boats for "U" boats in his best guttural gargle; or call on Priscilla Ruder as "Miss Roooder".

And there was the ridiculous: World Political Geography course, which was mandatory for those of us in the Reserve Officer Training Corps (ROTC). This course was required of all freshmen men as a result of the country's entry into the Korean War. It was taught by a very southern-sounding Air Force officer, a major who I doubt had ever flown or fought. He certainly knew precious little about world geography other than what was in our very dull textbook.

The class met once a week and for the other sessions we marched after classes on the football field in our blue uniforms, which made us look more like bus drivers than serious military officers to be. We never had any drills with rifles, nor was there any target practice. We all thought the whole thing was a complete Mickey Mouse operation and of no value. Nearly 150 of us were forced into the course and as it turned out after our second year, the Korean War was winding down and the Air Force realized it didn't need all these young officers from all over the country. So they told us that only about ten students would be commissioned. The rest of us gladly quit. What a waste! Those few who stayed on got their bars and went on to careers in the Air Force.

That first winter we were in Waterville was one of the coldest in several decades. For one whole week in January of 1951, we were besieged by continuous below-zero temperatures. Our dorm was at the far end of the quadrangle so the journey to the dinning hall was a brisk quarter-mile walk. If the north wind was blowing in our faces, as it often did, it became brutally cold. Some of our buddies preferred to fast rather than struggle on the walk through snow and ice for a meal. There were many requests to "bring back something between two pieces of bread." I had found a really heavy Army surplus trench coat and was perfectly happy to make the trip for my friends.

Both Tat and I were skiers. He was pretty good at it and I was just a novice as I had never done any real downhill. Colby had its own ski slope on the other side of the Meassalonskee River which was less than ideal since it was a south facing steep hill. That meant that it would melt from the sun during the day and then freeze at night and become icy. The slope was run by the Outing Club with some help from the college but it was strictly bare bones and low budget with no chair lifts. A rope tow went up a ravine that had been cleared of trees but was quite rough. There was no charge for the slope or tow; you just stood in a short line waiting your turn. The rope was a continuous loop, always moving; you grabbed the top which was going up. We all had heavy leather palmed gloves and let the rope run through our gloves, gradually increasing our grip. It worked well most of the time.

I remember Tat had a metal fixture just made for rope tows that fit on his ski pole which neatly grabbed the rope when turned. So off we went. Not so bad, I thought, as we whizzed up the fairly steep gorge hitting occasional rocks where the snow had worn thin. At the top was a little shed which housed the old Ford motor with a bunch of pulleys etc. Then somehow I made it down without a fall.

On the next run I learned one of the downsides to this homemade rig. After running for several hours the old Ford overheated and the tow stopped. I happened to be partway up the ravine when it quit. We stood, not knowing what to do, as we were spread out with someone every fifty feet or so. After about ten minutes the rope came to life. Before I knew if I should grab on, the person below me came full speed, running over my skis and I stumbled out of the way. The rope tow was definitely a challenge.

The best and most memorable event was the day that Smoky came straight down the slope. John "Smoky" Restler, a very muscular football player, was "Hunchy" Huffman's roommate across the hall from us in Averill Hall; both were from Columbus, Ohio. In his run down the slope, Smoky decided to shush the whole slope which was fairly steep with a number of humps and bumps. I watched him start straight down, going faster and faster until near the bottom, he hit a large mogul, went up in the air, did a perfect summersault and landed like a pro, totally in control. None of us could believe he'd done it.

Our third floor group in Averill became good buddies that first year and that spring we bonded further with a party in May put on by our proctor, Charlie Tobin. We all went out to Great Pond on the nearby Lakes where Colby had a camp. We brought beer and lobsters, drank too much, and as you can tell from the group photo. We all looked pretty far gone, me especially. I can still identify all of those kids by name. Several of them didn't return the next year and more have since departed.

One of them, Jack Richards, from Braintree, Massachusetts, had become a close friend. Jack had gone to Thayer Academy and was brighter than many of the others and well read. He was thin, short, and scrappy with a heavy Boston accent. He had come to my rescue on a chilly April morning when no one else wanted to come by joining me to race intercollegiate dinghies at Tufts College. We had agreed that he

In May of 1951 all of us on the third floor of Averill Hall had a party on Great Pond to celebrate our first year. That's me, sitting.

would meet me at the MTA bus stop by the college. I had spent the night in one of the dorms. I was sure I had told him to be there at nine o'clock that morning. So I stood in the bright sun expecting him to get off each bus as it arrived and looking incessantly at my watch. It was probably here that I became impatient in waiting for people. He finally showed up at around noon, as if nothing was wrong. Some people have no concern about time and being punctual.

We managed to join in the races with dinghies on the lakes although quite late and I vowed that the Colby Yacht Club had to do better than this. I always have wondered what became of Jack; Colby has no records of most of the freshman class. The Registrar's office simply said they had been lost, misplaced, burned or some such story. I had visions of Jack signing up for the Korean War. I think he said he wanted drive a tank. Was he lost over there in that first of a succession of the not "Good" wars?

That spring I decided to go home around Easter. The weather had turned milder and I thought I'd try my luck at hitchhiking even though it was a long way to Pennsylvania from Maine. I got a couple of good rides but by the time the day was beginning to fade I realized I'd have to find a place to stay. It was starting to get chilly and no one would stop. I was in central Connecticut. There was bar nearby so I went in and warmed up. It turned out that there were rental rooms up over the bar, both cheap and clean. As a safety measure just before I went to sleep, I took my wallet as I had a bit of cash and put it under my pillow. I slept well in spite of bar noise and awoke just before six o'clock eager to get on the road.

To my great surprise I got the first ride I thumbed and better still the driver of this delivery truck said he was going all the way to New York. Then suddenly I felt in my pants and realized I'd left my wallet under the pillow in the room. I got out thanking the guy and began a slow and frustrating way back getting there around eight o'clock. The room hadn't been made up and there was my wallet, untouched. Try as I may I can't remember the rest of my day. All I know is that I got home.

Shortly after our floor party in May came final exams, which were something I found particular pleasure in taking. I had studied and prepared for most of them. I left not knowing how I had done although I later found that while passing, the grades I got were hardly what you'd call outstanding. I took the train home that June and the whole way; I read the serialized article by Rachel Carlson in the *New Yorker* in what subsequently became *The Sea Around Us*. I'm sure this article helped me on the path to my future field of Oceanography.

The summer of 1951, my parents rented a cottage for the month of July in Blue Hill from a woman named Blossom Alcott. Who these days has a name like Blossom? And my father saw fit to charter me a "J" boat like the one Berto owned so I could take part in the club races held each Wednesday and Saturday. The boat belonged to Delight Weston whose nephew may have sailed it. And how many people are named Delight? I still have a color picture of the boat with its sick green hull color. In the photo my father, Berto and I are hard at work on it, with father painting the water line.

When I started my freshman year I wanted to major in English, but we didn't get to choose our major concentration until our sophomore year, which, it turns out, was a wise rule. Toward the end of this first year I was split in my thinking between English and of all stupid ideas, Psychology, which I saw later would have been a disastrous choice for me. So I had a talk with Charlie Tobin. He gave me a piece of advice: "English majors are a dime a dozen." This made a distinct impression on me. Since I had enjoyed Professor Don Koons's Geology 101 and Tat was definitely going to major in it, I decided to try it also. Clearly, I am easily persuaded! However, choosing geology was a wise and right move for me. It led me along the path that turned out to offer many interesting opportunities... the road taken instead of Robert Frost's *Road Not Taken*. My choice did make all the difference.

In spite of not becoming an English major, I did take several English courses. One of my favorite professors in this department was Dr. Mark Benbow. He made the course interesting by helping to interpret difficult passages of Shakespeare. Someone had given him the nickname of the "Happy Salamander" which visually fit him as can be seen in the photograph below. Some years later when I was class

Professor Mark Benbow taught some of us English literature, 1951-52.

president for our forty-fifth reunion, I invited him to be the guest of the class and to be the featured speaker. He was one the last living professors in 1999 and entranced us all with his remembrances of Colby days.

When I came to Colby I had several years of sailing gained in Blue Hill and I found that there was a yacht club of sorts which was mostly defunct. It had been organized and run by a very un-sailor like fellow named Bob. The group was recognized by the college but was given no financial support. Our purpose was to take part in intercollegiate racing in New England. We had no boats of our own so we would travel to the other colleges where there were boats. We either went to Bowdoin on the New Meadows River near Brunswick or down to the Boston area. The only race I can remember that first year when I was a freshman was scheduled to be at Tufts on the Mystic Lakes. Bob and I were scheduled to go but at the last moment he dropped out saying it was up to me to get a crew.

I met Pete Welles later that fall of 1951 and he helped me get a group of guys and girls who were eager and good sailors. We raised enough money that year to allow us to go to meets mostly on the Charles River where we raced against MIT, Boston University, Harvard, Northeastern, Tufts, and others. Of course, we were not all very good dinghy sailors and it took us several seasons to be able to win some races. Having no boats of our own, we had little chance to practice.

Pete Welles became one of the principal characters in my life at Colby. Pete's full name was Merrill Chase Welles, Jr. and he hailed from Belmont, Massachusetts and

Belmont Hill School. He was a year older than me but two years behind in school, entering Colby as freshman in 1951. Stocky, solidly built with a heavy beard even after shaving every day, he looked much older than the rest of us kids. I found as I got to know him that he was skilled at fabricating stories. The reason he was behind in school, he said, was that he had been in the Army for a short while. I later found this to be untrue. On the other hand, he told lots interesting stories that were true. You just had to be a little skeptical.

I often visited him in his dorm where he roomed with a guy named George Huether from somewhere in upstate New York. George was one of those freshmen who partied every night, threw his clothes in a pile in the corner, and never washed them. Over the fall the clothes pile in the corner grew larger until it nearly reached the ceiling. There was a definite odor in that corner. I don't know how Pete stood it. George only lasted through the first semester. Pete and I later went on to become roommates, fraternity brothers, car nuts, and sailing buddies.

Since I was the original organizer, I was later elected the "commodore" and held regular meetings and usually we would send three or four pairs of skippers and crew most weekends. Sometimes we had really long trips like the one to University of Vermont on Lake Champlain. It was mid-April and the ice had just gone off the lake the day before. It was windy and definitely chilly. My crew was Vic, a young freshman who was not an esperences sailor. As might be expected, he didn't shift his weight fast enough as we came about and over we went into the bitter cold water. By the time we had righted the dinghy, a rescue boat had come up to us and we were hus-

Merrill "Pete" Welles was my roommate in the DU house, 1953-54. Most of our time was spent on cars, sailing, and girls…not enough on the books.

82

tled to the warmth of the clubhouse. That was the only time I remember capsizing in college racing.

By the end of my junior year our racing record in New England was pretty good and when I entered my last year, I managed to get the attention of the Colby's Vice President, Galen Eustis, a kindly older gentleman with a thick Maine accent. He had a son in several classes ahead of us who later married one of our classmates, "Gige" Roy, and a daughter, Nancy, also in our class.

Mr. Eustis became interested in our boat-less plight and called me in to his office one day. He smiled at me and said he had managed to find a little bit of money if I could find three boats. By some good luck I just happened to know of some boats for sale in Blue Hill. Through my still-existing Blue Hill connection with Berto Nevin, I remembered that there had been a class of boats raced but now discontinued. When I first came to Blue Hill in 1949 there was a fleet of 12-foot cat boats called Wood Pussies built by the Palmer-Scott Company. I had raced in one of them with Tucker Cluett. They would be perfect for the Colby Yacht Club to race on Great Pond. I told Mr. Eustis that they could be purchased for $400 apiece and he authorized me to buy them.

In the spring of my senior year the boats appeared on Great Pond. Although it was too late for me to enjoy the boats in a race, I did take one for a sail with my then girl friend, Pat McCormack, class of '56. That fall after I had left, our picture

In the spring of 1954 the Colby Yacht Club acquired three racing dinghies which I took on Great Pond with Pat McCormack.

appeared on the cover of the alumni magazine with a brief write-up of the club and our new boats. I was proud that I had been able to organize and field a successful racing team that finally won the Maine championship, as well as get some of our own boats. It was probably one of my more important achievements at Colby, and it was the beginning of my starting various organizations over the subsequent years.

Incoming freshmen at Colby weren't allowed to have cars, so it wasn't until the following fall that I drove my car, a 1949 Studebaker two-door, medium green, from Pennsylvania to Waterville. I don't know why my father and I picked this car but it turned out to be a pretty good choice, as it got good mileage on trips back home. This was in part due to a new gadget Studebaker featured, called an overdrive. Although it was like a fifth gear, it was electrically activated with a switch. I don't remember much else about the car other than I taking a bunch of riders along on vacation trips home. But by the next summer I had met Pete Welles at Colby and was introduced to Boothbay Harbor and Southport Island. I sold the "Stupidbaker" and decided to buy a car all on my own. With the help of Pete, who was a big Ford fan, we found a local Southport car for sale – a 1937 Ford black two-door with a V8 engine.

The car belonged to Harriet Orchard, the town clerk of Southport, who wanted $125 for it. It seemed to be okay. Of course, I knew little about cars at this stage and was probably too eager. Harriet was happy to be rid of it and as I found out only too soon, the car was not in very good condition. Besides, it had the curse of having mechanical brakes. The brake shoes were activated by a pedal connected to two rods, one on either side of the car. It was, at best, an archaic system held over from wagons and was replaced in 1938 by hydraulic brakes. As I was to find out, these mechanical brakes were notorious for misbehaving in winter when ice and slush would freeze on one side, locking the rod and hilariously spinning the cars around. It happened to me more than once. But I didn't care; it was my car, bought with my own money.

The first calamity occurred when I decided to drive home with some friends. The engine was in bad shape and I found soon after leaving Waterville that it had an insatiable appetite for oil. Every fifty miles or so, I had to add oil. I guess the rings were cracked and oil just poured out in clouds of smoke. I realized the best way was to stop at a gas station and ask for drain oil in a large pail, usually free. By the time I got home, the engine was terminally ill. Good old Dad! He came to the rescue and helped finance a rebuilt Ford 100 hp motor instead of the original 85 hp one. I was happy but I felt badly burned on my first car. I often wondered if Harriet knew the car was sick. When I moved to Southport many years later too much time had passed to bring up the subject and she was quite old by then.

The new engine ran so well, it almost made up for all the body rust, the treacherous brakes, and the ravages of fourteen Maine winters. Clearly the car's days were numbered. Like a sci-fi thriller character, I went looking for a "new body." Cars had definitely become a big part of my college life. Pete and I searched the back rows of used car lots, junk yards, and peoples' yards for a car in which we could transplant the new engine. Finally, on a brutally cold February day, we found the perfect match at the Airport Garage right across from the Brunswick Naval Air Station. It was a beauty: pale blue, 1941 Ford Deluxe convertible which had a blown engine, all for the amazing price of $100.

Pete drove the '37, towing the '41 while I steered. The top was stuck down so I was in the cold breeze for the hour and a half ride back to Waterville. We used the standard trick of putting an old tire between the two cars to act as a shock absorber. A ride like that was good training for my Arctic adventures to come. We had already found a mechanic who would do the heart transplant. Although the blue car had sat outside without the top for a while, the leather seats were still in good shape. I managed to fix the top, making it a manual instead of motor driven.

Later that summer I repainted the car a two-tone dark and light blue. The car lasted me for quite a while braving the Maine winters and even starting in -35° mornings. Its heater was a bit wimpy for those bitter cold mornings but fortunately, someone before me had installed an Arvin gasoline heater that was so hot it almost melted the polish off my shoes. In fact, that good ol' car made a remarkable trip to Wyoming and back during the summer of 1953 when Tat and I went to work in the oil fields as roustabouts. The '41 was perhaps one of the best cars I ever had.

Over the next three years, being a geology major meant being outdoors a lot on field mapping courses. This was especially fun in a cold climate of interior Maine. It turns out that the early 1950s were among the coldest years in whole century. Nights with -20° to -30° were common and days never above zero could last a whole week. I will never forget those snowy days two of us would be standing out on windswept Mayflower Hill, stamping our freezing feet to keep circulation going, while one of us held the stadia rod marking an outcrop, and the other "shot" the rod-man using our alidade, a telescope mounted on a straight edge, and plain table as we directly drew our map on the paper on the board. We might spend several hours on our project area. As I found much later, Colby was the perfect preparatory school for the work I was to do in Greenland later on in the 1990s.

It was on one of these afternoon field trips that I met and worked with the "Bear" also from the third floor of Averhill Hall, although I also knew him from our episode at the Stand Up Bar. He and I were assigned the task of mapping parts of the quarry near the Colby ski slope across the Messalonskee River.I never knew where his nickname "Bear" originated; he was actually Paul Mc Dermott, a guy obsessed with drinking as were a number of our colleagues. He may have been there for two years but didn't graduate. I see from the departed list he is no longer with us, not a surprise at the rate he drank alcohol.

At the time our instructor was Mr. Richardson, a true Maine character who had field mapped for nearly forty years in the Southwest and could out tramp any of us kids. Late fall of our sophomore year, cold but not the depth of winter, we had a walk of several miles ahead of us to get to the quarry. Bear said he knew of a shortcut. There was, he said, a wire bridge of sorts across the river that would save us several hours of walking down to a road and over a bridge. We were carrying the plane table in a carry bag, the tripod for the table, and the box with the alidade. The "bridge" was made of two wire cables, one about five feet above the other, with occasional vertical connectors, with a span of several hundred feet.

Bear carried both tables and tripod and I had the instrument. We were smart enough to go one at a time. All I remember is getting about halfway across, having slid my way along cautiously when suddenly without warning the wire tilted and I found myself almost horizontal teetering about fifty feet above the river rapids. We made it, of course, but with lots of nervous sweat, deciding to walk back the long way instead of using the "bridge" after our mapping detail.

Not all of my class time at Colby was serious or academic. My fondest memories of Chemistry 101 were the tricks we played in the Chem Lab. Professor Weeks gave the lectures as he was senior faculty and Professor Richard Jacquith ran the weekly lab. Both were serious and not impressed with our bad behavior. My lab partner, Phil Tocantins, and I had a favorite experiment. While the other students were doing what they were supposed to be doing — the experiments in our book — Phil and I would take a 250 ml beaker, fill it with pennies, put it under the chemical hood with the exhaust fan, and pour on some concentrated nitrous oxide. The result was an evil, yellow smoke which was highly toxic, cuprous oxide, but was safely eliminated by the fans. Every minute or so, we would take one of the pennies out with a pair of tongs and compare it to a dime. When the penny matched the size of a dime, we poured in water to stop the reaction and lo and behold we had a beaker full of dimes or rather slugs since there was no letters left on them. That evening one of our ersatz dimes would buy a five-cent Coke, give back a nickel for a phone call to a girlfriend. It was another step in the life of a young criminal. Remarkably, I managed to pass Chemistry, but hardly with an outstanding grade.

I took my geology more seriously and worked hard during the three years of majoring, but Tat and I both tried to avoid Saturday classes. Why take Tuesday, Thursday, Saturday classes if you could get the same thing on Monday, Wednesday, Friday? As we entered our sophomore year Tat was "rushed" and pledged Delta Kappa Epsilon (DKE) fraternity. I had hoped to join also but I wasn't invited. Although I was disappointed, I learned a lot more about fraternities in the coming years — some good, much not.

Those of us not included in the "frat thing" were at that time a small minority group of slightly odd and different persons known as "independents," like those not included in one of the two political parties. However, there was another option. Because of the building schedule for the campus or "Hill," there was a push to get the women who were still living in the rickety, old dorms in the downtown Waterville campus up to the Hill. The new girls' dorms were a year away from being finished so the two dorms in the men's quadrangle were made available to the women. Here a number of the fraternities jumped to the rescue and a small number of men who were displaced were invited into the fraternity houses. I was one of those fortunate ones and wound up in the DKE house after all, where I had wanted to be.

It was some years later that I learned that for some unknown reason I never got an invitation join the fraternity; someone had "blackballed" me. It was a common practice for members to vote on a prospective pledge by using a white or black marble dropped secretly into a covered box. If, upon counting there was one black ball, the candidate was "excluded." Exclusion this way was one of the real drawbacks of fraternities. And, of course, there were all the other restrictive clauses which were racial or ethnic. I'll never know who blackballed me. But at the time, not knowing any of this was much better for me.

My roommate that fall in the DKE house where I was a one year guest was an interesting fellow from Buffalo named Wally Ward. He was a short, very muscular guy, with a round cheerful face and slightly bald. Wally was rarely around but could usually be found downtown drinking and playing cards. He was a Chemistry major and somehow managed to get good grades with almost no studying. The two things that were memorable about Wally were his physical and athletic ability and his skill at making lots of money at cards. He was the only person I've ever seen to do a standing push-up — a handstand against a wall, then a push-up with your entire weight on your arms — not easy at all. He was or had been a boxer.

To make money, Wally played cards or did amazing tricks which he bet people he could do. His favorite was to bet someone who was perhaps a bit drunk, that he could eat a cocktail glass or a light bulb. He did it and always won his bet; without serious damage to his innards. Many times I remember him coming home to our room at five in the morning after an all-night session. I would meet him early in the morning just coming in from a long night at a bar downtown saying he had made $500 that night. Wally also figured out how to get into the cafeteria at Roberts Hall one night. Being quite small, he squeezed into a dumb waiter from the second floor and smuggled out a bunch of metal trays. We all used them to slide down a hillside for late evening fun.

Years later he showed up at our thirty-fifth reunion at Colby now an executive in publishing with a PhD. He was living in Las Vegas and didn't look as fit as he had een in college. After that I had occasion to call him for alumni fund raising but could never get past his wife or answering machine.

I later learned, through his obituary, he had passed away in 2006. After getting his PhD in chemistry at Iowa State, Dr. Frank Wallace (as he was later known) had spent nine years at DuPont, then moved to Las Vegas to start his own publishing company, Integrated Management Associates. He also dabbled into philosophy. This, through possibly illegal acts, led to income tax evasion and a prison sentence. Among other accomplishments Wally wrote a book on how to make money at poker. While jogging on the highway in 2006 near Henderson, Nevada he was hit by a car and died. In spite of Wally's misdeeds he is listed as an outstanding alumni at Colby. Go figure!

For the summer of 1952 I landed a great job with the help of one of the girls in our Colby Yacht Club. Anne Isom, from Belmont, Massachusetts and a friend of Pete Welles knew of a summer job on a 60-foot schooner. I think her family had a friend who owned the boat. Whenever I think of Anne it makes me think of her father's sailboat which had a dinghy named *Soggy Biscuit*. I never saw Anne after graduation but recall she lived in Florida and is now among the "Departed.". I have her to thank for getting me into big boats.

I was hired by Herb Barlow, a patent attorney from Providence, to be his paid deckhand. I had a wonderful summer sailing experience where we worked out of Wickford, Rhode Island. The schooner, named *Onward III*, was built by Goudy and Stevens in East Boothbay, Maine in 1934. She was designed by John Alden as a 60 foot staysail schooner and was classic in every way. Herb and his son, "Skip," usually took out friends and business associates on weekends. Nearly every trip, we sailed to Block Island, about two hours away. It was a summer of learning for me as I had had little experience in large boats.

I remember hearing of a lad about my age who was used only to small boats. Without thinking he stuck his leg out to fend off the large boat he crewed on and broke his leg. I had several similar experiences but not so disastrous. We were out on Narragansett Bay running before to wind and Captain Herb asked me to jibe the main as he brought her around. I was holding the main sheet as the very heavy and powerful mainsail came over, burning the rough manila line through my hands. It taught me to snub the sheet around a stern bit just enough to check it, then let it go. Lesson learned. A similar incident occurred when I was letting go a halyard for a very large sail we called the "gollywobler" that stretched between the main and fore masts, with perhaps an area of a thousand square feet. As I let the halyard go off the cleat, I was yanked up the mast eight or ten feet with a great whoosh. By the end of the summer I felt confident that I wouldn't make these sort of mistakes again.

Most of the time I was the only one aboard *Onward III* while Herb and Skip were at work at their law offices in Providence. I spent what seemed like endless hours scrubbing the white topsides from a rubber raft, keeping all 120 feet of her clean when they would return for another Block Island run. On one of these we rendezvoused with a large fleet of boats from the Cruising Club of America (CCA). We all rafted up together, had cocktails, and then went ashore for a barbecue. I met Rod Stephens, was a young, hot skipper at the time with a boat named *Mustang*. He was president of Sparkman and Stephens (S&S), probably the leading designer and builder of the world's best sailboats.

Some years later I had the good fortune to meet and talk to his brother Olin, the even more famous designer at S&S. Then in his nineties, he detailed his long career before a large crowd at Mystic Seaport in Connecticut. He spoke for more than an hour and partway through he asked if anyone would mind if he sat instead of standing, which brought a chuckle from the crowd. He mentioned that in a day or so he was off to Italy where he was consulting on the restoration of a well-known racing boat, *Nyala*, one of the first twelve meters designed by S & S and built in 1938.

Olin was credited with the design of 2,200 racing and cruising boats, three of which I had owned and sailed. There were eleven of these 21-foot boats built in Blue Hill. As usual, when I sailed and raced that summer I hadn't a clue of the heritage of the boat I rented from Delight Weston. The other two were a 24-foot cruising boat called the Dolphin class and my present boat *Aurora II*, a 27-foot Tartan cruising class. Olin Stephens lived to be one hundred years old in 2008 and still racing in Maine into his late 90s. What a guy! I felt honored to have heard him speak and to have talked with him.

On another occasion we were on *Onward III* in Mattapoisett with another CCA round-up where we went aboard *Yankee*, a 90-foot steel brigantine rig, built in 1911 and owned by Irving and Electa "Exy" Johnson. The couple made numerous world circumnavigations with a crew of seventeen women from Bellville, Long Island, one of the first to offer at-sea training. Irving was a bull of a man, firm grip and all muscle. They had purchased *Yankee* in 1947 with the help of Sterling Hayden of movie and sailing fame who was partly responsible for the design and building of the Boothbay 21. As the story goes, Irving Johnson had once fallen overboard while single-handing in Long Island Sound, treaded water all day for twelve hours before being picked up by a freighter, and then climbed aboard on a rope ladder in good shape. I wish I had thanked Ann Isom for her getting me such a good summer job.

The summer of '52 was filled with good memories. One day a very pretty, attractive blond came down the dock pushing a pram. This is how I met the next girl in my life. Nancy Sudmann was an au pair who had somehow found her way to the dock. We met and she invited me to visit her. So, after finishing my job that summer, I took a trip to in East Rockaway, Long Island late in August. She lived with her parents in an older house in an average middle class neighborhood along with her older brother.

Nancy was a sophomore at Hofstra College where she was an all county track star. She was about my height, blond, with the beautiful body of an athlete, and a very heavy New York accent. Her mother was a chubby hausfrau; her father a strange and somewhat overweight man in his midfifties who most times sat in an enormous broken down easy chair. The room where I met him was dark and full of television sets. I counted at least six of them stacked two high. One had sound, another a picture only, another appeared okay. The rest of the room was crammed with fish tanks that were belonged to his son, Robert, who ran a pet store in the town. He was a younger replica of his father and about as large. It seemed like something out of a bizarre piece of fiction. Visiting a girl I barely knew was something I'd never done before. Nothing in my past and with all my previous girlfriends had prepared me for this. The Sudmanns acted as if their house and lifestyle were perfectly normal, making no apologies. The next day everyone went off to work leaving Nancy and me alone.

After lunch she and I somehow wound up taking a nap together in bed, totally nude. To say that she was a bit forward would be mild. I'm sure most any young man my age would have taken full advantage of the situation, but I didn't. She didn't give up on me, though, and during a college holiday she came to visit me at Sugarbridge. My parents were polite and tolerated her although I knew my mother well enough to realize she really didn't approve of Nancy's forwardness. One night when we had all turned in to our separate rooms, she managed to quietly sneak around outside, came up to my room and climbed in bed with me. It was sort of repeat of East Rockaway. I was totally nervous and whispered for her to go back.

That wasn't the end of Nancy Sudmann, however. That fall and winter we continued to write each other, and I decided to invite her to Colby for Winter Carnival. She came to Portland on the train and I picked her up in my '37 Ford in very cold weather. We drove up to Waterville, where I put her up in a hotel at considerable expense. I vaguely remember going to the formal ball at the college. In retrospect it was a bust of a weekend and it was clear that Nancy and I were not the right match. All told, I spent $150 or so that weekend, the money I received from my father for food allowance instead of eating at the college cafeteria. I spent the rest of the semester getting by on cheap food. Pete and I found remarkable deals like a hundred pound bag of potatoes for penny a pound! I guess Nancy finally gave up; I never heard from her again.

If being a geology major afforded me a bit of cold winter field work, living in the DKE house continued and heightened the experience. Of the seven fraternity houses, the Dekes had the distinction of having sleeping "ramps," a large room at the end of each floor that was just for sleeping with seven or eight double bunk-beds. Thus, our smaller rooms were for study and living while the big room was for sleeping. It was good if one of us wanted to study late and the other went to sleep early. The ramps were unheated and many of us had electric blankets or, like me, about seven blankets. We were all fresh air fiends and every night regardless of temperature someone would open the fire escape door. Essentially, we slept outdoors. Here I was out in the elements…again, I was in training for my future assignments in Greenland.

After those date-filled summers at Blue Hill came my four years at Colby. I had very few dates during my freshman year as we mostly went as a group drinking. It wasn't until I had my own car that I started to take girls out.

That spring I remember dating a wisp of a girl named Ginny Coggins who hailed from New Britain, Connecticut. She was a year behind me and very sweet and quiet, almost mousy. At vacations she would ride with me to New Britain where we were met by her father. Interestingly, many years later when I was living in Cutler, Maine in the 1970s I met her father, then quite elderly but still in good health as he came ashore with a crew off a cruising boat. I sent my greetings to her.

The winter of 1952 was the year of the Great Blizzard in Maine. I recall a special edition of the Waterville Sentinel which I still have somewhere, showing the incredible drifts twenty feet high, no cars able to reach the Hill, and all the hype that goes with a true blizzard that lasted three days. The college heating system failed when the fuel truck couldn't get to us. Some brave souls from our house skied or snowshoed down to the town and brought a case of beer back, realizing an enormous profit and, of course, totally illegal, but somehow unquestioned in this emergency.

My one-year stay with the Dekes ended that spring with no comment about staying on. I had never felt included with them, a little like my feeling of not fitting in at Haverford. More so here as the "brothers" had their weekly meetings which were held in secret. But as they say, as one door closes, another opens. That fall of 1952 as I returned to my junior year at Colby thinking, alas, I was going to be one of those dreaded independents, I was pleasantly surprised to be invited to join as a member the fraternity of Delta Upsilon (DU). I'm not quite sure how this came about at the time but found later it was at the suggestion of Pete Welles.

My third and fourth years at Colby were enjoyable partly due to becoming a member of the Delta Upsilon fraternity and because I was enjoying my major of geology. It turned out that the DU's were a much better group for me than had I joined the DKEs. The DUs basic tenants were non-secret, non-sectarian and did away with most of the exclusive discretionary clauses and traditions of other campus fraternities. In actuality, there were still the problems caused by our alumni advisors of the "old guard." These alums were local men from Waterville whose job it was to oversee who was being pledged as new members.

The DU chapter at Bowdoin College several years earlier had pledged an African American student and then suddenly found themselves being dropped from the DU national. In effect, according to our rather open bylaws, we could take anyone we wished to pledge…except the alumni wouldn't allow it. I wasn't aware of any incidents. We were a more liberal fraternity than others except maybe for the Lambda Chi Alphas who had already pledged the only two men students of color.

Looking back, of course, it was obvious that all fraternities were out of step with the changing times. Colby eliminated fraternities entirely around 1985. As I found out, there were several men from our class who felt strongly betrayed by the college and refused to donate money to the college or take part in alumni events because of this move.

After Pete Welles got me into the DU house we became roommates. Besides our mutual love of sailing and cars, Pete, whose major was history, inspired me to take a couple of history courses. It was in one of these classes that I first had Professor Paul Fullam for an instructor. As time went on, he became our favorite professor. He was a man of perhaps fifty, with grey to white hair, balding at the temples, a bit overweight but with a pleasant smile. In my estimation, he was a superb lecturer and storyteller. I took his American History course and really looked forward to each class. Professor Fullam was affectionately known as "Punchy Paul" because he always seemed a little out of touch and slightly bumbling. Actually, he was extremely sharp.

He would arrive in class always a few minutes late looking a bit disheveled, carrying a tired, beat-up leather briefcase which he would root through distractedly, searching for his notes. Out would come various non-academic items: a pair of undershorts, a golf ball, and scraps of notes. He'd mumble "never mind" and launch into a story, which would digress along a strange route. Where was he going? We'd all wonder if he'd lost it. But then we would realize we were being guided to a proper conclusion. In the last moments of the class he would expertly tie up all loose ends, his story complete and points made. Another great lecture.

After class several of us would join Paul in the Spa, our coffee shop-cum-bookstore where he might continue on the day's subject. He loved to talk to Pete and me about boats. He wanted us to tell him what we knew about tugboats, as he wanted to buy a tugboat in the worst way. An avid, unabashed Democrat and active in politics, he was a sharp critic of Margaret Chase Smith, the many-termed Republican senator from Maine.

We were still in the midst of the Korean War and she was most popular in Maine. In the fall of 1954, after I had gradated, Paul Fullam disagreed so strongly about the state of affairs that he took a leave of absence from Colby and entered the race against Mrs. Smith, something few politicians dared to do. I remember reading in *Time* magazine with some pride while I was at Texas A&M that fall that Paul Fullam had put up the best showing of any prior candidate running against Senator Smith. Then, to my dismay six months later I heard that he had died. I never knew any details of his death. He never got his tugboat.

Professor Paul Fullam taught us American History. In 1954 he came close to beating long-time senator, Margaret Chase Smith for the US Senate.

In the summer of 1953, ex-roommate Derek Tatlock and I took a long drive to Wyoming where my great uncle, John C. "Jack" Thomas, a former Continental Oil Company founder and Vice President, had gotten us jobs in the oil fields.

I drove my '41 Ford convertible from home to West Chester to pick up Derek in Pittsford, New York on a very hot June day. At one point the Ford boiled over but kept going up a long hill until I got over the top. Off we went, headed for the wilds of Wyoming and the town of Casper. The first night there we camped out in the city park, avoiding police. Then we rented a tiny two room shack for the week, expecting to be there a while.

As roustabouts we were the low men on the rig, not knowing what to expect. We rode in a giant truck weighing some 90,000 pounds, which carried the cable-tool drill rig. We took back roads because of the weight. The well was already drilled and the company was re-working it. We spent the morning dumping this enormous piece of machinery in place. Tat and I pulled and shoved and hauled heavy stuff. The tool pusher or driller, a big lanky, drawling cowboy type, called both of us "Shorty." It was hard work in the Wyoming heat but fun. After the second day, at noon, the boss called us over to his trailer to tell us the job was over and we weren't needed any more. The rest of the day we were put to work in the company's storage yard

*Derek Tatlock and me about to depart in my 1941 Ford to Casper,
Wyoming for jobs in the oil fields, 1953.*

picking up, cutting grass, and doing mindless work. Then we were paid off several
hundred dollars each, in silver dollars. That evening, all the oil gang gathered at a
bar reminiscent of a western movie scene.

The next day we decided to head for home but not before we had a chance to
see some more of this Wild West. We wandered north to the small, really western
town of Lander, a typical movie town if there ever was one. The population, then
around 3,000 has now doubled. The main street was enormously wide, like six or
eight highway lanes with what looked like movie set buildings on each side. It was
July fourth and a large street party was under way with everyone drinking beer. Two
things I remember: the crunch sound as cars drove slowly by flattening beer cans
and a good ol' cowboy passed out lying in the middle of the street. A long banner
stretched across proclaiming the Independence Day Party.

We continued driving north and spent a day in and around Yellowstone National Park. Even in 1953, in the park was overcrowded with bumper-to-bumper
traffic. The top was down on the Ford as we sat waiting to move on. Then one of
my most memorable wild life scenes occurred. A large grizzly bear ambled up to the
side of the car, raised himself up and placed both paws just behind the front door,
hoping to find a good morsel. Tat, thinking quickly, was able to grab a can of shaving cream and squirt the bear in the face. He shook his head and backed off. Clever.

Our final part of the western trip took us up over the mountains toward Red
Lodge, Montana. We tent camped by a large snow field probably at 8,000 or so
feet. Even with temperatures the next morning in the high thirties, mosquitoes still
buzzed around. From here we headed straight home, taking turns driving until we
got to his place in New York.

We celebrate 4ᵗʰ of July on a snow-covered mountain on the way to Red Lodge, Montana.

Lucky for me I was able to join my parents on their big trip to Europe later in the summer. Thus began my adventure on the Holland-American Line. My parents had booked our passage on the newest ship on the line, the *Ryndam*, an all tourist class except for fifteen first class cabins. It was my first time on a passenger ship. Today it would be called a cruise ship. The fare was about $175, cheaper than air, and it took maybe seven or eight days. While there were faster boats that probably made it in four or five days, no one was in a hurry. The ship carried about a thousand people and was not at all crowded. The food was wonderful and included in the price. Besides, for a young college kid like me, draft beer at 10-cents and Heineken to boot was a real treat.

I met a ravishing blonde from New Jersey named Norma Matusek, and we went to all the ship's parties. Toward the middle of the trip I fell in with an older group of teachers probably in their mid to late twenties. There was Maurice, a young man who I found later was suffering from some terrible terminal disease, his friend Fred a bit older, and a very striking, red head, Peggy Swikart, who must have been at least six feet tall. We all hung out together in the rarely used First Class lounge where no one bothered us and we had our own waiter, Jan, who brought drinks and when asked would sing wonderful songs, many in German, which must have been hard for a Dutchman.

The night before we were to arrive in Le Havre, as we were crossing the English Channel, I was in my favorite little bar on the main deck. A group of Dutch air force pilots were also gathered there, on their way home after a year of training at a base in Texas. It was amusing to hear their nearly perfect English spoken with a heavy Texas drawl. They were all drinking a bar favorite they called an "espanolke" or, a little Spaniard. It consisted of a shot of Dutch gin, a particularly strong liquor mixed with a Heineken draft and all for the amazing price of 15-cents. Two or three of these packed a real punch. It was here I met and conversed with a tall, slim, blonde Dutch girl. Some how we wound up out on deck on the fantail of the ship looking over at the distant lights on the shore and watching occasional flashes of a lightning storm. I remember her coarse wool sweater and her arm around me as we kissed. Her name was Leika and she was from Appledorn.

Fred, Peggy, and Maurice were planning to travel to Holland, Germany, Belgium, and then back to Paris. To my surprise they invited me to join them. My parents seemed happy for me to go along. So we struck off that next morning from Amsterdam by train and then by boat up the Rhine River. It turned out that we were good traveling companions. Fred and Maurice bunked together while Peggy and I had separate rooms. On our return to Paris ten days later, we saw Fred and Maurice off on the train to London.

I had an especially good time in Paris both with my parents and without. I recall spending a lot of time in the Luxembourg Gardens where I sat and sketched like a true artist. Every evening we would walk to local restaurant on the busy street, sit on the sidewalk and drink aperitifs, usually sweet vermouth. The waiter would stack the little drink saucers to indicate how many you'd had. Our favorite night spot was an incredibly smoky night club called "Lapin Agile," or the Agile Rabbit, a second-floor walk up fire trap with people packed in like sardines.

At some point my parents and I boarded the Orient Express from Paris to Vienna to spend time there with Hans Hatwagner, my mother's former husband. This was long before the 1974 movie, *Murder on the Orient Express*, but it still it had the aura of mystery about it. We boarded in the evening in Paris and the trip took nearly a full day. There were probably sleeper cars but we had a compartment. About midnight we stopped for a while at a station. My father and I got out and stood on the platform, smoked a cigarette, and watched people getting on the train. For me it was most exciting; perhaps it brought back many memories for my father. It would have been fun to talk about them. The next day we rode through the mountains and in the afternoon went through the Austrian countryside where we saw a group of Russian tanks on some sort of field maneuvers. We had special visas called "gray papers" required to travel through the Russian occupied zone to Vienna.

Hans met us at the station dressed in a proper grey flannel Tyrolian outfit with jaunty hat and a bouquet of yellow roses. In greeting us, he clicked his heels, as is the continental custom. He took us in his VW bug to a rooming house that he had arranged. The entire episode of the next week is wonderfully told by my mother in a rather long manuscript called "Angels on Holiday." It was never published but is a worthwhile and interesting account.

The Russians controlled and occupied most of Vienna. In 1953 the city still looked much as it had right after the war with many major buildings in ruins, much more evident than other parts of Europe we had seen. Hans took us on various tours of the city, pointing such things as an iron balcony where from the second floor Hitler had made his first address to the Viennese people as the Nazis were taking over the city. Hans had been an officer in the Army during the war. Supposedly he, like many Viennese, was conscripted into the German army. The Austrian army certainly had a bad attitude toward the country's Jews. He was imprisoned for four years by Tito in Yugoslavia.

I remember mostly the events such as the marvelous coffee shops on the "Ring" with the extra thick whipped cream (mit Schlag) and the pretty women in very fashionable dresses. I needed a haircut and went to a barber who spoke no English. He was a large, elderly gentleman with white hair, goatee, and a waxed mustache who chattered away in German frequently spitting on the scissors as if to sharpen them.

While we were in Vienna, Hans Hattwagoner had arranged a date for me with the daughter of an old friend. Mandi Payaruber was probably several years younger, a bit on the plump side, short hair, but tantalizing hazel eyes and a quick smile. She and a group of her friends and I spent some time at a bar, while they practiced their English on me. They teased me into saying German phrases like "thread spool" and "poople hoochen."

The following day, I took Mandi to the amusement park, the Wurstell Prater, better known as the Prater where we rode the roller coaster. It was much more daring than the Disney rides, going through water and steep curves. We sat up front while three Russian soldiers were behind us. They were only boys, I thought, maybe seventeen or so and the sort of rough farmer lads in shabby army drab, ill fitting uniforms with gap toothed smiles. They were having a wonderful time. It's as close as I will come to Russian soldiers. Although one night, while strolling along back streets, I came on a pod of armed soldiers guarding a building where I realized I wasn't supposed to be. They looked threatening but they laughed good-naturedly as I hurried away. There were overtones of *The Third Man*.

We left Vienna on the Arlsburg Express which went a different route through Switzerland. We stopped for a day in Lucerne where my father and I rented a sail boat and drifted around the lake in the fading days of summer.

Back in Paris, Peggy had stayed on and took a room at a hotel near where I was with my parents. I visited her a few evenings and suddenly we became romantically involved. She must have been a good five years older than I was and yet here I was making out with her. It was mostly hot and heavy kissing but still pretty exciting for me...an older woman. We said jokingly why had we had separate rooms? Think of

I sketched the deck on the SS Ryndam *on the way to Europe, 1953.*

the money we could have saved. A few days later my parents and I left for home. I think this first trip to Europe was probably my best.

The finale to my summer adventures came on the return trip in the middle of September. We had passage on a small ship named the *Sibyak*, a vessel leased from Rotterdamshe-Lloyd Company. She normally was sailed in the East India waters. We were about three days out when we were hit by a strong fall storm with winds up to Force 10 (sixty miles an hour). It took no time for an enormous sea to build. As I stood in the forward lounge watching each monster wave crash against the large glass windows, the ship pitched as if riding a roller coaster. Already the crew had strapped all the furniture together to keep it from being destroyed. Of the nearly 500 passengers who were immigrating to Canada, almost all were seasick and in their cabins. No one made it to meals.

At this point I met a most interesting girl named Barbara Adams. She had spent the summer traveling Europe and was returning to the US. Barbara was a student at George Washington University and her father, she told us, was in the diplomatic corps. She was hardly a girlfriend as my others encounters had been, but nevertheless a great person to share our rough ride home. My parents enjoyed her, too. When we arrived in New York the weather had turned to typical brisk fall. We all said our goodbyes and that was that.

It was a real surprise to run into Barbara about three years later when I was in Florida with Pete Welles on our Fort Lauderdale spring break. We were coming out of our motel room as we met her on the street. She was not the same as I remembered her on the trip on the *Sibyak*. She was disheveled and a bit wild-looking, like a street person who hadn't changed clothes in days. In fact, she was a total beach bum. She said she had no place to sleep and that she had been sleeping in phone booths. Pete and I agreed to let her sleep in our room while we were out for the day. I never had any kind of a complete conversation with her. I guessed she had dropped out of college. Perhaps she was on drugs maybe before drugs became so much a part of the culture. I'm not sure if she really remembered me but when I left Florida there were no goodbyes and no friendliness. It was some years later that I recall hearing, I don't know where, that she had drowned herself in a bathtub, the second of my female acquaintances to take their lives.

Pete and I coach the ADP sorority girls "Powder Puff" football, 1953.

During my senior year at Colby, my roommate Pete and I volunteered to coach a girls sorority football team as part of the Powder Puff league started in the fall of 1953. We drew the Alpha Delta Pi's (ADP), one of four of the women's groups. It was here that I met Pat McCormack, then a sophomore. The game rules made sure things didn't get rough; it was touch football with little body contact. The girls were quite good and after a bit of practice, we had games between our team and the other sororities. Pat was my favorite quarterback.

She, like Nancy and Arianne, came from Long Island and lived in Port Washington. That fall she became my steady girl on campus. We drank beer, parked around the pond, and made out. I visited her at Port Washington, and she later came to Sugarbridge. She was quiet, agreeable, and soft spoken and quite attractive but not exactly my type, whatever that was. Nevertheless, she was very sweet. The

ast time we met was in December during Christmas break of 1954. I was quite sick
n bed with some sort of flu. Pat had come all the way to Pennsylvania to see me. I
emember being sort of cool to her and I'm afraid I wasn't very nice. I guess I had
ost interest or maybe I had another girl. It was the same fall that she and I were on
he cover the Colby Alumni magazine sailing one of the new boats I had purchased
or the Yacht Club. I see her name in Alumni notes every once in a while. She is
narried and lives on Long Island.

Some years after I left Colby there was a program instituted called the "Jan
'lan" where students took a month off between semesters to pursue some type of
ndependent study. I spent my last semester doing something similar in the Geology
Department under the direction of our major professor Dr. Donaldson Koons. I had
lways liked Dr. Koons since taking his freshman survey course, but he was hardly
he sort of professor who we sat and drank coffee with as we did with Professor Paul
'ullam. He was probably in his thirties, although at that time he seemed older.

Don Koons had grown up in Seoul, Korea, a name that had become familiar
o us through the war we were in at the time. His father was a missionary there
nd Don came to the United States when he was seventeen. He had been a radio
pperator assigned to the OSS during World War II and told us he was stationed in
small hut at the end of a runway: "We'd listen as each B-17 loaded with bombs
axied down the runway, praying they clear our little house." After graduating from
Columbia with his PhD, his specialty became Quantitative Geomorphology and
ach summer he would disappear to Colorado or Arizona where, on an Office of
Naval Research contract, he did a special type of mapping. He said nothing about
he work. Maybe it was classified. All he said, with a little smile was, "everyone needs
a racket… and this is mine."

He had come to Colby in 1947 and taught until 1982. He lectured in Geology
01, a large class of over 200, maybe the largest class we had that year. Most of the
tudents were not very interested in his topics. Instead, they would keep track of
he number of times he cleared his throat. I believe 237 times was the record. But
ve no longer paid attention to this habit. We came to love his classes. There were
only about fourteen of us as majors so we got to know him well and to respect him.

The senior project he suggested I work on gave me a chance to get involved
using a brand new wave tank he had had built. I was the first to use it. It was about
ixty feet long by three feet wide with a large paddle at the end that generated the
waves. My project studied the effects of varying beach slopes, sand grain size, and
wave forms. It wasn't exactly something I knew much about, but it introduced me
o physical oceanography. Although there were very few reference documents in the
ibrary, it reinforced my intention to go on to graduate school.

Don Koons by the wave tank. My senior research was done using the
wave tank. A launch into oceanography.

As Dr. Koons was summing up our four years as geology majors and wishing us well in whatever we were about to undertake, he paused briefly to tell us what he should have told us at the beginning. "You know," he said with that slight smile, "you all should have been math majors in your undergraduate work, and then taken your geology for your graduate work." I didn't think too much about his comment at the time other than to say it's a heck of a thing to tell us now as we're leaving. In my case, with a weak math background it would have been most helpful. A great many of my graduate courses in oceanography would have been enormously more meaningful if I had taken more math, especially calculus. He was right.

Don Koons passed away in 2012, at age 94, another important person in my life who snuck away before I could say goodbye He was certainly an inspiration for me to follow my somewhat devious but rewarding career path. I had enjoyed seeing him over the years at Colby alumni reunions. The final chapter for Don Koons came in July of 2012 when Colby held a memorial service for him in the Lorimer Chapel on the campus. My wife, Ellie, and I attended, hoping that some of my Geology major students would be there. I knew that Derek Tatlock wasn't able to make it, but thought maybe some of remaining dozen or so of us might. But the only one was Bob "Whitey" Thurston who'd gone into a career with the Air Force instead of Geology.

The chapel was full, mostly friends of the Koons family, including three of Don's four children. The last I'd seen him was in 2009 where he was our dinner guest, very alive and alert and hardly showing his age. A number of his friends and family spoke. The crowning event of the service was the ending, where his son John Koons, introduced members of the Atlantic Music Festival who played Beethoven's *Ode to Joy*. Not knowing what to expect or anything about the group we watched as a lone young man in a T-shirt walked out and started playing the bass. And then a few moments later a young woman came out on stage with a violin. Then, to our amazement, one by one or in small groups a full orchestra came through various doors, each with instruments, playing in perfect time, sounding louder and louder. Finally, a man with a trumpet appeared from the balcony followed by a choral group. It was one of the most moving performances we'd ever seen and brought tears to our eyes along with many in the audience. We found out later from Karl Dornish, a local classmate, the Atlantic Music Festival played every year in the summer at Colby open to the public and free. Billed as world class musicians, they certainly were all of that! What a fitting tribute to Don Koons.

In 1953 when I was a junior, I met Carolyn English, a senior at Colby. We had a wonderful dating relationship that lasted an entire year until she graduated. An attractive brunette of medium height, Carolyn had grown up in Stoneham, Massachusetts, with a network of Colby girlfriends. She turned out to be my first Colby steady girl. Her nickname among her friends was "Muffin" English. Furthermore, she was one of the Colbyettes, an eight-to-ten woman singing group, the counterpart of the men's Colby Eight. Music was a big part of her campus life. She came from an Irish Catholic background and several of her siblings were involved with musical careers. We had fun going to movies, college functions, trips to the coast, and once she came to visit Sugarbridge. Unlike my past episode with Nancy, my parents liked her.

Carolyn was quite up front with me at the outset of our time together. She was in so many words "betrothed" to Joe Bean, her high school boy friend from Stoneham. She was sure she would marry him as soon as she left Colby. Even though I was the substitute, I found myself quite in love with her despite knowing there was no future. We were certainly fond of each other but she never let things get out of hand, so to speak. And so we parted as good friends at the end of my junior year. I never saw or heard from her again until 1990.

At that time I was starting a business in Bedford, Massachusetts and my landlord Ben Sears turned out to be a Colby graduate of the class of 1950 and fairly active as an alumnus. Somehow in comparing notes, I found that Carolyn was quite active also and was on the Alumni Council with Ben. In fact, she worked just a mile or so away at a company called Millipore Filter. So, after a phone call and thirty-seven years, we had lunch one day and renewed our friendship which continues to the present.

Carolyn English, a year ahead of me, class of '53, became my campus girlfriend.

The spring of 1954 as we were all getting ready to graduate, we held a class meeting in the big lecture hall in the science building. Dr. J. Seeley Bixler, our very likeable president, succeeded in drawing together our four years at Colby by trying to show the connection of the various courses we had taken. He wanted us to see the value of our liberal arts education. He told us that with our various tools we had acquired here we shouldn't be afraid to try anything we wanted to do. We were generalists equipped to tackle any job we wanted to. Through all the many different jobs I took on in the next years I always keep that statement in mind. It gave me a great feeling of confidence.

Colby graduation in June wasn't particularly memorable. Rain threatened so the ceremony was held in the field house and featured several interesting speakers and guests: Harry Emerson Fosdick, noted church leader who led the controversy between fundamentalists and modernist, Cyrus S. Ching, famous federal mediator who served under Roosevelt, Truman, and Eisenhower, Hyman Rickover, father of the nuclear submarine, E.B. White, later to become one of my heroes as a Maine essayist, and Andrew Wyeth, who at this time hadn't become nationally famous recieved honorary degrees. However, I knew Wyeth through my parents and greeted him on the stage, as we both recognized each other. Pretty impressive collection for a small Maine college!

After graduation I decided I would spend the summer sailing before going on to graduate school. But I also knew I would need some money to live on so I found a job at the Boothbay Harbor A&P market located right across from Boothbay Fruit Co. and the Smiling Cow. For close to full time, I worked stocking shelves, bagging, at the cash register, and anything else the manager, Henry Safford. needed. I was able to take off Wednesday and Saturday afternoons. This meant I could crew for Pete Welles in the Yacht Club races. The pay at the A&P was $3.50 an hour, which, while not great, was adequate. And as Tuesday was my day off it turned out I could drive cars for John Elderkin a.k.a. "Honest John," when he went to the used car auction.

At the time the Great Atlantic & Pacific Tea Company was still healthy. But its doom was not far over the horizon. The labor union provided excellent wages for long term employees like Henry but as time went on, especially in a mostly non-union state like Maine, the A&P couldn't compete with the newer supermarkets. Years later when I moved back to Maine in 1972, I ran in to Henry. He was still working for the A&P in his last year before retirement. The Boothbay A&P had long since closed and he and his assistant manager now had to commute fifty miles a day to Augusta if they wanted a job and a retirement. At that time there were only six A&P stores left in the state. It was, in many ways, a prelude to what the automobile unions did to bring about the downward trend we're seeing lately in the American car industry. I'm certainly not speaking out against unions, but the wage scales have made it hard for American cars to compete. Who ever would have thought those funny little Japanese cars would some day outsell our good old Detroit iron?

During the summer there was a big celebration in the Harbor one afternoon with quite a crowd gathered by the library and lots of people in the street. On the lawn stood none other than the great radio and TV personality, Lowell Thomas, in front of a microphone on a live broadcast. Over the loudspeakers he was telling all gathered about the schooner just down the street in the harbor that was about to depart for a summer's trip to the Arctic. The captain and leader was the well known Arctic explorer Commander Donald MacMillan, USN (ret). He and his group of young men from Bowdoin College were setting out on his twenty-ninth trip to the icy waters of Greenland. "Mac" was best known for his trek to the North Pole with Admiral Peary in 1909. Now at age eighty he was off again. Even more amazing I found later that "Mac" had made his final trip to the Arctic at age eighty-two. More seeds were planted for my future interests.

My other clear memory of my brief summer at the A&P was the day that my godfather, Claude Rains, stopped by to visit me. He strode in looking quite informal in a sports shirt and bought a few groceries. I proudly said I would take them out to his shiny Bentley convertible. I hadn't seen him in a few years. He looked well and was on his way to Portland to visit his dear friend Bette Davis who summered on Chebeague Island. She would years later star in the 1987 film *Whales of August* which was shot on Cliff Island. She and Claude had appeared together in several pictures and from what I gathered were quite close friends. I don't think anybody at the A&P recognized Claude. The next time I saw Claude was at my engagement party at Sugarbridge in 1957.

The rest of my summer after my graduation from Colby was spent sailing with Pete in his Boothbay 21. This sloop was designed by a naval architect from Bath

Iron Works, funded by Sterling Hayden, and built in Boothbay by Norman Hodgdon in 1936. It was more of a racing boat than the J boats I learned in at Blue Hill.

When we weren't sailing we cruised around in Pete's 1940 Ford or his father's 1953 Ford convertible. On one of my double dates with Pete where we were making the rounds to our favorite spots, we stopped at Newagen Inn at the waitresses' dorm. Two of waitresses agreed to go out with us in Pete's dad's convertible. This was my first meeting with my once and future wife, Karyl Mader. We had a grand evening just talking, which she did most of. Her last name, she said, was easy to remember. "If you just took the opposite of that spot at the top of the sky, you know the zenith — that is the nadir — it rhymes with Mader." I never forgot it.

We hit it off immediately and that was the start of a mild and long distance romance that lasted over three years. I left soon after this first meeting on my way to Texas A&M in the fall of 1954 and where I became totally wrapped up in my graduate work. Karyl faithfully wrote me witty letters from which I got to know her better. And I wrote back. I didn't get home much from Texas and then even less to her home in Needham, Massachusetts. I did manage to get to Boothbay Harbor the next summer while she was working at Brown Brothers Restaurant. Our long distance love continued for the next years and beyond.

So how did I get to Texas A&M? I knew I wanted to go on in the ocean sciences but I really got very little help from Colby. Somehow I was steered toward the University of Rhode Island where there was a school of marine sciences. In the spring of 1954 I drove to Rhode Island and ended up down by the shore at the old ferry landing where there was a small two-story cottage perched out over the water. The door was locked and no one was around, but the names of research staff were posted: Drs. Marie Poland Fish and Dr. Charles Fish, her husband, both ichthyologists. Later, as I was about to apply, I learned through the University that the graduate school only had classes beginning every other year. I knew I couldn't wait a whole year without enrolling and risking the draft for Korea. After exploring possibilities at University of Miami and Washington, both with good oceanography departments, I found my way to Texas A&M where there was a very active and rapidly expanding program in oceanography.

Chapter Five

On to Texas A&M
1954 - 1958

Late in the summer of 1954, I bought a real car, not one of the many heaps that Pete and I had always pushed and towed around. So just as Hurricane Carol, one of New England's most destructive hurricanes, was about to sweep up along the coast in late August, I said goodbye to my Boothbay friends, briefly stopped to say another goodbye to my parents at Sugarbridge, and then cruised by car down through the deep south. I missed the major destruction that Carol brought to New England by a day or two, but I recall all the photos in the news of boats stranded high on rocks. I was glad not to be a boat owner.

My dad and me at Sugarbridge behind my '49 Ford about to depart for Texas A&M, September 1954.

I have pleasant memories of driving my almost-new '49 Ford with its loud glasspack dual mufflers along the old, narrow two lane cement roads in Mississippi. The edges of the road were grown over with thick vines like a jungle, most likely kudzu. It was unbelievably hot and humid and I wondered if Texas was going to be like this. I stopped in Jackson, Mississippi for gas, which was much more expensive than in the east. I made a comment about the high price to an older gentleman who was pumping the gas. "Yassuh," he said, in typically slow Southern drawl, "they rob you here without a gun!" An apt phrase.

My choice of A&M was hasty and without much background information as I realized I had to enroll before the draft caught up to me. In fact, the only thing I knew about the school was its highly recommended Oceanography Department. My first surprise was the college was for men only and, to boot, the undergraduate school was all military Army ROTC. But I wasn't about to turn around and go home after the nearly 2,000 miles that it took me to get there.

The graduate school professors and students turned out to be a friendly bunch who hailed from all over the country. The only problem that I had to face was Dr. Trotter, Dean of the Graduate School and a typical Texan, who had a low opinion of those of us from back east. He looked over my transcript and shook his head. "Your grades from Colby aren't good enough," he said. "The eastern schools just don't measure up to our Texas A&M standards."

I knew my grades weren't outstanding, but still his attitude was tough to take. If I wanted to get into the graduate school, he said I would have to take some undergrad courses that fall to see if I could meet their criteria. I saw no way to object or get out of this requirement, so I took a freshman biology course, along with couple of introductory oceanography courses. The biology course was ridiculously simple... not even on par with something I might have taken at Haverford. It was taught by Dr. Larry Dillon whom I got to know later on. I found him to be a first rate scientist. Because of him, I wound up taking a minor in biology specifically in limnology (study of lakes) and some very special techniques offered as a "one on one" course with Dr. Dillon. Taking that simple biology class wasn't so bad after all. I got A's in all my courses and Dean Trotter begrudgingly admitted me into the graduate school the next January.

The college, with its military establishment, was something to behold; it was nothing like Colby and its relatively insipid Air Force ROTC. These poor guys were in the Corps twenty-four hours a day and in uniform, albeit World War II issue army khakis for summer or browns for winter. It was constant discipline and hazing in which the freshmen, mostly kids off the ranches of the Texas plains, were called "Fish" and were the lowliest scum. Their heads were shaven and anytime they would meet an upperclassman walking outside would have to assume a "brace" or rigid "at attention" position. Their enemies were the sophomore who were called "piss heads." The seniors got all sorts of privileges. They wore jodhpurs and high leather shiny boots and could do most anything they wanted, like breaking empty Coke bottles on the sidewalks and making underclassmen clean up.

When they graduated, all these men were obligated to serve in the Army for four or six years as officers. It was said that A&M turned out more officers than

West Point. I always wondered if they were as good. I doubted that the academics at A&M were anywhere close to those of the other service academies.

My first year in Texas took a bit of getting used to, at a totally different kind of college. I was placed in a graduate dorm and had a roommate, Walter Polestak, who was from Brooklyn Poly Tech. Proud of his Polish heritage, he was a most pleasant person. He was working toward a PhD in chemistry and was a teaching assistant (TA) for freshmen classes. Each day after class he would just shake his head and pound the desk as we studied and worked. He couldn't get over his students' lack of basic training. He kept saying they weren't able to do more than sixth grade level work. He told me he had found out that the freshmen didn't have to pass any kind of entrance exam. They just came to A&M right off the ranches and farms. Later we also found that at the time most Texas high schools only had eleven grades. And of course, all of them were in the Corps which meant four years in uniform, constant drilling, marching, and being hazed by upperclassmen. Academics weren't of much importance. What a change from Maine and Colby!

While I was living in the dorm one evening someone came into our room and offered to give me a shotgun. Thinking it would be an interesting experience, I said sure and took it. Then I realized it was a 10-gauge sawed off shotgun, the kind that gangsters use to kill ten people at once. It had a great name, too: "Shoot-More." It was highly illegal and not something I wanted to keep around.

Then there was football! When I arrived, I was fairly impressed with Southwest Conference football. It was big and then some. On top of all this there were the Aggie rituals that went on at every game. There was the "Twelfth Man" or the student body, based on an episode from 1927, when too few team members went to an away game at Baylor and at some point in the game, after lots of injuries, there weren't enough men on the field to make the required eleven players. A student had come dressed in a football uniform and stood ready. He supposedly raced down on the field so the game could go on.

From that day on the entire student body including guests, dates, and graduate students had to remain standing during the whole game, symbolizing readiness as the "Twelfth Man." The college thrived on tradition and ritual and we did stand through every game. If you didn't stand you couldn't see. It was so different from my quiet, staid life at Colby that this all seemed like great fun. Graduate students were also called "non-regs" that is, not regular because we weren't in the "Corps."

There was also the long-standing tradition of the bonfire the night before the University of Texas versus Texas A&M football game at Thanksgiving. In the style of "bigger is better," which is the theme of Texas, each bonfire had to be bigger than the one from the previous year. The freshmen were organized by upperclassmen to build this display. I remember it as being over seventy feet high, made out of logs and telephone poles and built on one of the playing fields. At the top there had to be some symbol of completion. Usually it was an old rickety outhouse that the freshman "fish" stole from a poor family in the countryside. After a lot of pep rally talk with the entire student body of nearly 8,000 watching, the fire was lit. It was all very tribal and primitive as we watched the flames consume the 70-foot tower.

During the first or second year I was there, a couple of University of Texas boys secretly got a T-33 training plane from Bryan Air Base and buzzed the field where the fire was ready to be lit with some crazy idea of trying to light it ahead of time. They did some sort of dive bomb at the pile of logs but they failed to pull out and crashed. Although both were killed, it didn't stop the ceremony.

The bonfire ritual went on for a number of years after I left in 1957. Recently, there was an incident where several Aggies were killed, as the whole towering pile fell on them. It was in the news all over the country. Akin to this was another ritual called "Silver Taps." Whenever an Aggie was killed in a car accident or some other mishap, a service was held for him at ten o'clock in the evening. The entire college would be blacked out and utterly silent as the Corps bugler played taps three times over the PA system. One year I recall seventeen silver taps funeral services. These accidents usually involved drunken driving on the weekends by the members of the "Corps," a sad commentary on the youth of Texas.

Instead of being a TA like my roommate Walter, I was lucky to have a graduate assistantship in the Oceanography Department. There were no undergrad classes in Oceanography, so we didn't need TAs. As far as I know every graduate student in the Department had a part time job and support. Most of the money came from Navy contracts through the Office of Naval Research (ONR). I say that I was lucky to get this job because it was the beginning of a series of research jobs with practical training, not correcting freshman quizzes and tests, which would have seemed to me dull and not useful.

When not in the classroom, a good deal of my time was spent on our research vessel, the *A. A. Jakkula*, in the Gulf of Mexico. After my three years working on my master's degree, I found some years later that I had a great deal more practical seagoing oceanographic experience than most graduate students from other universities. My full year at sea allowed me to get a Coast Guard license. I don't think many of us realized how good a school A&M was until we got out into the professional world.

I really enjoyed my classes in the Oceanography Department that first year. We had excellent professors who made our course material interesting. At some point in the graduate work, I realized nearly everything we had learned in college was wrong, or, if not actually wrong, then oversimplified and long out of date. I was fortunate to have two of the world's leading marine geologists teaching our courses that first fall, Dr. Philip Kuenen and Dr. Lambertus Van Straaten, both from Holland.

The Department was divided into five disciplines: Physical, Geological, Biological, Chemical, and Meteorological. All these topical areas came into play in the ocean, so we had to be somewhat proficient in them all. Some courses had textbooks but in others we got the latest scoop in notes only or mimeo handouts. *The Oceans*, considered the granddaddy of all oceanography books, contained a bit of everything, although much of it was somewhat outdated since it was published in 1942. The author, Harald U. Sverdrup, a prominent Norwegian scientist, had been the Director of Scripps Institution of Oceanography starting in 1936. He was also cousin of Otto Sverdrup, the famous explorer who drifted around the North Pole on Nansen's *Fram*. I was delighted to find out later that H. U. Sverdrup had been the Chief Scientist aboard the *Nautilus*, during Sir Hubert Wilkins failed attempt to dive a World War I submarine under the ice to the North Pole in 1931; a topic that I became interested in some years later writing an article on the *Nautilus* expedition.

Dr. Dale Leipper, Head of Oceanography Department at Texas A&M. He started the department after leaving Scripps Institute of Oceanography in La Jolla, California.

One of Sverdrup's outstanding students at Scripps was the Head of our A&M Oceanography Department, Dr. Dale Leipper, who taught the Introduction to Oceanography class. Sverdrup recommended Leipper to head the department and he took over in 1949. Just as a prophet is not respected in his country or city, at the time we all had little good to say about our department head and leader. At the time, he was not well respected, but we should have realized how important Dale Leipper was in starting our Department. We would all snicker as he played *Asleep in the Deep* on a tuba at our Department parties. I also found that in 1932 he had played this same tune as a high school student in Salem, Ohio. I remember him telling us that the jobs we would wind up with weren't even created at this time. How true, as I look back on my job record.

My assistantship job sponsored by the Navy's ONR was what was called Project 24, the Hydrography and Deep Circulation of the Gulf of Mexico. This part time job paid enough for me to live on since the tuition at A&M was only $125 per semester the first year and $25, once I was no longer considered an out of state student. The project was headed by a mild mannered Texan named George Austin who, along with his wife, Sarah, worked full time. There were three or four graduate students, a couple of technicians, and a Japanese physical oceanographer named Saito. Dr. Saito was extremely bright but he was highly frustrated because he neither spoke nor understood much English. Luckily, there were several other Japanese in the department for him to talk to.

Dr. Ray McAllister, formerly of Scripps who started our courses in SCUBA at A&M in 1955.

In 1955, the Department offered a course in SCUBA Diving taught by Ray McAllister. Ray had been at Scripps where the first SCUBA diving course began with Connie Limbaugh about 1951. Ray taught his first class in 1952, later coming to Texas A&M. With fifteen or so of us starting out in the A&M pool, the school furnished the then very new Aqualungs, those with two hoses that came to California around 1950. From the pool, we moved to a local quarry and finally our open water dives were in the Gulf of Mexico. We had to make some fifty dives, getting to fifty feet before we were certified. Ray was a good instructor and emphasized safety and the strict rules of diving. But he had his bullshit side, too, with all sorts of unlikely stories from his Marine Corps days in World War II. He walked with a slight limp which he claimed had come about when his foot got caught in the blow hole of a whale. Needless to say, we were a bit skeptical.

I still have a textbook which he stamped with his own rubber stamp reading "Bunny Snowshoes." He loved to make fun of our Department Head, Dr. Leipper. He left A&M to spend the rest of his career at Florida Atlantic University. I'll always remember the story of his violent temper when he disciplined one of his children, as the story goes, by picking him up and hanging him from a coat hook. Ray departed us in 2012 with many tributes from his Florida friends. I guess I owe him a thank you for getting me started in SCUBA diving.

That fall on a cold, gray day in November, three or four of us decided to go diving in Lake Travis in central Texas on the Colorado River which stretches for 65 miles and is 210 feet deep at one spot. The water felt equally as cold as the day. We had fashioned our own wetsuits since the first commercial suit wasn't available until 1956. We took sweatshirts and pants and tried our best to coat them with liquid rubber. A noble effort but quite unsuccessful. We weren't in long or went very deep but I have never been as cold as on that day when I surfaced. I'll bet my core temperature was less than 90° and I couldn't stop shivering and shaking. A few years later it was such a pleasure to wear a White Stag 3/8" foam suit with farmer John pants. I was comfortable even in water with lots of ice.

After my first year at A&M where I lived in the dorms, I decided to move out and find a better living situation. All of us who lived in the dorms ate in the chow hall which served the whole college. A year of this, too, was enough. It was rather amazing that 4,400 students on two floors were fed in about twenty minutes but it was hardly a relaxing dinner. Most all were in uniform of the Aggie military in which the food was passed up and down the long tables and followed the "reg" procedures of Army names for each food. For example, Worcestershire sauce was "Winchester," because it was easier to say. Whatever it was, you had to say "short stop" or it would go right past you. Dining was hardly a calm, pleasant experience.

I found two other graduate students, Ben Miller and Ben Edwards, who needed a third roommate. Their house was a single floor, typical ranch style, and painted a sick green color as most were, but it was such an improvement over the dorm. Both Bens were graduate chemistry majors from Texas and lots of fun. They had a black and white cat named Thomas, who was playful and loved to attack us after being provoked. Ben and Ben enjoyed seeing who could brew the strongest coffee. It was here that I used a Vespa scooter for getting around on the campus and stayed with the Bens for a whole year.

In 1957, I was invited to share a room with Dick Adams, who owned a house just off campus. Dick was an administrator in the Department and a really nice guy from Indiana. He also was a Chief Scientist on several cruises. Dick's nephew, an undergrad named Gary Staley, was one of the boarders. Dick and Gary did most of the cooking, mainly typical Midwestern, dull meals with overcooked vegetables and gray meat, but still far better than the dorm.

The other border to join us was Walter "Wally" Charm; he was one of my favorite characters. Wally, a marine technician who hailed from Winthrop, Massachusetts, went on most of the cruises on our various vessels. A true hippy with beard, shorts and sandals, he played guitar and ukulele and was a great folk singer. Wally had also been a SCUBA diver who went after abalone when he lived in California where he was a member of the Pacific Grove Loony Gooney divers. Wally was gone to sea a lot, so sharing the same room was okay. During the late summer and fall, I began sleeping out on the screened porch on a folding cot and sleeping bag, which was more private and pleasant. After my training of sleeping in the really cold of the Deke house at Colby, this was mild.

After A&M, I thought I'd lost track of Wally, but a decade later, I found he was alive and well in Miami when Karyl, daughter Amy, and I moved there. By this time, Wally was married and maybe divorced, with a daughter named Vicky. He was even more of a hippy, still singing, and now made wonderful custom made leather sandals. I bought a pair and have cherished them to this day. The last I heard from Wally was 1999, he was part of a large string band.

Research Vessel A. A. Jakkula *a converted 120-foot steel schooner, which served the department from 1953-56.*

Every month or so, a group of students, marine technicians, and a chief scientist would make a cruise out of Galveston on our research vessel. Our ship was a 120-foot, three-masted schooner, the *A. A. Jakkula*, named after Dr. Jakkula, the first director of the A&M Research Foundation. The ship, built in 1923 by Bethlehem Steel Company, was later purchased by the Ulhlein brothers of Milwaukee, who owned the Schlitz Brewing Company and named her *Moby Dick*.

During World War II, the schooner was used for submarine detection by the Coast Guard. In 1953, the Ulhlein brothers donated her to Texas A&M. A fine yacht in her day, by the time she arrived in the Gulf, she was in need of a lot of upkeep. Jerry Stein, one of our graduate students relates the story of bringing her down the Mississippi River with her masts out and on deck. At one sharp bend in the river, she failed of respond to the wheel and gracefully put her bowsprit through a building. It happened to be into the ladies room of a Sears, Roebuck store — a good start for our research vessel.

The *Jakkula* had been converted to an oceanographic vessel on a shoestring budget, as was the case with most research vessels at that time. When I first went aboard I noted that the masts had been shortened, her large ten-foot deep center board removed, and her once fine Krupp diesel traded for a puny underrated GM 671. I don't think the Coast Guard was nearly as strict in 1953 as now, because the *Jakkula* was barely seaworthy even in the Gulf of Mexico. On many a trip out into the Gulf in moderate seas, we rolled forty-five degrees side to side. Most of us experienced some amount of seasickness, at least for the first few days out. Our mission was to make measurements of the temperature and salinity to depths of at least 4900 feet. To do this we had a winch with about 10,000 feet of wire cable on which we attached a series of cylindrical bottles that took a water sample and temperature at set depths.

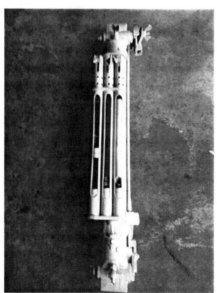

A Nansen bottle invented by Fridtjof Nansen in 1910; in 1955, we used these to samples of water temperature and salinity to determine the deep circulation of the Gulf of Mexico.

It was a slow and somewhat archaic process started long ago by the Norwegian scientist and explorer Fridtjof Nansen, inventor of the Nansen sample bottle in 1910, but even in 1955, it was the most accurate way to determine deep ocean currents. We were able measure temperature to one hundredth of a degree Celsius and salinity to two hundredth parts per thousand. The use of electronic instruments to make such measurements was still decades in the future. Each location or "station" took several hours or more; this meant that the science crew worked around the clock on shifts of six hours on and six off.

One of our cooks named Blackie would switch on the lights in our bunk room, yelling "drop your cocks and grab your socks!" at midnight and six in the morning. This was how I learned to awaken instantly and be on deck within ten minutes to start grabbing Nansen bottles off the wire cable, with seas on each roll washing over the man in the "bucket," a grated platform attached to the side of the ship which every so often would dunk the occupant in the warmest waters of the Gulf. I learned to enjoy this job but I more liked running the winch and 10,000 feet of cable. Years later I would find myself involved with a similar winch and 10,000 feet of one-inch cable drilling through the Arctic ice sheet on the Greenland Ice Sheet Project.

Our cruises would last one or two weeks, most of the time in hot, steamy weather. The Galveston water we had to drink aboard the ship tasted somewhat oily, due to a certain amount of salt intruding into the water supply. We had no coolers, instead we used Kool-Aid to mask the taste. On one of my first cruises, as we came out beyond the breakwater into the Gulf, the old *Jakkula* began to pitch heavily into the head seas. My office mate, Jim Henry and I sat up on deck munching on saltines, believing it might put off seasickness. It usually didn't. After the first whole day the queasiness would pass. A couple of the guys were sick for days, and one, Juan Gonzales from Puerto Rico, had to be put ashore by The Mississippi Delta after continuous sickness for seven days. On many of our cruises to survey the outflow of the Mississippi River we would encounter bad weather where conditions didn't allow us the work.

Our skipper, Harry Moors, would take us up to the protected area and the little town of Burrwood, Louisiana, about seven miles up the river. We tied up at the US Weather Bureau station and dock. There was a tiny store and post office, which at first seemed quaint but after three or four days of waiting out the weather, became incredibly boring. Burrwood had been an Army base started in 1938 and manned in 1942 to spot enemy subs. There had been six officers' buildings according to old photos. By 1956 all that was left was the Weather Bureau and a couple of observers. More recently the town is now uninhabited and photos show it under water, potentially an effect of rising sea level and climate change.

Our skipper, Harry, retired from Lykes Lines as a top notch captain to be closer to home instead of months at sea. He was an extremely heavy American Samoan who resembled a South Seas native wearing shorts and sandals or a sarong. When we pulled into Galveston after to or three weeks at sea, he would be neatly dressed ready to go ashore looking like the big ship's skipper, not the South Seas native.

I still awaken some mornings with the vivid picture clearly in my mind of an early dawn, far at sea in the middle of the Gulf of Mexico. The sea is a brilliant blue seen only in mid ocean with a slight ripple. I'm hanging on to a thin railing in the bucket, the floor of which is a wooden grating mounted over the edge of the ship's gunwale as we go through deep rolls. As the ship rolls, the occupant — in this case, me — gets doused in the sea sometimes up to the waist, but the water is warm. I've been attaching the Nansen bottles every hundred and fifty or three hundred feet. They're painted a bright yellow for better visibility when they come back up. I clamp the bottle to the wire, tighten the thumb screw, release a spring, invert the cylindrical bottle so that the valves allow water to flow in, and snap it to the wire. Finally, I attach a "messenger," a heavy stainless steel weight and a release pin. All the while, the ship has been rolling, as well as drifting to leeward adding to an awkward wire angle. The ship is impossible to maneuver so we are in effect towing our cast of fifteen bottles worth many thousands of dollars. Now we have to wait a while for all the thermometers to stabilize each at a particular depth and pressure.

Finally, the Chief Scientist says to go ahead. I reach in a bag, grab another messenger, clip it on the wire and shoot it down the cable. My hands are now thoroughly coated with black, sticky cosmolene grease. I hold onto the wire which vibrates with tension and feel each bottle reversing and releasing the next messenger so on down and knowing or hoping each thermometer has registered the exact temperature. But it's not over yet because we now have to bring them all back, rack them on the side of the lab, and read both protected and unprotected thermometers with a special magnifying glass. This routine goes on day and night as we work our way across the Gulf. It was a slow and tedious process that ultimately added to our knowledge and understanding of the movement of deep currents. How simple it all became years later when a single electronic package did it all in one quick lowering, painting an immediate picture in the lab.

I went on my first long distance foreign cruise in the spring of 1955. We had made a long string of Nansen stations across the center of the Gulf and then headed into Havana, Cuba for a short break. As flagship of the Texas Navy, the A. A. Jakkula struck the colors with a large Texas flag as we entered the harbor and sailed by Morro Castle. In return, we received a twenty-one-gun salute as all of us scientists stood on deck. I had with me a letter of introduction, written by one of the Post editors, to Ernest Hemingway who was supposed to be living there. We didn't stay in the harbor long enough to try to make contact and, over the years, I lost the letter, but it makes a good story.

Instead of something noble like meeting a literary giant like Hemingway, I went out drinking with the guys, and with a bit too much decided to walk up an off limits approach to some fortification with large signs reading "No Entry." A guard with a machine gun came out to meet me. At this point, one of my ship board buddies rushed up to grab me. This was pre-Castro times in Cuba but the Batista military was just as bad. We left the next morning for another twenty days at sea along the Yucatan Peninsula.

Upon our return in April, I took some time off and, with Phil Moore, one of the ship's marine technicians, headed to West Texas and Big Bend National Park. This part of Texas is at its most beautiful in the early spring with the desert in full bloom and nothing but open space. The only people we saw were prospectors with Geiger counters looking for uranium. We slept out on the cold desert hoping a rattlesnake wouldn't try and snuggle into our warm sleeping bags; Phil had a beautiful World War I Luger 9mm pistol that he carried just in case. The next day we built a raft from driftwood and floated down the Rio Grande River through some amazing canyons never seeing anyone.

Later on, we drove in my '49 Ford to a crossing in the river where someone had said you could just drive over to Mexico. And we did. It was a shallow, rocky ford one or two feet deep that was regularly used but there were no officials, just a place to cross. On the other side, we drove a short distance to a cantina — several buildings in a typical small Mexican village — for a few beers. This spot now has some sort of remote border control where you can call to a central station 260 miles away to get permission to cross. On our return to A&M, Phil sold me his 9mm Luger for $60. It had a wonderfully worn leather holster and all the parts had the original matching serial numbers stamped in them. I had it for a while and then sold it, as guns became less popular.

I had an earlier experience with a 9mm Luger that belonged to roommate Pete Welles in the fall around 1953, when he and I went on a day trip to visit Blue Hill. We were walking up the trail on the mountain; there was no one around and Pete had his Luger with him when he saw a deer some distance away in heavy underbrush. Suddenly, without warning he pulled the gun out of its holster and fired at the deer. I jumped, as the cannon-like noise was deafening. He missed, thank God; we could have been in big trouble. My final episode with that Luger came one night as I returned to our room in the DU house at Colby. I had been drinking more than I should have and was by myself. I believed I was able, although barely, to field strip Pete's Luger. I proudly proceeded to disassemble the gun into its many pieces and reassemble it, a move more stupid than dangerous.

At A&M, our Oceanography Department was in an old brick building, dark and dingy inside with worn, squeaky wooden floors. One of the original buildings on campus, it was in serious disrepair and apparent danger of collapse. It was my first introduction to the southern cockroach, otherwise known as the palmetto bug, a long-time resident here. I was given a desk in an office that I shared with Jim Henry, another grad student who hailed from Port Arthur, Texas and was working on his doctorate also in Geological Oceanography.

Jim was immediately friendly and helped get me settled in to the Geology section. He convinced me that cockroaches were a normal occurrence in old buildings. Occasionally, we had to look for records stored in the third floor attic. It was full of roaches nibbling away on old paper. I got used to coming into our office at night and as I turned on the light all the roaches would go skittering up the walls. On hot nights in the dorm without air conditioning when sleep was impossible, I would sleep in my office. At first I tried sleeping on the floor but after having a giant roach come up and explore my face with his feelers, I moved up on the desk.

Jim and I became good friends and shared common interests in our marine work. We later tried to put together a small research company called Marine Research Co. Our venture involved the purchase of a 36-foot long unfinished wooden shrimp boat hull. We named her *Mareco* and one night after we bought her for a mere $2,000, we towed her with Jim's 14-foot outboard runabout along the Intracoastal Waterway to the home of Vernon Harness, the Chief Engineer on the *Jakkula*. He joined up with us and had agreed to install a diesel engine. We had great plans of leasing out the boat for research projects. As you might imagine, good ol' Vernon never came through with his part; he was mostly talk. Jim and I finally abandoned our boat next to Vernon's house. It was a lesson in trust.

Jim and his wife Judy, daughter Caroline, and son Jeff lived off campus in married students' quarters. They made me feel welcome that first fall and had me over frequently for dinner. Jim also would invite me to his home in Port Arthur on the coast for weekends. I later went to have dental work done by his father. Both he and Jim's mother, Jodie, were so warm and made me feel at home, like surrogate parents. On May 2010. dear Jim, like many of my colleagues, passed away making me wish I had kept up with him more. We last spoke by phone a year before his departure.

Ken Drummond, one of my other long-term friends from A&M, had a lot to do with marine operations. I soon learned Ken had gone to Bates College in Lewiston, Maine, class of 1942. Like many at that time, he went into the service as a naval officer and finally finished at Arizona University. Tall, lean, and easy-going with a quick smile and deep laugh, he seemed more Texan but was originally from La Jolla, California. We became good friends over the many years that followed.

The section secretary, Katie Blaine, took care of our various typing and office needs. She was a bit brash and loud — very much a Texan type — and quite attractive. Katie had been there for a couple of years and worked for Dr. W. Armstrong Price, my thesis adviser and boss. Katie seemed to like all the men, but me especially. She began inviting me over to her place for meals and such, although she was married to an undergraduate in the Ag Department. Katie was probably the first real southern girl I had met; I was soon to find out that she was in the process of separating from her husband.

I ate dinner at her house in Johnson City on several occasions and she later invited me for Thanksgiving. The town of about a thousand people was the home of Lyndon Johnson, then in the US Senate. Katie wasn't my type and like most of those come-on-strong affairs it was over soon after.

Several of my courses were in the Geology Department, quite separate from Oceanography. At that time Geology on campus was dominated by the importance of the oil business both on land and offshore. Under the graduate school arrangement, I was supposed to have a minor in Geology, which meant two courses and a field project. This involved spending a summer mapping a quadrangle in west Texas. The thought of tromping through the dusty desert of some godforsaken piece of west Texas in 100-plus degree heat did not sit well with me. As much as I enjoyed the courses I had already taken in Geology, I changed my minor to biology and bowed out of the Geology Department altogether.

As time went on I found I was required to choose my thesis topic. Dr. N. Armstrong Price wasn't much help as he was a few months away from his retirement. Somehow I wound up with an area in the southwest in Matagorda Bay not too far from Corpus Christi. Several other members of the Department were working here. I sampled the surface sediments of the Bay while others took cores of the bottom. We chartered shrimp boats, rather ill fitted for this kind of work. It was hardly the slick new and custom designed rigs like those I knew at Woods Hole or other first rate Oceanography schools. But still we managed to get our field work done over the course of several months during 1955.

I wish now that I had had better guidance and mentoring as I progressed on my field problem and the required thesis. The new incoming chairman in our group turned out to be the wrong person for most of us who had already started our research. Dr. Richard Bader was a geochemist who had no interest in sediments and infauna animals. He had recently been in Washington, DC as a National Science Foundation rotator and was more into the bureaucratic science and the money game for getting funds. He had made it clear to me that I would be taking chemistry courses if I were to stay on after my master's degree.

During the late summer of 1956, I decided to attend the twentieth International Geologic Conference, to be held in Mexico City, at the idea of my office mate Joe Scott Creager. Joe had come to A&M from Colorado College after a two-year hitch in the Army. He gave me good advice that if drafted I should get a critical MOS (Military Occupational Speciality) and be put in a geology holding company as he had. Thus, no marching and peeling potatoes.

We struck off in my Jaguar XK-120, the car I'd bought in Florida. We left Texas taking the rather rough and not ready Pan American Highway through Mexico. I recall a narrow winding two lane road with poor surface and no guard rails looking out over deep canyons.

Me and my 1950 Jaguar XK-120 in Fort Lauderdale, Florida. In 1956.
Pete Welles bought it for me. It had been a rental car.

We stayed the best part of a week listening to numerous papers. The only one I remember was presented by Dr. Maria Klenova (1898-1976) from the Soviet Union. She was a well-known marine geologist who produced the first complete Antarctic atlas and spent much time aboard ice breakers. Few women were in oceanography in these times and she was one of the first for the Soviets.

I learned to drive in the crazy Mexican traffic especially at rotaries. It was many times more challenging than anything I had seen in Europe. On the way home, as Joe and I were bumping along a terrible piece of the famous highway strewn with potholes just after the afternoon rain, we smelled and saw smoke coming from the behind the seats. I stopped and pulled the battery cover away to see flames. Here we were in the middle of nowhere with no fire extinguisher. There were small puddles from the rain so we both madly scooped water over the burning fabric and the fire went out. But the battery, still smoldering, was badly shorted and the engine wouldn't crank over. Then, like an answer to a prayer there came a band of young school boys gaily marching along. We quickly made them understand we needed a push and off we went, but for how far? The nearest town as best we could figure was many miles away. Several miles up the road off in a field there appeared a large barn on which were even larger letters, bold and faded …ACUMLADORES. It was a battery factory way out here. I drove up, disconnected my battery, and with a few words gave it to the shop foreman. In about thirty minutes they had completely rebuilt my battery. Talk about divine providence!

During that same fall, while on a trip to Maine, I met up again with Pete Welles. He had at the time a Jaguar C type racing car and Karyl and I took it for a ride. The C type was famous for winning Le Mans in 1951 and 1953 with one of our driving heroes, Stirling Moss, at the wheel. Jaguar had only produced fifty-three of these 150 mph cars. There was also a rather amusing incident when Pete and I went to gas up this racer. We stopped at the Amoco station in Wiscasset, Maine, located where the police and fire stations are now. He told the attendant to fill it. After the pump read twenty-five gallons, the guy began to get suspicious as it kept pumping. We said nothing, just stood there. He stopped and looked underneath, expecting to see gas pouring out. Finally Pete told him it took fifty-five gallons to fill.

Although a master's thesis, as I understood it, was basically supposed to present data, while the PhD was to solve a problem, I undertook an effort to show the relationship, if any, between the mechanical properties of the sediments and the distribution of small one- celled animals of similar size called foraminifera. This meant I had to identify these organisms of which there were literally many thousands of species. I also had to characterize and measure the particle size of the sediments such as the sand, silt, and clay portions. This process took the best part of a year and a half because my job there took me to sea for nearly a year. Eighteen-hour days were common as I sat in my office, now in a much newer, nicer building, straining over the binocular microscope, "picking bugs" and putting them on black grid slide tray with twenty-four compartments so I could count them. It was tedious, as you would lick the tip of tiny bristle paint brush and pick up one of these sand-size shells, a critter with a name like *Rotalia beccarii*, or *Quinnquoculina* something or other. We had a catalog showing pictures of the shells, or tests, of these species. In fact, the Ellis and Messina catalog came in nearly sixty large volumes.

In the spring of 1957, I hitched a ride with Ken Drummond to Washington, DC to attend the annual meeting of the American Geophysical Union that brought together lots of geoscience people from all over the east. In the large ballroom of the hotel for cocktail hour, I met all sorts of marine scientists, many of whom were from underwater technology companies. I was beginning to think about what I might do next in finding a job or project to work on and meeting these people was useful. Over the years, I met up with these same guys at various conferences even though they were working for different companies or agencies. One of the topics of great interest was underwater sound tracking systems. Although most of the information was classified it wasn't too hard to piece together systems such as Caesar, SOSUS, and others which were part of our early warning network along the continental shelf against Soviet submarines. Although it interested me, there was no place for me and my geology in this area.

In June of 1957, I submitted my thesis after the usual revisions that thesis supervisors require simply to prove their power and control, and I received my degree. I had played the game with Dr. Bader and had an easy time on my oral exams by answering questions like "what six books would you take with you to a desert isle and why?" While there was no great celebration I passed the exam, I was just happy to be done with it.

My first published paper from my master's research in the
Gulf Coast Association of Geological Societies, *1957.*

The best part of my master's thesis experience at A&M was that my thesis and one of my colleague's, Dave Fagg, were accepted for presentation and publication that fall. We went to New Orleans in November and presented our papers at the Gulf Coast Association of Geological Societies meeting. Several well-known scientists from the various oil companies commented favorably on my paper. One of them, Bill Walton, of Pan American Oil Company, wrote me a long letter a week or so later commenting with interest on the results. He pointed out that it was too bad that I hadn't taken time to stain my samples so I could have been able show the percent living to dead. Of course he was quite right as much of my work was not as useful as it could have been. If I had had a good thesis advisor, I'm sure this would have been corrected. Nevertheless, I was still proud of my first paper.

In the summer of 1957, I had finished my MS degree but went on working in the Department. I took a week's break to fly back to Boston to visit my long-term romance, Karyl Mader. Although I had spent very little time with her over the last few years. I realized that I loved her. It was, as I have said, the classic long distance love affair

I stayed at her house in Needham that summer. One night, as we sat smooching in the car on a high hill overlooking the city lights of Boston, in a moment of emotion, I said maybe we should get married. As I look back on it now I guess it was rather hasty and maybe a bit rash. I was twenty-five and she was twenty-one. Without much hesitation we set a date for December 22. It was a short courtship, with little time together as I had to get back to my job in Texas. She made all the arrangements for the wedding including picking the local church, her dress, and the ring. She was a Christian Scientist, and they don't have weddings in their church so we hired the Methodist Church in Needham.

Then on October 4, an event occurred that I paid little attention to but would have great importance in my future… the successful launch of Russia's Sputnik, the world first artificial earth satellite. I was totally involved with my oceanographic work and had little concern how this event would effect all our lives. In 1958, I became deeply involved in the US Satellite Tracking Program.

My parents and I arrived the day before the wedding, and we stayed in a nice inn in Wellesley. Andy Marvin, from among my sailing friends at Boothbay, had agreed to be my best man. I had hoped that Pete Welles would stand up for me but he was in the Army in Germany. I recall absolutely nothing of the wedding service except Karyl's father, Burt, proudly walking her down the aisle. We had a reception at the church, with no liquor, as dictated by her relilgion. Gordon Converse, a well known photographer for the *Christian Science Monitor*, took lots of pictures. We escaped in somebody's car and, of all places, spent our first night together at Karyl's parent's house in Needham. The parents discreetly left us alone. Her brother, Burt, wrote us a kind and tender note welcoming me into the family.

The next day we made a quick honeymoon trip to our favorite Boothbay Harbor spot and got a room at the Fisherman's Inn right on the water. The town was deserted, bitter cold and very Christmassy. We had the 1948 Olds that Karyl's father had given us as a wedding present. On our way back to my job in Texas, we stopped briefly to visit with my parents at Sugarbridge. I recall listening to the radio in the bedroom and the Cassius Clay (before he became Mohammed Ali) fight which was one of his first big appearances.

Karyl Mader and I were married on December 22, 1957 in Needham, Massachusetts.

Karyl's father gave us the wedding gift of his 1948 Oldsmobile 98 convertible

The next morning we were on our way south where we stopped briefly in Wil-liamsburg where I had been some thirteen years earlier as a boy. The town had aged and began to look like it had always been there. From here we went on to Charles-ton, South Carolina where many of my relatives from Scotland had landed or later been born starting in 1787.

A day or so later we wound up in the magical city of New Orleans for New Year's Eve, staying at the well-known Court of Two Sisters in the heart of the old city. It was unusually cold and we shivered as there was no heat in the rooms al-though there were charcoal braziers downstairs. Being "non party" types we went to bed early but were kept up most of the night by revelers and some sort of football game excitement. In those days, New Orleans was still fun and not overrun with tourists nor had the 2005 Hurricane Katrina yet occurred.

Our life in Galveston certainly had humble beginnings. Our first home was called Island City Housing and was run by the City of Galveston — what we would today call Project Housing. The rent was minimal, around $50 a month; the units were single floor and much like an army barracks, likely what they had been during World War II, with thin walls and no insulation. It snowed that winter, a rare event for the coast of Texas. The only other thing I can remember is it here that we had our first pet. He was a Beagle mutt named Fred, a stray Karyl had taken pity on. Soon after he wandered away. As spring came on Karyl and I decided it was time to move to better digs. We found a second floor apartment on Winnie Street in Galveston. The bathroom was right off the kitchen which seemed wrong somehow; you could sit on the throne and cook on the stove.

My job with Texas A&M was an interim one that had been a real lifesaver. Some time in the previous fall I had received my final draft notice and taken my pre-in-duction physical in Houston. The Korean War was still active but definitely winding down. My notice gave me thirty days before I had to report to the US Army. I had tried in the previous year to join the Naval Reserve, which would have required two weeks active duty each year and two months each year for eight summers. Unfortu-nately this option was too good to last and was filled up when I applied.

Luckily, my Department Head, Dr. Leipper, came up with a good solution. He decided to make me acting Head of our Galveston Marine Lab and kindly wrote to my draft board located in Coatesville, Pennsylvania, saying that I was vitally needed at the Lab. The board had plenty of farm boys from the countryside to fill their quota and granted me a deferment. It turned out that A&M had just acquired a new building which had been part of the US Marine Hospital at 45th and Strand. I became the Acting Director of the Lab. Most of my job was to paint and fix up some of the rooms. I really didn't want to go into the Army and this was the perfect out. I was, in effect, a draft dodger. As soon as I turned twenty six, I was too old fo the draft. Karyl was able to find some advertising art work but hardly what she liked or what was worth doing. And I was writing everywhere all looking for something better that the lab job.

Late in the spring, I managed to land a job along with one of my A&M classmates, Fred Marland, a biologist, in Woods Hole. He wound up at Woods Hole Oceanographic Institution, the most prestigious of oceanographic institutions on the east coast. I was hired by the US Fish and Wildlife Service, based on his recommendation.

Since we had already accumulated a fair amount of furniture and household goods, Karyl and I decided to sell the '48 Olds as it really couldn't carry all of our belongings so it went on the block, so to speak. What we needed was a small truck because we were on the move again. Then by good luck I found a great deal in a 1949 Dodge half-ton pickup, for sale by the A&M Agricultural Station with sealed bids. My bid of $300 took it. The truck had just been serviced and newly painted a pretty dark blue. Not only did Karyl and I fill the truck but we wound up pulling a fourteen-foot trailer. We were on our way to my first job, as a Fishery Aid, GS-3, in Woods Hole.

Chapter Six

Back to New England
1958 - 1962

What I remember most about the trip from Texas to Massachusetts is that the good ol' truck never missed a beat as we struggled up long hills through the Appalachians. My friend Fred had planned ahead knowing that there was an acute housing shortage during the summer in Woods Hole. Somehow, he and his wife Sarita had found one of the last available houses for the summer. Karyl and I, however, found it futile to search as prices were prohibitive, even if you did find something. Fred's house was a tiny converted chicken coop about twenty feet from the railroad track. It had all the basics but was about $500 per month, which was big money in 1957. Further, as Fred learned after they had moved in, the first train to Boston, a two car Budd Liner, would sit every morning beside their bedroom, with its very loud diesel engine chug-chug idling at four thirty.

My only reasonable alternative was to find a cheap apartment and commute to Needham where Karyl was staying with her parents. And I did find the almost perfect arrangement through my employer, the US Fish and Wildlife Service. The original lab from 1889 or so had been torn down and was in the process of being totally rebuilt that year. Luckily for me one of the buildings still stood. It was the bachelor officer quarters (BOQ) and it was free. I had a bunk and kitchen privileges and we were right on the water to boot. Every Wednesday, I would drive the two hours to Needham to break up the week, then return on the weekend. As soon as I this set up, I realized the truck was not made for this type of trip and I sold it. It had done heroic service and I was ready for something a bit more sporty.

I had been impressed with brother-in-law Burt Mader's MG-A he had brought back from Germany. He had given me a fast ride around Newton and I was hooked. So now I went and found one for myself, a 1956, medium green. This, as I look back on it, was my third green car, not a color I would ordinarily choose. The MG had been one of first sports cars from Britain to show up in this country. Its ancestors the MG-TC, like the one Jane Nevin had, and the TD were true classics but were a bit too "tweedie" for the young American family. The A was an inexpensive, sporty two-seater, seemingly less of an import. It was fun that summer on my commuting and taking it on trips to Pennsylvania to visit my parents. The trunk or boot was tiny and hardly big enough for one suitcase. But we were still young and didn't care and it was "BC" — before children.

My job was really only a summer position but nevertheless a perfect way to get up north and have employment. I went to work for Dr. Roland Wigley, an authority on marine worms and benthic infauna or the bottom organisms. I was always amused by "Wigley the worm man." In later years I encountered several of these name/vocation connections: Bob Citron, the station chief in Florida and Claude Knuckles in South Africa. Our USFWS research group was comprised of mostly marine biologists; I was probably the only marine geologist of twenty or so there. Dr. Wigley therefore gave me assignments searching the literature for information to do with sediments and bottom feeders. I had expected to be working right on the water among all the famous labs in the crowded narrow streets of the town. Instead, we were all housed in an ancient cottage just on the edge of Falmouth, six miles away. The cottage was an enormous turn of the century elegant home converted to offices and labs situated on a hill far from the water.

My work was to compile everything I could find in the feeding habits of haddock, pollock, and other bottom-feeding flat fish, hardly exciting or cutting edge oceanography. Here I was at the dream location for a young oceanographer with all the research vessels imaginable and I wasn't able to go out to sea. Instead I was stuck in a hot, stuffy, garret room away from the water. The best I could do was enjoy my cool BOQ digs which were very much on the water. And at night there always a gang that would hang out at the Captain Kidd the best known bar and restaurant right across from the real mecca, Woods Hole Oceanographic Institution, (WHOI) or just the "Oceanographic."

On many nights, distinguished scientists held forth at the Marine Biological Laboratory, the other famous lab run in the summer. An offshoot of Harvard, it hosted prominent scientists from all over the world. I attended a fascinating lecture by Dr. Roman Vishniac, a Russian-American biologist and photographer who specialized in capturing pictures of live microorganisms such amoeba and paramecium. He was one of the first to devise a mirror system that would provide enough light to photograph these tiny animals without cooking them under the strong lights usually used for microscopic examination. He became better known for his remarkable photos taken in the 1930s in Europe of Jewish ghettos.

When my summer appointment was about to run out, I received a call from my old friend and former boss at A&M, Ken Drummond, better known to us all as "Ol' Drum." He had left Texas about a year earlier in 1957 to work for the Smithsonian Astrophysical Observatory (SAO) in Cambridge, Massachusetts and was now was firmly entrenched there. He asked whether I would be interested in joining him on the Earth Satellite Tracking program. "You bet," I replied even though it wasn't the Antarctic that I had so hoped for. This project, he explained, was also part of the IGY, the International Geophysical Year, a major scientific undertaking. I bade Ro Wigley goodbye and, thanked him for two months of interesting work in Woods Hole and I headed for Cambridge to join Ol' Drum and several other A&M acquaintances including Walt Lang who was in Hawaii and Dick Adams who had been an administrator in the Oceanography Department. I had also lived as a roommate in Dick's house in College Station. Ken became the overall administrator at SAO and a very good friend and supporter.

Ken Drummond, known to all as "Ol' Drum," was at Texas A&M in charge of marine operations then moved to Smithsonian Astrophysical Observatory. In 1958 he asked me to join him on the Satellite Tracking Program where he was in charge of operations.

Over the Columbus Day weekend, Karyl and I took a short vacation in Boothbay Harbor. We sailed with Pete Welles on his Hinckley 36 yawl and visited his island off. When Pete's parents died, they left him a large sum and he had bought Cape Island, a rustic small island that sits in Newagen Harbor on Southport Island. He had purchased it from Margaret Hamilton, the actress who played the Wicked Witch of the West in *The Wizard of Oz*. Although the island was only a few hundred yards from the mainland there was no power brought over from the mainland. There was, however, a large old farmhouse with a grand view of the harbor and Newagen Inn, where I had first met Karyl.

The island was mostly forested, with great crashing surf on the sea side. It also had a small cantankerous electric generator that rarely worked. I recall Pete standing by the door of the generator shack, scratching his head wondering why it wouldn't run. There was a dock and float for landing a dinghy, but after summer the float was emoved, making it very hard to land in the winter. Along with that, carrying bags of groceries up slippery rocks in the rain at night presented quite a challenge. Pete became disenchanted with island living and sold it after several years. Perhaps the witch had the same experience.

Toward the end of August 1958, I had reported to SAO to be a satellite observer. It was my first real job and I was thrilled. Imagine in one month jumping from a GS-3 to a GS-9 with a starting salary of $5,440 per year! While it may seem paltry these days, then it seemed pretty grand.

The Astrophysical Observatory was a bureau of the Smithsonian Institution in Washington, DC and one of only two bureaus not located in the city; the other was in the Canal Zone Biologic Station. SAO had moved to Cambridge in 1955 and shared quarters with the Harvard Observatory. A small group of scientists and administrators had been formed to take on the International Geophysical Year Earth Satellite Tracking Program scheduled to start about 1955. Smithsonian was a quasi-government agency that received funds from Congress each year but also had private funds making it a sort of hybrid group.

Nearly all hired for the Satellite Tracking Program were paid on the private side although we used the GS pay scales. Interestingly, we carried Special Passports, drove government vehicles, and appeared to be regular government employees. Yet we didn't swear to uphold the constitution or whatever rigmarole went with real government employees. I only found this out later when our status was scrutinized by Frances Knight, head of the passport agency. Thus, several years after I started here, we lost our Special Passport status. It had meant that we would travel as diplomats, getting preferred airline seats and quick processing in foreign countries. The head of the operation was Dr Fred Whipple, Director of SAO, a distinguished astronomer best known for his dirty snowball hypothesis of comet composition, and a fine gentleman. I had the pleasure of getting to know him while I was there.

A group of astronomers from Northwestern University had recently arrived for this new program. It was headed by Dr. J. Allen Hynek from Northwestern University, who was later to be better known for his deep involvement with the Air Force's UFO investigations and the famous Blue Book. Dr. Karl G. Henize, from University of Michigan, was co-leading the group, and later went on to become a NASA astronaut, flying a Challenger mission. Unfortunately, Karl died of a heart attack while climbing Mt. Everest in 1993.

The Satellite Tracking Program, (STP), had gotten off to a rough and inglorious start by being behind schedule and then was suddenly upstaged by the spectacular launch of Sputnik I by the Soviets on October 4, 1957, that took the Americans by surprise. Sputnik I, also known as "co-traveler," was a small, shiny aluminum sphere weighing 184 pounds and emitting a beeping signal from four antennae for the whole world to hear. It also was able to measure cosmic radiation which was picked up by a station in Australia. It only stayed in orbit three months but it ignited an enormous race that changed all our lives forever.

This date turned out to be the dawn of the space age. The US program was far behind and underfunded. Our satellite package was to be a geodetic surveyor in orbit by this time but due to a series of failures and explosions of the booster rocket on the launch pad, we were unable to put anything into an earth orbit until January 31, 1958, with Explorer I. On the other hand, the Russians — or Soviets as they were then called — had enormous rocket capability; enough, it was said, to put a railroad car into space.

The best the US could put into orbit was a tiny satellite, six inches in diameter and weighing three pounds with very limited electronics, mostly a radio transmitter. This first one was affectionately called "Hagen's Grapefruit" after John Hagen, an astronomer and one of the originators. It went into orbit on a Vanguard I rocket. The satellite, Vanguard I was launched on March 31, 1958. In Washington our program was managed by the National Advisory Committee for Aeronautics (NACA) which in late 1958 became the National Aeronautics and Space Administration (NASA) and began to organize the manned space program. Our job at SAO was to provide the worldwide optical tracking camera network. Our longer range goal was to determine important basics of geodesy, that is, the shape of the earth and the precise location of the continents. In reality such information could only be gathered from a platform in space. When I arrived at SAO in the fall of 1958, we were a very long way from that goal.

Baker-Nunn photographic satellite tracking camera. One of twelve cameras world wide, part of the International Geophysical Year Program operated by Smithsonian.

Several years earlier, work had begun at SAO and Harvard on developing instruments and equipment for optical photography of this mission based on some existing cameras. The optical system was designed by Dr. James Baker and modified from a smaller meteor camera, the Super-Schmidt. Our cameras were to be manufactured at Boller and Chivens in Pasadena, California. The mechanical tracking apparatus was designed by an engineer named Joseph Nunn. The first Baker-Nunn camera was assembled at Organ Pass, New Mexico early in November, 1957, although it was not operational for Sputnik I. The telescopic camera stood over ten feet high and nine feet across, with an twenty-inch aperture, and an f1 focal length. The primary mirror was thirty-one inches in diameter. Early in 1958, this prototype camera photographed 1958 Beta, the six-inch satellite at a height of 2,500 miles, similar to taking a picture of a .30 caliber bullet at distance of 200 miles. Large 1,000-foot rolls of 55mm film especially formulated for us by Eastman Kodak had an ASA rating of 1200 for photographing faint objects and stars and captured the images.

But the photos for all their precision needed highly accurate timing and this was a serious problem in 1958. The only available timing device off-the-shelf was a large rack mounted set of electronics about six feet high. The Normann clock was manufactured in Wisconsin by a man named Ernest Normann. It looked good but unfortunately, as we found out, it was not nearly precise enough for our requirements. The problem was identical to that encountered by an eighteenth century navigator described in Dava Sobel's fascinating book, *Longitude*, who needed a better clock than existed to determine the east-west component. In our case we needed a one millisecond or better accuracy. The Normann time standard was close to ten times less accurate depending on radio signal propagation quirks. It would take three or four years to resolve this problem. Consequently many of the early photographs lacked the precision required for the program.

When I arrived at SAO in the beginning of September, I spent a short time reading up on everything I could about the system. Then I found myself on a plane bound for our tracking station in New Mexico where I would receive about three weeks training on becoming a satellite observer using Baker-Nunn camera No 1. My immediate boss was , a very warm and personable fellow, who was totally different from all the scientific colleagues I'd been around for many years. Dave had been an administrator at Edgerton, Germershausen, and Grier, (EG&G) a firm known for a variety of scientific projects. A master of office procedures, he was constantly grabbing his Dictaphone and rattling off memos and notes.

Dave had been at SAO for less than a year and was responsible for communication with all twelve of our tracking stations around the world, most of which had just been established in the last six months. I was to be one of three station coordinators who would assist Dave in supporting the field stations. To be able to understand the technical operations in the field, the three of us would receive the same training in station operation that the regular observers did.

The week before going to New Mexico was spent in an office environment — a first for me. I had my own separate office. Our project had grown so fast that we were moved across the street from the main SAO building in the Harvard Press building where *Sky & Telescope* magazine also was located. I even had a Dictaphone and a secretary to type my memos and letters to the stations. Most of the women were wives of Harvard graduate students.

Our travel department was headed by a gal named Midge Nelson, who was kept busy coordinating travel to our different countries. Most of our travel was first class, especially overseas as required by our Special Passport status. This meant good seats, great food, and other perks. Joining me in training were Bill Hughes, an astronomy graduate student from Indiana University and Len Solomon. Bill was scheduled to go to our station on Curacao, then still part of the Netherlands Antilles. Len was headed for Spain where we had a station in San Fernando next to the astronomical observatory there.

Shortly after arrival in Las Cruces, New Mexico, we were given a brief orientation on the whole satellite tracking system by our trainer and station chief, Chuck Tougas. Station # 01 was located in Organ Pass and overlooked the White Sands Missile Range, the largest military base in the US spanning more than 600,000 acres. Our twelve optical tracking stations were located roughly between 30° N and 30 degrees 30° S latitude. From these positions we could easily see, with our telescopic cameras, satellites launched from Cape Canaveral (later called Cape Kennedy) Florida. Of the twelve stations, nine were operated and staffed by US personnel, while the others, Australia, Japan, and India were operated by those foreign nationals. Besides New Mexico, there were Florida, Curacao, Peru, Argentina, Hawaii, Spain, Iran, and South Africa. Over the next few years I was lucky to have the opportunity to travel to all of the US stations except Hawaii — eight of the twelve.

For the next two weeks, I tried to learn everything I could about station operations, even though I didn't really expect to put this training to use in the field at the time. I came to understand the value of what the US Navy calls the Blue and Gold teams. Crews on ships, especially submarines, are regularly rotated between headquarters and sea duty on sixty day periods. As we later learned, such routine trading of places helps to minimize hard feelings and antagonisms that arise between field and headquarters. It would have been beneficial if some of our prima donna stations chiefs could have gone through the same team rotation and put in time at headquarters in Cambridge.

We immediately began our lives as satellite observers by going on the nighttime schedule which meant going to work around six in the evening and photographing several satellite passes throughout the night. In those early days of the program, the US optical satellites weren't visible to the naked eye. We were looking for objects that were from six to eighteen inches in size and were very faint. Usually, we could pick them out on film as they were moving against a stationary star background; the satellite would appear as a tiny dot against the trailed stars. The camera tracked the satellite at its same speed. We had predictions of time and location calculated by the astronomy folks at Cambridge from previous passes that told us about where to point the camera. The Soviet satellites were enormous and easily seen as objects sometimes as bright as any of the stars or planets. As observer trainees, we wrapped up our day as dawn approached, like werewolves, and retreated to our air-conditioned rooms in the motel. It was a perfect routine for the extreme heat of the desert. This nighttime drill was familiar after my several years of shipboard duty at Texas A&M where we were regularly up most of the night.

Chuck Tougas was a good instructor and also was good at keeping us entertained with a large repertoire of stories through the long nights as we waited for the next satellite pass. He hailed from New Hampshire, was handy at most trades and made an effective station chief. Chuck was transferred later to our Argentine station where we had had serious problems in station construction. Little did I know I would be visiting him there several years later. One of the early observers who left the program before I arrived was Walt Webb. He was sent out to the Hawaii station December of 1957 before any of the Baker-Nunn cameras were in operation with a smaller older camera, the Super-Schmidt, where he got one of the first US photos of Sputnik II on January 27, 1958. I had the opportunity to meet and visit Walt at his home in Norwood, Massachusetts many years later in 2010. We had both been close friends with Ken Drummond.

SAO was in charge of the optical tracking part of the earth satellite program which was the high precision part but there were two other components in this IGY program: Moonwatch and Photo Reduction, also located in Cambridge.

SAO had organized a very effective lower precision tracking effort that involved the use of volunteers all over the world. Under the name Moonwatch, the program was brilliantly conceived by Dr. Fred Whipple, and was under the leadership of Leon Campbell. Leon had a long association with the Observatory, where his father had been known for his work with variable stars. Following in his father's footsteps, Leon enlisted and organized amateur volunteers for satellite observations.

These amateur star watchers and eager volunteers, each with a thirty power apogee scope, would look every night for the larger satellites in a line, each covering a small sector of the sky. These teams of typically fifty to seventy-five persons were organized in many countries and played a very important role in early days when we had little idea just where and when the numerous objects might be coming along.

134

The networks were in place by 1956 in preparation for the IGY satellites. As many as 200 of these teams that went into action quickly when we were all taken by surprise with Sputnik I on October 4, 1957.

The sightings were relayed to SAO headquarters where the early version of the IBM computer turned out the first orbital projections. Moonwatch is hailed as the largest single scientific project ever undertaken in history. In short, the problem they helped solve was finding the extremely small objects in a vast area of the sky where we had a very imperfect idea of the satellites' positions. The original plan in 1954 had called for a one hundred-foot diameter balloon to be placed in orbit in space, where, in reality because of problems with the launching rocket, we started with something not much bigger than a golf ball or grapefruit. So the low accuracy program proved of highest value.

At SAO we had a whole group involved in photo reduction of the film from the Baker-Nunn cameras. These rolls of film were shipped back by slower freight, usually by sea, and arrived several months later. Here they were painstakingly examined under higher magnification and accurately measured to high precision coordinates.

Working under Leon Campbell was a young man named Ned Bullis. The name Ned, I found, came from Edmund. Karyl and I became good friends with Ned and his wife, Anne Shepard, the niece of Alan Shepard, the first American in space. One of the moments of great excitement at SAO in those early days was his suborbital flight. The head of our communication department, an ex-Navy Chief, "Pete" Peterson had arranged for us to tap into the radio link with Shepard so we could listen to the launch. These were launches before broadcast television.

A group of us crowded nervously into the tiny com room and heard Shepard describing his fifteen-second ride to 116 miles above the earth as he was fired off on *Freedom 7* mounted on a Redstone rocket on May 5, 1961. Part of everyone's apprehension was due the large number of failures with the first series of US rockets on the launch pad. Few people today realize how brave it was for Shepard to make this first flight, without total confidence in the launch rocket.

A year or two later Karyl and I were guests of Ned and Anne as we attended Shepard's wedding in Derry New Hampshire at his parents' farm. We had a brief chance to meet him in the reception line and shake his hand. Afterward, his father told us that he was dismantling the old barn on the property and we were welcome to browse around it and take anything we wished. To my amazement I discovered a bag of valuable antique, handmade rose head nails dating from the eighteenth century. Several hundred of these were packed in a linen bank bag marked $1,000, meant to carry money. It was a great treasure both because these nails were quite valuable and because their connection to Alan Shepard. The rose head nail was made by hand and while red hot, the head was struck with a hammer on four sides, giving it a rose look. Later on, nails were made by machines, although still with four side. I still treasure that bag and have used the nails sparingly over the years, mostly on restoration of the house Karyl and I owned in Amesbury, Massachusetts.

For the next three to four weeks at SAO, I was broken in as a tracking station coordinator and given three stations to help remedy their operating problems. Each tracking station was required to send a written weekly report of activities, progress, and requests for action or supplies. The two US stations, New Mexico and Florida, had telephones, teletype, and were in good communication with headquarters. The foreign national stations, Japan and Australia, were of less concern as they were all staffed by nationals and presented fewer problems for us. The reports from other stations, where local conditions were far more rugged, made fascinating reading and gave us continual problems of logistics and personnel. Among the worst were India because of primitive conditions, and Peru and Argentina, where our station personnel had to construct buildings, fight seeming insurmountable customs problems amid revolutions, warfare, sabotage, arson, and primitive labor. Each mail delivery brought reports with cries for help and support we in Cambridge were usually unable to provide.

In addition to the two US stations, I took charge of the stations in Spain and South Africa; both had fewer problems than the others like Iran. The two South American stations, Peru and Argentina were difficult because of the import and custom regulations. Every shipment of film, electronics, or other high tech equipment was usually held up for months until various officials were bribed or convinced they wouldn't lose their jobs if some item was released. Even though Smithsonian had negotiated high level agreements with local universities and observatories, the local officials seemed powerless to help us to get these important items necessary for operation to our stations. In all, I managed nine of the twelve stations.

Another difficult problem in those early days was the basic one of communications. Since most of our communication was by mail with written reports and no telephone, it was sometimes hard to understand just what was needed or what the background was. With the exception of a very few upper management persons, we in Cambridge had no onsite experience at these foreign locations. Many of our station personnel had been working extremely long hours, under harsh and unfamiliar conditions without any breaks. Most of the station personnel had a dim view of us in our comfy, soft offices with secretarial help, living in the "land of the great PX." I'm sure we really didn't understand how hard a job these early pioneers had. In my first month or so at SAO, I received weekly reports that ranged from fairly polite and civil to some of the most sharp, cutting, sarcastic letters I had ever read. The frustration was clear. For example, a letter report from Clarence "Clancy" Truesdell, the station chief in Spain, expressed that he felt he wasn't getting what he needed and that we back home just didn't know or care what their little isolated group in a very foreign country was up against. In great frustration he wrote, "This is Spain, where sopa is not soap, and ropa is not rope, and mantequilla is butter." He felt we just could not appreciate his situation. It wasn't until sometime later in the next year when I went out into the field and found out what he meant for myself.

Toward the end of 1958, I was offered a chance to join the field crew and live in Iran for an eighteen-month assignment. At first, it was tempting. In those days anyone living outside the US for more than eighteen months didn't have to pay a federal income tax. I had done a small amount of overseas travel in my earlier years; maybe this would be worth doing and maybe even fun. But already I knew that the station located in Shiraz had a history of especially difficult living conditions. We had received a number of reports describing in detail the hardships that new incoming station personnel faced. Our chief there, first Morgan Thomas and later "Chic" Capen would relate how all food had to be washed thoroughly even if bought at the local military base or one would suffer horrible dysentery or other intestinal attacks.

When I ran the overseas offer by Karyl she decided, wisely, against any such move. We were not in any way pioneers enough to take on this difficult assignment. I recall seeing pictures of Mr. Pahlavi, the Shah, and a friend of the Americans coming to the grand opening of the station in 1959. This was long before he was deposed and the revolution of Persia occurred. Some years later I remember reading when the Americans left our station in Iran we donated the camera and other equipment, or rather we weren't allowed to take any of it from the country. I did get to visit this station for about a week several years later and found the country among the most interesting of our twelve locations.

But soon enough in January of 1959, I got my chance to travel when I was assigned to one of our better and less difficult stations. I found myself hustled on an aircraft headed for South Africa. It was to be a temporary assignment, so Karyl wasn't able to go. The situation had come up rather suddenly and the station chief, Bob Cameron, had to be replaced. Bob, an astronomer, had been one of the original observers sent out to these far-flung outposts. In the early days, the work load was brutal — usually 90 to 120 hours a week — especially where the stations were understaffed and the satellite load was growing dramatically. In reading letters from Bob, we felt he might have been having a minor mental breakdown, and there had been complaints from the station observers that work wasn't getting done. My orders were to proceed immediately to Johannesburg to relieve Bob and take over as station chief for the time being.

Toward the end of January, I found myself on an aircraft to New York, next on a short but exciting helicopter shuttle to JFK (nee Idlewild), and then to a Pan Am DC-7B. Flying was a pleasure back then; there were no security measures and a government employees, we all flew first class. On this night flight, we settled down to great comfort on the first leg to Lisbon, Portugal on the four-engine propeller plane. The food was excellent with a multi-course meal with wine and finished with fruit in the best European style. We arrived early the next morning and by nine o'clock, took off on the same plane flying south over the Mediterranean and then across the, vast stretch of the North African desert and the famed but tiny town of Timbuktu.

There were eight people in first class and it took all of that day to fly across Africa. I became bored and moved forward into economy class and found several interesting people to talk to. By the time we landed in Accra, Ghana, the deepest, darkest part of Africa around midnight, I realized this had been the longest day I'd ever flown. We all got off the plane for a stretch and walked into what looked like a movie set from *Casablanca* with slow turning paddle fans and rattan chairs. Then we were back on the plane. Early next morning, the pilot woke us to see the falls where Stanley met Livingston. We circled slowly twice around so people could take pictures.

Finally, we landed at Johannesburg — the end of my thirty-two-hour journey. My welcome to South Africa was hardly what you could call warm. The customs and immigration officials pulled me aside and into a special room and treated me with great suspicion. First of all I was an American traveling on a special US passport and further, I had no return ticket and relatively little money. I was detained for nearly an hour as I tried to convince them I was there to work at our tracking station. At the time, Americans were viewed as anti-South African government because of their support of racial justice. The country was undergoing a major change as the once ruling British-controlled government was preparing to pull out and turn the rule over to local Afrikaners (Dutch), who had been a minority group. And it was this very element who treated the native South African blacks so harshly that later led to unrest and uprising. I guess you could say the English had been disliked by the predominantly black population but the Afrikaners were hated with their oppressive apartheid rules.

I managed to get through of the airport where I was met by Terry Edwards, a giant of a young man and the only other station observer. He told me he had been running the station nearly single-handedly, as Bob had been unable to pull himself together enough to be on the work schedule. He gave me a brief history of the station as we drove into the city. It seemed so strange to drive on the wrong side of the road, but even more so in the station truck, an American Ford three-quarter -ton pickup with the steering wheel on the left side, while all the local cars had the wheel on the right. He dropped me off at my hotel where I would have a room for the next four months.

Johannesberg was very modern with tall buildings and wide streets. My first experience the next day in the city was almost a disaster because I just naturally looked to my left as I stepped out into the street only to have a car blow his "hooter" from the other direction. It took a while to learn to look the correct way. The other thing we all had to learn was which way to turn in a roundabout or on a single dirt track when you just naturally go to the right, and the look of horror in the oncoming driver's face.

A few days, later, Bob left for home, relieved to be leaving behind the pressures of starting up and running the station. Recently, I came across a comment in *Sky Rangers*, the book by Ken Drummond, that Bob, in the early start-up days of 1958, had produced the best predictions for acquiring the satellites. Clearly, he was a competeht astronemer, but not the best chouce for a field assigment.

Part of my job back in Cambridge was interviewing candidates for our field positions, although I was only one of several interviewers. In my experience our most successful observers turned out to be geologists or someone with similar training where rugged field work was the norm, compared to the more academic or theoretical type of person at a large observatory with lots of support facilities. Visiting nearly all the stations over the next few years, gave me a great opportunity to work with many different observers . . . some good and some not so good.

For the next several weeks, Terry and I worked every night trying to get the station on an even keel. I'm sure the desk clerks at my hotel wondered what I did as I left each night at six o'clock, then came back in around four in the morning or later if we had had a busy night of satellite passes. Our station was located about twenty-five miles north of the city in a small community called Olifantsfontein (Elephants Fountain).

Our station buildings were on the grounds of the government radio station ZUO. Unique to the local architecture, the buildings were called *rondavels* and resembled the thatched huts indegenous to the area, but were round prefab metal structures about fifteen feet across with a conical roof. The main camera building was a more conventional and rectangular, made of cement blocks with the split roof that rolled open in halves. The compound was surrounded by wire fence to protect it from vandals.

We had employed several local watchmen and laborers to protect our equipment; meeting them was my first contact with indigenous people. The one I remember best was Moses; the others had similar biblical names. They spoke only fragments of English and were paid an incredibly low wage equal to $15 per month but I gathered it was a good job with better than average pay. These men all addressed us as "Bas" which, although it sounded like boss, really was in fact their word for Sir.

The saddest part of my experience in South Africa was fully seeing the apartheid system in operation. Most of the wealth of the country came from the natural resources, principally gold and diamond mines. The wealth was enjoyed by the British and Afrikaners but was earned on the backs of the country's black population, which, at the time numbered about seventeen million as opposed to maybe a million or less white inhabitants.

Blacks were as separate from the whites as could be imagined. Signs to this effect were everywhere: "European" and "non-European." We saw these in the post office, at drinking fountains, rest rooms, government offices, and on the transportation system. Suddenly, I found myself as a European when I walked into the post office to mail a letter using a separate entrance. Although the city couldn't exist or operate without the black labor, the male population was excluded from living there. The men and children were forced to live in villages some thirty miles away, while their wives who worked for the white man as cooks, nannies, or other domestics were allowed to live in their masters' homes. How close to slavery was this? I well remember the hordes of men commuting every morning before dawn on bicycles or if lucky to have enough money, on local trains.

Apartheid not only separated black from white but brutally tore apart the family structure. The country was run on a basis of fear; fear of the black man uprising and revolting. As we saw over the succeeding years, the tighter the screws were turned, the more likely became the uprising. The first of these visible to the outside world was the Sharpsburg Uprising in 1965. I suspect the even harsher treatment by the Afrikaners hastened the government's overthrow. This was a subject of conversation we continually had with our British friends who saw it coming and decided to leave. Of course, one had to admit that the white Afrikaners had been there and owned the land for over three hundred years, although they probably stole it as we did from the American Indians.

I had been in Johannesburg for a couple of weeks before I received mail from home. The only way to communicate was by air mail, which probably took a week or so. Karyl and I wrote each other frequently but that ten thousand mile gap seemed awfully large. Telephone was possible but very expensive and not very satisfactory. Several months later I recall making a phone call. You had to book a call with an overseas operator which needed to be nearly eight hours in advance. Then you had to hang around until the operator called, and the call became like a marine telephone where you said "over" on each end — hardly what you'd call an intimate conversation.

The next local event was the arrival of a new observer, Ted Sorenson, a pleasant young fellow, thin, medium build, and a crew cut. Ted had an airplane and in his spare time, he was able to do some exploratory local flying. I never saw the plane but he would regale us of his exploits. One of these was a solo trip he made to Kruger National Wildlife Park some distance away. The park was world-famous and I always regretted not taking the time to see it.

One day Ted was flying his older single engine plane, a Piper J-3e Cub with fabrid coering, when suddenly he began to lose altitude. To his horror, he saw that part of the wing covering fabric had ripped away and was streaming in the breeze. Below him was the enormous expanse of veldt, flat and easy enough to land on. He managed to bring the plane down safely but as he climbed out he was totally surrounded by a large tribe of natives, similar to the scene from the movie *The Gods Must Be Crazy*, where a strange object falls from the sky. At first he said he worried that maybe they were hostile. Luckily they were only curious. As all good small plane pilots, Ted managed to make some sort of innovative repair with the torn fabric and off he went. I hoped that I might fly with him sometime but never did.

I made some good friends while in Johannesburg. We had an afternoon tea group that met in the hotel lobby around four o'clock every afternoon. Among them were several United Kingdom aircraft technicians whose job it was to oversee the service and maintenance on the Vickers planes that South African Airways flew. The Vickers Viscounts flew within the country and were a very successful prop jet. Larry Finucane, an Irishman whom I best remember from the group, was like many of his countrymen with a good sense of humor and hilarious and entertaining aircraft stories.

When he and his crew were getting ready to pack up and move out with most of the British groups in the area, we gathered for a proper English-style tea and were usually joined by several young women. In many ways, it was a small group like the one I had known on the *Ryndam* trip to Europe in 1953. I usually had to leave for my nightly satellite work about the time we were breaking up. After a while I got be quite friendly with a girl named Marion who had emigrated from Germany. I found she had an interest in motor sports, so on Sundays we went to the local racetrack where they were running such races as the South African Gran Prix with Formula 3 (F3) cars. I hadn't been to a car race since Pete Welles and I went in Texas and it was great fun.

By the end of March our satellite team was working well together. And by this time, the predictions which were sent to us each day by teletype from Cambridge had improved to the point we were fairly sure to photograph each passage, even the very faint objects. Most times, even with a dark, clear sky we never saw the satellite with the naked eye. The camera shot continuous exposures on special Kodak 70 mm film. As soon as a camera was finished, one of the two night shift observers would take film and wind it on a specially designed reel while in total darkness in the dark room. Then it was processed in a developer bath and dried; next, we would both scan it on a light table looking for a faint image, usually stationary against a background of streaked stars. In this case, we had adjusted the camera's tracking rate to match the satellite speed based on what we knew from previous passages and predictions from the IBM 7090 computer at headquarters.

There were lots of other tricks that the hotshot stations had perfected to capture lost objects or those with uncertain orbital data. For each of four or five passages in a night, we had to locate the satellite against star background, reduce it to sky coordinates, encode these into a message in number groups, and finally, at the end of the night take these sets of numbers across the road and transmit them to CAMBMASS on the NASA TWX line. The films were then shipped back to Cambridge for a much more precise process in our Photo Reduction group. The ultimate objective of the program was to obtain very high resolution observations for geodetic purposes. Much of this work had to wait a few years until we had better timing devices at the camera stations. The ultimate goal was to make more accurate determinations of the positions of the continents and the shape of the earth.

There were times when we prayed for rain or clouds so we could take the night off. This didn't occur very often. There also were times when maybe our station was the only one in the twelve station net to capture an elusive "bird" and we felt proud. Many times, we would be weary and tired driving the truck back to town to collapse for a day's sleep feeling good about having accomplished something worthwhile.

One of my extra assignments from the SAO in Cambridge was to visit other facilities in South Africa. I traveled to Bloemfontein and Capetown, a nice change from the nightly grind. I also flew south to Capetown, where I was met by Bill Hurst, head of the local Moonwatch team. He very graciously put me up at his home. Bill was the ultimate British character with the brisk humor and set of expressions we associate with them.

"I've got to stop here and put in little wind in my tires," he would say cheerfully. Later he referred to his brakes as "binders." He was a delightful chap. I was given the grand tour of the region visiting Table Mountain by aerial tram. From here at about 4,000 feet we could see the vast sight of Table Bay, the harbor for Capetown. I was reminded of an interesting movie we were shown by Basil Wilson, one of our professors at Texas A&M. He hailed from South Africa and took time-lapse photography of a strange oscillation. In a fifteen-minute period you could watch all the moored yachts all move in one direction and then all turn 180 degrees the other way. This was a clear example of a standing wave, or seiche, which we had learned about in Physical Oceanography. As Bill and I descended in the afternoon we watched the table cloth, a thin vaporous wreath of clouds slide down over the mountain top. This made the visit perfect.

My other experience back in Johannesburg was going to the Sunday entertainment at a large sports stadium where the mine dances were held. It was the day off for the mine workers who came here in tribal teams and had dance competitions. These men were dressed in spectacular bright colors, feathers, and headdresses, all joyfully doing their own native dance. They sang and chanted and did all the things that most tourists would expect, yet I doubt the working life of an African mine worker was a very happy one.

I did manage to buy some souvenirs. There were some carved masks, a heavy wool blanket and a book called *Blanket Boy's Moon*. I remember hearing that the book was banned by the South African government because it told more of the natives' plight than they wanted the world to know about. I also went to a play starring Miriam Makeba, who was becoming more well-known as a recording artist. She later left South Africa for the United States and a career, finally returning home. At the invitation of Nelson Mandela she became known as "Mama Africa."

By April of 1959, the station was now fully manned and there was no reason for me to stay around. I said goodbye to my tea friends and four months of a pleasant stay in a beautiful country. I had become a good friend to Marion. I especially recall seeing the Southern Cross that is only visible in the southern hemisphere. She later wrote to me at my Smithsonian address and sent pictures of our day at the races which I've kept.

On my way home, the aircraft stopped briefly at Nairobi and Khartoum but I saw nothing except the airports. I wasn't feeling so hot and was just happy to be going home. I spent a day or two in Rome, but I will admit that I'm not a good solo traveler. I also stopped off in Edinburgh, Scotland to do a bit of ancestral research on George Heriot (1563-1624) — both my mother and I have Heriot for our middle names. The two days I was there were glorious and brisk spring days that felt like New England.

I wanted to find more about George and the school he started in 1623, the George Heriot Hospital. I found the location of the school still with the same name, Heriot's Hospital, but the entrance behind a large iron gate somehow seemed unwelcoming and I was still not feeling well from my journey. Instead, I found an interesting library where I took some notes. I learned that George was the royal goldsmith to King James VI and Queen Anne of Denmark. George was quite wealthy and was supposed to have loaned money to Mary Queen of Scots shortly before she was beheaded; there was no mention whether he recovered his loan. He also was in Sir Walter Scott's, *Fortunes of Nigel*. He was better known as "Jinglin Geordie," for all his wealth. There is a pub in the town now with that same name. It was definitely a worthwhile side trip.

I then took a train ride on the famous train from Edinburgh to Glasgow and later, a four-engine Constellation to Boston via Gander, Newfoundland, where we stopped for fuel. It was still winter in Boston as our plane made the descent at about midnight into Logan Airport and its extremely short runway. The pilot warned us to be prepared for bumpy landing as there was ice on the runway and he was right. We skidded sometimes sidewise and then straight ahead and came to a stop near the runway's end. It was one of the more hairy landings I recall. It was, to say the least, good to get home and renew my life with my wife after four months.

At this time Karyl and I had been living in the upstairs of small but quite new house in Medford, Massachusetts on Gordon Road. It was adequate but hardly roomy. Our landlords, Sandy, a Scotsman with the genuine accent, and his wife Judy lived downstairs and were nice enough. Still, as with any young couple, there's that yearning to own your own place. I was always scanning through the Sunday paper looking at what was for sale. Here it was in an innocuous ad: "Older house on lane with other similar houses...Amesbury, Massachusetts. $9,500. Call Anne Soule." Next thing we knew we had called and made an appointment with Mrs. , the first realtor I had ever dealt with.

Anne Soule was a plump, pleasant woman, the perfect model of a realtor, telling us all about the town and especially to the Point Shore neighborhood where the house was located. She explained that The Point, an upscale part of town, had once been part of the town of Salisbury but sometime in the previous century had been annexed by Amesbury, which at the time was a thriving factory town known as the "carriage capitol of the United States," producing up to two million carriages a year.

We drove by beautiful houses along the banks of the Merrimac River. Just behind Main Street was a parallel small road known as Andrews Lane about half a block long with about seven houses on it. I was immediately smitten with Number 5, which was a good example of a saltbox and appeared to be in near to original condition. Behind the house was a long narrow lot with some woods that backed onto the Powow River. We were really excited and with little hesitation said that we would take it.

In those days house inspections were rare so we passed on that. The price was right. How could we lose? But where would the money come from? Luckily, Grand-pere Caffoz, Karyl's grandfather of French decent offered to loan us the down payment of $2,000 and the bank loan was $101 per month at 5 percent. This house was truly a fine antique and probably the best of all the houses that I owned. We moved in June and I began the life of a country gentleman commuting every day to Boston.

Before the move, my job was becoming more demanding and I had found myself going into work on weekends or staying late each day. Now that I was about forty miles away I couldn't do that sort of thing. Besides, the assistant director, Carl Tillinghast, had carefully lectured those of us in middle management that if we weren't able to get all our work done in the forty-hour week, then there was something wrong, advice that I've always cherished.

Later that year at SAO I was promoted to Chief of the Tracking Stations, which carried with it the grade of GS-12. I'm sure it was Ol' Drum who recommended this move. As non-government or private employees, we were able to advance more rapidly than those with true federal jobs. Still, to come from a GS-3 in two years was quite a jump in pay grade. I'm sure the regular GS people, although there were only a few in the Satellite Tracking Program (STP), were jealous of us newcomers. Now I had three station coordinators who worked for me and a growing hierarchy above me and we were finally getting organized. Still there were lots of problems at the field stations. We tried to rotate station chiefs by bringing them home on leave and reassigning them to other stations if they wanted. Later on, we had all of the chiefs come back to Cambridge for a week's conference to try and iron out their problems. It may have helped, but there some who continued to feel neglected, misunderstood, or just not supported.

As chief of the tracking stations, I was suddenly in charge of about seventy men in the field. My boss, Ken Drummond, thought it would be good for me to visit most of the twelve stations. So, in January of 1960, I found myself on a plane again this time bound for South America. I was in the company of John Grady, a highly specialized engineer and technical advisor on the cameras who had joined us from our Australian station and who had worked there since the beginning. John was a delight to travel with and full of amusing stories and Australian expressions. We flew in grand style on the first of the jet liners, a Boeing 707 from New York to Buenos Aires in the remarkable time of twelve hours with brief stops in Caracas and Asuncion. The distance was about the same as my flight the year before to South Africa but almost three times faster. The Pan Am meals and treatment was still as good as before.

We were impressed with the city of Buenos Aires, or as it was referred to by the locals, "BA". Our problem, however, was the extreme difficulty in getting various specialized electronic equipment for the station through customs. The present government had inherited a multitude of problems from the corrupt days of Peron that had persisted on from the 1950's. Argentina was now trying to start its own manufacturing industries and had added incredibly high duties on most imports. Ford and Kaiser had set up assembly plants within the country to build cheap and affordable cars. Unfortunately, most of these cars were too cheap and flimsy for the really rugged dirt roads and potholes in much of the country, and they disintegrated in six to twelve months. Those who wanted a good car, either American or German, were faced with paying a steep import duty. An ordinary Ford from the US might be $15,000 in 1960. All of the electronics, were bringing to the station, were impounded even though we carried letters explaining our situation from Dr. Gratton, head of the University's Observatory. None of the customs officers wanted to take any responsibility to release them for fear of losing his job. We couldn't leave for Villa Dolores without our cartons and crates, and neither John nor I spoke enough Spanish to do any good.

Fortunately, Chuck, now station chief for Argentina, who was more fluent in the local language, flew the 500 miles from the station and helped to make our case and retrieve the equipment so desperately needed. Chuck trained most of us in the New Mexico station in 1958.

We paraded from office tof office in the customs area with growing sheaf of papers as each official elaborately signed his name, then carefully pushed a pin through the papers, as staples hadn't appeared in BA yet. We stayed in a very nice hotel in the city and had some time to wander around. In many ways Argentina's principal city reminded me much more of Europe than other parts of South America — the dress, the shops, and the layout of the streets was definitely European.

After three days we finally managed to get all of our precious cargo cleared and got aboard an ancient DC-3 operated by Aerolineas Argentina. This type of two-engine, highly dependable aircraft which had started flying in 1935 was still the basic workhorse in most of the remote parts of South America and would continue through the rest of the twentieth century

Chuck and his wife, Mal had been assigned to Argentina to get things running after a series of fires, sabotage, and other difficult events three years earlier, had plagued Walt Lang, the first chief to set up and build the station.

The Argentina tracking station was located outside of Villa Dolores, a small country town, in the midst of beautifully kept fields and ranches as the hills began to rise toward the mountains in the west. John and I were taken to a room in the local boarding hotel called the Estancia. Our hosts were European, probably originally from Germany. Beef, for which Argentina was famous, was the staple in the daily diet. There was a definite feeling of well being and plenty, so different from what we were to see in Peru and Chile in later days. This was in no way a hardship post, such as Iran and India.

John Grady and I worked our way into the satellite observing schedule during the week we were there. Much of our nighttime work was spent passing time between satellite transits telling stories, just as I had years before on oceanographic cruises on long night duty. Chuck was a marvelous storyteller and highly animated. He loved to tell a long-winded, shaggy dog type of joke in the early morning hours, just as our bearded friend John would be falling sleep. As John's eyes drowsily closed Chuck would shift to a different subject for a while, then adeptly shift back to the joke whenever John would awake. Chuck's story could last for at least an hour or longer.

My favorite story of Chuck's concerned a local Argentine politician who was strictly from the out back country and not well educated. One of his aides had prepared a speech for him to read. The text went on about certain agricultural crop harvests and forecasts stating various percentages. When he came to the figure, "25%" he was totally unfamiliar with the percent symbol. To him, it looked like "ojo," the

Spanish word for eye. He proceeded to read all the symbols as "ojo" and, as the local custom, pointed to his eye, a gesture used to mean, "it is true or I have seen it with my own eye." Needless to say, the crowd he addressed was either confused, amused, unimpressed with their local guy.

John and I learned a lot of local customs, such as the morning coffee gathering. Actually the workman at the station would gather at around ten o'clock and have tea. They all had their own cups, which were handmade clay pots with a narrow opening. They would add more tea leaves each time, never emptying the cup and drinking it with a straw. The tea was strong and bitter, unlike the much better local coffee.

A few years ago, while speaking to our friend, Irwin Shapiro, the Director of SAO, we were rambling on about the good old days. I had lost track of Chuck Tougas; Irwin related how at some time in the past, Chuck had been accused of stealing government property and actually served jail time. Although he did show up as field manager at Mt. Hopkins Observatory in 1966, somehow I couldn't imagine Chuck being involved in stolen property. Chuck, one of my idols of that whole STP experience, passed away in 1995.

At the end of our nearly two weeks in this rather idyllic setting, John and I flew back to BA and then on by jet over the Andes to Lima, Peru. This city of about four million people (now it has more than nine million) on the west coast of South America was the absolute antithesis of Buenos Aires. The majority of the population was Indian with varying degrees of Mestizo. As we first saw it from the landing in the plane, the city was a strange mix of very modern architecture amid the squalor of cardboard dwellings spread out along the edges. Many of these really were nothing more than cartons for roofs and sides, great poverty among a small bit of wealth. We changed to a smaller aircraft and flew on to the village of Arequipa nestled in the mountains at an elevation of 7,000 feet. Like most of our stations this one was chosen for its excellent visibility conditions, the lack of city lights, and clear dry air for maximum telescope performance.

We arrived in Arequipa right after there had been an earthquake and were told this sort of event was fairly frequent. The road to the station was littered with rocks that tumbled down from the walls along the roadside. The station personnel we met seemed to accept these minor rumbles casually. I remember standing in the main room and feeling a strange dull roar like a subway going by close and then realizing it was just another tremor. Our visit was short and uneventful. I can't recall who the station chief was. John and I were ready to be heading home which we did in several days.

Coming home to Amesbury was always a great treat after one of my trips. I usually managed to miss much of the winter, which was too bad as I truly enjoyed the cold weather. When we moved in the year before, we had torn into the restoration with a vengeance. The house layout was typical of an eighteenth century saltbox with a large central chimney and two small rooms in front. The rear was the "keeping room" running around thirty feet, the entire length of the house. The central feature of this all purpose living-cooking-dining room was the enormous fireplace. When the house was first built around 1745, the central fireplace was probably always burning in the bitter days of winter. Once warmed, the massive brick structure, which also served three other smaller fireplaces, retained the heat very similar to the Russian ceramic fireplaces that are presently popular.

The brickwork was hidden behind wood panels. Sometime in the recent past, a former owner had bricked over the entire fireplace and only the mantle remained. I could hardly wait to open it up and soon after we moved in I started to knock through the brick wall. What a find! Inside was a 5-foot wide by 4-foot high opening that you could almost stand up in. It was beautifully preserved condition with an oven in the upper right corner. The brick inside showed faint traces of whitewash, a common practice used in times past to increase the reflectivity at night for better lighting. A second fireplace in the parlor had been filled in and a stove was probably there. This too, I opened up finding another medium sized fireplace.

5 Andrews Lane, Amesbury, Massachusetts. Karyl and I bought this c. 1745 saltbox house in pristine condition restoring only fireplaces.

Our first big project that year had been to restore the fireplaces. Someone had referred us to a delightful expert on early housees, named Reggie Bacon. He and his twin brother, Roger, Bacon had been Shakespearian actors, and now specialists in early Pilgrim period antiques. Reggie had recommended we hire Arthur Cronin, a restoration mason. When he saw our fireplaces he was excited by the possibility of rebuilding the hearths with a type of very old, worn smooth street brick. He had found a load of these that came from the Newburyport poor farm for a real bargain price only ten cents each. Reggie acted as the consultant and each day would oversee Arthur's plans for work. The house had settled over the years and they were careful to have the hearth slope with the floor rather than make the bricks level.

Karyl and I went off to Boston early each morning and when we arrived home in the evening there would be a scrawled note from Arthur describing what he had done and why, as well as his hours and the cost. In the big fireplace the crane hooks were still there and we found a proper antique crane for it. We added dampers in both to stop heat loss. The heat loss without a damper must have been enormous in those cold days of the eighteenth century. In the end the restoration was perfect, closely resembling the original.

This was our beginning of a long love affair with old houses and antique furniture. Roger Bacon became our favorite antique dealer of very rare pieces; we were lucky to have bought them in the 1960s while they were still affordable. Roger was to become one of the best known antique dealers in the country in following years. He had sold us a beautiful rare early pilgrim desk for about $2,500, which we sold back to him some years later for $6,000.

While I enjoyed my job at SAO, "this old house" experience was more engrossing and doing the restoration correctly became an obsession. I think eeverything I had subconsciously absorbed from my parents and our old houses came back to me.

We purchased this rare c.1745 bun foot desk from Roger Bacon for $2500 in 1960, similar to several pictured in Nutting, Furniture Treasury, 1928.

For the next couple of years in our Amesbury house my life became focused on the house and the right furniture for it.

Like most eighteenth century New England homes, the house had a balanced arrangement of rooms and windows. In front there were four windows, two up and two down, on each side of a central entrance with large front door, whereas a seventeenth century or earlier house usually had windows in an asymmetrical arrangement. The clapboard siding on the exterior had been correctly attached with the lowest strakes, near the ground, spaced three or four inches apart instead of the usual five and a half, affording greater protection from snow and ice near the ground. The house was sited properly with the long axis facing the south for winter warmth. This fact was important when the house was built, as the effects of the last Little Ice Age still made winters very cold.

What made the Andrews Lane house such a gem was the fact that the house had had minimal improvements and modernization, unlike most of the others on the lane. Virtually all the hardware such as hinges, latches, doors, and floors were original. The windows were nine over six pane sashes and one the on the west end was for sure original with thick mullions and very wavy handmade glass. The two upstairs bedrooms had interior sliding shutters made of wood over the lower portion. Locally they were called Indian shutters but they were likely more for stopping the drafts as there were no storm windows. Fortunately, there was modern plumbing with a single bathroom on the first floor in what had been originally the "borning room" not far from the warmth of the great fireplace.

If you were to come to the front entrance you would have found a beautiful double door painted a bright barn red that stood out from the dark brown stain

Front door to Andrews Lane, called a "coffin" door where two unequal doors opened to 40 inches.

of the house. There were two doors about four feet across and unequal in size; the larger for regular use while the smaller was usually locked. Called a "coffin" door, it was used for hauling large objects in and out. Front doors were mostly used for visitors, not friends and relatives. We did have fun when visitors came. The larger door had no lock only a huge wrought iron bar on the inside that went across both doors which opened in. It was straight from the Bible verse which cautions: "Bar your door against thieves..."

Upon entering this door with its beautiful hand wrought "lima bean" latch, there was a tiny hallway, met by a set of stairs that turned after three steps and then went almost straight up. Reggie Bacon had said when he first saw it, "it's a damned ladda," which was entirely accurate. On the first floor to the right had been the parlor which we decided to make into a comfy kitchen-dining room with its all new old fireplace. The previous owners had their kitchen in back in the keeping room. On the other side was the more formal sitting room; all the floors in the front sloped slightly where a sill had dropped. This room also had a small fireplace that we rarely used. A nicely paneled door with hinges that may have been from the seventeenth century period made for the room's outstanding feature. The hinges were a pintle and gudgeon style such that you could lift the door right off its hinges.

At the other end of the keeping room, a recently-added back stairway led up to a long, narrow and hardly usable space due to the sloping saltbox roof. The local pine floorboards here were nearly sixteen inches of soft local pine, and amazingly unblemished without a knot. At the west end of this space was a tiny room that I made into a sort of office and used only occasionally.

On a bitter and snowy day in January, 1961, Karyl and I sat in this very room watching television on a small, black and white set. Work for both of us had been cancelled, due to several feet of snow. We were witness to a great moment in history as John F. Kennedy, bare-headed on a blustery day in Washington, DC was sworn in by the Chief Justice, Earl Warren, as the thirty-fifth president of the United States He gave his famous and oft-quoted speech: "Ask not what your country can do for you..." In the same telecast, national poet laureate Robert Frost, then eighty-six, recited "The Gift Outright," which I had heard him give in person three years earlier in Ford Hall, Boston. This was the last we were to see Frost as he died two years later. I'm sure we didn't appreciate how historic a moment this was.

There was no central heat in the house but there was a kerosene stove for cooking and heating in the large keeping room. The main heat source, such as it was, was a floor furnace in the front between the hall and living room. Nor was there any insulation. We chose to put in a new baseboard, hot water system that kept us warm and toasty. Recently coming across the bill for the complete heating system I was amazed to see the price of $1,227, about a tenth of what it would cost today. But since we only paid fourteen cents per gallon for heating fuel in those days, instead of $4 a gallon, we thought little of the escaping heat from a non-insulated house.

I did a little research through the old deeds for the property and was able to get back to about 1775 but prior to that things became confused. At one time I believe our house was the only one on the lane and may have had more land. It was interesting to see that in 1829 the house and its two acres had sold for $900, but that just after World War II this one and all the rest on Andrews Lane had also gone for $900 each.

In February of 1961, I climbed aboard an aircraft bound for Florida where my successor-to-be at SAO and I visited the Jupiter station near Cape Canaveral, now Cape Kennedy. The Station Chief here, Bob Citron ran a very organized station. But it was some years later he and others at Cambridge discovered that the station's location was two or three miles from where we thought it was. When the STP system finally produced the highly precise data it was designed to, we found there was an enormous error from early land surveys. When the hundred foot diameter balloon, Echo 1, was in orbit and three or more Baker-Nunn cameras simultaneously photographed it, we could finally determine the Florida station within feet not miles. Bob Citron went on to found a new group in 1971 called Earth Watch, patterned somewhat on the model of Moonwatch using volunteer observers all over the world. He also started the Smithsonian Center for Short Lived Phenomena. He also founded a number of private sector space ventures competing with NASA. Bob died in 2012 after a very eventful career.

From West Palm Beach we headed to Miami and on to Curacao in the Netherland Antilles. I boarded a 727 with rear stairs like the kind that D. B. Cooper had jumped out of in 1971, taking with him $200,000. Suddenly I saw a vaguely familiar face. The stewardess was Jodie Peary, and she recognized me from our days at Colby; she and I had a double date with Pete Welles in 1953. Jodie was Admiral Peary's granddaughter and lived in Brunswick. Our date occurred long before I had the slightest interest in the Arctic and the Admiral's adventures. Jodie was amazed to see our tickets which were for Kingston, Aruba, Curacao, Lisbon, Madrid, Seville, Rome, Beirut, Teheran, Shiraz, London, Glasgow, and Boston all in one month. She said she normally flew around the east coast and had never seen such a batch of tickets.

Our visit to the station in Curacao was a brief one at a hot, salty spot, where dry winds blew constantly and the temperature was always about 80 degrees year round. Rainfall was a meager few inches; it was paradise for beach people and SCUBA divers. The only things going on in both Aruba and Curacao were tourism with lots of gambling and oil refining. The station was run by Jan Rolfe, a Dutchman, and Gus Van Loon, with no apparent problems like those we had in South America, Iran, or India.

Our next destination was Lisbon, Portugal with a fuel stop at Santa Maria. This KLM route still used the older Constellation Super G propeller planes which were comfortable but slow, taking fifteen hours to across the Atlantic. Here we changed to Iberia Air stopping at Madrid and finally after several more hours we got our next stop at Seville, Spain. From here the best way I was told was to take a train from Seville to Cadiz in southern Spain. I'm not sure what became of my successor, George, but I do know I had to find my way by myself from the airport to the train station using my best Spanish. The year before I had found what little of the high school Spanish I could recall was of little use in Peru or Argentina. But here the language was a more pure Castilian and much easier to understand.

I had been warned by the station chief, Clancy Truesdell, not take the Expresso train because, contrary to its name, it was incredibly slow. The preferred train, the Rapido, only managed to average about 25 miles per hour with frequent stops. It didn't matter; I was in a compartment with several Spaniards and enjoying myself. I suddenly found that I could understand most of what was being said. I started a conversation with an older woman, whom I'm sure was kind and spoke slowly. But still we carried on a reasonably intelligent dialogue on various things that took most of the night. My two years of Spanish at Haverford had definitely been worthwhile.

The station was located on the grounds of an observatory in the town of San Fernando, a small village near Cadiz. This station had experienced some problems with mail, shipments, customs, and such but not nearly as bad as the South American ones. We were able to get some support through an American Navy base at Rota when things bogged down through the Spanish channels. Still as Clancy explained, an enormous effort was required to keep the station operating. It was useful for me to see all the hurdles they had to jump over besides their normal work load every night. I was reminded again of the Navy rotating crews from sea duty to desk jobs back at headquarters and how beneficial it was to trade places.

Among the few things I recall now after fifty years were the dreaded Guardia Civil, the special police that patrolled the streets of every town and city. They were recognized by their three cornered hats and snappy green uniforms that set them off from the regular police. I was told in no uncertain terms to avoid any confrontation with them.

After my stay of several days, I was driven in the station truck across the border to Gibraltar, which I believe then was British controlled. With less than three square miles and a population of 30,000, it is now mostly self governed except for defense and foreign relations which are still the U.K. responsibility. The airfield was near the famous "rock" but somehow it looked all wrong because it didn't face the sea as we think of it in insurance company ads. Gibraltar was also well known for the apes that inhabit the rocky mountain and many times attack tourists.

From there, I took a British European Airways Viscount to Rome. When I flew out from "Gib" I encountered for the first time the backward seating arrangement that BEA was doing then. It was a bit disconcerting at first as everyone sits in seats that faced aft instead of forward as a safety measure. I recalled somewhat later the standard joke about the two older lady tourists on a BEA plane where one says to the other "Don't worry, dear, when the plane gets up to altitude it turns around."

I met up with George in Rome and we flew to Teheran with a short stop in Beirut. We spent the night in a modern hotel in Teheran but had little chance to see much of the city. What I did see was not impressive. Long streets with low buildings of one or two stories, all sort sand colored brick, and no trees to speak of. I recalled reading about the primitive sewage systems that much of the Middle Eastern cities had with open sewers called "jubes" on the side of streets. Much has been written about being "jubed," as in walking along the street and being crowded off the sidewalk into the open sewer gutter, although we didn't see any of these either.

We were taxied to the airport again and met by someone from the Embassy who knew of our trip to Shiraz. Since we were not just tourists and we still had our special passports, the Embassy had been advised not to let us use the regular flights but had arranged a chartered plane for us. Here we went in a vehicle across the airport, past all the big jet planes and other commercial planes, until finally we came to a tiny Piper Tri Pacer, a four passenger light plane. As the Embassy man explained as we went along, the Embassy was aware that the service and maintenance on the Iran Air aircraft was considered to be unsafe and rather shoddy, thus no official travel to Iran was allowed on Iran Air.

We were introduced to the Iranian pilot who put our baggage aboard who spoke no English, only a bit of French. Somehow he conveyed to us that we would flying over a group of high mountains on our way to Isfahan. The plane was normally limited to an altitude ceiling of 11,500 feet. OK, we thought, sounds good. As we flew over a fairly flat desert at several thousand feet, the pilot gestured at various wrecks of aircraft that had crashed sometime in the past, a fact certainly not too reassuring. Then we saw an impressive mountain range in the distance and realized we had to go over it.

As we began climbing we heard familiar American voices on the radio that he pilot had left on. We looked above and saw the Iran Air, a Convair aircraft on its way to Shiraz, flown by an American crew. Here we were, struggling along in a toy plane trying to get over the mountains and the American plane whooshes past us. At about 12,200 feet we sneaked through a mountain pass and headed down slope for Isfahan. We stretched our legs while the pilot filled the wing tanks, being careful to strain the gas through a chamois to eliminate any water from condensation getting in. We made it without event and went on to spend an interesting week in Shiraz, the "city of nightingales and poets." Friends later scolded me for not buying the highly valued woven Persian rugs, as they were extremely cheap.

The Shiraz station ranked along with India, Argentina, and Peru as those with the most problems. Iran, or Persia, as it was popularly referred to then and sounded much less threatening, was a land most unfamiliar to us westerners. The food, culture, and language were all so different as I listened to tales from the station observers. I was especially glad I hadn't accepted the offer to go there two years earlier. Most of the horror stories of building the station, importing the camera and equipment were in the past and things now were more normal. The station had recently been officially dedicated; many pictures were posted showing the Shah being shown around. To find favor with the government, SAO had agreed to hire two local observers from the university as well agreeing to leave the camera and all equipment when we finished the project.

Before going on this trip, I had read the continuing saga of, an Englishman in the employ of one the many foreign missions, who had disobeyed the standing order not to drive a vehicle on the local roads in town. Although he knew there was always the risk of an accident he chose to ignore having a local driver. Sure enough some very poor and desperate person, desperate to collect insurance, jumped in front of him in the street and was killed. Owen was summarily taken to jail with no way of getting out. Week after week, Chic Capen from our station related the attempts of various western authorities trying to intercede without success.

The most impressive memory from my Persian trip was the day we went out to Persepolis or "Takht-e Jamshid" as the locals call it. We joined a tour on a bus and drove forty-five miles northeast of Shiraz in the wide open desert to these amazing ruins of the most famous city of Persia. Many of these beautiful examples of early sculpted figures still remain even though they were first built in 512 B.C. We also visited the dark and smelly cavelike tombs of Cyrus the Great, who chose the site and Darius the Great, who built it. We all marveled at bas relief carvings of bulls and other animals and how perfect and real they are. The Persian society was very advanced, something we as westerners have failed to appreciate.

I was happy to be getting back home after another month long trip and also as spring was approaching. This meant planting a vegetable garden in our large backyard and trimming and neatening our pine woods, a job in which I took great pleasure. One day in these woods I met a six-year old boy who came boldly up to me and showed me a pocket knife his Aunt Barbara had given him. He told me his name was Brian Lees and his parents were Philip and Patsy Lees who lived two houses down the lane. Brian became a good friend and regular visitor who liked Karyl. One morning, he brought us a stray cat. He stood outside the back door holding this cat almost as big as he was, and asked if we wanted it. We hesitatingly took the cat and named him "Perky." He became the first of a long line of family cats.

Brian was a cute kid — a surrogate son before we had a child of our own. Long after Karyl and I parted ways, she kept up with Brian as he grew up. Thirty years later, I met up with him again. I was in the role of cameraman for a local TV station at a New England Republican convention in Boston doing an interview with the then-Secretary of Defense, Dick Cheney. Brian was minority leader of the Massachusetts House at the time. We had a brief handshake but not enough time to reminisce about Andrews Lane. He'd come a long way with a successful career.

Meantime, things were changing at SAO. The satellite tracking program had begun to mature as the stations and the personnel evolved from the pioneer stage to the settler phase and everything started to run smoothly. Many of the original station chiefs had decided to move to more challenging things. In the spring of 1961, I was moved over to Project Celescope, an ambitious effort to map all the UV or ultraviolet stars. The concept had been hatched by Dr. Robert Davis and others at SAO in 1958 and required a fairly large space vehicle to be placed in orbit above the earth's atmosphere where it could clearly see the UV spectrum that wasn't visible from earth. Celescope was the first of many subsequent space stations and, in the NASA lingo, was called the Orbiting Astronomical Observatory. Because of its strange configuration with an opening door on the end used to protect the sensitive optics which looked like a toilet seat, we all called the "orbiting outhouse."

My job was more administrative and I found myself helping to meet our various project deadlines as the launch date grew closer. It was fun in some ways because we had an interesting group of scientists and engineers on the team to put this device together. This group, under the direction of Bob Davis, a Harvard astronomer, was to assemble three video cameras operating in various UV frequencies, called "vidicons" or for our specific use they were "uvicons" together with some optics that used sophisticated telemetry to beam the data back to stations on earth as it orbited. The goals was to map 100,000 stars.

Under Bob Davis was the staff engineer, Dr. Mario Rossi, an electronics expert recruited from Italy. He was amusing and very effective at bringing all the various parts together and he told marvelous stories from projects in Italy. Then there was Al Baez, a noted optical specialist and co-inventor of the X-ray microscope who had a joint appointment at MIT and Harvard and had recently come from Redlands University in California. But more importantly, Al was the father of Joan Baez, new young singer just starting her career in Cambridge about 1958. And among the team was a bright, young Israeli engineering student named Efriam Arazi, who also entertained us with jokes and stories and who was always eager to get a date with Joan, although at the time she was married to David Harris who later was sentenced to jail as a draft protestor. In all, we had a most interesting international mix of scientists.

But I began to miss being involved in field operations and the ocean sciences. It was nearly time for me to move on. As the SAO door slowly closed, Dr. Whipple, our director, called me in one day to give me a new assignment, the inglorious job of organizing the Red Cross drive for the Observatory. It may have been his polite way of saying I should go. However, he told me to take as long as I needed to find suitable employment. How different an organization like Smithsonian was compared to most every large company where you're given a few hours at best to clean your desk and leave.

My four years at SAO had been among the best of jobs that I was to have had. I heard sometime later that Project Celescope had been a huge success but never found any details. As a footnote, Celescope and the STP were ultimately responsible for transforming SAO from being in the ranks of almost near death status in 1955 to one of the largest and most non-traditional astronomical observatories in the world. It turns out I had been there at just the right time.

My pal and supporter, Ken Drummond, left SAO before I did, joining Roger Revelle at Scripps Institution of Oceanography in La Jolla. He and his family visited us in Amesbury sometime in 1960. I then lost track of him until sometime around 1978 when he nominated me for The Explorers Club, an organization he had belonged to for some time. I always hoped he might show up at one of the annual meetings. When I last spoke to him he sounded very cheery, like the Ol' Drum I had known, and was living in Seattle with his second wife. He passed away in 2009 at age 87 and was buried at sea.

In my search for my next job, I wrote letters and sent resumes to various oceanographic groups and in one case I answered an ad in the local paper for technicians to recover photo packages in mid air. The project, "Corona," was one of the first CIA spy satellite operations, although I didn't know that part of it. The job sounded exciting as it meant I would be on a team that made high altitude recovery of film packages nabbed in mid air. But of course it also meant I would be stationed small godforsaken island in the Pacific. Karyl and I both agreed to nix it.

But as is usually the case, it's not what you know but who you know that comes through with the job. David Scott, the former student of my father at the Academy of Fine Arts and sailor friend from the time we chartered his boat, *Heron*, in 1946, called me out of the blue. He said the company he worked for as art director in Annapolis, Maryland, was looking for an oceanographer. I called them and the next thing I knew I was told to get my things together and show up in Annapolis, Maryland. Looking back, as I can now, this seemingly small gesture on David's part was a most important turn of events for me. He is one of "the big three" that played so importantly in the events of my life.

Our wonderful old house on Andrews Lane was easily rented to our friends fro SAO, Ed and Anne Kohn. As I was ready to take up my new job in Annapolis, I realized I was back on track in my marine science career.

Chapter Seven

On the Road Again
We Pack for Annapolis

We arrived in Annapolis in June of 1962 in a large, 24-foot U-Haul truck that Karyl, Perky, our cat, and I drove from Amesbury. We had found a house to rent from a friend of my parents named Judy Offutt. She lived out in the Maryland countryside but owned a vacant rental that was perfect for us on Cornhill Street in the center of the old part of town. A mid-eighteenth century rowhouse, it was extremely narrow, on a one way street that radiated out from the State House in the center of this old colonial town. Our house was one room wide with a narrow winding stairway quite similar to the one at Sugarbridge in Pennsylvania. The kitchen was barely adequate, certainly not by modern standards — a tiny galley with no place to sit, much like many older apartments in New York City.

Our new home at 58 Cornhill Street in Annapolis.

The house had been remodeled at a time when everyone had servants, especially in the south, and kitchen eating hadn't yet arrived. Above were two bedrooms, a bathroom, and a stairway leading to a large third floor open room from which we could get a glimpse of the harbor and beyond to Chesapeake Bay several blocks away. Rent was in the low $100 range. In getting accounts set up in town, I paid a visit to the gas company which would run our furnace. Being from New England I

159

hought it perfectly natural to ask about winter heating and how many days or times he temperature dropped below zero. I was met with an incredulous look. "It don't iever get that cold here! Welcome to the south."

Soon after our arrival I reported for work at The Geraldines Ltd., a small privately owned marine product and research group recently founded by a flamboyant cientist and promoter, Jim Fitzgerald. Although the Limited designation made it ound foreign, it wasn't. Our offices were located, by some good fortune, on a dock ight on the water in the harbor next to the Naval Reserve building. We were just cross from the city docks and parking lot where at that time there were lots of oyster boats and not many yachts and when there was still a commercial fishery. At the nd of this narrow cut was the town market about two blocks from our house. The back of our office had been an outboard motor repair shop and was now our workhop for underwater gear. It was a wonderful place to work and just a five minute walk from home.

My first assignment was to develop and organize an "Instructional Cruise on Dceanography." Jim had conceived the idea as a way to get the company some ecognition in the field. The plan was to take a small number of students from ndustry and prominent corporations who wanted to jump into the field with a wo-week cruise and become familiar with the instruments, procedures, and terminology aboard an oceanographic ship. This was a perfect project for me since I had ecently spent four years doing this exact sort of thing in graduate school. But it was ı big job that Jim gave me since I had to prepare a course outline, put together the ıdvertising to get the students, configure the ship we were going to take on the trip, ıs well as deal with the Coast Guard regulations for taking passengers for hire . . . ll of it within one month while the weather remained good around the Bahamas, ınd just before hurricane season began. A tall order but nevertheless one I relished.

The plan, I learned, was to use the company's 90-foot ketch, the *Earle of Desmond* and transit to Nassau, in the Bahamas, then to work in the Tongue of the Dcean, a deep water basin to the south. Marty McDonald, a young geophysicist and ny new officemate, was to help me on the course. Marty had recently been at the Vational Security Agency (NSA) as a Japanese language specialist. He worked hard ıelping me but unfortunately didn't get to go along.

At first the whole job seemed so idyllic like a dream project but all too soon I ound out that budget limits were going to make it even harder than I thought. I vould have loved to make the *Desmond* over into a real oceanographic research vesel with proper instruments and gear but the short time and too little money meant ı lot of improvisation. Most of our instruments were borrowed from the US Naval Dceanographic Office where we had good friends. The Coast Guard regulations lidn't allow for me to be a scientist as I had been, aboard the Texas A&M vessels.

160

They said the only classifications were passenger, crew, or stowaway. Thus, I became part of the crew which meant in addition to my other duties I had to study up to become a licensed member of the US Merchant Marine. After taking a four-hour exam in Baltimore I became a deck hand "wiper, any waters, twelve months," whatever that meant. Actually, I later found out that I could have gone to sea on my "Z" card on a merchant marine ship and earned something like $1,200 a month, pretty good for 1962.

The Geraldines Laboratories was a spinoff from a larger corporation in Shady Side, Maryland named Chesapeake Instruments where they produced specialized towed sonar arrays for the US Navy. Jim Fitzgerald had been a principal in that company but, when they parted ways, he went on to start his own group. Jim claimed to have numerous patents and rights to some of the instruments and planned on continuing to produce and sell these sonars. Our tiny research division, the Oceanography Department, made up of Marty and me, was to live off the proceeds of the hardware sales. Jim was optimistically sure that the anticipated boom in ocean sciences and instruments was upon us. Although things rarely work out as one hopes for that brief summer we were able to carry out our preparations for the cruise.

Again David Scott came into the picture this time he introduced Karyl to her friends at *Skipper Magazine* where she soon found herself in demand and put to work. *Skipper* was the wonderful creation of H. K. Rigg, a well known yachtsman and Victor , a journalist and World War II photographer. Henry Kilborn Rigg "Bunny" to most of his friends, was a close friend of Pierre "Pete" DuPont. The magazine was a small but elite independent, monthly sailing journal with too few advertisers to really turn the corner financially; but never mind, Uncle Pete footed the bills. Vic and his sidekick, Fenno Jacobs, had both been well-known Navy photographers during the war. They took care of the editorial work while Karyl and her boss Mike Hall chased potential advertisers. Mike's full name was Monroe Bostwick Hall II, and was from a well to do Connecticut family as you might suspect with such a name.

Skipper's advertising department had one angel, Avard Fuller, who owned Brush Company and always ran a full page back cover for his brushes. Karyl wound up doing some small sketches while David Scott was part time artist. It was, as they say now, a fun place to work and was located right on a dock in the Trumpy Yacht Yard a classic power boat builder, across from the Annapolis Yacht Club. Karyl rode to work on her Vespa motor scooter. We were, in short, quite happy in our new life on Chesapeake Bay.

Vic was famous for his VJ day photo of a sailor kissing a girl during the celebration published in the *New York Times* only to be one-upped by the more famous exact same picture by Alfred Eisenstadt, which appeared the following day in *Life* magazine; the latter became far more well known. Fenno, whose real name was Charles Fenno Jacobs, was a naval aviation photographer whose pictures are respected in many World War II collections. From these accounts it seems they had pretty exciting times during the war.

While Karyl was enjoying her new job at *Skipper*, I was frantically getting the *Earl of Desmond* ready for our big cruise. Our date was cast in stone from August 4 to August 25, and only in the last week or so did we manage to sign up four students which was about the right number for the 90-foot ship. The fee for two weeks was roughly $2,000, not bad compared with the prices that cruise ships get these days.

We had enlisted a Dr. Paul Bauer as the guest oceanographer or professor and lecturer. Paul was an older gentleman (USN Ret.) who was a long time friend of Jim Fitz and although somewhat garrulous and old school, was quite good in his role. Furthermore, he was associated with American University as well as being a consultant to the House Committee on Merchant Marine and Fisheries in Washington, DC This allowed us to offer our course for three college credits even though none of the attendees was enrolled or interested in credits. Jim wanted our course to have the appearance of a true academic venture.

The Perry Cubmarine, a two-man early submersible.

To make the Instructional Cruise in Oceanography even more of an attraction, Jim had added the latest in underwater technology, a small, bright yellow submarine called the Perry Cubmarine, PC-3A, a two-man submersible. In his inimitable way Jim named her *Sub Rosa*. One of the first American submersibles, it had been designed and built by John Perry, a wealthy Florida newspaper owner. Perry Submersibles was destined to become a major player some years later in the development of advanced submersibles and the oil industry.

I had the good fortune to dive in the Cub in Chesapeake Bay when it first arrived from Florida. The pilot was a small, quiet guy named George Beasley. The sub was about sixteen feet long and the pilot and passenger sat fore and aft, as in a Piper J-3 aircraft. As we left the surface, George sat forward and very nonchalantly said: "See that metal bar? Put it in the slots below the hatch." Before I could ask why he went on to say that it was necessary to keep the hatchway from collapsing. It made sense but the bar, now tightly held in place, meant there would be no way to escape through the hatch as it completely blocked the way.

We descended to about a hundred feet on the bottom and, sure enough, when I reached up to try and wiggle the bar it was firmly held in place due to the outside pressure on the hull. Fortunately, we returned without incident. I realized that I had no fear of small confined places and went on to dive in many other subs. It all started when I was ten years old on the farm and delighted in crawling through drain pipes and under hay bales stacked in the barn. In my later years I have recurring and less pleasant dreams of crawling in confined spaces where it gets smaller and smaller with no escape… until I awake in a sweaty panic.

Our four students on the cruise came from a variety of backgrounds, although three of them were sent by companies not wanting to miss out on the rush into the sea for business. They were Gene Veslage, from Grumman Aircraft; Don Marquis, from General Electric; and Edgar Davis from North American Aviation. The fourth, Bill Mote, was by far the most interesting and memorable. Bill was an extremely wealthy and retired man from Florida who spent time going on fishing trips for black marlin. He wanted to learn about the marine sciences so he could start a marine lab of his own.

A few years later I learned there was a new lab called the Mote Marine Lab in Sarasota, Florida. Over the years it has become a well-respected facility and one of only a few privately run marine research labs. I wish I could have had a chance to meet up with Bill in later years to hear how he did it. I found out then that Bill was a fishing buddy of Mortimer May who owned the May Company, a large department chain in the Midwest. His son, David, became the founder of the Window Quilt Company, my employer to be some years later.

The students and I joined the crew of the *Earl of Desmond* in Annapolis to make the six day trip to Nassau. The crew consisted of four or five. Captain Herb Williams, US Coast Guard, retired, had been a full Captain for thirty years and was an excellent skipper. While mentioning the skipper of this ship I can't fail to also tell of the Chief Engineer, Walt.Kennedy, Walt must have been in his mid-60s; and, more amazingly, he had been with the ship since she was built in 1934. His term had begun with the original owner, an executive from RCA, then a stint with the Boy Scouts, and for a while with the US Coast Guard during World War II when the vessel was commandeered for coastal patrol.

I conduct oceanography class in the Bahamas in 1962.

Walt faithfully stayed with his ship and was, in fact, the ultimate of a permanent fixture. He was invaluable to whomever owned the ship because he knew all the quirks and secrets of the engine room including the direct reversing main engine. This meant that there was no transmission. To go into reverse, Walt had to stop the engine and throw a lever of some sort which made the engine run backwards. It took a good man like Walt to assist Captain Herb in maneuvering the ship around at a dock. Oscar, sailing assistant to Walt and two other deckhands comprised the crew.

A few days before, we had done some trial runs with our new scientific gear and tested the winch in a deep hole in Chesapeake Bay. Captain Herb had given the order to the deckhands to let go the anchor. The heavy anchor descended pulling the clanking chain. We were near a deep spot in the otherwise shallow bay, about 180 feet. As I stood in the bows I heard a muffled cry from the chain locker, "Bitter end!" Before anyone knew what was happening as the end of the chain snaked through the hawse hole and disappeared over the side. Gone was anchor and chain. Captain Herb was not amused.

Out in the Atlantic we motored most of the way, as it was glassy and calm. The great variety in organisms living in the vast masses of seaweed in the Sargasso Sea was memorable. Once in Nassau, we stayed a day at the Purple Onion, a local bar, restaurant, and hotel which was owned by the Geraldines. Here I had a chance to teach my students a quick SCUBA course in the hotel's salt water pool so we could get them under water later on. After this brief stay we headed south into the Tongue of the Ocean, an enormous bathtub shaped enclosed basin 6,000 feet deep, which, in years to come, would be used by the US Navy as a test site. Halfway down the Tongue on the western side was a shallow bay called Middle Bight which was to be our home port for the next week.

Each morning and afternoon Paul Bauer held classes in the ship's wardroom, covering as much as he could of the five disciplines of oceanography. By this time the Cubmarine and her mother ship rendezvoused with us and we made a series of shallow dives. I spent as many hours as I could get in demonstrating ocean measurements with instruments we had borrowed from the Navy. I was even able to do a simple cast using several Nansen bottles and showing how to collect physical data. I never knew how much, if any, of this I was able to get across to the students; I should have given quizzes. We also had time to do some SCUBA diving with gear we'd brought. Instead of diving in the bay with unknown creatures of the depths, we moved ashore on North Andros Island. Several hundred yards from the ocean was a Blue Hole, a circular pond connected to the bay and filled with salt water. It was about forty-two feet deep and perfect for beginning divers.

On one of the days we all went through very shallow waters by small boat to a fabled fishing resort called the Bang-Bang Club on Pot Cay that was known for its excellent bone fishing. This camp, like the Purple Onion in Nassau, was also owned by Jim Fitzgerald. Hardly a fancy resort, it was a genuine fishing camp of the old days, very simple and without air conditioning even in this hot humid climate. I gathered real bonefish aficionados paid dearly for this rare opportunity. We of course, rode for free.

The interesting back story here was how the club got its name. As Jim told it, in his usual understated quiet tone, and as he always did squinting and pushing his glasses up on his nose; the Duke and Duchess of Windsor were visiting the Club perhaps about 1940. They were real royalty, he being Edward VIII, briefly King of England until he decided to marry Wallis Simpson, an American, twice divorced, and he was forced to abdicate. The Club, small as it was, faced with this royal visit but unable to produce the expected traditional cannon salute resorted to the only thing available, a double barreled shotgun. Two shots were fired. This, as the story goes, was how the Bang-Bang Club got its name. I recall being shown the guest book and sure enough in faded signatures were those of the Duke and Duchess of Windsor. Knowing Jim and his eternal bullshit he could have faked it, but it made for a good story.

Our week in Middle Bight went quickly and students and other dignitaries flew home from Nassau while I rode the "*Earl of Demons*," as we called her, home to Annapolis. As hurricane season was approaching, our skipper decided to take the Intracoastal Waterway to avoid going around Cape Hatteras. We went inside at Charleston, South Carolina and proceeded up the ditch used by many power and sail boats, which ends at Newport News, Virginia. This leg was the best part of the whole trip because we motored slowly through fields and jungles of the subtropics, small villages, and countless bridges. At ninety feet in length, we were one of the larger ships to go through. I would climb the ratlines of the main mast and sit comfortably for hours on the large thirty foot spar, the horizontal part of our brigantine sail rig, and scan the distant countryside. We usually stopped before dark as the canal had no lighted navigational buoys but only reflectors on posts which were too hard pick out in the dark. Several times in daylight when the channel was poorly marked, we nearly went aground, dragging on the soft, muddy bottom. The *Desmond* drew about ten feet. The trip took about four days.

Back in Annapolis, I felt the cruise had been a great success and I received various kudos for it from Jim. We sent out press releases and printed a brochure touting the first trip and advertising a second. Several articles followed in trade magazines as well as a nice looking report that I was asked to put together summarizing the trip. We announced the second cruise for February of 1963. But it all went nowhere and was quickly dropped, as Jim had lost interest. It wasn't a money maker and there was no demand for it. It fit well into the curious statement by Ken Kesey, "Never give a second annual anything."

Sometime in the fall of 1962, we had an addition to our Geraldines group. Bruce Parker joined as a film producer, diver, and general PR man. He was a short but stocky, muscular guy, built like an ox and with a certain film star aura. Tanned with white hair, he was in his late forties. His lovely and much younger wife, Diana, also had that starlet glow but there was something tough underneath. She very soon rented space on Main Street and opened an upscale women's clothing store. Bruce had come from TV land where as he told us he had taught Lloyd Bridges not only how to SCUBA dive but how to swim for the show *Sea Hunt*. Bruce told us he played the bad guy, always in the black rubber suit. "I knew Lloyd was in trouble when we first got underwater and his eyes bulged and he began panicky breathing," he told us.

Bruce was a strong and confident swimmer and I recall him directing us in the water out at the West Virginia quarry, our test site. He had the kind of resonant voice which he could project over great distances. The next summer he and I flew over much of mid-Chesapeake Bay in a rented Cessna 140 float plane looking for areas of clear water where we could dive the Cubmarine. We took the minimum of diving gear because the plane had such a small payload. At one spot we landed and Bruce dove to check water clarity, but then we had a really hard time taking off. It was a very hot afternoon — in the 90s — and the water was dead calm flat. Bruce tried several times but the old Cessna didn't have the power too break the suction or surface tension to get the floats off the water. Then he told me to hang on; he would try an old pilot's trick. He gave it full power and put the plane over on one float, being extra careful to avoid putting the wing tip in the water (that would have been curtains) and gracefully left the water on one float and then was able to pull the other out. He was certainly a skilled pilot.

Bruce Parker, "Mr Water Skiing" head of our diving group.

As it turns out, Bruce was best known as a water skier. In fact, he was known as Mr. Water Skiing. He began to water ski in 1935 at age nineteen, using snow skis and a motorboat — the first person ever to do so. He organized a major show for the New York World's Fair in 1939. Among his various records he was the first, and maybe only person, to ski on one ski from Nassau to Miami fully dressed, holding a briefcase. He was crowned the National Water Ski Champion and was later inducted into The Water Ski Hall of Fame in 1983.

I also knew the darker side of Bruce, who, while he was living in Nassau, got seriously involved the recovery of underwater treasures. He had been finding various antiquities underwater and selling them. The Bahamian government had strict rules that all such treasures were the property of the Crown. Bruce was caught in a sting operation and spent a year in a Nassau jail. He told us it was the worst experience of his life.

While SCUBA diving, I had met an instructor who was at the Naval Academy who gave training courses and certification for SCUBA divers. Dr. Joe Bodner was a naval officer and good instructor. He had asked me to give a short lecture to one of the classes he ran for the National Association of Underwater Instructors (NAUI). My lecture was a general and very brief bit on oceanography. After the usual training in a pool, I tagged along to watch the final exam. Most all the students were civilians who were already trained divers and needed certification to train newcomers. The NAUI dive required the students hold all their gear: tank, regulator, mask, flips, etc., and jump off the stern of a moving boat in about fifteen or twenty feet of water. Each guy (there were no women in those days) had to put his gear on while sitting on the bottom and return to the surface.

One afternoon, on a weekend in December, I got an urgent call from Joe. It seemed that a retired admiral on his power boat at a marina on South River had lost something of great value, could he come quickly? We grabbed our diving gear including wet suits and got right over. The admiral was nervously waiting and told us his wife had come out on deck of his 45-foot cruiser when suddenly her diamond wedding ring flew off into the water.

By the time we were geared up, it was almost dark. We slipped into the water with our flashlights and descended about fifteen feet to the bottom where a thick coat of silt was easily stirred up. I probably inflated my vest so I could avoid hitting the silt. We moved nimbly looking for the ring. On the first scan I spotted something that looked like a piece of tin foil just peeking out of the mud. I managed to carefully slip my little finger into the ring. What luck! In less than a minute we'd found it. Joe made signs to say "let's not rush." So we poked around in the forty-five degree water for a while then surfaced to tell the anxious admiral we had it. He seemed greatly relieved because, as he confided to us, he had recently cancelled the insurance on the $1,500 ring but hadn't told his wife. He gave each $50 and got off easy at that.

I was involved in one more incident with Joe Bodner. This was also another search type dive and it involved a crime. It seemed a Navy chief was at his retirement party the day before his official mustering out on a dock at the local Navy base. Somehow he managed to steal a safe with money and throw it over the side of the dock late that night. We were asked to find it. How could we not find a large metal safe? There were three or four of us in about twenty feet of extremely murky, black water. We were joined together by a line but right off we got disoriented and then got tangled in old cables on the bottom. That was enough. We climbed out and said, "No, thanks!" Not all treasure dives are successful.

I'm sure Jim realized that things weren't going well for his small struggling company. He wanted to move into more productive areas and put Marty and me to work writing proposals mostly to government agencies. Most of these were on topics which we had little chance of winning. I can remember one of many in which we had to design a method for the detection of chemical, biological, or radiation weapons for some super secret agency. Neither Marty nor I had the slightest knowledge of this field and we stumbled along, writing gibberish. And at the very last moment Jim would call in several of his stable of consultants, highly paid I'm sure, from the Naval Academy and local universities to help us out. Of course, they weren't much better. A whole group of us would sit around most of the night writing and helping assemble the proposal. We would stuff half a dozen PhD scientist's resumes in the back, print it all up in the wee hours of the day it was due and then rush it off to Washington.

One of these really longshots was for a Navy group on the West coast. It was late as usual and finally Jim realized it had to be hand-carried to California to make the deadline. This was before the present day reality of overnight delivery. He picked one of the secretaries to be the courier. Most young women would be thrilled for this assignment, but she was terrified because she'd never been out of the state of Maryland and she'd never been on an airplane! Regretably, we won none of these. It was clear that the Geraldines were in a cash flow bind. Although we all received our weekly paychecks on time, that fall our VP of Finances, Jack Tynan, a tweedy dressed, preppy looking man, would loudly announce on Friday afternoon, "Please, gentlemen, don't cash your checks until next Tuesday because there isn't enough money in the bank to cover them 'til then." This was my first encounter with the joys of a small struggling, privately owned company. I wondered what I had gotten myself into.

One of the more interesting contracts The Geraldines had that summer was with Bell Laboratories in New Jersey. I had no part in the initial contacts; all I remember was the cruise we took on the *Earle of Desmond* from Annapolis to the Jersey shore. Captain Herb was the master and Marty and I the scientists. We had a group of Bell Lab scientists and technicians aboard. Our mission was to find and examine with cameras some cable just offshore. The background was that AT&T, Bell's parent, had been having continuing problems with numerous breaks their overseas telephone cables. These cables came from the shore going across the continental shelf in depths of several hundred feet and then down the deep slope and across to Europe.

The cable we were observing was TAT-3, put in service in 1963 with 276 channels. The suspicion was that Russian trawlers operating legally beyond the twelve-mile international limit were involved. When the trawlers would drag their nets along the bottom many times the nets got fouled by the cables. To avoid losing an expensive net, the trawlers added cable cutters on the leading edges of the otter boards. Bell wanted to see any evidence of this conflict. We made several attempts to get pictures but after numerous tries it was a failure or maybe as Karyl used to say "an unsuccess." The interesting point here is that in talking with Bell I found that the method used by the Labs was to approach such a problem from many angles. We found that there were most likely several separate groups working on the same problem with no coordination or in some cases no knowledge that other groups in Bell were engaged in the same effort.

At this time, 1963, Bell had plenty of money and bright people that afforded them this luxury. Although I never knew the results of our investigation off the Jersey shore or what became of these Bell groups, the most obvious solution came along soon after: trench the cables in these shallow areas deep enough below the sea bed to avoid being cut. It was an added expense but nothing compared to splicing a broken cable or laying down a new one. There are now seventeen such cables in use which have become much more common and competitive than satellite communications. And an amazing number of innovations and inventions came from Bell over the years including transistors, solar cells, lasers, fiber optics, and many other digital devices.

I can't remember exactly when the *Earl of Desmond* exploded but I do recall the incredibly loud boom that resounded throughout Annapolis one early morning around three o'clock. It was winter and the boiler for her heating system had violently exploded, causing a fire aboard, and blowing a hole in her side so that she sank at the town dock by the parking lot. She was in shallow water so she was only partly submerged. Jim Fitz worried that the ship was vulnerable and that vandals might strip her of valuable equipment. So, I and several other employees were assigned night watchman duties. I still can recall vividly the sharp, acrid odor of smoke and burned wood as I sat in the bridge of the *Desmond* as she was partly filled with water. It was very cold and dark. No one attempted to break in.

Amazingly the next week a salvage crew came aboard and managed to raise her and take her across the harbor to Trumpy's yard for complete renovation. Poor engineer Walt was beside himself with worry for his home of nearly thirty years. And he couldn't have been happier when she was afloat again.

In the fall of 1962, a major political-military crisis was looming. The United States was suddenly confronted with the fact that the USSR had been building missile bases only ninety miles south of Florida in Mr. Castro's Cuba. I recall sitting in the basement room in Annapolis and watching the nightly news show the increasing tension as Soviet fleets converged on Cuba. President Kennedy and his brother Bobby were deliberating whether to launch air strikes on Cuba. Karyl and I were a bit apprehensive and we hadn't even seen *Dr. Strangelove* yet! Eventually, it all blew over although I'm sure there were those of us who began making plans for bomb shelters.

Soon the Oceanography Department consisting of Marty and me was augmented by the addition of an older, seasoned researcher who moved in as our boss. R. K. Salin had recently retired from the US Coast and Geodetic Survey in Washington, where he had spent most of his working life doing serious, coastal marine surveys. He had a wealth of government connections and contacts especially at the US Naval Oceanographic Office. We were pleased with addition because we reasoned maybe now he would get us the contracts we needed to get some business. But no such luck. However, Bob Salin, (a great name for a marine person) was fun to work with and he told lots of good ocean stories.

Bob also had a small company of his own called Geonautics. This group of six or seven retired navigational experts was already well on their way to success. Their prime contract was with the astronaut pilots from NASA. It seems the pilots were worried about the upcoming planned missions especially the ones to the moon. They weren't at all comfortable with their dependence on the onboard computers to accurately make the final calculations for the landing. The Pilots Association asked Geonautics to prepare a series of tables and guides to be used in an emergency if the onboard computer failed at the last moment or was erratic. A true professional, Bob quickly grew disenchanted with the sort of Mickey Mouse atmosphere at the Geraldines and departed sometime in mid-1963. It was too bad to lose him both as a friend and a mentor.

My life on on Cornhill Street was good at this time. Karyl and I were happy in our jobs even though the signs of possible doom at The Geraldines were looming. Marty and I were told that we had to keep writing proposals and that, in essence, we were responsible for our own projects. It certainly was a different feel from that at SAO and the government. Apart from the regular job I got to know the gang at *Skipper Magazine*. They began to get books for me to review which both augmented my library but gave me only meager pocket change. And, through the continued help from David Scott, I got to know the editors at the Naval Institute, located on the grounds of the Naval Academy. David did a fair amount of art work for their publication, *The Proceedings of the Naval Institute*.

During our stay in Annapolis I managed to write and sell several articles for this monthly magazine. And to keep it all in the family, my father, now in his late sixties and needing some work, with the demise of book illustration had collapsed, was occasionally drawing for both *Skipper* and *Proceedings*, again through the help from David Scott. My article "The Challenge of the *Challenger*" on the US *Challenger* Expedition (1872-1876) was well received by the *Proceedings* and some years later was reprinted in the *Explorers Club Journal*. It was good to have another iron in the fire besides The Geraldines.

I had brought my Firefly twelve-foot dinghy along from Amesbury. I had bought the boat, which I had never named, from Tommy Tavenner, whom I'd known in Boothbay Harbor and sailed it in Marblehead one summer. I kept it in Amesbury on the creek at David Scott's house. I didn't sail it much but I do recall one afternoon when Karyl and I sailed it across Chesapeake Bay. It was a busy thoroughfare for a twelve-foot boat to be calmly sailing in the path of freighters on their way to Baltimore. But I was young and foolish then and luckily, we had no hair raising encounters.

David and Joanne had been most hospitable to let me keep the boat there; in return they asked if we would be willing to babysit for them. Of course, I said yes before consulting Karyl, who was perhaps less excited at the prospect of watching four children ranging in age from toddler in diapers to a near teen and for a week! Not that this was grounds for divorce but I think Karyl was slightly overwhelmed as it was she who had most of the kid duty. Actually, they were well behaved kids especially by today's standards but the instant family aspect was daunting.

The house was hardly modern, more farm cottage style, on a bluff overlooking Mill Creek on the edge of the Bay. My most memorable recollection was the diaper pail. Karyl had the diaper detail; there were two kids still in them. This was before disposables. At some point we noticed a foul odor and traced it to the white enamel pail that was used. The bottom had rusted out and liquid contents had seeped out. What a mess I had to deal with! But overall, those kids were pretty good and some-how we made it through the week. The experience didn't make us say we'll never have children but certainly made us think about how many.

David Scott was such a talented person, and the day he asked me to go flying with him was special. He had gotten his pilot's license, at a very young age, followed by time in the Navy as a fighter pilot in Korea with P-51s. This day he said he had an assignment from a real estate agent in Annapolis to provide complete photos of the old ferry dock near Sandy Point on Chesapeake Bay. My job was to be co-pilot while he manned the camera.

He picked me up early one very cold December morning in 1963. It was well below freezing as we climbed aboard a bright yellow, rented Piper J-3 Cub at the Annapolis airport. The J-3 had always been one of my favorite small planes. My father and I had once said we would take lessons on such a plane, but unfortunately, we never did. Now as we got up several thousand feet over the old ferry dock and adjacent land, David opened the door and snapped it in a clip on the wing. We made sure our seat belts were nice and tight. He dipped the right wing to ninety degrees for better view, put the plane in a slow descending spiral, and asked me to hold the stick steady while he fired rapid camera shots. Needless to say, I was bit nervous. As we neared the ground he pulled us out of the spiral, finishing the cam-era work. Then, with his boyish grin said, "How about a quick illegal pass under the Bay Bridge?"

How could I say no? I think it was a Sunday morning and there was little traffic on the bridge. This was when there was only a single span, two lane bridge across the Chesapeake Bay, and we were maybe thirty feet off the water, with about the same thirty feet above. No sweat... piece of cake, as under we went. But it was definitely against FAA rules.

I lost track of David Scott when I moved away from Annapolis in 1966. In 1978, while I was living in Cutler, Maine I heard a radio news account of his death. I clearly remember sitting in the kitchen rocking chair by the stove. He had been returning to his home in midcoast Maine late one night on a small commercial aircraft in a heavy fog at Owls Head. The pilot missed the runway and crashed into a hill. How tragic I thought, was such a good pilot, had gone through all the hell of flying F-80s in Korea, and many other adventures, and now to die at the hands of another pilot. He was a real hero to me. His wife Joanne has gone on since to become a painter and a published poet. She spends summers on Monhegan Island. I finally found her address in Maryland and we exchanged letters. In the summer of 2011, I had a pleasant visit with her on Monhegan. I had found a copy of her book *Legacy* (1999), which she autographed. It's a summary of all their some thirty boats in poetry with David's drawings. A final footnote: David's ashes were spread at sea.

Shortly after our flight in the J-3 the Westinghouse Underseas Division, located in Baltimore, purchased the land and dock that we had photographed for their new facility which is where I would be working for the next several years.

Back at The Geraldines, Jim Fitzgerald's flamboyant and desperate actions to get business only seemed to lead us deeper into a hole. The harder we tried, the fewer opportunities occurred. Sometime in 1963, we were informed that The Geraldines had been acquired by Bell Aerospace Corporation. I'm sure Jim reaped some of the profits from the sale but as always is the case, he lost control and his child, The Geraldines was no longer his plaything. Marty and I, neophytes in the acquisition world, thought we were in for good times with a major corporation and all its money now available for our various projects.

Bell Aerospace sent us an executive who was, we thought, going to make the company more efficient and thus a more profitable business. His name was Jack Steele, whose last name formed a most appropriate image, directly out of central casting. He was the epitome of the company man, white haired although still young with a firm jaw and a most fitting deep, authoritative voice. Needless to say, we were impressed. We were in good hands, or so we thought.

It was now the fall of 1963. I had been on one of our desperate and usually fruitless marketing adventures to some government agency on the outskirts of Washington one afternoon, and I was somewhere on the Washington-Baltimore Parkway that November 22, just before Thanksgiving, when there was radio news flash that President Kennedy had been shot in Dallas and died shortly after. It was the first major tragedy to our country in my lifetime. Looking back it may have been the beginning of a series of events that changed our lives and the course of our country. Karyl and I sat at home on Cornhill Street watching the funeral procession as we went through two days of mourning. How many times since then have we seen the black draped wagon pass by, the rider-less horse with boots backwards, and the gallant tiny figure of John Jr., saluting as he stood at attention on the curb?

Sopranino, *a 19-foot sailboat and one of first to cross North Atlantic, 1952.*

It was sometime in this stretch that I was bitten by the boat bug, feeling that with all the activity of a harbor like Annapolis, I should have larger boat than the Firefly. One of the editors at *Skipper Magazine*, Hugh Whall, had a remarkable small boat that intrigued me. A native South African, Hugh had owned a 19-foot English designed and built transatlantic vessel for a few years and was looking to sell it. I took a loan out to pay him the asking price of $5,000, no small amount in those days and found time to sail it in the several years I had it on the Bay.

It was almost the death of me and Karyl that first summer. Since she was working at *Skipper*, she felt it would be proper to take part in the boating world. Hugh had told us that his boat was one of ten from the UK that had found its way here. The prototype for the Junior Offshore Group (JOG) was *Sopranino*, meaning smallest wind instrument. He suggested reading the story of its transatlantic voyage which we did. The book, titled *Sopranino* by Patrick Ellam and Colin Mudie, was No. 39 in the Mariners Library. Of course we were excited to own a sister ship to such a famous small boat. She was named *Picolo* and, ignoring the old curse that would come by changing the name, and in keeping with wind instrument boat name, we named it *Ocarina*, as she was of a similar shape of a sweet potato. In retrospect perhaps we shouldn't have made the change.

On one of our first sails we started out on beautiful bright day from Annapolis Harbor. We headed down Chesapeake Bay with a pleasant following breeze on our stern. After sailing for five miles or so I realized the wind was picking up as afternoon breezes do and we would have to sail home into the stiffening wind. It's always a shock to jibe and head back upwind. Karyl was a good soldier and took the occasional spray over the bow without complaint. Then I looked below to see that we had a bit of water coming in through the lapstrake planks — not good. The planks above the waterline hadn't swollen. Somehow we struggled back to the harbor after maybe eight or ten miles just after sunset picking up a mooring. We were exhausted but had brought along our dinner which we ate. We turned in early in our very comfortable berths in the tiny cabin.

We slept soundly for several hours, dead to the world, when a sudden crashing sound woke us, following a twang that sounded like a broken guitar string. I leaped on deck to see the departing stern of a rather large power boat heading straight for the city dock. Moments later there was a resounding crash as the boat hit the dock head on, knocking over a Coke machine. *Ocarina* somehow had sustained minimal damage; the power boat had just scraped the hull, but the outer shroud, a substantial steel cable that supported the mast, had popped. We were visibly shaken. If the monster boat had come a foot closer our boat would have split in two with us in the water. We immediately hopped in our dinghy and I called the Annapolis police to report the ramming then went home to bed.

Next morning we found out that boat belonged to a prominent Washington lawyer who, we learned, had passed out drunk at the helm. He contacted the Trumpy Yacht Yard to immediately replace the broken shroud at his expense. The police said all they could do was to issue a reckless driving ticket for $25. We met with the US Coast Guard who said there was nothing they could or would do. The $400 bill was paid by the owner and we chose not to get into a tangle over it, but it did dampen Karyl's outlook on sailing. I did a lot of single handing and had great sailing times for a year or so. I kept looking for a trailer to put the boat on and finally found the perfect setup. One of the Geraldine employees, Doug Chamberlin, had come by a Star boat that wasn't worth saving but it had a good trailer. I remember that he had torched the Star boat, salvaged the lead keel, and sold me the trailer for $75. Thus, I avoided yard storage fees. The sad end of *Ocarina* came the next year.

Karyl's connection at *Skipper* gave me a chance to go sailing and racing with the big boats, too. Late one fall day in November I was invited to join the after guard to race in the *Skipper* Race, about fifty miles down the Bay and back. The boat was a classic named *Freedom* that was used for training at the Academy. Built in 1931, she was an 88-foot wooden schooner. She had been owned originally by Sterling Morton, founder of the Morton Salt Company. There were seven older men including David Scott and Robert de Gast, a top flight photographer, and eighteen midshipmen. It was a gray, cold, and windy day with gusts to thirty knots, perfect for *Freedom*. We had a downwind start and a real sleigh ride leaving all the smaller boats behind, then out of sight. Our mark was a lighthouse, Point Lookout, which we had to round and then beat back up the Bay. I guess we old guys weren't that good at jibbing in these winds; suddenly, with a loud sound, our mainsail ripped half way up. Robert took a classic picture of pile of the middies, David and me trying to get the torn sail down. It looked like the even more classic one of Iwo Jima and the flag raising. In going forward on the bowsprit to pull in the jib staysail as we pitched into the steep waves, I went under water once or twice. Luckily, I had my harness and safety line attached. We didn't finish. I think of this race whenever I see a Morton Salt container.

David Scott and I try to haul sail down aboard 88-foot Freedom.

As time moved us into 1964, it became evident that things weren't going well at The Geraldines and now we saw that Jack Steele had been sent to Annapolis for one thing only. His assignment was to close down our little struggling effort in the typical way large companies do after a quick look at the profits and losses and decide the best way out is to write off their investment.

It's said that timing is everything. And so it was as several of our group were returning to the office on the afternoon of February 14 from another one of marketing attempts, that our favorite secretary, Myra, smilingly greeted us at the door. "Guess what gentlemen, you don't work here any more!" It wasn't a huge surprise, but it was a blow and fitting as the Valentine's Day massacre. There was no severance pay or any help to find placement elsewhere. It was for me the first of several firings which were to occur in coming years. How different this was from the time before when Smithsonian was so generous and gave me a month or two to look around for something else.

What was I to do? I had foolishly not been as diligent as I should have been looking for possible employment. I immediately set about sending out letters and Form 57s, the government employment application, all of which were, sadly, as fruitless as our Geraldines efforts had been. I realized it was unlikely I would be able to waltz into a new job in a week or so. Marty and I and several others appeared weekly at the Maryland unemployment office willing to work but finding nothing; we gladly took our meager $175 or so a week without feeling guilty.

While I was focused on my own future there in Annapolis, I wasn't aware that the Beatles had come to the United States that February and had been a sensation with the young crowd; Cassius Clay had scored an amazing victory over Sonny Liston; and President Johnson, unelected, was about to change our whole country's outlook on race and poverty with the Civil Rights Act of 1964. These were the best of times and the worst to come. I just wanted a job.

I was a member of the Christian Science Church in Annapolis and that spring one of the members, Bob Davis, offered me a project to paint his older 35-foot powerboat. He didn't pay much but it made me feel useful and lasted for several weeks. I also got a similar job from Judy Offutt, our landlady, to paint the inside of our home. But this work hardly filled the gap. Karyl was her usual calm self and not in a panic at all even though we had known for a while that she was pregnant and expecting our first child. In those days it was common not to know the sex of your child before birth so we had no idea whether it would be a boy or girl. Nevertheless, the soon to be birth made me feel it was urgent to get some sort of full time employment. The due date was late May. Karyl had been seeing Dr. Stevens who lived just down Cornhill Street.

Then, out of the blue and just in time, came a phone call from a person whom I had known at Haverford School. Bill Maguire from the class of 1949 was someone whom I vaguely recalled, hardly a close friend. He'd heard that I was an underwater expert and wondered whether I would be interested in joining the new company that he had recently formed to explore the ocean for deep sea minerals. I jumped at the chance. What wonderful timing!

I immediately drove up to Bill's house in Wayne, Pennsylvania, trying to remember what little I could of him from my Haverford days. I found when I met up with him again that he had been in investments with family money. One of his clients had told him of the great promise of unlimited treasures lying on the ocean floor. Promise maybe, I thought, but a long way from a reality as it is still is. Bill had been hired to invest this family's money with a group of engineers at Battelle Institute, a well known non-profit company located on the campus of Ohio State University. He had already entered into a contract with Battelle who were to develop a tethered unmanned submersible. This vehicle, the General Purpose Underwater Device, went by the name of GEPUD.

He proudly showed me the proposal booklet from Battelle. It was completely conceptual with very few hard specifications and lots of artists' renderings. He was about to pay $50,000 for something which was not well defined. I was not impressed but, of course, he believed he would be getting the vehicle for this amount. Dream on Bill, I thought, they've taken you for a ride. We were at the very dawn of the remotely operated vehicle (ROV), but Battelle was hardly at the cutting edge. As I found out later there were others out in front on ROV's, mainly the US Navy at the Naval Ocean Test Station (NOTS) in California. Most of the effort was being concentrated on manned submersibles; things on long cables in the deep ocean had a bad history. Although I was not an expert, I was aware of the difficulty of Bill's project. Had I the chance, I would have advised Bill against this course. But it was too late and I wanted a job, so why spoil his fun?

Bill agreed to pay me a weekly salary. A bit later he and I made a visit to Columbus, Ohio to meet his design team. There was little or no progress to see for his $50,000. Even in 1964 that amount of money didn't go far with a large R & D outfit.

Bill was eager. There was no point in telling him to watch out. He now needed (or better phrased, wanted) a boat which would act as the mothership to carry his pet GEPUD to sea. Nowhere did I ever see his plan for what would come next or what funds would be needed. He had been pouring over magazines and papers like *Boats and Harbors*, a weekly listing of work boats, looking for a boat. Low and behold he had found just what we needed. The boat of his dreams was in Florida and was named the *Maurice F. Fitzgerald*. It was none other than the 85-footer The Geraldines had put on the market sometime ago. She was, in fact, well suited for his project and I'm sure the price was right. Bill was even more excited when I told him that I had been working on the *Maurice F.* that previous winter and knew her well. At that time she had been under contract to the Navy for towing various instrumented bodies or underwater shapes associated with sonars. Coincidentally, I had been part of the crew and had just learned how to pilot the twin engine boat under the eye of a very seasoned skipper. And here I was a few months later back on board. Off to Fort Lauderdale we flew and prepared to bring her back up to Annapolis.

The *Maurice F.* was lying at the same marina where Pete Welles and I had hung out in 1956, coinciding paths again. Bill, the new owner, proudly took the wheel and we began our journey north choosing to take the Intracoastal Waterway. Bill was a strange looking tall, gangly fellow with a sallow complexion and a prominent Adam's apple and a receding jaw, an Icabod Crane sort of character. We figured the trip would take five or six days without pushing too hard. As I measured out our progress on the charts I began to get a bit anxious because Karyl was approaching her delivery date of the third week in May and Bill and I were still nearly a week away. I couldn't miss being there. In those days of limited communication, I called only when we stopped at night. Few pleasure boats ran after dark as most of the waterway didn't have lighted buoys. I could recall being on that earlier trip on the *Earle of Desmond* late one night blindly searching with a spotlight for the reflector on a day mark in a wide shallow bay and feeling very lost.

While the *Maurice F.* was in relatively good condition, it had not been converted to diesel power so we still ran on two enormous gasoline powered engines probably the originals from World War II. These monsters guzzled great amounts of gasoline. Somewhere in North Carolina, Bill decided to stop at a fuel dock. I watched in amazement as the dials indicating gallons at the gas pump whirled around. In 1964, highway gas was around thirty cents a gallon and marine high-test was closer to thirty eight cents. When the marina attendant presented Bill with a slip for $640, he deftly handed it to me saying he didn't have that much cash. Anxious to please, I foolishly stepped up to the plate and said, "I'll put that on my Gulf credit card if you'll pay me back." He never did pay me back and that was the beginning of the end of my relationship with Bill Maguire and GEPUD. In subsequent weeks each time I would call him asking for payment he would repeat the mantra of "I'm sorry but I don't owe you anything…it's the corporation that owes you…and unfortunately it's broke." I never knew whatever became of Bill and his GEPUD or for that matter really cared except for the $640. At least I got back in time for the birth of our child.

By now it was the first of June and Karyl was at least a week overdue. The usual humid swelter of summer was upon us; we waited patiently in the heat. On the night of June 6, we decided to go to the air-conditioned comfort of a movie, since most homes did not yet have air conditioning. Luckily, the theater was about a hundred yards up the street just around the corner. About halfway through, Karyl began to feel labor pains so we walked home. Soon after as she sat in the living room her water broke on the small couch we had had made from an antique hired man's bed, a piece of furniture Karyl still has.

We got in the car and drove across town to Anne Arundel Hospital. This was it, I thought. I spent the long night in the waiting room expecting news at any moment. But as time slowly dragged on into the early hours near dawn with no word I began to worry, never having been a father. Fortunately, all was well, just slow. Finally, Dr. Stephens, came in. With a smile he said I should go home and get some rest as it would be a little longer. As it was, the birth took about twenty-four hours but was all completely normal with no complications. It was June 7, 1964 and Amy Webster Shenton had finally arrived, about two weeks late.

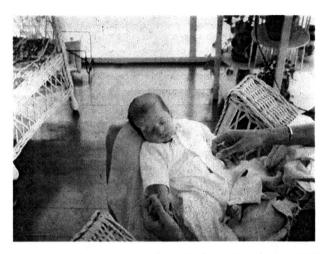

Amy at two months at Granny Mader's in Sudbury, Massachusetts, 1964.

In Anne Arundel Hospital, Karyl had spent much of the time lying alongside a friend, Kathy Hall, who was also giving birth to a child. Kathy was wife of Mike Hall, Karyl's boss at *Skipper Magazine* and it was her third or fourth child. The two births were almost simultaneous but we never kept up over the years with Monroe Bostwick Hall III, the Hall's son. However, my path and Mike's did cross again some years later when he had become the mayor of Belfast, Maine and I was involved in the design of the Belfast waterfront. But this was Amy's day and we proudly took her home. Karyl had chosen the name which meant much loved.

We were now in the real heat of the summer over those first few weeks of Amy's young life and the house on Cornhill Street was hot and sticky day and night without air conditioning. I did my share of diaper changing in the middle of the night and we had a service that supplied freshly washed nappies. For the most part Karyl took charge. After Amy was three or four weeks old I recall taking care of her while Karyl was out. We would stand in front of the large mirror in the bedroom and do a little dance as I held her giggling and I sang a song called "Baby Amy." She was a good and always a happy child.

At this point Karyl decided she had had enough of the Chesapeake Bay humidity so we fled to her mother's in Sudbury, Massachusetts and the relative cool of New England. The two of them stayed on for a month or so while I drove back to Annapolis and the eternal heat. At this time we were driving in a shiny, bright red Saab 850 GT Monaco, a car that performed exceptionally well.

All this time since my peculiar episode with Bill Maguire, I had had no income or job. And then came another major turning point of my life; I was offered a job in the Westinghouse Undersea Division in Baltimore. Undersea, I was to find out in my interview, was one of nearly 172 divisions of Westinghouse Electric Company where the whole company had some 100,000 employees. The company was started in 1886 by George Westinghouse as the Westinghouse Air Brake Company grew rapidly in the twetieth century.

Underseas was principally involved in the design and production of torpedoes and sonar equipment for the Navy. The company was heavily staffed by engineers and was perhaps too light on sales and management. At that time, there was a small group of engineers, encouraged by the Division VP, directed to explore whether there was a market for small manned submersibles, a promising new field in its infancy. Apparently, my background in marine sciences and submersibles like the Perry Cubmarine, SCUBA experience, and my brief time with GEPUD was enough for them to offer me a job on their team.

Several members of this team were already aboard and had conducted a one-month trial session in February of 1964 using the Diving Saucer developed in 1959 by Jacques Cousteau and his remarkable French group. Cousteau had been approached by The Westinghouse VP, Jack Clotworthy, and agreed to bring his vehicle, the *Soucoupe Plungeant 300* and a team of French pilots and divers to California. During this one-month period Westinghouse took a variety of marine scientists from local labs on a series of free dives along the coast and islands to demonstrate the capability of the manned sub. The marketing manager, Tom Horton, an ex-IBM salesman, had a real talent for getting these scientists involved in this new venture. This trial run was so well received that he now had been able to put together a six-month project for the upcoming fall and winter again in southern California and Mexico using the Diving Saucer. The projected cost of the Saucer and French crew, transport by MATS plane from France, a support ship and the nine-man Westinghouse team was split between the various labs. It was what was called in the oil patch a "group shoot." My role was to be the science coordinator and work with the scientists who would be diving.

The team leader was Fred Willet, an ex-Navy and former geodetic specialist, probably late in his late forties and newly hired for this job. His role was to mobilize the whole effort and get us out to sea. Fred did this admirably. The next member was Jerry Burnett, a longtime Westinghouse field engineer who had been on the February Saucer trials and had become close friends with French crew most of whom were back again. Joe Thompson, was our official photographer and a potential pilot for the Saucer, and a seasoned SCUBA diver originally from the Philadelphia area. Larry Somers, in his mid twenties, was an ex-Navy explosives ordinance disposal officer. The last member of the original team, Val Boelschevy, a diver of unknown background, was a large, goateed fellow with underwater experience and shrouded in a bit of mystery.

We were due to leave for San Diego in early October where we would be assembling our equipment aboard a ship; the Saucer was being flown in from France in early November. However, before all this, the team first had make some practice dives and each of us had to qualify as swimmers and divers. We had to swim 300 yards in a river estuary, which I found was a struggle since I hadn't done any serious swimming for quite a while. I made it all right but realized I needed a lot of practice if I was to be part of this very competent team. Our practice dives took place in a quarry in West Virginia in September — the same quarry that Marty McDonald and I had used a year or so earlier for experiments for The Geraldines. We spent the day trying out all the SCUBA gear that Westinghouse had bought us as well as our own personal gear. Karyl and Amy came along as well as the families of Jerry, Joe, Larry, and Val.

Here I was, with a good job as a senior engineer at Westinghouse, even though I was really a scientist. I was about to embark on an exciting adventure with the Cousteau diving team in the Pacific. My father was equally excited and had gotten me an entrée to the publisher, W. W. Norton, to discuss a book contract. Bob Farlow, VP of Norton, and long time friend, and editor of my mother's books was eager for me to submit a proposal. I hastily dashed off three chapters and an outline. I subsequently visited Bob at his house near Doylestown, Pennsylvania to discuss my upcoming expedition and boldly mentioned that I might be a pilot of the Soucoupe. In his jaunty way, Bob said that it would be a dandy book, probably what he said to all new authors. Just before we packed up for the West Coast, I received a contract and an advance check for a $1,000.

One final event took place before our departure. The crew at Woods Hole Oceanographic Institution invited several of our Westinghouse group to witness the first set of experimental dives they were making with their new submersible, *ALVIN*. I was one of the ones to go along with another engineer, Pete Ianuzzi to Woods Hole, Massachusetts. Little did either of us realize that *ALVIN* was to become the longest operating, most successful submersible in the world over the next fifty years. I got a brief dive in her in the harbor to a depth of maybe thirty feet. *ALVIN* was the result of several creative scientists and engineers at WHOI. The leader of the group was Alyn Vine for whom she was named, the project was funded by the Office of Naval Research, built initially by General Mills (maker of Wheaties, etc.) and completed by Litton Industries.

When Pete and I first saw her the pilots were placed sitting upright, side by side as in an aircraft. As Cousteau found many years earlier in 1958, this arrangement didn't allow the pilot and observer to see out of the portholes. WHOI was able to change the layout in those first months to let the pilot and observer lie down with faces close to the port as in the *Soucoupe*, greatly increasing the field of vision. Cousteau had designed his vehicle to be a type of shell for a diver where the prone position was natural. We also saw how this sub, measuring fifteen feet long and weighing three tons, needed a dedicated support ship. The Soucoupe was much easier to handle with the move from ship to ship as Westinghouse was about to demonstrate. Getting to know the *ALVIN* crew even for a short time was most valuable.

ALVIN's christening June, 1964.

One of my jobs as a senior engineer at Westinghouse Underseas in the mid-60s, was to select a group of underwater sensors, cameras and lights, available "off-the-shelf" and able to operate at 20,000 foot depths. This was all highly classified so we couldn't ask what it was for. Rumors were that it had something to do with salvage from the ocean bottom, but nobody really knew. Later, at an assembly of all project engineers, we were warned that we were never to divulge what we had seen or heard, even if we read it in the newspapers. Everything we did were black secrets.

Sometime later, we pressure tested these sensors to 10,000 psi. On one occasion in a separate building behind a curtain, I happened to glimpse an enormous claw three stories high. Nearly five years later the *New York Times* broke the full story. I and all my fellow engineers had been part of the Howard Hughes ship the *Glomar Explorer*, specially built to recover the Soviet sub, K-129 from 16,500 feet deep. The wreck was 450 miles NW of Hawaii. Since then several books have been written about our remarkable feat, Project Azorian. I felt priviledged to have a peak at "the claw".

The "claw" mechanism from the Glomar Explorer

Chapter Eight

On to California

Karyl and I sublet the house on Cornhill Street to an elderly couple with the approval of our landlady and packed what we thought we would need for a six to twelve month absence into boxes shipped by rail by Westinghouse. We even managed to include Karyl's Vespa motor scooter. Our immediate needs were stuffed into our Saab 850 GT for the drive to the West Coast.

Our flashy red Saab 850 GT got us from Annapolis to San Diego in great comfort.

My last chore was to do something with *Ocarina*. I didn't have time to haul her and I had met a young Navy guy who said he would take care of her so I hastily said fine, which later turned out to be a mistake. When I returned that next year I found he had, against my instructions, closed the boat up much too tight and, in the local humid climate, mold and rot had taken over with terrible results. I took a large loss on her.

At four months, Amy was carefully cradled in a heavily padded car carrier and strapped in the back seat. It was early in October, and fall was rushing down from Canada. We took the northern route through Madison, Wisconsin. I was delighted at how well the small Saab purred along at speeds of 70 to 80 mph, feeling solid and safe. The western states still had speed laws of "reasonable and proper." The car was a fine touring machine with incredibly comfortable front seats evolved from Saab's experience in fighter aircraft. There was even a movable lumbar pad so that even after a full day's drive I felt no fatigue.

Our goal was Yellowstone Park where we were to rendezvous with Joe Thompson, wife Lorraine, and two kids, Joey and Jeannie. Also joining us would be Larry and Barbara . In 1964, the lodge at Yellowstone Park was still the original, built about 1880 with an enormous great room, gigantic fireplace, and vaulted ceilings nearly thirty feet high, with the all the character of the hotel from the movie *The Shining*. Although I've never been back, I hear the new lodge built some years later has lost much of the grandeur and charm of the old one.

Arriving on schedule, we all met that day in the vast central hall and sat toasting by the roaring fire with six foot logs while the outside temperature fell to near zero at night. Our rooms were very plain, one step above camping, with cottage style wood-paneled walls. Although the rooms were chilly and unheated, the experience was definitely pleasurable and very much like the huts in the White Mountains that I would visit many years later.

The wait staff in the dining room were all young college students preparing for the seasonal closing. We spent the next day watching moose, deer, and elk calmly grazing in bare patches of frozen fields and marshes. The ground was already well covered with snow. A park ranger explained the various animals we could see at certain times of day. We had been allowed to take seven days on our cross country trip of nearly three thousand miles, which was fully paid by Westinghouse on expense account instead of the US government's stingy per diem that most of us were used to. So we took a day of rest without feeling guilty

Karyl, Amy, and I arrived in San Diego several days later and began a brief search for housing in various beach communities like Point Loma and Pacific Beach, where most of the others of our group had already settled in. Finding nothing to our liking, we decided on a small apartment on a monthly rent just across from the La Jolla Beach and Tennis Club in what was called La Jolla Shores. We had been told that our operation might only be there for six months, although it could be extended to a year. For the next few weeks our crew spent time putting all our gear aboard a 120-foot vessel called the *Hugh Tide* which was to be only a temporary home until our designated ship, the 136-foot *Burch Tide* was ready for us. These vessels were known along the Gulf coast as "mud boats" because they carried thousands of gallons of drilling mud for the oil business. They had a clear deck which was perfect for placing our trailer vans and crane.

On November 2, we all trekked to Los Alamitos Naval Air Station to watch the arrival of a MATS C-124C Cargo Master with the Diving Saucer and its French

The Diving Saucer with French crew arrives aboard a MATS C-124-C
Cargo Master at Los Alamitos Naval Station.

crew. All the details of this operation and of putting together our traveling "rent-a-sub" show is fully described in my 1968 book *Exploring the Ocean Depths*.

During this outfitting time, the ship was docked at Long Beach, which gave Joe Thompson and me a chance to pick up our motorcycles that had been shipped from Baltimore. We got them out of storage late one afternoon and headed toward San Diego. We knew that neither of our bikes were freeway approved so we had to ride along California Route 101 which is equivalent to Route 1 on the East Coast. As we left the Los Angeles area, sunset was upon us. We also knew we had a slight problem ahead around Oceanside where the 101 stops and, for about five miles, joins the freeway where motorcycles were required to be faster than ours. In the dusk, we entered the four lane freeway with cars and trucks rushing by at 65 mph or faster, as we struggled to make it to a mere 45 mph. We wisely remained in the breakdown lane.

We had nearly covered the five miles when a car pulled up behind us with red, blue and yellow lights flashing. A pleasant California Highway Patrol (CHP) officer informed us that we shouldn't be on the freeway, but also said he knew there was no other way. This was my first exposure to the CHP and I was very impressed with his polite manner. He proudly mentioned his qualifications, including his attendance at UCLA. I have yet to hear any police officer ever stopping me and then telling me where he had gone to college; welcome to California! What's more, the officer escorted Joe and me along the rest of freeway behind us with lights flashing until we were safely back on the 101.

For the next month or so, we all got used to our new life in California, beginning with parents and other family members a whole continent away and a Christmas without snow. The team's work at sea quickly became all consuming. Many times we would get the order from Fred Willett to show up at the dock of the Naval Electronics Lab (NEL) on Point Loma at three o'clock in the morning and we would steam up the coast in the dark to be off one of the Channel Islands for a couple of dives with Scripps or NEL scientists during the day, arriving home long after dark.

While we were doing local test dives for the Scripps scientists, I had a chance to make a deep dive SCUBA dive with Joe Thompson and the Saucer. We accompanied the Saucer at the edge of La Jolla Canyon, descending gently as the Saucer scientist examined the canyon walls. Joe and I were both on single tanks, which meant we shouldn't go below 150 feet to be safe. Of course Joe felt we could go deeper and I, breathing minimally, agreed. This was well before gauges and alarms and all the safety accessories. Finally, at 190 feet we waved goodbye to the Saucer guys and began a fairly rapid ascent knowing we were low on air. At twenty feet, Joe made us stop to soak or decompress for five minutes. We surfaced and all was well.

I sold an article on this and other dives in 1965 to *Skin Diver* magazine, with lots of photos by Joe and Ron Church. This was my first publication in a national magazine and amounted to nearly four thousand words. They paid me a paltry $38, a penny a word. I should have written more! I visited with Joe several times after this West Coast adventure; he had become a well-known photographer. Sadly, Joe departed at age seventy-four, at an assisted living home in Pennsylvania.

Before we left for Mexico, we were paid a short visit by Captain Cousteau to see if all was going well. I later had lunch with Cousteau, who was correctly called Commandant Cousteau, along with several of the Westinghouse Underseas management folks from Baltimore. Cousteau spoke perfect English, although in public appearances his accent was more pronounced. His topic of discussion for us all was "what do you think the world would be like a hundred years from now?" It was an interesting discussion. Then Joe Laing, one of the Westinghouse engineering bosses started to ask him about financial matters. Cousteau brushed him off saying why should we talk about such dull and everyday things? He put Joe in his place.

At an evening lecture to a group of scientists in San Diego, Cousteau went on to describe how he had gotten started in the US It was 1950, he said, and he came to Los Angeles and found someone who he thought could interest prospective SCUBA divers in his Aqualung. Cousteau and Emil Gagnon had invented and patented the Aqualung in 1943 and Cousteau's company, Le Spirotechnique, wanted to get a start in the US He brought ten Aqualungs and asked a well-known Los Angeles diver to try to sell them. He came back a year later and, finding this person, asked how he'd done with the ten units. The rather amazing answer was, "I sold them all, but I don't think there's anyone else who wants one!" Shortly after this negative forecast, Cousteau founded US Divers and the race to get us all underwater was on.

Another great story took place right here in San Diego at the NEL facility near the docks where we worked. A few years earlier in 1960, the Navy had staged the world record dive of *Trieste* descending 35,800 feet into the Challenger Deep, in the Mariana Trench. This effort had started seven years earlier with Professor August Piccard's invention of a large vehicle designed to reach the deepest part the world ocean. He was the first to ascend in a balloon to 53,000 feet. Piccard's son, Jacques, along with Lieutenant Don Walsh of the Navy, had made this historic seven hour dive, described in my book, *Diving For Science*. Jacques Piccard went on to dive in his boat *Ben Franklin* in 1969. I had the pleasure of meeting him once at a scientific meeting. Don Walsh, co-pilot with Piccard in 1960, was a fellow Texas A&M oceanographer and Explorers Club member with whom I have kept up over the years. *Trieste* went on to be part of the Navy's manned search vehicle program and is now on display at the US Navy Museum in Washington, DC.

In March 2012, James Cameron, filmmaker of *Titanic* fame, made a solo dive to this same deepest point in a $7 million hi-tech vehicle, *Deep Sea Challenger*. To put things in perspective, in 1958 the US Navy had purchased *Trieste* for $250,000. In

Jacques Piccard and Lt Don Walsh surface in Trieste *after an historic seven-hour dive to 35,800 feet in January 1960.*

Deep Sea Challenger *designed and built by James Cameron for a solo dive in Marianna's Trench in March 2012.*

2014, my step daughter, Julie Palais, and I were invited to a premier showing in New York of Cameron's dive, where the actual sub was on display.

Meantime, back on the job, we would be gone for a week at a time. And then sometime in mid-January, the *Burch Tide,* our larger mud ship, was to head south for an extended stay in Baja California. Our team of ten flew to join the ship in Cabo San Lucas at the very tip of Baja.

Karyl, Amy, I had a few days before I left, so we spent time in Julian and Alpine in the inland hills of San Diego County, where there was a bit of winter at 4,500 feet. It was like a sneak visit to back home. The rest of any time off was spent on the beach or in our tiny apartment. As I look back, it did seem that I was at sea for about 90 percent of the time that year.

Our first series of just-completed dives near to San Diego had been good preparation for this longer cruise to Mexico. Our French counterparts rode the ship the seven hundred miles to southern Mexico while we all flew by commercial air to Mazatlán and then by a small charter plane operated by the local hotel. There was only one hotel at the time, operated by Americans, and Cabo San Lucas was hardly a big tourist destination, just a sleepy village and a fish cannery. All the food for the hotel was flown in by the same aircraft.

By the time we came across from Mazatlán it was dark and the air strip was a rocky, dirt strip with no runway lights. Two pickup trucks were parked, one on each side of the field trying to light it up. At the last moment on the approach, a loud horn went off in the cockpit where the door was open. The pilot had failed to put the flaps down. At that point, the plane fell like a rock the last twenty feet or so, and we took a giant bounce as he somehow got things under control. We all cheered and clapped. We were all young and brave. I could picture Karyl reading the paper at home..." Small plane crashes in Baja — all passengers killed."

The time went by quickly and our operation of taking many different scientists for dives of up to four hours at a thousand feet deep went well. After a couple of weeks, Fred Willett and I were called back to Baltimore for a meeting. He had told me he would be re-assigned to another position there and had recommended that I take over his duties as the Westinghouse manager aboard the ship. Our team had complained to various upper bosses there about the way Fred ran things. Now it was going to be my turn getting dives done and keeping the complainers happy; or, as it was called, my "day in the barrel."

None of our success would have happened without the French team that came with the Saucer. The leader, Andre Laban, was the Technical Director of the Office of French Undersea Research (OFRS), Cousteau's group in France. At thirty-six, Laban had a good sense of humor, spoke English perfectly but with an accent, and was a qualified Saucer pilot. He stayed with us for several weeks to make sure all was running well. He was most notable, especially in those days, with a clean-shaven head. He also helped as our official barber. After our expedition he spent three weeks underwater in an underwater habitat and continued in producing Cousteau films. Laban went on to become quite famous as a painter and was the first to make paintings underwater. I recall Andre's amusement with our language. One evening after we had our dinner and we were sitting around he said with a faint smile, "After supper, motherfucker," which became one of our favorites.

Andre Laban, Technical Director of Cousteau OFRS and leader of our Diving Saucer program.

Jacques Roux, the Chief Maintenance Technician, had been with the Saucer since the very first edition in 1956 and probably knew more about the workings than anyone else. Always in black coveralls, he had been on the first Westinghouse Saucer project 1964 in California and now spoke some English. He went by the nickname of "Gaston." The third member of the team was Raymond Kientzy, a former combat diver with the French Navy and had been with Cousteau since 1952. He spoke a little English, was quiet and serious and frequently smoked a large curve-stemmed pipe. He, too, had a nickname, which was "Cano-e" since as a young boy he'd paddled a small canoe. He was our head pilot and very capable.

Without these talented men we never could have carried out our "rent a sub" project. The French were like fish in the water, utterly at home making us — even those we called "pros" like Joe and Ron and some of our ex-Navy divers — look most amateur. In his quiet way, Andre would say, "Slowly, Joe. Do not rush around." It was a pleasure to see them work in the water with the Saucer. One of the most re-membered phrases was uttered by Gaston one morning at breakfast as Little Joe, our cook, was serving French toast: "French toast…American bread." Another favorite of the French were the doughnuts Little Joe made frequently. They called them "O" rings after the round rubber gaskets used to seal connections underwater.

"Gaston" and "Cano-e" discuss operations and maintenance with Commandant Cousteau.

One of our more interesting diving adventures took place around San Clemente Island. The island belonged to the US Navy and we were asked to spend a week there using the Soucoupe with their scientists. Purchased in 1934, the island was used in Navy training operations and no civilians were allowed there. Our team was flown out on an old Constellation chartered from Capitol Airways for Navy contractors while the ship transited the seventy-five miles from San Diego. Some of the most the fascinating kelp forests I've ever seen were off the east side where we worked and dived. We swam between the tall kelp plants that were in forty feet of water; it was like a jungle with the sun's rays streaming through. We stayed in old Navy barracks where up to three hundred others spent time here on projects.

The most exciting part of the visit was our day off, when a couple of us took a truck over to the west side which was completely wild with no signs of humans. Here, looking down from a cliff a thousand feet to the sea, we watched a pod of orcas threatening some sea lions perched precariously on rocks surrounded by water. This scene went on for some time until one poor sea lion lost his footing and was devoured by one of the whales — a true chapter out of nature's playbook. The steep cliffs were teeming with feral goats, with the faded brown coloring of deer. Legend has it that Spanish missionaries had brought the goats to the island centuries ago. With no natural predators, the population had grown to more than eleven thousand. Recently, they were hunted, and with the intervention of an animal protection group, the remainder were airlifted off the island and relocated. That scene with the goats, killer whales, and sea lions still remains most clear in my mind even a half-century later. Soon after this we also visited and dived off San Nicolas, Anacapa, and the other Channel Islands. San Clemente was by far the best place I had visited.

Before the change of command between Fred and me, headquarters in Baltimore wanted us both back for a briefing. Having spent a lot of time at sea and living the straight and narrow life aboard the *Burch Tide* with no chance to go traveling across the country, this was exciting. Conventional in his approach to everything, Fred had proceeded me by going east to Baltimore via Los Angeles much earlier for our meeting next morning. I managed to hitch a small plane ride to Mexico City determined to beat Fred back by some alternate route. Suddenly, at the airport in Mexico City, I realized that I had only $20 cash to my name and no ticket to continue on. This was in the days before credit cards and somehow I hadn't brought a blank check. I went to the Pan Am Clipper Club where I had been a member since the SAO days. It was now a little past midnight and the last plane to New York was leaving very soon. I was able to talk the club manager into letting me have a blank check, cross out the name insert mine. He obliged in cashing it for $150 and I dashed to the ticket counter and, with luck on my side, boarded my plane. By greater good fortune I got to the meeting at seven-thirty the next morning, easily in time to greet Fred when I met him in the men's room. His surprise was worth all fuss of the flight.

My time with the team and the Cousteau crew went fast although not without incident. Besides nearly losing the Saucer when it leaked at a thousand feet and later celebrating our three-hundredth dive, among other events, we had a really successful six months. These details are all chronicled in *Exploring the Ocean Depths*.

Just before leaving our California paradise, I made a visit along with Karyl and Amy to my great uncle, Roderick Sherwood, who was living in Long Beach at the time. He was Pansy Webster's brother and a wonderful character. We found him living alone in a typical turn-of-the-century California cottage. I recall walking in with Amy in my arms. Uncle Rod, while in his nineties, was still extremely alert and cheerful, and although slightly stooped, still quite tall. His desk was piled with papers and books. He proceeded to tell us the family history of our Scottish heirs and especially our McKenzie connection, this being his middle name. All of the true McKenzies, he said with some gravity, had a barely visible sort of birthmark across the forehead. He, like his ancestors, had been called "Rorie." I wish now I'd heard more of his tales. I still have lots of his letters to my mother in nineteenth century penmanship. Of all the Sherwoods, he was the most interesting.

We celebrate Dive 300 of the Cousteau Diving Saucer, March 1965.

A final memorable event before we left for the East Coast occurred while the Westinghouse crew was working of the naval facilities at Point Loma. Our ship was docked there and in between cruises there wasn't much to do, so one of the favorite pastimes was to SCUBA dive off the docks and search for items tossed over the side of Navy ships. Over to the side was a large garbage can of odd items. One of the crew surfaced one afternoon, holding up something he was excited about. It turned out to be a bronze plaque, about three-by-twelve inches, with letters stamped in it reading "Perry Is a One Way Prick." Who, but a bored Navy sailor, would make such a thing? We all got a good laugh until our marketing manager, Tom Horton saw it. He decided to make it an award called the Perry of the Month Award for whatever stupid mistake or bone-headed trick that had been done by one of our crew. We never did find out whbo Perry was but the award continued for a while.

Chapter Nine

Back East We Go

Karyl, Amy, and I left La Jolla and the lovely Southern California climate in early June, 1965. My time with the team was up and I was needed to be back on the East Coast, as things were getting very busy with new contract work for the Navy. The Saucer team was now increased by four or five new members as they prepared for the arrival of *DEEPSTAR 4000* being built by Cousteau and company in France.

We had made plans much earlier to return home via train. I had always wanted to travel across the entire continent by train and here was the chance with Westinghouse paying all the expenses. The Saab we drove out the previous fall was put aboard the moving van with the rest of our belongings. By this time, Amy, our pride and joy, was just one year old. We took the local train to Los Angeles and then climbed aboard the *Super Chief*, which was nearing the end of its cross country runs before nearly all trains vanished, forced out by cheap, fast, jet air travel.

The *Super Chief* had made its maiden trip in 1936 and became known as "The Train of the Stars," as nearly all the Hollywood stars traveled from Los Angeles to Chicago on this all-Pullman sleeper train in only thirty-six hours. It was the first use of diesel engines with 3600 horsepower made by GM. Famous for its gourmet menus and five star meals, the *Super Chief* ran until 1971. We felt lucky to have had the chance to ride it in all its elegance.

The train was elegant with a quality dining car and behind it, an observation car with an all glass upper deck. We saw wonderful expanses of back country in the west, not visible from any of the main highways. Amy was snuggled in blankets in a large laundry basket that Karyl and I carried between us to our compartment, a good sized room and slept much of the way to Chicago; I wished she had been a little older to enjoy this fast-disappearing mode of travel. In Chicago, we changed trains for a less fancy style of coach to Baltimore and then returned to Annapolis.

During my Saucer days, I had started writing a weekly report of events and activities occurring on our mobile dive ship for the various interested groups and upper management in Baltimore. Our Westinghouse PR representative, Jim Shober, and marketing manager, Tom Horton, got the idea that this firsthand report "from the front" might be good PR for the Corporation in Pittsburgh, where they were going through price fixing scandals along with their competitor, General Electric. My report told quite frankly of our un-successes as well as occasional triumphs each day in our struggle to carry out as many dives as we could for the scientists. We had had a variety of near catastrophes always saved by the ever-vigilant French crew. It made for good reading and was widely circulated to upper echelon corporate members. It was printed each week under the name "Westinghouse Log" and, as it turned out, became the basis for my book, then under contract with W. W. Norton.

As we arrived back in Annapolis and our former life, I had a fairly easy time of writing my first book using the "Log," as well as with the debriefing interviews I had taped. After each scientist-observer returned to the ship with fresh memories, I conducted a five or ten minute interview. The actual writing took about three weeks but the revisions, editing, pictures, and final production took much longer and the printed book didn't arrive until 1968. I dedicated the book to Dr. Fred N. Spiess, who at the time was Director of Scripps Institution of Oceanography. It read: "To Fred N. Spiess, whose inspiration and foresight brought together those scientists who used the Diving Saucer."

The drawings had been beautifully rendered in exquisite detail by my brother-in-law, Burt Mader. I still have the original drawings that he did for me at no cost; I've always felt guilty that I should have paid him for them. In those days, Burt was an excellent artist but was struggling to get a start. He went on to become very well-known for his highly detailed renderings of classic aircraft. Some years later, I remember going to see a show of his drawings he put on at Owl's Head in Maine at the Transportation Museum near Rockland, Maine, about a year before his death in 2003. A number of his posters and artwork of airplanes are available on a website managed by his wife, Gloria. The book title, *Exploring the Ocean Depths*, was hardly my doing but that of my editor, Bob Farlow. I'm told editors usually pick titles knowing what will sell or, in this case, what has sold. He recalled an earlier ocean book by Helen Raitt that Norton published called *Exploring the Deep Pacific* (1957). She and her husband, Russell Raitt, a Scripps oceanographer and geophysicist, had conducted deep sea research in the 1950s. The suggested title sounded pretty good to me. Both of the literary review weeklies gave a reasonably good review as well as a nice commendation from one of the Westinghouse VPs. But the best and most prestigious mention came from *New York Times* double-crosstic where there was a 150-word quotation. Although the publisher and I could have done more to promote the book, I was content to sit back, collect my meager royalty checks and bask in my fifteen minutes of fame.

At the invitation of Bob Farlow, Karyl and I went to New York City to meet for lunch in the private back room of a swanky and famous Manhattan restaurant. I briefly pictured myself as a successful author. Overall, the book sold nearly five thousand copies — not bad, but hardly a moneymaker. It even went into a third printing and I autographed quite a few copies, mostly at Westinghouse.

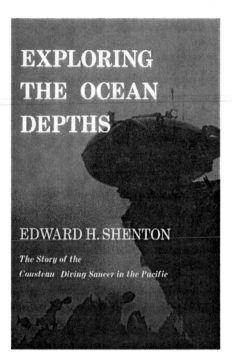

My first book, Exploring the Ocean Depths, *was published in December 1968*

After completing the book, Karyl, Amy, and I decided it was time for our own house. We moved from our rented small brick row house on Cornhill Street to a house we found and bought on Market Street. The street came down a steep hill and ended by a creek, rather typical of Annapolis. We had a spectacular water view. The house was a two-family, joined-together home common to Annapolis, with three floors and a large semi finished basement with a half bath and a long, narrow back yard. Our neighbors on the other side of our common wall were a family consisting of Anne May, a single woman with three children.

We later learned that Anne was the niece of commentator-journalist Drew Pearson, of Washington fame in the 1940s and '50s. A diminutive strawberry blond, Anne was quiet, reserved, and, it turned out, a former TV soap opera actress from the daily *As the World Turns* series. She confided that the previous name of the program had been *The Storm Within* but when Alka Seltzer took over as sponsor, the name seemed a bit much. She and Karyl became close friends.

We paid around $15,000 for the Market Street home. By this time we had decided to sell our Amesbury house for somewhere around $13,500. While the Market Street house was certainly not as unique as our 1745 Amesbury saltbox, and our choice pieces of seventeenth and eighteenth century furniture were slightly out of place in a 1920s duplex, having our own house again was comforting. It soon became our home.

Up the front steps was a porch that ran about fifteen feet, the width of the house. Upon entering the door there was a corridor off which opened a living room adjoined by a dining room. Farther down the corridor was the kitchen. The stairway to the second floor ran up along our common wall. Our bedroom was in the front looking out on the street and the creek, which really was a broad stretch of water that lead eventually to Chesapeake Bay. We were the next-to-the-last house on the street and beyond was a lovely open field that went right to the water's edge.

My job at Westinghouse began to take up much of my time. I would have liked to stay on with the West Coast diving team as they prepared to take the new submersible, *DEEPSTAR* from California to Nova Scotia over the next year. I didn't get that chance because the folks back in Baltimore needed those of us with submersible experience for their new special black project. Westinghouse had been awarded a major unsolicited, sole source contract. (That is, there had been no competition as I understood it.) The Navy needed the design and fabrication of equipment to locate and retrieve certain "things" suspected of being on the bottom of the Pacific Ocean at about 20,000 feet.

"Black," in this case, referred to highly classified and Top Secret information, as we later discovered. Val and I were tapped for this project, which was to go under the code name "Winter Wind," but even that name was classified. All of us on the project were given top secret clearance and normally would have had a different stamp on our ID badges, except the powers that be decided that having so many top secret badges would attract attention, so we didn't sport the much envied blue stamp, or as they were called, "bugs" on our badges. The whole thing seemed a bit ridiculous. Were there really any spies in the plant? I doubt it. I still have my ID badge which was supposed to be surrendered when I left Westinghouse…a memento to all the spooky charades that went on.

The project went on in various buildings in the Baltimore complex. Much of it was in more secure areas, like the Surface and Aerospace Divisions. In these areas, access was only for those whose names were on cleared lists. We would enter an enormous room the size of an airplane hangar, where we saw a large mechanical arm suspended behind a curtain. We were told not to ask any questions.

Prior to this event, a number of us had been assembled in an auditorium for a briefing. Some government official told us that none of what we saw or heard could ever be divulged or discussed. "Ever," even if you read about it in the newspaper. These guys from Washington struck the fear of God into us and demanded all to sign a document to this effect. If anyone was ever caught talking the penalty was…Death! Of course, it all sounded pretty funny and over dramatic, a bit like the old "burn before reading" adage. The Navy and intelligence people were very serious about the secrecy. I couldn't even tell my wife what I was doing, although I likely did.

DEEPSTAR DS – 4000, *designed and built Captain Cousteau and his group in France, was operated by Westinghouse Underseas Division.*

The New York Times finally revealed the CIA secret mission to recover a Soviet submarine from 20,000 feet in 1974

The project was cleverly designed to secretly protect the goal of the mission, so that there were many levels in the hierarchy, each with its own cover story that contradicted one another. Everything was on a need to know basis and based on how each level was compartmentalized. I was truly unaware of true the mission until sometime in 1999 when I read *Blind Man's Bluff, The Untold Story of American Submarine Espionage*, which was a revealing account of the undersea war with the Soviet submarines. The book divulged the story of a secret salvage of an older diesel Golf class Soviet sub using a giant claw from a drilling barge, a fact that had been buried by the CIA all this time. My job had been to oversee a group of engineers to procure certain off-the-shelf electronics such as cameras, lights, and associated devices to be used at depths of up to 20,000 feet. We were the very early stages of this project.

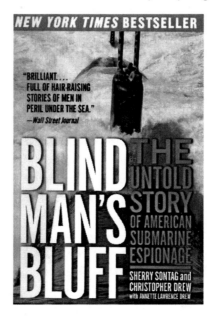

Blind Man's Bluff published in 1996 told the history of undersea espionage between the US and the Soviets.

All documents relating to the project were kept in secure rooms in locked files behind doors, where upon entering, yellow lights flashed. We all signed in and out of special log sheets. The whole spook thing seemed a bit overdone. On one occasion we went to DC, with several upper-level Westinghouse bigwigs. We were ushered into a large command center in a Navy building that was right out of *Dr. Strangelove*, and sat in high backed swivel armchairs arranged around a large circular table. On the wall about two stories high was a map of the world and each of the sixty or so US nuclear subs on patrol were detailed.

Here I was, in the heart of inner workings of the struggle between free world and the enemy later to be branded the evil empire and our race to nuclear superiority, pretty heady stuff. Dr. John Craven, one of the key Navy personnel, was the Chief Scientist on the project. Our discussion had to do with the completion of our instrument packages and whether they would be ready in time. In time for what was not mentioned, a real "don't ask, don't tell" moment. Some years later in 2001, Craven published his book, *The Silent War, the Cold War Beneath the Sea*, which detailed a lot of what we didn't know at the time. "Winter Wind" is not mentioned by name in the book but much of the project was. Craven was also instrumental in the technique he used to discover the missing H-bomb off Spain and the location of the nuclear sub USS *Scorpion* (SSN-589), which sank with all hands in 1968.

To complete our task we had to prove that the off the shelf equipment would able to withstand the pressure at 20,000 feet or roughly 10,000 pounds per square inch. Our engineers had modified the gear enough to meet this depth. But to prove it, we had to test each piece under these pressure conditions. For this we needed a test tank to simulate such pressures. While there certainly were a number of Navy facilities capable of this, someone had decided to find a non-government lab. The only one close by belonged to the Benthos Company, a small business located in Falmouth, Massachusetts, the next town to Woods Hole. Benthos was well known for building oceanographic instruments, and the Woods Hole Oceanographic Institute was one of their best customers. Their test chamber used a World War II sixteen-inch naval gun barrel, enormously strong and able to withstand pressures of 10,000 psi.

Sometime in the late summer, Joel Rizzo, his wife Linda, and I piled all our array of cameras, lights, sonar, pan and tilts, and such into a rented vehicle, left Annapolis and headed for Woods Hole. Our Westinghouse colleagues were, to say the least, jealous as it appeared we were going on a company paid vacation. Joel, better known to us as "Joby," was a Westinghouse Field Engineering Service (FES) employee, in a different group than ours, but very involved in the project. Also, he was my neighbor in Annapolis just several doors down on Cornhill Street.

We got rooms in Woods Hole at the Nautilus Motel overlooking the harbor and the Coast Guard base. Each day we went over the Benthos Lab and proceeded to put our gear down to a simulated 20,000 foot test hoping not hear some kind of an implosion. The 16-inch gun was mounted vertically with the loading door opening at the top. I later saw an ad for these guns which were declared surplus after the war. There was a picture of a jaunty gentleman in shorts and a large mustache, amid a field with hundreds or even thousands of the gun barrels for sale. The only place I ever saw these guns in action was in news reels of battle ships firing these enormous guns at sea. On land many were mounted at shore batteries on the east and west coasts. I discovered that Peaks Island where I later lived in Maine still had several of these enormous concrete batteries, but the 16-inch guns were long gone.

Our test program went on for about a week. In the evening we played tourist and went out to dinner occasionally at elegant restaurants. We didn't feel guilty, as Joby and I put in long days. On one evening, the three of us went to an especially nice place in Falmouth, the Coonamessett Inn. In those days there was a dress code. Since neither Joby nor I had on the proper attire, the maître d' reached into a closet and gave us each a jacket for the evening. We both felt that we had come to the right place. To start off we all had large bowls of clam chowder. Then, on cue, Joby leaned forward, squinting through his thick glasses, spotted a fly in his soup. He could hardly contain himself, calling the waiter over as Linda tried to stop him. Of course, he had to ask, "Waiter, what's this fly doing in my soup?" Instead of the famous reply "the backstroke, sir" the waiter, unamused, glowered and took the bowl away. It was a once in a lifetime occurrence and a good laugh.

There were several times the Westinghouse search team was called out to find lost objects such as an aircraft in Lake Michigan or a railroad car carrying toxic chemicals in a river near Baton Rouge; I was able to attend some of these searches. The one I wanted most to be involved with was the lost H-bomb off Palomares, Spain in 1966. Underseas Division had developed the best side-looking sonar for use by the Navy and our team was requested to fly it to Spain. I was all ready to go with them until someone from the Navy in Washington said I wouldn't be allowed to go because of my Top Secret clearance. Did they expect me to blab to a Russian agent? After a couple of months of much searching involving *ALVIN*, *Aluminaut*, and other manned subs, good ol' *ALVIN* found the bomb in 2,400 feet of water and rescued it.

Sometime around 1966, all of the Underseas Division moved into our brand new shiny quarters at Bay Bridge on the piece of land that David Scott and I had photographed years earlier. We all felt we were finally in our proper home right on Chesapeake Bay with our own dock, the former ferry landing and the spectacular view of the Bay Bridge. I now moved from the black program to a more interesting small group of a half-dozen scientist-engineers who took on special projects.

One of the jobs we had was to design a swimmer delivery vehicle (SDV) for the recon forces of the Marine Corps. These especially tough guys' mission was to make a reconnaissance on enemy territories by swimming ashore underwater for up to ten miles from a submerged submarine. Then, upon completion of their mission, if they were still undetected, they had to swim back days later and be picked up again by the same or another sub. Our job was to design them a two-man wet sub to take several teams to the beach underwater. Although there were a few commercial vehicles that could do part of the job, none was fast enough, with such a range or with sophisticated navigational instruments. The initial contract was for $25,000 hardly enough to do the design. But we took it on anyway as it was a challenge and sounded like fun.

My design mates were two very capable academic types, Kurt Keydel and Bill Hammel. We had a Marine Corps liaison, Buck Kauffman, who, being one of the swimmers, was a big help in working with us and keeping us on the right track. Buck was the epitome of the tough Marine: shaved head, bulging biceps and he rode a Harley. We spent about half a year on specifying available parts and turning out drawings.

Buck entertained us on his visits with tales of his adventures. One of his fellow Marines had written a book on how to survive under extreme conditions. He had been blindfolded, taken to a wooded area, and dropped off with no equipment and no clothes, to be picked up a week later. His book told the story of how he survived to be picked up, living off the land. Buck took on the job of trying to lecture and tell his friend's story and sell the book. Apparently, the author managed to feed and clothe himself before his pickup. While I never learned whether our SDV was built or not, I still have an artist's rendering of it.

An artist's rendering of the swimmer delivery vehicle (SDV) we designed for the US Marine Special Forces in 1966.

The "black program" continued to grow but I was less involved as Westinghouse started to write elaborate proposals for continued secret work in the ocean depths. My days there were becoming numbered, as newer, brighter horizons beckoned. Jack Clotworthy, the Underseas Division VP and visionary who had planted the seeds for all the submersible activities with Cousteau was getting restless for his next act. He felt there was a promising future in non-military ocean ventures.

Jack, who had been a long time Westinghouse executive, decided the time was right for a small company to venture into the recreational aspects of the ocean. He also saw that the good times we hoped for in building and operating small subs might not come to pass. The ever larger war in Vietnam was devouring so much of the formerly available federal budget for research subs that none was left for groups like ours. Further, Captain Cousteau and his TV series had been immensely successful in showing the watching public his exciting underwater world. Jack felt it was time to take John Q. Public underwater.

I doubt that Jack Clotworthy or any of his advisors conducted much of a market survey in the spring of 1968 on what the potential for underwater recreation was; it was an unknown field at the time. But 1968 was better remembered as the beginning of nationwide unrest with demonstrations, the assassination of Dr. King and Bobby Kennedy, the Tet offensive, violence by Students for a Democratic Society at Columbia, and a multitude of other disturbing events. In spite of all this, Jack Clotworthy began assembling the players and funds for what was to become Oceans General Incorporated (OGI) located in Miami, Florida.

Jack Clotworthy, VP of Underseas Division, collaborated with Cousteau on submersibles. Later he took a small group of us to Florida to start an underwater recreation company.

I was one of about six or seven engineers, mainly from Underseas, invited to join the company. The company prospectus was exciting to read and sounded like an underwater Buck Rogers world. Among a variety of proposed ventures the gem was to be an all glass underwater restaurant located several miles offshore off the Keys in ocean depths of sixty-five feet. It glowed with Captain Nemo excitement. At Westinghouse, I had just been promoted to the much desired position of Fellow Engineer, the top level before moving up into administrative jobs. The idea of the slow, sedentary life of the aging, pipe smoking engineers that I had observed had little appeal. What the heck, I thought, I was only thirty-six, hardly time to slow down. So I accepted Jack's offer. The underwater restaurant beckoned like some mythical Greek god. Florida here we come!

Chapter Ten

We're Off to Florida

Karyl didn't have many misgivings about leaving Annapolis and moving south; at that time the itinerant life of the oceanographer hadn't become an issue. She and I took a quick trip to Miami to scout out possible places to live. After looking at a few grand, older mansions with green pools full of algae we found a small, fairly modern one-story house in Coconut Grove in what seemed like deep jungle. It was what the realtors typically called "grove-y."

The backyard came complete with an above-ground pool; the large lot contained a separate garage that I was to later convert into an office/writing room. A trellis, with a profuse crop of small orchids, was next to the house, and alongside this was a Florida Room, a sunny space with glass jalousie louvers which allowed tropical breezes to blow through the house. The living room was several steps down from the front, giving a feel of more space. The kitchen, a tiny galley maybe eight or nine feet long was barely wide enough for two people. We made an offer on the spot and returned to Annapolis to pack and move.

The Recreation Group of Oceans General was staffed by three people. The leader, Haven Emerson, had previously headed up the diving division at Westinghouse which started up soon after the submersible section but now was a large part of the company. Haven had been one of the principals of the J. H. Emerson Company, founded in the 1930s by his father, Dr. Jack Emerson, the inventor or developer of the iron lung, an important device in the medical world. It turned out that Jack was the great-grand son of Ralph Waldo Emerson and cousin of Maxfield Parrish…a pretty distinguished heritage.

Soon after World War II, Jack went on to develop specialized underwater breathing apparatus. During the 1960s, his son Haven, and his colleagues, Alan Krasberg and Jerry O'Neill, had made notable advances in exotic mixed gas techniques used in deep diving for the oil patch in the Gulf of Mexico. This small company was acquired by Westinghouse, who saw the exciting possibilities of men working in depths to 700 feet. Krasberg had invented and patented a small regulator that allowed a diver to use mixed gas to great depths and required no hoses or tethers from the surface.

Through these men, I was introduced to an up-and-coming bunch of young divers whose company became New England Divers of Beverly, Massachusetts. The founder, Jim Cahill, was a former Navy SEAL and the first SCUBA diver in New

England. I had attended a lecture in the past by one of the team members named Frank Sanger, a most remarkable person. Frank, a one-armed and one-legged man, became a diver at an early age, using a single giant Duck Foot fin. He was incredibly skilled, as he demonstrated how he could light a cigarette one-handed using a book of matches. He was also quite strong as I recall his crushing grip when he shook hands. He related how he had done the inspection of the *Texas Tower 4* which was an air defense radar platform off the coast. In 1961, the tower had failed in a storm with all crew lost. Frank was asked to dive down inside of one of the three legs making a camera survey of stress cracks. He described the descent with the camera on his head in a nineteen-inch pipe. The tough part was that the tower leg was used for diesel fuel storage. "I really had to bite down hard on my mouthpiece," he laughed.

Frank then related how he and Jim Cahill solved a murder case that took place near us in Amesbury; apparently, New England Divers took on all sorts of assignments. It seems a woman named Lorraine Clark who worked in a diner in Salisbury had been murdered, most likely by her husband after a "key club" party. The body had been tossed over the Rocks Village Bridge on the Merrimack River. Jim and Frank determined the tidal current at the supposed time and, drifting along the bottom, found both murder weapon and the severed hand with the wedding ring still on a finger.

In his new role, Haven was going to be charged with looking for ways to get the public involved in underwater recreation. He and his wife, Judy, and son, Daniel, had lived on the river in Annapolis where he had his boats and water activities. Haven's mother had been married to a Forbes, whose family owned Naushon Island near Woods Hole. We had been there in 1946, anchored in the harbor with David Scott on the schooner *Heron*. Here, again, we verge close to six degrees of separation.

The third member of our venture was Peter S. Stevens, an old childhood friend of Haven's. A tremendous asset to our group, Peter was trained as an architect with a degree from Harvard but held a very non-traditional outlook. And he was a disciple of Buckminster Fuller, famous for the geodesic dome and the "Dymaxion" design principles. Peter also had a strong background in physics, was an accomplished musician, and innovative song writer. He had been picked to conduct the design and construction of the underwater restaurant. Peter was from Belmont, Massachusetts, and was married with three young children. They had found living quarters on Key Biscayne. The move for all of us was planned for June. Peter wanted help in driving to Florida and I agreed to accompany him in his elderly VW bus.

Our respective wives and children would follow us in their cars. He and I had a very slow trip south as his VW had a regulator on the engine that keep the van under 55 mph. The trip in the VW was especially challenging when we encountered strong headwinds. Peter and I had a jolly time, however, reviewing our lives and goals and frequently took turns driving. One of our thrills was to get close behind a big truck on the open highway and suddenly feel the van pick up speed to 65 mph as we were dragged in the slipstream, yet we were only a few feet behind the truck. This was a trick I had learned in California with the tiny Vespa motor scooter — unsafe at any speed — but fun nonetheless. We arrived intact and set about putting our houses in order and getting families settled. And soon after, we all met in our new office overlooking a part of the industrial Miami waterfront.

For several weeks Karyl, Amy, and I had to live in a motel before our house sale was closed. Our dear rescued cat, Perky, had ridden all the way from Amesbury with Karyl and Amy. Suddenly, when confronted with an entirely new location, the cat bolted for the vacant lot adjacent to the motel. I spent hours searching and calling for him to no avail. After a week or so we moved out to our new house, feeling saddened over the loss. I kept going back hoping maybe he was still there. Nothing. Then, nearly a month later on one last try of calling, out from the jungle in the lot came a bedraggled, hair-matted, cat full of burrs, really none the worse, and extremely happy to see me. Amy couldn't have been more pleased. He had used one of his lives, but he was good for many more years.

Our group consisted of Haven, the diver; Peter, the architect/designer; and me, the oceanographer. We didn't have much of a plan nor had we been given a budget, but we had lot of ideas and enthusiasm. Our goal was to convince prospective investors that we knew how to design and construct a futuristic restaurant some eight miles offshore in about sixty-five feet of water in the Florida Keys. This was not a small task, because it had to operate at a profit. We were in virgin territory. In his research, Peter discovered that a similar venture in had been attempted in Australia, but the end result was unclear.

There were certainly others in the Oceans General bunch with equally wild ideas, but we had no paying contracts. Among them was Lloyd V. Stover who, went by the name "Smoky." Smoky had been recently employed at GE in Valley Forge, Pennsylvania, where he was part of a group working on ocean technology concepts. Without a doubt, he was a great concept person and talked a good game. His project at GE had to do with creating a type of luxury living quarters on the ocean floor, the sort of thing that was popular in the 1960s with conceptual drawings rendered by an imaginative artist. As VP of Oceans General, Smoky was tasked with reviewing our ideas and plans.

Many years later in the 1980s after I had moved on from Oceans General and all but forgotten Smoky Stover, I ran into him in a dockside restaurant in Belfast, Maine, looking almost unchanged from twenty years earlier. We chatted uncomfortably and then I discovered he had somehow met up with my sister-in-law, Marcia Ellery, who was living in Cambridge, Massachusetts and had invited her to join him to go hang gliding off the beaches of North Carolina. She had wisely declined the offer.

It was never clear exactly what Smoky did for us; perhaps he contributed money for startup fees. We were all given the opportunity to invest in our own company; Peter, Haven, and I each put up $2,000 for private shares of stock. It was a move we all would later regret.

Karyl, Amy, and I managed to adapt to the oppressive Florida humidity and constant temperatures in the mid-eighties. We were saved by the steady afternoon breezes off the Gulf Stream. While the house had air conditioning, we discovered early on that we did better without it and used it sparingly. We acclimated, moving slowly about, and avoided the sharp changes of going outside from cool air conditioning to a hot then cool car, and so on. Just before turning in for the night we would take a leisurely dip in our pool; it did the trick. After a while, we felt we were old-time Floridians living comfortably in a time before AC.

The summer began with the three of us designers doing the initial planning and contacting suppliers for information on the materials we might be using. Toward the end of the hot summer, I lucked out on an assignment to do some literature research for an unnamed and anonymous oil company. I was sent to Washington, DC to find all I could about the occurrence of ice off the coast of Southern Greenland in preparation for drilling there. For nearly a month, I got aboard a plane every Monday and spent the week in the Capital, digging through everything I could find in the government libraries. I found precious little, and this was most frustrating because I knew there were lots of valuable and classified data residing with the Navy, especially for the US submarine activities throughout the Arctic. I'm sure the oil company could have found a lot more than I did; perhaps they wanted to remain anonymous.

In any event, it was a nice break from the heat of Florida, as Washington was beginning to cool down. Every Friday, I would be back on the plane heading south. I suspect my flights cost more than we made on the job although it could have been a cost plus contract. And we did save on hotels since Oceans General had an office and adjacent apartment in DC where I was put up. Our resident DC rep, Dave Harvey, also previously from Westinghouse, made the rounds prospecting for potential jobs for the company, albeit unsuccessfully. Each time I arrived back in Miami as I got off the plane I found the near 100% humidity so stifling, it felt like a giant hand closing around my throat and I questioned why I had decided to move to this wretched place. As we slipped easily into fall, however, I found the climate became really quite pleasant.

Haven, Peter, and I worked on our design for the restaurant. The shape was to be a geodesic, perhaps a form of a decahedron — multisided and strong, but easier to assemble than a sphere. Each face would have a triangular window. Peter prepared sketches and preliminary specifications. To get a better idea of the environment we expected to be working in, we took a several field trips to the John Pennekamp Coral Reef State Park. This was the target for many divers and tourists and was a spectacular undersea garden. The day we dove there it was typically windy and rough. We realized how challenging it would be to transport tourists, non-swimmers, and the general public to our "dining room" sixty-five feet beneath this turbulent sea surface and eight miles from shore. We played with conveyor tubes of high strength glass, vertical shafts, and other improbable schemes that became more frightening as we looked at them carefully. It was a bit like Smoky's conceptual futuristic drawing and not very practical.

Under the mantle of recreation we also explored other more conventional areas such as child play units; Peter had built geodesic plywood structures in the backyard for his kids. We tried various marketing approaches after looking at the phenomenal success of toys from companies like Wham-O, the creator of the Hula Hoop, Frisbee, and dozens of successful fads. None of what we had in mind seemed to find a tangible market. As time rushed by us that fall, we realized we were creating pipe dreams. Peter began to construct cardboard architectural models using Fullerian concepts and multisided bases for the restaurant. I spent time on the physical oceanographic aspects including water temperatures, currents, and bottom sediments for anchoring. None of us was an engineer — that would come later, we believed. But Oceans General never got to "later."

At home, I had set up an office for my writing projects. Not long after my first book, *Exploring the Ocean Depths* was published in 1968, I had managed to sell my publisher, W. W. Norton, on a second book. What I had in mind was to be a popular survey of manned submersibles in the US and worldwide. I had been busily collecting data on each sub while at Westinghouse and realized with growing interest that there was a market for a book of this type. Norton had gladly given me a contract for the book, a feat not so easy these days. I had advised that it would involve a fair amount of research, unlike the quick writing of *Exploring the Ocean Depths*, filled with personal experiences.

My office was in the small garage in the back of our tropical lot. The garage had not been used as one for some time as a car could not get through the thick jungle-like overgrowth. I installed a dropped ceiling, painted it, and bought some office furniture, including a beautiful white leather swivel chair. Now I had the perfect, quiet getaway for my weekends and spare time.

Late that summer of 1968, Haven and I were interested in becoming dealers for a small sailing/racing boat he had done some research on. We agreed to each buy one with the idea racing them and perhaps selling a few. The boat, called an OK Dinghy, was fourteen feet long and similar to a Finn, the Olympic class. It was a cat rig, sailed single-handed and arrived on a trailer. The boat was very fast and quite tippy, but I had only sailed it once since we weren't near the ocean. Very close to my maiden voyage came a day long-remembered by submersible people: October 16, 1968. On that day, *ALVIN* was lost in 5,000 feet of water, although subsequently recovered. Alyn Vine, father of *ALVIN* once said in a lecture, "You can count on a cable to do one of two things, either get fouled or break." On this day two cables on Lulu, *ALVIN* 's support ship, broke. Luckily, the pilots escaped before she sank.

ALVIN *after 50 historic years of diving can still dive to 21,000 feet.*

And it was this same day in 1968 that I crashed through the glass door of the Miami house, changing my left-hand dexterity forever.

I was working in my garage office on a weekend afternoon, when Karyl called across the backyard saying I had a telephone call. Although it was October, Florida was still quite hot so we were still using our air conditioning and Karyl had closed the glass slider after calling me. As I ran across the backyard, I stupidly failed to notice this and assumed the door was open. It is said that "assumption is the mother of all fuck ups" and how true! I ran into the solid glass and at the last moment put my left hand out in front of me as it took the brunt of the impact. The glass shattered but it didn't crumble, as safety glass is supposed to, and there were sharp shards lodged in my wrist.

I severely cut my left wrist with much blood spilled. It was quite a shock and I was a bit fearful. Karyl immediately took steps in Christian Science which had a calming effect on me. We didn't rush to the hospital, but instead Karyl called a practitioner and the CS nurse whom came right over and expertly dressed and bandaged the wound. I spent a week or so away from work. I recall the three of us taking a day or two to get away in the Keys. Over the next month or two small bits of glass worked their way out of the wound area and I regained some of the function of my left hand. To this day, I've continue to wonder who called me on the phone.

Perhaps I would have had better use of my hand had I gone to the hospital and seen a doctor. But this incident encouraged me to learn more about Christian Science and practice its principles and faith, which have been most beneficial to me throughout my life.

Late that fall, Karyl got a bit of disturbing news. Our former neighbor in Annapolis, Anne May, was being held in prison for murder. The story was quite bizarre. Anne, a quiet, petite and almost timid woman, was being held for the stabbing murder of her boyfriend.

As the story goes, one Saturday night, Anne and her boyfriend, Jay, a local Annapolis man, had been drinking in her kitchen. There was a partially frozen turkey involved, along with a large carving knife. An argument ensued and Jay lunged at Anne, who was holding the knife. It went through his heart, killing him. Jay was a "townie" and Anne was the rich hotel owner's sister. It didn't look good. Karyl was called as a character witness and flew to Maryland for the trial. Fortunately for Anne, it was deemed an accident and she was freed after a month in the Annapolis jail. Like so many of my stories, Anne returns into our lives later on in Maine.

Pete Welles at Sebring, Florida in his Jaguar XK-140 MC where we drove around the track, an old airport, just to say we did it, April 1956.

The following spring, I decided to attend the famous international sports car race held every March at Sebring, in the middle of Florida. I had been there some years earlier with Pete Welles and his Jaguar XK 140 MC but we had missed the race by a month. The track used the runways of Sebring airport and thus it was flat with no banking, making it much more difficult as speeds were fast on the straightaway and slow around corners.

The race began at ten in the morning and would be twelve hours long. Since it was an international affair, most of the drivers were foreign with several classes including Ferraris, Jaguars, as well as the smaller ones. The race started LeMans style, with the cars lined across the track from the drivers in which everyone sprints to a car, jumps in, starts and roars off. I sat with hundreds of race fans in the bleachers. It was a hot day, but not quite as bad as summer.

By afternoon, the initial excitement began to wear off as cars dropped out and it became hard to know who was leading and who was lapped. Finally, the race finished, well into the night. I had decided to camp out by my car, a 1947 Plymouth. I had just begun to drift off to sleep, as the parties and drinking got serious. Suddenly several very loud motorcycles began chasing each other up and down the aisles between parked cars in the large field. Realizing I might squashed, I quickly rolled under my car in my sleeping bag where I spent rest of the night, uncomfortable but safe.

The real treat was the arrival of Briggs Cunningham from Connecticut with a very rare Jaguar XK-SS, an extremely fast car evolved from the Jag D-Type originally run at LeMans. The XK-SS was to be a road car that could be operated legally, but still very fast with top and side curtains. This one was one of sixteen cars built just before the disastrous fire at the factory in 1955. There was to be a production model it but never made it. Driven all the way from Connecticut for this race, I've never seen another one and gather they bring a price in the millions.

The rest of our time in Miami was spent trying to make a go of the underwater venture at Oceans General. Peter Stevens and his approaches to to architectural design as well as his musical talents made for an entertaining office mate. But by spring it was becoming clear that our small company could not hold up. In late May of 1969, what we all dreaded came to pass. Jack Clotworthy sadly told us that the company was going to sell its stock in the market. Shortly after, a group of investors bought the remains and the following day Peter, Haven, and I were out of jobs.

I kept up with Haven over the years through our mutual friend Chic Ransone from our Annapolis days. Haven became deeply involved in mixed gas diving and was most successful in the Gulf where there was need for diver hook ups at great depths for the oil and gas business. Later, I heard that Haven had suffered a fatal heart attack. I ran into his first wife, Judy Emerson, at church some years later and fairly recently at the 2010 Thanksgiving service at church in Boston. She recognized me but sorry to say, I didn't recognize her and we had a brief chat. She re-married, has a couple of now grown kids, and seems happy. We never mentioned Haven.

A rare Jaguar XK-SS, one of only sixteen that survived a fire at the factory. Pete and I saw it at a race in Louisiana. Photo Courtesy Chelsea Auto Legends.

Peter Stevens went on to work in some capacity at Harvard. Then he moved to New Hampshire where he still lives. Peter has become well known for his book, *Patterns in Nature* (1974). He and I had collaborated in the design of an educational science kit for oceanographic sampling which we took to SEE, a local developer in Newton. The company showed an interest but along the way other things interfered and we dropped it. I still have the prototype that fits in a small case. It had a mud sampler, water sampler, and several other gadgets, all easy to manufacture. We called it Oceanokit.

I ran across Jack Clotworthy some years after we all left Florida and the failed Oceans General adventure. He was the general manager of the Joint Oceanographic Institutions for Deep Earth Sampling, a major government deep sea drilling program with ships like our "black" project with the Hughes group. I must have been looking for work when I visited him in DC. He passed away at age eighty-seven on Christmas, 2011 and had been living in Annapolis. His move at Westinghouse to bring The Cousteau Diving Saucer for its scientific program was truly visionary.

First, it was the St. Valentine's Day massacre at The Geraldines in Annapolis in 1964 and now the death of Oceans General. And worse, the $2,000 stock investment each of us three had made in good faith in the company was also gone. Although there wasn't a lesson to be learned for future ventures due to the amount of risk in a new, startup business, our time in Florida had been a chance to see another part of the country and add something new to my resume. I was still young and resilient and ready to try new endeavors. Karyl had seemingly grown used to the wandering life of the itinerant oceanographer by now and Amy, at age five, was still quite portable.

I immediately began a series of networking phone calls to friends and business associates putting out feelers in the job market. We had already planned a summer vacation for June and rather than cancel, we went ahead and drove to Gloucester, Massachusetts where my parents had gone for years. It turned out to be a nice chance for them to have some time with us and to see Amy as she was growing up. Their usual vacation spot was an older row of room rentals in a waterfront apartment building, right on the harbor and looking across to the town. It was run by an elderly couple, who had owned it for years.

We spent lots of time that week sitting on the porch watching commercial fishing boats coming and going as Gloucester was still an important harbor to land fish. Evenings we sat on the porch, peacefully rocking in our chairs. My father entertained Amy with his classic storytelling skills. One of her favorites was of the traffic light across the water being an old woman putting her umbrella up and down as the light changed from red to green I always liked that. It was here that dad introduced Amy to the "Magic Seagull." While she was asleep or out The Magic Seagull would come and leave a small present. She loved our visits and dad's games.

We went to Crane's Beach frequently that week; the vacation was idyllic and unhurried. I spent a fair amount of time in phone booths, exploring career opportunities. The usual adage prevailed and the opening door did it again, this time with

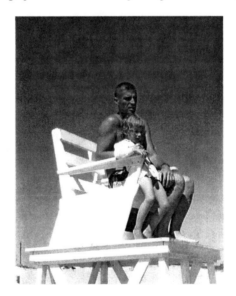

Amy and me at Crane's Beach, Massachusetts on vacation ready to move to La Jolla.

215

a small group in San Diego. The firm, Dillingham Oceanographic, was a part of the parent company of Dillingham in Hawaii. They were eager to find an oceanographer for a recently-awarded contract.

I was asked to report immediately, and felt it was great break for me as I had really liked California from our last episode there in 1964-65. And I was never ever one to turn down a new opportunity. The west coast had much to offer over the Florida coast so the family voted a resounding "yes." All too soon we would be off to the other end of the country robbing our parents of a chance to see their only granddaughter grow up.

As soon as we returned to Miami, we quickly packed up of all our household belongings to be shipped in several weeks at company expense. The house sold immediately and we hired a company to drive the Volvo wagon to San Diego. In short order, we were aboard a plane including our intrepid cat, Perky. He was sedated and rode in the belly of the plane in his carrier. Poor fellow, I bet he was terrified. He was to go on many more cross country trips by car, but never again, we promised him, in the hold of a jet plane.

Chapter Eleven

California Redux

While our belongings were slowly wending their way across the country, we set out to look for suitable housing in La Jolla. Luckily, we were familiar with the town from our first time there several years earlier. We began our search in the $30,000 to $40,000 price range, but found the houses totally unacceptable. These were small bungalows from the 1920s sitting cheek-to-jowl along the main street and not for us. We found ourselves looking above $50,000 — a scary sum in those days.

We met a real estate agent, John Bancroft, through friends from church, Ted and Peggy Joyner, who ran a real estate agency in La Jolla. John, who looked a bit like Spencer Tracy, drove us all over the hills of the town in his VW convertible. Very quickly we came upon a place that immediately got our attention on Carrizo Drive. The house sat high above the golf course with a view of the beautiful slopes to the Pacific Ocean. John referred to this prime location as giving him "whips and jingles," a marvelous sort of nineteenth century term. Among its many definitions, the best refers to excitement from too much caffeine.

When you find the right place, you can almost hear it say, "Hello, buy me!" For us, this was it. The house sat on a pad back from the street on a gentle moderate slope. We guessed it had been built in the 1950s by someone from the east, because although it was only a single-floor house, its unusual double-hung windows with multi-paned glass were very un-California features and quite a change from the Florida jalousie, crank-out windows.

The property also had a large two-car garage and no lawn, just lots of ice plants and other succulents. We said yes in spite of the $50,000 pricetag; we'd make it work, somehow. Having lived in the Florida house with only one floor, we had no trouble adjusting to the same here. The layout was a basic U-shape with bedrooms on one end, a narrow passage looking out on a patio and living room on the other end. The kitchen, utility room and garage extended out that end. From most of the windows, we had a long views of the canyons below and in the distance, the vast Pacific Ocean. Our street dead-ended in a cul-de-sac, so there was virtually no traffic.

We moved in soon after and were faced with camping out without our furniture. It was definitely sparse. Amy suffered the most being in an empty, unfamiliar house without her belongings. Finally, our possessions arrived and we began to settle in to life in La Jolla. Amy found several playmates her age in the neighborhood and by September, she was enrolled in the local public school where she was placed in the gifted class.

I started my job at Dillingham a few days after arrival. Their offices were in Sorrento Valley, about five miles north of our house. The Oceanographic group was comprised of five or six men all with marine, geologic, or engineering backgrounds. The leader of the group, Dr. David D. Smith, was a marine and Arctic geologist who at first seemed like the nicest guy you'd want to work for. I quickly found that things would change as I got to know him, and not for the better.

Our first project or contract was with the American Petroleum Institute (API). Most all of us were fairly new hires and didn't know much about API, while I had at least been familiar with them some years ago at Texas A&M on a study called API Project 51. Our job here was to design a response team for oil spills that had been occurring too frequently and were harmful both to the environment and the public image of the oil industry. While our group was more on the academic side, most of the employees of Hydro Products Division designed and built oceanographic measuring instruments such as salinity, temperature, and depth (STDs) and more exotic cameras and lights used by many of the deep sea expeditions.

Many of the sensors that Joby Rizzo and I had tested for Westinghouse were made right at this plant. The parent company, Dillingham Corporation, was located in Hawaii where among other things they raised pineapples, cattle, and owned a big chunk of Hawaiian acreage, but were now mostly in construction and transportation. The Dillinghams were among the early settlers of Hawaii and certainly among the wealthiest.

The California facility was located in a narrow and fairly steep valley, with La Jolla to the south and Del Mar to the northwest. Miramar Valley was also in the flight corridor for Navy jets returning from carriers in the Pacific and landing at Miramar Naval Air Station a few miles inland. Every few minutes there would be a deafening roar as two or three jets rocketed up or down the valley. If one of us happened to be talking on the phone, we'd have to stop talking until the jets passed. After a while, we got used to it.

I had forgotten how nice it was to be living in La Jolla again, one of the most pleasant places that we had lived. And this time around, we felt more permanent. Maybe, I thought, we'll stop moving and stay in one place. Amy settled in to her school, found friends, and seemed happy. One of her friends, Jennifer Nail, was a cute red-headed girl who in my memory stands out like a Little Orphan Annie character. She was famous for things like managing to get her shoes on the wrong foot but it never bothered her. Jennifer and her family lived down the hillside from us closer to the golf course.

Then there was Mark McCaffery, who may have been five or six but was seemed quite grown up. I was always amused and amazed as I listened to his conversation from the back seat of the car as he described his visits to Disneyland in Anaheim. I felt he had trouble telling real from unreal. To him, Disneyland was reality. Maybe that's where this younger generation began to go off the rails. Real and unreal in California were easily confused. I'll always remember Mark saying "impoor to the people" but I never knew what he meant.

The first of what might be called a bad experience occured that fall, not long after we moved in. Suddenly, the house was under attack by fleas. We guessed the former owner had had pets with fleas who were now starving and took it out on us. We were overcome by them as they leaped up on our legs from the carpets. The only solution was to have the house tented by an exterminator to kill the fleas. We had to vacate for several days while everything was fumigated. When we returned, the fleas were no longer a problem.

The next thing to go was our lovely, almost-new Volvo wagon. The local dealer said there was little that could be done, because the gasoline in California was of an octane rating too low for the car. They claimed there was no remedy at the time a great excuse to buy another car.

We could clearly tell that La Jolla was a German car town with its plethora of Mercedes, Porches, and VWs. I had always admired the Mercedes, so here was my chance. We found an older Mercedes 190 which was solid and, as with all west coast cars, rust-free. One of several more Benz to follow, it was a black, four-door, not very jazzy but slow and comfortable.

Amy and me on the hood of our Mercedes 190 at our new home in La Jolla, California, 1968.

At work, our project on oil spills and how to respond to them was put on a fast track for a preliminary presentation in New York in October. Although we hadn't completed all the tasks assigned, we were scheduled for October 15. I was one of several chosen to make our pitch to the customer and we were hastily put on an eastbound jet. We arrived in the city near midnight the night before. By the time we got a cab to our hotel, it was after one in the morning. What we hadn't realized was that this was right in the midst of the World Series where the Mets were playing the Baltimore Orioles.

The hotel clerk looked up and down on his list and said there were no reservations for us. We weren't in any mood to be sent off, and after much shouting and threats, we were given a couple of not-so-good rooms. The meeting with API went well, but it was clear our study was window dressing for the big oil companies to show they were going to be careful about any spills and perform complete clean ups. Of course, many spills followed with much damage. It was good to be back with the large company with all its benefits and perks after the brief flirtation with the Florida operation.

Meanwhile, a number of changes had occurred in La Jolla since our last tour in the mid-1960s. Most noticeable was the enormous and ugly wall of high-rise buildings along the once beautiful and unspoiled coast. It turned out some well-heeled developers had found a legal loophole in the building codes and one summer, while the town fathers were away on vacation, had slipped it through the Town Council. By 1968, what had been open views of the water and rocky coast were now mostly shut off from the road along the shore.

In addition, the arrival of U C San Diego, along with an entirely new collection of buildings around the once-empty spaces above Scripps Institution of Oceanography suddenly popped up, along with 5,000 new students. And, this being California, new freeways also emerged, along with thousands of new homes that lined the hills and canyons. For years, La Jolla's population hovered around 34,000 residents. That, too, was changing, although the town itself was surrounded on all sides and couldn't expand much further.

At home, Karyl was doing freelance commercial art and advertising. About this time, we decided to adopt a dog. An only child must have a dog, as I did when I was about the same age as Amy. We saw an ad in the local newspaper with a cute picture of a black dog wearing a "please rescue me" look that appealed to us. A mixed breed of German short-haired pointer, St. Bernard and Irish setter, "Jack," as he was called was just what we were looking for.

We found after we picked him up from the rescue kennel that he was hard to discipline. Perhaps, we thought, he had been mistreated; maybe all adopted dogs are like this. But he became a wonderful pal for Amy, riding proudly in the back seat of

Jack and Karyl somewhere in Montana on one of our cross country trips from La Jolla to Boston.

the car, alert and attentive, and enjoying the ride. On our annual cross country trip to Boston, Jack was completely at home and got along perfectly with Perky the cat, who draped himself along the car's rear deck.

My fondest memory of Jack was the day that he and I were on a walk on our street up above the country club golf course. Jack was properly on a leash as we passed by a house on the road when suddenly with no provocation, a large dog leaped out from a court yard. A rather ugly dog fight followed. The owner was nearby but unable to control his dog. Neither of us wanted to get involved but as I tried to pull Jack back, out of fright, I think, he turned and bit me on the leg. At that moment I remembered a trick I'd learned. At just the right time I grabbed his hind feet as the dogs were snarling and biting; and somehow managed to swing him in a circle. Like magic, he let go, the evil dog spell was broken, and Jack and I quickly departed the scene. I'm sure he didn't mean to bite me and would have apologized had been able to speak (or rather had I been able to understand what he was saying).

I was shaken, however. Jack was deemed an uncontrollable and unmanageable pet. Karyl and I decided quickly that he must go back to the shelter. Sadly, we returned him but felt relief that there would be no more dog reliability problems. Then, after several days, all three of us began to experience a lonely and guilty feeling like "what have we done?" I knew Amy missed him as a companion.

We called the shelter. "Is Jack still there?" we asked, fearing maybe he'd been adopted by someone else or, worse still, put down. But the voice on the other end said "he's still here." The next day we had a sweet reunion; Jack was overjoyed to see us at his re-adoption. He became our permanent pet for the next twelve years and Amy got a special friend back.

My work with Dillingham continued over the next several months but there were growing problems between me and my boss. David became very hard to satisfy and was always directing my work and looking over my shoulder in the most critical way. I found later that he was having his own problems and was seeing not one, but two, psychiatrists. In the spring of the following year, 1970, I was given the assignment of going alone to Hawaii to gather data for a pollution study around Honolulu. Here was a major city of 50,000 people with absolutely no sewage treatment and total raw discharge into the ocean. Someone had sent us a flyer from a bulletin board that said, "You swim in your own sewage!"

I was told to spend up to a month digging through city and state files as well as interviewing people at various agencies. Just before I was scheduled to leave around early April, David and I were not communicating well at all and there was a new player involved. Dr. Jerry Stein, formerly an oceanographer colleague from Texas A&M, had become a board member of the company. He wanted to get in on the study and decided to come out later to review my work. I remember leaving San Diego feeling unsupported in the days ahead. I spent a month doing the data search but feeling a bit lonely with no friends or colleagues there. I wasn't enjoying Hawaii as much as I should have.

The best part of my stay was on April 22. There was a large celebration, for it was the first Earth Day and there was a great deal of emphasis on the environment. I had been reading Paul Ehrich's book on all the things we should be doing for the earth. Senator Gaylord Nelson, founder of this day, had originally conceived the idea in 1962 with the backing of President Kennedy. It was exciting to see the enthusiasm of the movement.

Toward the end of my stay in Hawaii, Jerry Stein flew out to see how I was doing. I had hoped he would be friendly but instead it turned unpleasant. He was most critical of what I had accomplished. I don't take criticism well and returned home feeling very down. Not long after coming back to California two of the upper management of Dillingham, Ro Favreau and George Hatchett, who lived up to his name, decided it was time to close down our oceanography group and devote all their effort to Hydro Products hardware. It was one of those fabled corporate scenes where on a Friday afternoon all seven of us were told point blank that we had 15 minutes to pack stuff and clean our desks and leave. There were no "thank you's" or explanations.

Here I was again, out on the street with a flashback to Friday Valentine's Day massacre at the Geraldines eight years prior in Annapolis. I never learned what became of David Smith, or whether he stayed on there. In his defense, he told good stories and had been involved in some very important work with ice islands and such, living on "T-3," one of the first floating Arctic bases in the early 1950s. He was a member of the Explorers Club, a Fellow Emeritus, '53. He remembered meeting up with Sir Hubert Wilkins at the Club in New York when it was definitely an "old boys" club. David was still listed in the Club directory in 2004 and was living in La Jolla. In spite of this background, I was not his biggest fan.

Here we were, seven fairly accomplished marine scientists out of work. We had or should have realized that a "think group," as we were, was at risk as part of a company that produces hardware. Unless we could generate enough contracts, we would be the first to go. Nevertheless, I felt I had been kicked down again through no fault of my performance.

I don't know what became of Jerry Stein. He was originally part of a Westinghouse group that had started off in a beautiful lab just up the road in Sorrento Valley. The lab was part of the Pittsburgh headquarters of Westinghouse Research Labs. Dr. Roy Gaul, also a classmate of mine from Texas A&M and now a well-known oceanographer, was the lab's director. Roy had hired me in 1967 to edit a fancy color report of a series of dives called Gulfview using *DEEPSTAR 4000*. The lab had also been disbanded around this time, which brought Jerry Stein to the Dillingham Corporate games.

Shortly after that, through some sort of networking now long forgotten, I got a nice offer to join a competitor also in the ocean hardware business about ten miles away. Plessey Environmental Systems, a British owned company, designed and built temperature salinity measuring instruments similar to the Hyroproducts STDs - the eternal grail of the physical oceanographer. The income from this activity allowed them to employ a small group of marine science guys. In those days there were almost no women in oceanography. Dr. Lela Jeffrey had been the only female oceanographer at Texas A&M during my time there in the 1950s and was highly respected for her chemical work. Women were more prevalent in the larger and more prestigious institutes like WHOI and Scripps.

Plessey, formerly known as Bissett-Berman, was a most pleasant place to work. Our work team, like the now-defunct Dillingham group, consisted of a half dozen oceanographers working on contracts. The group leader, Robert P. Brown, was a quiet, easygoing fellow with a good idea of the sort of studies that he could sell to the feds in Washington. He had been an Underwater Demolition Team (UDT) diver in Vietnam and, like many of his diving buddies, his ears had been blown out by numerous underwater explosions, causing the need for a hearing aid.

Bob's special interest was the regulation of ocean dumping. He and my nemesis, David Smith, had collaborated on several studies summarizing the field of ocean dumping, especially the illegal aspects. One particular study for the newly-formed Environmental Protection Agency (EPA) was the definitive effort in the field. It described and listed the volumes and contents of hazardous, toxic, radiation, or other dangerous pollutants that were regularly dumped into and along the Atlantic, Gulf, and Pacific coasts with virtually no regulation. This practice had gone on for many decades with little thought to the possible disastrous consequences.

By examining records, ships' logs, and personal interviews, Brown had shown by 1970 that there were numerous violations. The most obvious of these was cited as "short dumping" where a barge load of garbage, sludge, or maybe highly toxic waste was likely dumped at ten or twenty miles offshore instead of at the designated site forty to sixty miles offshore at a depth of a thousand fathoms. There was no evidence of this out of sight, out of mind practice, but he knew it existed. And since there had been no sampling of these illegal areas or any of the designated dump areas, a starting baseline study was necessary.

Thus began the basis for my one and only exciting deep ocean dive to inspect a number of reported dumping sites off the California coast. Based on data gathered for EPA in 1970, Bob had received a contract from NOAA's Manned Under-Sea Technology group to make a series of deep dives on different types of dump sites. Several of these locations were in water more than 6,000 feet deep which meant there were few submersibles capable of such depths. Of the several choices, Lockheed's *Deep Quest* (*DQ*) turned out to be best suited. Lockheed had one of the best diving operations in the industry but was quite expensive.

I found *Deep Quest* in an entirely different class, in comparison to my experience with Cousteau's Diving Saucer. *Deep Quest* was a 50 ton, 40-foot long vehicle that took three scientists and two crew to depths of 8,000 feet and had been built for nearly $50 million. With its size and weight, it needed a large mother vessel. Lockheed had specially built the *Transquest* for this purpose. It was clear the company was serious about entering the manned submersible business. This was all very exciting at the time; although not long after the market for such ventures totally collapsed.

Lockheed Deep Quest. *Bob Brown and I went on a series of dives to inspect ocean. dumping sites to depths of 6,250 feet in 1972.*

Since I'd had prior submersible experience, Bob enlisted my help with the promise of letting me make the dives. We planned on fitting *DQ* with lots of instrumentation, most from our company. One of advantages of a large vehicle was the capability of carrying a large payload. We could strap on relatively heavy instruments requiring lots of electrical power something not possible with the Saucer or *DEEPSTAR* with their severe limitations in battery capacity.

We adapted the salinity/temperature/depth device (STD), a multi-rosette water sampler, a transmissometer, and sediment sampler. All this equipment weighed nearly 200 pounds and was installed in early June of 1972 aboard *DQ* on *Transquest* in San Diego. On June 22, we left en route to a spot twenty-one miles south of Santa Cruz Island, a total distance of about one hundred and twenty miles. There were about thirty people aboard on this cool grey day with high swells and head winds, hardly a pleasant southern California day.

Our first dive was to be in 6,285 feet of water. We were searching for three thousand or so 55-gallon barrels of low level radioactive waste that had been dumped in the 1950s by the Atomic Energy Commission (AEC). We began our dive around noon in a nearly calm sea. Our team included a Lockheed scientist and two pilots, Don Saner and Larry Shumaker, as well as Bob and me.

After my experience in the Saucer, *DQ* was most spacious and very high tech. And, since it was the product of an aircraft company, the layout in the cockpit had all the looks of the latest aircraft with a multitude of gauges and dials. As with my first visit to *ALVIN*, here also the pilots sat upright in seats, as in an aircraft. However, the design of *DQ* didn't allow for any change as *ALVIN* had. But with all the space, the observers were able to lie down close to the forward-looking ports with good vision.

We had been cleared for a ten-hour dive and now the long two hour descent began. The light from the cloudy day on the surface began quickly to fade, yet there was the thrill of seeing the journey through darkening "Maxfield Parrish Blue" into utter blackness somewhere around five hundred feet. We landed gently at 6200 feet, stirring up a cloud of fine sediment that took ten minutes to settle.

Bob and I lay looking out the ports for most of the dive as we photographed, sampled, and made notes. The pilots used a very sophisticated forward looking sonar to spot these targets that were beyond the short range of our lights. Besides lots of smaller marine life, we observed dumped munitions and some of the AEC's radioactive barrels, the object of our mission. These barrels were intact and did't appear to be leaking. Much more detail is presented in the report that Bob and I put together in 1973. It's amazing how fast time goes by in such an exciting situation at six thousand feet beneath the sea. I don't think there was a moment that I was ever nervous or anxious about that mile of water lying on top of us, although had anything gone wrong, there was no possible rescue. After about ten hours underwater in *Deep Quest*, we took a break for lunch and to share what we had seen.

Don Saner was in occasional contact with the surface ship on our UQC underwater telephone. About ten o'clock that evening, they told us that the sea conditions were quite rough and getting worse with twenty-three knot winds and six foot swells. The surface ship said they might not be able to recover us and retrieve the sub on its platform. Instead, they might have to tow us into the lee of Santa Cruz Island at a speed of two knots or less, a ten hour trip. We were told to conserve our power.

Our ride to the surface took about two hours and was uneventful. When we surfaced a little after one o'clock the next morning, we could really feel the rough weather. I was familiar with the recovery process from my days with the Saucer when I had been the recovery crew commander and I recall how nervous I had been at times as the ship and the sub pitched at different frequencies.

With the Saucer, we had to have divers in the water to connect the helicopter hook to a lifting bridle, a very tricky process in rough conditions. Here, Lockheed had designed a better but more costly system, and it worked well. *Transquest* was a catamaran, a twin-hulled ship similar to Woods Hole's *Lulu*. The design was ideal for sub recovery, you just drove into the garage on an elevator platform. Any contact between sub and ship could be extremely dangerous and damaging. There were usually several line handlers to guide the sub. Luckily, all went well and we clambered out and aboard the ship. Had it been any rougher we would have been towed to quieter water, an uncomfortable ride at best. We all felt good having our deepest dive accomplished and behind us.

We made several shallower dives over the next few days. At 2,500 feet, the dives were still far deeper than any of the conventional nuclear subs normally went, even at the present time. On all the dives, we took photographs to document the locations and types of items we found in the dumping sites. These were things like bombs, mostly unmarked, and unexploded weapons. Most familiar were the "hedgehogs," the anti-submarine weapons which showed up clearly on our sonar screen.

Bob and I pulled together an extensive report of the trip with data and photos. Titled "Submersible Inspection of Deep Ocean Waste Disposal Sites off Southern California" (1973), it told the whole story. While the results were hardly dramatic, they were perhaps the first records of a deep ocean dump sites. Ocean dumping of nuclear waste was halted in 1970.

The summer of 1971, Bob invited me to meet his brother, commander Chris Brown, who was the commander of the USS *Hawkbill*, an attack class submarine and very special nuke boat. Its role was to carry the Deep Sea Rescue Vehicle, (DSRV), the Navy's rescue sub also based in San Diego, aft of the sail. The *Hawksbill*, SSN 666, was known as the "Devil Fish" for references from the thirteenth chapter of Revelation.

226

Bob Brown and I were invited aboard the USS Hawkbill *SSN 666 by his brother who was the commander. The* Hawkbill *was fitted to carry to carry the Deep Submergence Rescue Vehicle DSRV-1.*

Chris Brown gave us a complete tour of his boat which was commissioned in February 1971. It was most impressive. With compartment after compartment, the size and amount of space was like a small village, totally self-contained for one hundred and thirty men for two months or more. Earlier, I had a chance to see and go aboard the DSRV, which was designed to rescue up to fifteen men from a downed sub to the depth of 5,000 feet.

The list of retired submarines has grown over the years. The USS *Hawkbill* was retired and cut up for scrap at the turn of the millennium. DSRV-1, *Mystic*, was launched in 1970 and decommissioned a decade later. The sail of Hawkbill is on display in Arco, Idaho, a remnant of the Cold War. *Deep Quest* was also retired since 1980 and on display in Washington State. Our dives were recorded in the relatively short history of manned submersibles, with 1972 being the height of the industry.

In the twenty-first century, there have been plenty of deeper dives, although still by a relatively small group of scientists. In the seventies, we in the submersible community all believed our trade was destined to be continued; that putting man in the deep ocean was really the best way to make observations and on site decisions. And while I still treasure the card I received on that dive of 6,285 feet, over the following years we were sadly proven wrong.

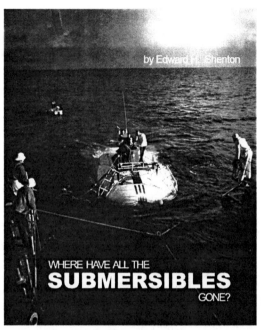

by Edward H. Shenton

WHERE HAVE ALL THE
SUBMERSIBLES
GONE?

An Oceans magazine *article I wrote describing many no longer in use (1972).*

In writing this article for *Oceans*, I had conducted an extensive survey of the field and was surprised to find that most of the more capable and thus, more expensive, subs had been shelved. I predicted this lack of funding and softening market for the large corporations like Lockheed and Westinghouse would continue. The only survivors of any significance over the next several decades turned out to be *ALVIN* with its Woods Hole Oceanographic and Navy backing. Outside the United States, the Russians and the Japanese continue to conduct important deep dives. It was amazing to think that at one time in early 1970s there were more than 150 manned subs. Much of what followed their disappearance was the growing importance of unmanned or Remotely Operated Vehicles (ROV) which turned out to be safer, cheaper, and more effective. Underwater exploration became analogous to space exploration in this sense, although it took a number of years before the ROVs replaced the manned vehicle.

I had several other memorable experiences while at Plessey. One of the several marine scientists working there, George Grider, became a good friend. He was a Naval Academy graduate and always apologized for the Navy habit he said he couldn't get rid of. He would turn away from you, unbutton his pants, and neatly tuck in his shirt very tight. Stocky and short with a round cherub-like face, he had his pilot's license, and was an avid hang glider pilot.

228

He invited me to join him aboard his airplane for a local tour. I could hardly believe that the worn, fabric-covered aircraft with numerous patches was what George had been telling me he flew all along the California coast. The plane, a 1946 Aeronca Chief, had a tail wheel better known as tail dragger. He had bought it a while ago for $800 but had to do some work on to make it airworthy. As we strolled up to the plane, I touched the faded red fabric. It had a taut, drum like sound, yet it seemed incredibly frail.

A 1946 Aeronca Chief like the one George Grider owned. We flew around San Diego County landing in small fields (illegally).

"Oh, it's safe enough" he assured me. "I've had the airfield mechanic certify it, but at $45 an hour that gets expensive."

I recalled George first describing how he would fly from San Diego on weekends to San Francisco in the 85 hp craft with his four-year-old son strapped in behind him, bucking head winds and making a ground speed of about 80 mph. More startlingly, what he really liked to do for practice and experience was to fly into the busy airport of Los Angeles (LAX) at night right along with the "big boys" on the main runway.

"Those tower controllers are sure good," he said. "Even though I don't have a radar transponder or a very good radio they've always helped me in."

According to George, there was no law that his Chief had to have a transponder, although nearly every plane large or small did have them; he saw no need for one. His radio didn't work on transmit but he could hear the controller talking to him and giving reassuring instructions. "Never had a problem at LAX."

The plane was first produced in 1946 and featured side-by-side seating. I sat inside while George completed his required walk around checking surfaces, struts, patches, or anything suspect. Although I had flown in a variety of small planes I'd never been in such an elderly one.

"Switch it off," he called as he stood outside pulling the prop around. Then with a confident smile he climbed in and cranked the engine into life. We warmed up for a short while then taxied slowly down the strip to the far end of Montgomery Field. After the run up of the tiny engine and a careful check of the few instruments on the dash, he gave it full throttle and we ran along easily. We were off the ground in what seemed like a few hundred feet, rising above the sea of low flat-roofed development houses that stretched in every direction for miles, gently undulating over what, not long ago, had been the barren soft beige hills of Southern California.

I had told George earlier that I wanted to get an aerial view and photographs of the way the land of San Diego and surrounding countryside was being gobbled up by the monstrous home building machine. It wasn't possible to comprehend from the land level so I cranked away on the camera and was amazed to see the wave after wave of housing coming over every hill side. Since 1972 there have been a number of impressive books describing in detail this overwhelming invasion.

At one point in our tour George said, "How about we land down there in that field?" Before I could say yes or no, he swooped in below some high power transmission lines onto a grassy field and with a quick bump we were down. He pointed out that such a maneuver was against all flight rules, but no one would know. We briefly strolled around, climbed back in and were off again as though it was the most common everyday event.

He and I made one more exciting flight later that year. He and two others from the Bissett-Berman group had a one-day contract to inspect an oil company facility in the Bay Area. He chartered a very fancy Navion, a four-place aircraft, and we all went for a joyride somewhere north of San Francisco. I recall nothing of the actual job but on the return flight, George suggested we might try a flight maneuver he called a "chandelle," he thought we would enjoy.

Making sure we were all tightly strapped in our seats, he put the plane into steep dive rolling at first left with wings vertical and then right as the dive bottomed out and then climbing again. We slightly exceeded the approved aircraft speed of about 185. It was a very smooth maneuver and didn't seem at all dangerous.

George and I corresponded through the 1970s and beyond. He was then working freelance as a tech writer. He had left his wife and was living somewhere in Pacific Beach, California. He had great hopes of becoming a writer he said but wasn't too sure if it would work out. In his last letter, he described his attempts at hang gliding from Mt. Whitney. He had searched in vain for a pilot that would take him to the mountain top so he could hang glide down. No one would take him.

A few years ago I found a posting from George in an open letter to his classmates of the class of 1963 at the Naval Academy. It's a wonderful letter written in 2004, asking his classmates to write to President Bush and demand that Donald Rumsfeld, then Secretary of Defense, step down over such issues as Abu Ghraib and all the horrors of our wars.

I reconnected with George again in 2014 through Veterans for Peace, an organization in which he has been a member of for some time. I spoke to him at length and we exchanged email addresses. He now lives in Memphis and is involved with rescue dogs and beekeeping.

Another experience while at Bissett-Berman was a short contract to examine the possibilities of using remote sensing satellites for estimating fish populations in Alaska. I spent two weeks in the summer of 1971 with another scientist to learn as much as we could by visiting labs and canneries in Alaska. We were to concentrate on the salmon industry so we visited and interviewed dozens of those working in Juneau, Kodiak, Fairbanks, and Anchorage.

I really loved Alaska; it reminded me so much of Maine. I spent an afternoon walking up to and inside of the Mendenhall Glacier outside of Juneau. What a thrill to be inside under the ice in a cave that was all blue and sparkling! It was my first encounter with a glacier, a glimpse of more to come in later years. I suspect in the subsequent forty years that glacier has now retreated several hundred feet or more. Our study report concluded there was little hope, at least during that era, of using satellites for salmon population observations.

There was also a several month EPA-funded contract in which I visited state, federal, and university labs and offices in fifteen western states the winter of 1971 to gather all data on fish populations related to fresh water temperatures. It was the sort of job I loved. I got to travel through places I never would have had the chance to see, and mostly in the winter.

The summer of 1972, Karyl, Amy, the pets and I piled into our 1957 Mercedes 220S and headed for a two-week vacation and a visit to Granny Mader, Karyl's mother in Sudbury, Massachusetts. While there, we made several forays to our old and familiar grounds in Boothbay Harbor, Maine. Each time we visited, we would start by saying "You know, over all the years since we first came here in 1954, the area really hasn't changed very much at all," when in fact it probably had.

We sat at a table on the deck at Robinson's Wharf on Southport Island, on one of those perfect sunny but cool northwest breeze days, the way one always remembers Maine and I asked Karyl, "Why can't we live here?" I don't recall her answer but it must have been positive because we began looking at places for sale. We visited Ethelyn Giles, a popular regional realtor, and after a few unlikely houses, she showed us one in Southport just across from the water on a cove. It had once been called

Chestnut Lodge, a farmhouse built about 1840, with a separate garage and a melodious brook running along the western edge of the five acres. It belonged to Richard Conant, who also owned a beautiful home on the same cove across the street. The asking price was $50,000 firm.

Karyl and I spent a major part of our return trip to California discussing the pros and cons and what ifs of a move east. The house and land seemed too good to pass up and soon after returning to California, we made our offer on Chestnut Lodge. We immediately put the La Jolla house up for sale and had no trouble selling because the market was rising. We were amazed to get our price of $72,000, a sizable gain over four years. When I tell this story, most people say I should have hung onto the house and made ten or twenty times that amount. But I had no regrets at that point; it was time for us to move. Our old house has now been totally rebuilt in a Spanish style and is for sale for $3.9 million, about fifty-five times the selling price in 1972.

It was to be a pretty bold move on my part with no job in a state where salaries were far below what I'd been accustomed to in California. But the excitement of going back to Maine overcame any panic over my future employment.

My path again crossed with an interesting character, "Waddie" Owen, whom I first met when I went to work for Westinghouse Underseas Division in Baltimore. Part of our group was involved with the highly classified, the Ocean Bottom Scanning Sonar (OBSS), a side looking device used for searching and mapping by the Navy. Waddie and a bunch of bright ocean engineers were working on this and he in particular befriended me. Wadsworth was his full name and he had grown up in Florida where he liked the sea, flying aircraft, and racing an Ariel Square Four, a 1000 cc. motorcycle, on dirt tracks. After a degree in physics from Johns Hopkins, a tour in Korea as a Marine sergeant, and oceanography at Johns Hopkins, he came to the Underseas Division. We had lots in common as he loved Maine — his parents had a home in Friendship where he spent time — and motorcycles and boats. Waddie was of slight build, with sandy hair, glasses and a friendly smile. He did not look the part of motorcycle riding Marine. Some years later after we both left Westinghouse, aka "Circle Bar W," he moved on to become the Director of Marine Science at University of Delaware. I visited him there hoping to find some sort of role being employed in his Department. The best I could do was to write an article for the University newsletter and their new oceanographic research vessel.

After I moved to Maine in the 1970s he and I flew in a plane he had rented from Boston to Wiscasset, Maine to inspect a small submersible in South Thomaston. The sub was designed and built by retired US Navy captain, George Kittredge, as a one-man, 250-ft. depth sub. His company over the years had made forty nine of these midget subs. Waddie was asking me to evaluate the sub for some company where he was a consultant. I recall Capt. Kittredge checking me out in the sub and then down I went to about thirty feet. alongside a dock. The K-250 was very simple and I'm sure adequate for pleasure diving but as I told Waddie later, I doubted if it could be certified or insured. It was a fun adventure and added to my diving list. In 2012, I stumbled across a long list of all the submersibles produced by Frank Busby in 1976. It did list the K-250 and bigger brother K-350. Both were probably safer and more effective than so many others on the list which even included Jim Helle's wooden vehicle. At the time there were seventy five subs listed and presumably in existence at one time. I also found a site called Midget Subs, with a lot of data about K-250, which also included some about the Navy's nuclear powered research submarine, NR-1. And more recently in 2012, durng my birthday celebration, I found,a K-250 at South Thomaston, Maine. on display as a memorial to Captain Kittredge who died in 2010.

Captain George Kittredge built over forty nine of these one man subs to go to 250 feet. This one is one display in South Thomaston, Maine.

In 2005 or 2006, I decided to visit Waddie who had retired to his parents' house in Friendship, where he was living alone. He and his wife had divorced some time ago. It was a comfortable older Maine house and barn and a lot of land near or on the water. What more could a guy ask for? But I got the distinct impression that it was a lonely life in a very small town. His four daughters, now grown, lived else where. We exchanged Christmas cards for a while and I recall talking to him once when he told me one of his daughters had just gone to Iraq in the service. Then as usual not long after, I read of his passing in 2009 as another one of my friends escaped.

Chapter Twelve

The Last Move for Karyl and Me

My life as an itinerant oceanographer continued as we packed up all our belongings, took Amy away from her friends and out of her excellent school in La Jolla, knowing she would be going to a small island school in Southport. In early October, 1972, we made our last cross country trip with Jack and Perky to our new home. We sent our household belongings ahead by a moving van generously paid for by Karyl's mother, who was eager for us to be back on the east coast. The $3,000 moving fees later became a bit of a contention when Karyl and I divorced. Driving along the Maine Turnpike, we were amazed at how few cars there were. Gone were the California eight-lane freeways, everyday traffic jams, and the feeling of teeming millions everywhere you went.

I knew finding a job in Maine might not be easy. As we approached Boothbay, I took the opportunity to stop in Bath at the Maine Employment Office for listings of jobs I might apply for. When the interviewer asked my salary requirements, I casually mentioned a sum based on my California income. The fellow sat up and exclaimed, "Why that's more than the governa' makes!" I remembered the sorry pay scales from my Colby days in Waterville where those who worked at the mill were bringing home $100 a week. Those employed at Bath Iron Works, Maine's largest employer, weren't paid much better. It was then I realized I would have to create my own job.

About a year before I left California, I began subscribing to the *Maine Times*, a weekly newspaper started in 1968 by two journalists, Peter Cox and John Cole, formerly with *The Times Record* in Brunswick. I had become familiar with Maine state agencies, as well as the names of most of the players in environmental activities. *The Times* featured full coverage on key environmental issues, with the majority of activities centered in Augusta, the state capital. In fact, I had created a whole card file of agencies and names, so the move to Maine was, in a way, premeditated. But before finding work, I had to get our new home ready for winter, which was hovering just above the northern horizon and about to pounce on us.

Chestnut Lodge with its beautiful chestnut tree. It was once heated only by woodstoves but in 1972 we added a furnace and hot water baseboard system.

When we arrived at Chestnut Lodge the weather was deceptively warm, as October can be, in the last golden days of autumn. But we knew our priority was to install a heating system for the drafty old house that had been only a summer rental for years. Before that, it had been heated by woodstoves and the large attached living room had been a woodshed. We never gave the idea much thought because our former houses in Amesbury and Annapolis had always been heated centrally with hot water baseboard systems.

Our realtor recommended John Stark, a plumber for the job. In addition to a specializing in heating and plumbing, John had once been a marine engineer, a truly versatile individual. He drove a beat-up old truck which seemed to be on its last legs. As I was to learn, he never seemed to have the right parts, often sending a gofer to Lewiston or Brunswick for a missing elbow, tee, or valve. In many cases, I was that gofer. Perhaps we should have chosen a more professional company but we were desperate to have heat. And John turned out to be an interesting person. I offered to help and he gladly took me on as we had lots of copper pipe to solder or sweat. He taught me how this was done as we crawled about in the dirt cellar in tight spots. This skill proved most helpful in years to come when I installed another heating system all by myself.

Nor was John your average plumber. He seemed well educated, well read, and when we played classical music on our radio he hummed and whistled along to familiar tunes as he soldered pipes in the cellar. Amy enjoyed dropping small hand-written messages through the cracks in the floor for him and he would write back. Karyl got such a kick from all this that later she wrote an article where she established a local column for the *Boothbay Register*. Titled "Snow Before Heat," she related our race against time as the mornings became frostier and then into early November, when it was just plain cold.

Fortunately, Mr. Conant, the previous owner, had left us a tiny antique stove in the front room, a definite help. As the first snow fell on November 22, we shared a collective "Hurrah!" as the monster furnace in the basement roared into life and spread glorious warmth along all the baseboards. At last, we felt ready for winter.

My parents had driven up to spend Thanksgiving with us and see the new place now that we had settled in. The weather continued mild until December 3, the day they had to leave when, with little warning, the temperature plummeted and blowing snow covered the driveway. Winter had arrived.

The northwest wind howled down the cove as we stood saying our goodbyes. The thermometer dove to three degrees and our new heating system struggled to keep up as the strong wind blew in through all the cracks and minimal insulation. The dining room, which faced north toward the cove, was not the least bit warm. I began to worry that even with the new furnace, we might not be able to survive here.

Ironically, a year later the price of oil and gasoline doubled during the oil embargo of 1973. With everyone suddenly becoming energy conscious, Karyl and I patriotically made the switch back to wood, leaving the expensive oil fired heating system unused. I found a beautiful Queen Atlantic cook stove made by Portland Stove Foundry. This classic-style cook stove was popular in a number of Maine farmhouses until being replaced by kerosene or central heat. It seemed so romantic, until I realized it had a voracious appetite for wood. I soon learned I should have opted for an airtight stove. It was then that I became adept at stove duty every night. The Queen, old and warped, had me up every few hours. And, with the air leaks common in an old wood stove, smoke often puffed into the room when the wind backed down the chimney. Our clothes had that faint but definite aroma of wood smoke that wood burners were known for.

Making that complete switch to wood showed us how easy it was to walk away from the fancy oil heating system we had gone to so much trouble and expense to install. Later, we installed two more new, airtight stoves which made all the difference in warmth. It didn't matter if the temperature dropped below zero; we always felt warm enough.

As soon as the family was settled in that first winter, my job search began in earnest. It was refreshing to be able to walk into nearly any state government office in Augusta where few were dressed up; most wore casual Maine clothes, especially in wintertime. Maine, however, was the antipathy of California, with layer upon layer of bureaucracy which made getting a consultant's job nearly impossible. Everyone I talked to seemed to indicate I should look into The Research Institute of the Gulf of Maine (TRIGOM), a group in Portland involved in marine sciences, but somewhat outside the confines of the conventional academic regime.

After several visits to the TRIGOM office on the University of Maine campus, I convinced the director, Dr. Don Horton, that I would be able to help his group by writing proposals for work in marine sciences. We agreed on a casual arrangement where I would be paid around $300 a week with no benefits. With the commute of more than a hundred miles a day, it hardly paid off, but I was happy to get work of any sort at this point. I started at the end of 1972, with an understanding that this was a trial period for both TRIGOM and me.

TRIGOM had been conceived several years before as a consortium of various Maine and New Hampshire colleges including the University of Maine, all of whom had marine science research projects. In 1968, Democrat Vice President Hubert H. Humphrey had been promoting this type of collaborative idea as Chairman of the Marine Fisheries Committee. A similar concept already existed in the very successful Sea Grant Program.

VP Humphrey had been visiting at the University of Southern Maine's Portland/Gorham campus at the launching of TRIGOM. When I came on the scene, eight or nine colleges were loosely affiliated with a small amount of funds from the Maine legislature. Direct funding came from grants and contracts of various soft-money sources. The one holdout, the Ira C. Darling Center, a laboratory of the University at Orono located on the Damariscotta River, refused to join with us, adamantly stating that the University was not coordinated by anybody. Academics, I found, took a dim view of working with groups outside their own institution.

TRIGOM was located in a small former residence that the University had purchased, just off the campus. Horton, a biologist/ecologist with a marine background, held a doctorate from the University of Rhode Island. A pleasant person, he was also frustratingly slow both of speech and physical motion. Both close in age, we shared a number of mutual friends in the ocean community. Along with his wife, Eva, he had started a small business on the side and which had just started to grow. Eva was an attractive Norwegian woman whose brother in Norway was well connected in the furniture trade, helping to establish the Hortons as a key importer for Jotul wood stoves. Little did any of us realize the financial importance that wood stoves were about to play in this country.

My office mate on the second floor of TRIGOM's old building was a young, eager and very knowledgeable woman named Kathy. She and her husband, who went by the name of "Bear," lived as tenants on a farm and orchard of a family whose daughter was also one of our TRIGOM secretaries. Bear was a wonderful large, wooly, bearded fellow whose name fit him perfectly. He drove an oil truck in winter.

We were now becoming acclimated to Maine. My meager earnings weren't enough to support us, so Karyl returned to freelance artwork, which meant long drives to Brunswick or Lewiston in the middle of winter. By this time, we realized that we needed two vehicles for our jobs in different locations. We had noticed a pickup truck with a For Sale sign in a driveway along Route 1 each time we drove past; it looked just right for a second car. We drove up a long driveway to an elegant estate looking out over the Sheepscot River and were met by a pleasant man named Stuart.

He told us he had used the truck, a 1950 Chevy half-ton, to haul manure for his garden but it was in good working order. Bright blue with a rough broom paint job, red stake body and yellow wheels, Karyl immediately fell in love with it. We paid the asking price of $250 and off we went. By the time Karyl needed heat, we found the truck's heater was pretty wimpy. But here was her chance to use that ridiculously heavy raccoon coat that had belonged to her mother and a pair of heavy, warm boots. She was a sight as she climbed into the truck on her way to Lewiston on a sub-zero morning.

Cozy Harbor restaurant and gas pump run by "Gussie" and Emolyn Pratt. It and "Gussie" are now replaced by a fancy large restaurant better suited for upscale tourists.

And Amy, at eight years of age, began at Southport Central School which housed Kindergarten through eighth grades, roughly sixty students. It was a three-room schoolhouse with three grades to a room, each taught by one teacher. Although it seemed the teacher was doing a juggling act in a three ring circus, Amy received a quality education.

Amy started in third grade, and was taught by Emolyn Pratt for third, fourth and fifth grades. Emolyn's husband, Earl, otherwise known as "Gussie" Pratt, owned and ran the Cozy Harbor Restaurant and gas station which also featured Southport's only bowling alley. Gussie's had been part of my most pleasant memories in Maine when I first came to Southport in 1951 with roommate, Pete Welles, while we were at Colby.

Twenty years later, here I was, back in a time warp. Gus, a typically dour Mainer, looked as though he had just stepped off a movie set and not a day older than he had in 1951. When Pete and I used to drive up from Colby for gas in his father's shiny, new 1953 Ford convertible, Gus would amble out in his apron, grab the gas nozzle, turn the handle and say in his best Maine accent, "Did you boys want regula' or super-chaaghed?" Pete insisted Gus was originally from Malden, Massachusetts, but I never found out if this was so.

As my work at TRIGOM progressed, I was involved in several interesting projects. One was a survey of the history of oil spills and subsequent effects on the Maine coast, especially Casco Bay where most of the oil was handled. In 1972, before I arrived, there had been a major oil spill when the tanker *Tamano* ran aground on Soldier's Ledge in Casco Bay, spilling nearly six hundred thousand gallons of No. 6 oil. I enjoyed this type of work, which was similar to what I'd done earlier on the west coast jobs.

In 1973 I produced a lengthy report that TRIGOM published, "An Historical Review of Oil Spills Along the Maine Coast." Although the press always focused on the large and spectacular spills, it turns out that in many cases the smaller, more repetitive spills over long periods were far more damaging to organisms, especially the infauna in the sediments. But typically, the pictures of oil-coated birds and dead fish stuck in the public's mind. A respected US Fish and Wildlife Service marine ecologist with whom we spoke had developed a quick test for oil pollution. "As you walk on the sandy beach, pick up a hand full of clean-looking sand in your white handkerchief and rub it together," he advised. "If it comes out slightly black, it's a sign of spilled oil in the sediment from some previous time."

In other oil-related research, Don Horton and I conducted a literature survey of marine environmental data for Eastport, Maine, in 1973. The Pittston Corporation was proposing to locate a deep-water oil terminal there and they asked us to gather background data. Eastport offered the only deep-water port on the entire

Atlantic east coast where supertankers, drawing up to eighty-foot depths, could land crude oil.

Pittston operated coal mines in West Virginia and was known to have had an extremely poor safety record with numerous accidents in their mines. They had approached TRIGOM and commissioned us to gather environmental data. Surprisingly, they did not lean on us to draw any conclusions in their favor. We, as scientists, and familiar with fragility of the area, were quite opposed to the thought of an oil terminal in the pristine shores of Passamaquoddy Bay with its twenty-eight-foot tides and swift currents of up to five knots.

What I really liked about this assignment was that it gave me lots of opportunities over the next few years to learn more about Downeast Maine and to visit this far eastern part of Washington County. Although most of our work was done in libraries and data centers, I seized any chance to travel to what was usually referred to as the poorest part of Maine, if not all of New England.

In 1973, Eastport at first glance was certainly a most depressed-looking town with nearly half its storefronts closed or boarded up, no hotels, a few shabby restaurants, and little else. This town, actually a city, had a peak population of 5,300 in 1900 when it was a thriving port for herring, with numerous sardine factories employing eight hundred people or so. By 1970, there were less than two thousand residents. Since the 1930s as the herring either were overfished or had disappeared from coastal waters, jobs disappeared and times became tough.

The grandest scheme proposed for the area was from the Roosevelt administration and the New Deal to construct an enormous tidal dam that would produce great quantities of electricity and provide numerous construction jobs. Unfortunately, the plan was on such a large scale that it became a typical political football for the next thirty years with no action and nothing but disappointment for the local residents. Most learned how to subsist on seasonal jobs as much of rural Maine does...clams, blueberries, lobster and ground fish, as well as woods work. Much of the economy went underground where things like bartering was common and published data on per capita income were misleading. The present census data show a per capita income of $14,864 with seventeen percent of the population below the poverty level of $21,000.

Yet, as is the case in many such situations, these data just aren't true at all. As part of my study effort, I visited the home of a US Fish and Wildlife Service employee as I was looking for local fish data. His wife, assistant manager of the bank in town, said she recalled few, if any, repossessions of cars or snowmobiles for non-payment. Nearly everyone owned or paid on one or more such vehicles. There was certainly cash around, but Uncle Sam was none the wiser. As far as I could tell, no one went hungry and everyone lived comfortably even if it meant in some cases that husbands and wives were divorced or separated for tax purposes. Food stamps were quite rare. Few, I guessed, who had adapted to this way of life would be interested in the typical eight-to-five job. And I had heard that various attempts at light industry such as electronics had not prospered because of a lack of a reliable work force.

Over the next two years, Pittston pushed its proposed terminal with local pressure and connections. I regularly attended a number of hearings put on by Maine Department of Environmental Protection, in both Augusta and Eastport. Eastport residents were split over the issue at first. Some saw the influx of jobs and money as a possible boon after years of promises and disappointments. There was, however, a definite negative climate in Eastport. None of the proposed projects starting with the Passamaquoddy Dam had ever come to fruition. Even with the power of President Roosevelt who summered on nearby Campobello Island, no federal monies ever flowed their way.

To give a classic example, one morning before a hearing was to begin in Eastport, I was sitting on the end of a dock by the waterfront. It was a sparkling, clear and crisp Maine morning and I commented to a local inhabitant nearby about the beauty of the day. His reply took me by surprise. "Yeah," he said, "but we only get one or two of them a year." Talk about a glass being half empty! But as I was to learn, this was the general Eastport attitude: few, if any, economic promises ever came true.

The local newspaper, *The Quoddy Tides*, took a strong stand against the Pittston project and Pittston as a company. During my visits to Eastport I had gotten to know the editor's assistant, Marie , and her husband, Bob, a cantankerous but interesting retired geologist from the US Geological Survey. Both were originally from Washington, DC, first living in Eastport as summer people and now full-time residents. I spent time at their farmhouse along with their two sons Robert and John. Amy, Karyl, and I visited them several times in our summer vacations to Downeast.

The Pittston-Eastport oil terminal and refinery project dragged on for nearly ten years, long after I was involved. I had spent a great deal of time at hearings, reading environmental impact statements, and listening to the pros and cons. To bring large supertankers through the torturous and narrow Head Harbor Passage in Canadian waters would, in many experts' estimations, be suicidal and threatening to the thriving marine life of the Bay.

By 1983, Pittston finally withdrew its application, saying the cost of construction of the terminal and refinery had escalated from $350 million to $1 billion and it was unfeasible. The real reason Pittston withdrew was that the Canadian government was adamantly opposed to large tankers transiting through their territory and would never have permitted it. Yet long before this final resolution, Eastport had given up again and returned to its sleepy, territorial ways.

Eastport, Maine is a five hour drive from Portland either along coastal Route One or inland Route 9 better known as the "Airline." Eastport was the scene of a ten year battle over a proposed oil refinery.

The last time I visited, there were definite signs of a revitalized town, with nearly all stores open and a brighter future ahead without an oil terminal.

I had clearly benefited from the chance to see and experience a part of Maine that most visitors to the state and, in fact, many southern Maine residents never get to experience. With no commercial airports east of Bangor, the respective five hour and seven hour drives from Portland and Boston are too far for most would-be visitors. Karyl, Amy and I also drove out this way to visit friends we had known in Annapolis. Our next door neighbor, Anne May, had decided to flee the organized world, as many of the "back to the earth" people had in the early 70s. She, her three children, and newly acquired man friend, Bob Dale, had found an idyllic cabin in the woods and left their former lives in an escape. How romantic it sounded!

Bob, a rugged and resourceful pioneer type, had been a World War II Navy pilot and later the skipper of the National Science Foundation (NSF) ship, the *Hero*, sailing each year to the Antarctic. With Anne's help, he had made this summer camp into an acceptable year round dwelling on a salt water bay. The only trouble was that the cabin was a one-and-a-half mile hike from the nearest road in the small town of Pembroke, a town fifteen miles from Eastport. Bob had left his wife and children in Annapolis to join Anne on this adventure. Although Bob and his former wife had lived only a block from us on Market Street, I never knew them as a couple then.

Leaving one's family and dropping out was quite common in the early 70's, as I was to find out soon enough. With Bob and Anne, I believe, things started out pretty good, although I'm sure there were lots of strains. The children were home-schooled—no small task if done correctly. Living as they did far from the town, they weren't part of the community and were viewed as people "from away." Their car, parked by the trail head to their cabin, was vandalized several times. Tensions between Bob and Anne grew over time and sometime later, I'm not sure when, Bob moved out and went to live at the Lincoln House in nearby Dennysville.

I don't know how long Anne stayed on at the cabin. Long winters, unfriendly townspeople, harsh and somewhat primitive living conditions all contributed to their split. Karyl received letters from Anne describing the fights and disputes she had with Bob and I heard Bob's side some years later. The whole story was quite typical of such relationships: the thrilling escape from the real world to an idyllic life then the hard, reality set in.

Bob went on to buy an island in Woolwich, just north of Bath, where he built a log cabin for which he felled the trees, and lived there for many years. He and I are still close friends. More recently he and his wife Jean have moved into Brunswick on a lovely spot near Bowdoin College. Bob celebrated his 90th birthday in the fall of 2014.

Chapter Thirteen

Life in Maine

During our entire marriage, Karyl and I had led a somewhat nomadic life: Galveston, Amesbury, Annapolis, Miami, La Jolla, and now Maine. Much of the time, we were a long way from our parents, whom we saw perhaps once a year. My father had been going through tough times as the demand for book illustration declined and then disappeared altogether, leaving only a few magazines still interested in his work. This may have been an early indicator of harder financial times to come in the publishing business, as well as in many other areas.

Dad never would admit being in need of any financial assistance and I probably didn't do enough in trying to help him and my mother. But later on, I recall a few phone calls in which he asked for a small loan and I would send $100, not knowing what the need was. From what little I found in my mother's scribbled notes some years later, she had put up with a lot. My father was still drinking, enough that it interfered with his work and with life at home. One or two drinks were enough to make him sleepy and he would wander off to bed half way through dinner, much to Mother's consternation.

Around this time, he started avoiding paying his bills especially his taxes. I doubt that Mom knew about this, and at some point, the IRS came after him. He had been unable to face this problem and had thrown all his unpaid bills and tax returns into a cardboard box in his studio for well over a year. Like my mother, Karyl and I were totally unaware of the situation. We weren't the best at staying in touch with our parents; phones weren't used as much then.

Luckily for dad, a member of the Episcopal Church he and my mother attended, together with a member of Alcoholics Anonymous came to his rescue. Although I never knew who the churchgoer was, he was likely an accountant or IRS employee and realized my father's dilemma. With their assistance, my father's accounts were reconciled and he was in no further trouble with the IRS. And soon after, dad stopped drinking with the help of AA, and stopped smoking at the same time.

Shortly after these events in 1968, my parents decided it was time to sell the farm. My father had been commuting to Philadelphia a couple days a week to teach at Moore College of Art and the trip by train was becoming increasingly difficult, especially in the winter. He was now approaching seventy-three years of age and slowing down. And the mounting costs from deferred maintenance on the farm house and barn were worrisome.

It was hard to give up the country living, most of all for my mother, who thrived on this kind of life. The recent move from the quiet and serenity of Sugarbridge to the twentieth-floor city apartment in The Philadelphian wasn't easy. Prior to the final move, they stayed in temporary quarters in a fleabag hotel downtown and I helped them drag their suitcases down the street. Once they were comfortably planted in the new apartment with much of their antique furniture collection from the farm, they appeared to be much happier.

We visited them when we could. Amy loved the twentieth story of the apartment and the elevator ride even more than she liked motels. One of my fondest recollections of Philadelphia is walking with my father along the Schuylkill River. At seventy-four, he was beginning to have trouble with his feet. Unlike my mother, who loved to walk, my father began to walk less and less as he got older. As my father and walked together, I was reminded of our earlier Sugarbridge walks up the lane at dusk, a family ritual with a bounding dog and complaining cat trailing behind.

The location of The Philadelphian was ideal for my parents, especially my father, who was still teaching at Moore College of Art only a few blocks away. He'd been at this all-women's school for a number of years since leaving the Academy of Fine Arts. I met some of the students in Annapolis when he brought the class on a field trip.

Since his work had changed from book illustration to magazine drawings, he now took occasional jobs from editors like Roger Taylor and David Scott at the Naval Institute, although this work was hardly enough to support him. Thus, his teaching became more important. He loved working with the students; it kept him in touch with the field. And, in turn, they appreciated his help in starting their careers. At least one student from the Academy, Dorothy Gilman, became a somewhat famous mystery writer. She dedicated one of her books, *A New Kind of Country* (Doubleday, 1978) to my father: "For Edward Shenton, artist, author, editor, instructor-who taught us all how to see."

Dorothy and I corresponded in the late 1990s, but I never had a chance to see her at her home in Connecticut, as I had hoped. At her death in 2012, she had written nearly twenty-five spy novels with a large fan following.

I have such fond memories of my father, always kind and understanding and never punishing in any way. He was instructive, a good teacher and wonderful parent. Although he may have been physically slow and deliberate, he possessed a quick mind and true sense of integrity. And, of course, he adored his only granddaughter. Like some younger children, she had a habit of finger sucking at age three. My fa ther would say "finger out, raisin in," popping a raisin in her mouth each time. This positive approach worked and is one my daughter still remembers.

He also taught me how to shoot a rifle before I was ten and before I learned at summer camp. Having a gun on a farm was a very normal thing; all of us farm boys had one. Dad had been a marksman in the Great War. Although he never mentioned it, I found his medal in his belongings several years after his death.

My first gun was a BB rifle. We all had BB guns: Stacy Wood, Petey Edmiston, and my other country friends. An air gun that you cocked with either a pump handle or a lever, it was really fun to shoot. With a range of fifty feet, at best,. Petey once unwittingly shot at me and hit me in the back. No harm, but did it sting!

On my ninth birthday, I invited my whole class from the High Street School to Sugarbridge. Here my father had all the boys try target practice with my new BB gun.

My father was in charge of the shooting range on the farm. We shot at birds, rarely hitting them. I graduated to a .22 caliber Remington single shot rifle a few years later, used mostly for bottles and cans. Dad also had several pistols, which he never fired. Of the collection, my favorite was the .22 cal. long barrel for accurate target work. This had belonged to my grandmother, Pansy Sherwood Webster. She was the true "Annie-get-your-gun" gun-toter.

All these guns became mine in the late 1960s when my parents moved from Sugarbridge to Philadelphia. When the riots over civil rights broke out in 1968 in Washington, I decided I didn't need or want guns in my house. I donated them all to the police station in Annapolis. I later heard that in those days, the police may have given them to their friends and that the weapons might be on the street again.

My great aunt, Phoebe Thomas, with the deer she just shot and hung from a tree.

Roads End, Boothbay Harbor, Maine, the last address for my parents in 1973.

247

With great dismay, I watched the TV news coverage of the burned out buildings in the poorer sections of Washington. Later, I drove along those streets filled with boarded-up houses, thinking that guns only get you into trouble.

In the late 1960s, my father had become somewhat overweight, partly from less activity and likely also due to his alcohol consumption. In his final ten years he slimmed down a bit with remarkably few health issues. And by this time he had finally retired from Moore College.

I'm not certain whether Karyl and I convinced my parents it was time to consider a move to Boothbay Harbor or whether they got the idea first. Regardless, we looked about and found them a reasonably priced house almost on the water. The address, Roads End, always amused my father and, in fact, it was the end of the road for both of my parents about four years later. The house, three-bedroom and built at the turn of the century, was situated on nearly an acre set back one row from the water on the east side of town. For a reasonable $26,000 selling price, there was a good glimpse of the harbor from the front porch and second floor when the leaves were gone. And there was ample room for a garden for my mother, a hobby she had greatly missed during their Philadelphia sojourn.

I helped them with the move, far more simple this time since their current apartment had only two rooms. I rented a 24-foot U-Haul truck, the largest available and, with the help of several apartment employees, we began lugging furniture and boxes from the twentieth floor down the service elevator. Even though we packed everything tightly, it was clear that those two rooms were larger and filled with more belongings than I had realized and there was no way to make it all fit. So back I went to the rental agency and picked up a 14-foot trailer. Once packed up, we were bound for Maine with my parents following in their 1968 Volvo.

The truck and trailer was fine on the highway but no fun when I had to back up all thirty-eight feet of the rig. During a pit stop for gas on the Connecticut Turnpike, I noticed a couple standing on the exit ramp looking for a ride. Thinking it would be pleasant to have company for the trip, I stopped for them. They quickly explained that they were on their way to Lubec, Maine. They lived in the woods in a cabin outside of town, a perfect example of the back-to-the-earth wave of new settlers in the seventies. True to form, they introduced themselves as the Woodsfellows, a name they had adopted when they shed their urban skins in New York.

They had lots to talk about: eastern Maine, the environment, and people we knew in common. They had been married by a well-known minister in Lubec, whom, coincidentally, I knew since he was also an authority on shore birds and had been a contributor to TRIGOM's Pittston report. All our talk of eastern Maine made time fly by and soon we pulled into a parking lot in Sudbury, Massachusetts next to my mother-in-law's house and said goodbye to the Woodsfellows. I never ran across the Woodsfellows again but it had been fun and made a good story. The rest of the trip was uneventful.

About this time, Don Horton had landed a major job for TRIGOM with the US Bureau of Land Management (BLM) in Washington. The contract required us to collect all available data for areas around Georges Bank and put it into a report, as there was to be proposed exploratory drilling for oil and gas. It may have been a competitive bid but as a non-profit consortium, TRIGOM was a perfect entity because we had a large number of available scientists from universities that lent credibility to such studies.

The project was funded well enough to hire several dozen and respected scientists from all over New England. My role was coordinating these various people and assigning the tasks in areas such as sea birds, benthic fauna, and marine mammals. Then Don and I were to weave it into a complete report. There were to be no conclusions or opinions toward drilling for offshore oil, merely an assemblage of all available environmental and socio-economic data that would be useful in the decisions whether to drill or not on Georges Bank. Most of my time was spent editing and gathering the various consultants' papers for the final report. Karyl dubbed it "Deposits and Withdrawals From Georges Bank." The job lasted a full year.

By now, TRIGOM had grown and moved from our humble, cramped quarters in Portland to a much grander location on the campus of Southern Maine Vocational Technical Institute (SMVTI) in South Portland, which provided far more of a marine setting. We also had access to a biological lab there. It was a wonderful spot on hot summer days, being so close to the cool waters of Casco Bay. The only problem was that I lived sixty-five miles away. Working until midnight many nights, only to leave the next morning at six o'clock took a toll on me.

Chansonetta Stanley Emmons, noted photographer from Kingfield, Maine, sister of the famous Stanley brothers of the "Steamer". She was best known for photos of rural Maine scenes.

On days that I wasn't staying late at TRIGOM I carpooled with Boothbay colleagues. I was then driving the 1969 Saab 96 that I had bought when we first arrived in Maine. One of my riders, Stan Chenoweth, was a fisheries biologist who had been a longtime employee of the US Fish and Wildlife Service in Boothbay Harbor. When the lab closed in 1973, Stan had come to work at TRIGOM on the BLM project. He had grown up in the Harbor and was related to the Stanley brothers of Stanley Steamer fame along with their sister, Chansonetta Stanley Emmons (1858-1937), a noted photographer in the 1880s, also from Kingfield, Maine where most her now-famous photographs are held in the Stanley Museum.

My other rider was Peter Holmes, also a biologist, who taught at University of Maine at Portland. Peter lived on the River Road to Damariscotta, which was a bit of a detour on our run to Portland and South Portland. His old house and barn were typical of many Maine farmhouses in its weathered look and usually referred to as scrapped or ready to be painted, although they probably hadn't been painted in many decades. The house and barn were perpendicular to the road and in large, bold painted letters was the message "Come Home Mummy." It seems that Peter's wife would leave her home and children for somewhat extended periods. As the story goes, when she was expected home after one of her jaunts away, her kids painted on the weathered side of the barn in large bold, white letters, "Welcome Home Mummy." After some time, possibly weeks when she did not return and the kids were so disappointed, they went out and erased the "WEL." So forever, after there was the touching plea, "Come Home Mummy." Eventually, she did.

On some days we swapped around and rode in Peter's car, a small Chevy Chevette, known as a "Shovit." He had what we called a peanut habit and loved to shell and eat peanuts on his commute. I've been known to have the same habit. But Peter left all the shells on the floor of the car where they were three and four inches deep in certain places. Stan, in his quiet and down home way, never made a comment.

While working on the BLM project, I gathered an informal group of marine science colleagues together, which we called the New England Coastal Oceanographic Group (NECOG). I compiled a list of about ten or fifteen names, some fairly important in marine sciences and asked if they would be interested in consulting if I were to obtain small contracts. Most expressed some interest. To kick things off, I invited the group to my place in Southport. There were a number from Boston/Woods Hole, but Bob Ballard was the only one I can remember.

Bob was still easy to approach then and hardly the terribly important person he was to become after the discovery of the *Titanic* and all the *ALVIN* submersible events. Before the group's arrival, Karyl and I made a large stew pot full of haddock chowder to be served with biscuits. Although all those gathered listened politely to my pitch, nothing really came of NECOG at the time, but it was resurrected somewhat when I moved to Cutler years later.

After lunch, Bob and I strolled down in the small meadow by the stream behind my house. I had first met him when he was a Lieutenant while visiting Westinghouse as a Representative for the Office of Naval Research, Now at Woods Hole, he told me how his life of constantly being on research cruises had its downside. He was at sea at least nine to ten months a year even when WHOI flew the scientists home from far away places like Australia. He felt he had no home life. Of course, if he had not continued on that career path he never would become the famous person he is. Although I chatted briefly with Bob some years later when he was a featured speaker at the Explorers Club, I was glad to have had a chance to see his personal side.

About this time our BLM report was nearing completion and I had assumed the position, although informally, of deputy director under Don Horton. He had begun to formulate the concept of the Gulf of Maine Aquarium, a public aquarium in Portland to be operated by TRIGOM. This concept finally came to fruition in 2005, although not under Don Horton.

With the BLM project coming to a close, TRIGOM had succeeded and all was well with the world. It was September of 1975, and my life was about to change forever.

We were in the process of interviewing for a secretarial job in the TRIGOM office. Don and I usually both interviewed candidates in the kitchen, our makeshift conference room. Our most memorable candidate, a woman wearing a red and blue checked suit and white gloves, quite impressed me and we hired this "woman with the white gloves." And thus began my relationship with Judy Ellery Blaisdell.

Over the years, I had found a few women attractive in my various jobs. But right from the beginning, my work relationship with Judy was different. I had known Judy a very short time when she began to tell me the details of her life and marriages. Her eight-year-old son, John, and she were living with her second husband, Ernie Blaisdell, on what sounded like a very tenuous basis. She planned to move out at any moment.

Initially, I was flattered by her compliments and comments. I guess you could say I was ready for my midlife crisis and couldn't resist this pretty young thing more than ten years younger. We spent lunchtimes together, walking out on the breakwater toward Spring Point Lighthouse where we sat and ate. All seemingly harmless, yet I was being enchanted away and not resisting.

In the beginning, Judy wrote me letters, which I, in turn, answered. She had left Ernie and taken an apartment in South Portland not far from the TRIGOM office. I visited after work and took her son trick-or-treating on Halloween. Like an addict, I was hooked and decided to let the affair take its course. On one of my usual late nights, Judy invited me over to her old apartment for dinner where Ernie was still living. I'm not sure if he realized what was going on, but I felt most peculiar. And one afternoon, not long after, I got a desperate call from Judy that Ernie had attempted suicide, asking if I could come over to her apartment immediately and help her.

I was about to leave TRIGOM for home and had my rider, Stan Chenoweth, with me. Stan agreed to come along. By the time we arrived, Ernie had been taken away by ambulance and Judy with him. She had asked me clean up. What a mess! Ernie had tried to slit his wrists and bungled it in the bathroom. The walls ceiling and floor were covered with blood like a scene from a horror movie. Poor Stan, he'd never seen anything like this but with his quiet Maine way just grabbed some towels and we became good cleaners as the guys in *Pulp Fiction*. On the way home I tried to explain what was going on to Stan although I'm sure he didn't understand. The soap opera continued to play on.

In the meanwhile I continued my life in a normal way at home in Southport; Karyl was completely unaware of my affair. I could have (and should have) told Judy that this closeness was getting out of hand and just said goodbye. But I was too weak or maybe too entwined so I let things proceed. Judy suggested that we run away from it all and we chose Alaska. It didn't really dawn on me that this was going to be a disaster in my life and more so to Karyl and Amy. Reason and good sense had been abandoned. Up to this point, Judy and I shared nothing more than a few kisses and handholding.

The next stage was "The Plan." Like two high school kids about to elope, we sat and plotted our escape; hers from an unhappy marriage and mine, hardly an unhappy marriage, more for the excitement of an adventure. How was I just to decide to disappear? Here one day and gone the next? Furthermore, winter was upon us as we entered November. I had wood to split and lots of fall chores at home. And one of my political friends proposed that I run for the Maine legislature, an exciting idea in itself.

To raise money for this Alaskan escape, which now suddenly became real, I had decided to sell my cherished 1957 Mercedes classic 220S driven all the way from California — a car that I had so lovingly cared for. Karyl seemed oblivious to this. Judy and I planned to take a bus cross country to Seattle using the Greyhound $76 fare to anywhere in the nation, in honor of the country's Bicentennial anniversary. Through my connection I had with Bill Reed and his coastal planning business in Gardiner, I was offered a job in his Juneau office as a Program Manager. Thus, we had a goal and maybe a job. But what about Karyl and Amy, not to mention my aging and not too well parents in Boothbay Harbor? I could find no way to tell them of my intentions, coward that I was!

On Veteran's Day, under the guise of working at TRIGOM, although it was a holiday, I went to Portland, and of all things, I took Amy along. She and I met Judy and her son, John. We took the Casco Bay ferry on an island trip to Peaks Island and Long Island. I had found out earlier that Judy had spent her younger years on Peaks. Strolling the beaches of Long Island that chilly November day seemed surreal and bizarre, as I think back on it, making my daughter a partner in my crime. Amy and John had a great time playing on the beach. John remembers his first meeting with Amy, two years older than he. He kept asking her "How old are you?" It became one of our favorite family jokes years later.

My wonderful 1957 Mercedes 220 which I bought in San Diego for $950 from a Navy chief and drove to our new home on Southport Island.

The previous night, I had attended an Armistice Day celebration at the American Legion in the Boothbay Harbor where my father was the featured speaker. It was wonderful to hear him, as I had many times before, tell of the night that he his brother, Don, were waiting for a train in a French railway station. It was near midnight and only a handful of people were there. Among them was a typical peasant woman in traditional black clothes with a shawl and a basket on her arm. At this moment, the startling news of the Armistice ending the Great War was announced. There was a moment of silence followed by much jubilant celebration. Then, in slow motion as if rehearsed, the woman wanting to be a part of this joyous occasion, took one egg at a time from her basket and tossed it up in the air, each one landing with a resounding splat as all there watched in silence. The group of old timer vets in Boothbay listening were moved, as was I.

That evening I returned to my home in Southport after a day on the Casco Bay islands. I had fallen in love with my secretary, decided to leave behind my whole life, nice home, loving wife and daughter for another woman. That evening after dinner, I finally felt I had to say something to Karyl. I partially confessed that I had met with Judy that day. Naturally, she was shocked and implored me to do the right thing, get a hold of myself, and put an end to the affair.

The next morning, I went off to work in Portland with a faint resolve to do just what Karyl had said. Instead, I picked up Judy at her apartment and I told her of last evening's events. I could have still firmly said "No, I'm not going," but I didn't. Instead, she said that we have to leave at once, that very day and I caved in. I really wanted the adventure, the heck with the consequences.

Things began to fall into place except at that critical moment as we were riding in my 1969 Saab, my master hydraulic cylinder failed. It meant the clutch pedal didn't work at all. I had learned long ago how shift without the clutch and somehow we made it to my bank in South Portland, where I withdrew everything from our joint account. Judy did the same with hers. I was reminded of a scene from *Divorce American Style* where the runaway couple does the same thing. I felt like a criminal.

Chapter Fourteen

I Run Away from Home

Our impromptu plan called for us to take the first leg in our cross country trip to Boston where we would stay with Judy's sister, Marcia Ellery and regroup. Before we left Portland, I called Karyl and told her in a very matter of fact way that I was parking the car at the bank parking lot and Judy and I were leaving for Alaska. Talk about an abrupt and cowardly way to leave! I had stashed a backpack with a few personal items at Judy's. By early afternoon, we were on a Greyhound bus to Boston and I felt even more like a criminal making an escape.

We arrived at Marcia's apartment in Cambridge. Marcia cared for Mique Kennedy, an elderly man in his 70s, who lived in her apartment. I enjoyed Mique immensely for his wise and sage outlook on life. Part Native and part African American, Mique received various government benefits, including a stipend for Marcia's caretaking services. In a quirky story, Mique, always fuming at the outrageous prices stores charged for spices, once hid a handful of various spice bottles under his poncho and left the store without paying for them, with Marcia prepared to say her "uncle" was a bit daft.

While Marcia and Mique may have privately wondered about our wild escapades, they didn't show it and were most supportive of our adventure. Judy and I left for New York the next afternoon but missed our connection to Chicago and had to spend the night in the New York City Greyhound bus terminal, definitely a weird experience. In 1975, there were a lot of drifters, street people, and assorted homeless persons who were allowed to spend the night in the bus station. Sometime around midnight, the police herded everyone into a holding room and gates were locked so no one could come or go. It wasn't clear whether we were being held or protected. Although there were a few benches; many of these loud, drunk, or sleepy people lay on the floor, seemingly just one step from jail.

Early the next morning, we were released to the regular and much more pleasant waiting room. We took the nine o'clock bus that morning, sat in the way back and discussed our nebulous future in Alaska. In previous assignments, I had been sent to Alaska several years earlier to study fisheries and remote sensing, traveling to Juneau, Kodiak, and Fairbanks. The prospect of returning was exciting but under the circumstance of having a new partner, I found it a bit scary.

We arrived in Chicago early the next morning with a short layover. Our next bus took us all the way to Minneapolis late that night where we spent the night in a nondescript hotel. The following day found us rolling along through the beginning of the real west with enormous expanses of wide open plains and prairie I recalled from all my previous trips. We were on the northern route, now showing signs of an early winter. The bus driver expertly wheeled his bus through windy passes, and later in the day we started up the long slope to the Rockies. On each new leg of our trip Judy and I made a special effort to be first on board the bus for the best seats the first row on the right where we would have a full panoramic view ahead, a true bargain for just $76 each. Every four hours the bus stopped at a restaurant or gas station; most of the stops offered barely edible food, but it was a good chance to stretch. The farther west, the quainter it became. In one of the tiny towns where we stopped, I went into the men's room and saw two very western looking boots, toes up, connected to a pair of jeans, and sprawled, out cold, in one of the stalls.

When we finally pulled into Seattle it was a perfect clear day, with all the pale buildings shining in the bright sunlight, unlike the typical picture I had of the Pacific Northwest as being eternally rainy and raw. We felt the sunshine was a special treat just for us. We immediately went to Seattle-based Recreational Equipment Inc. (REI), the catalogues of which we'd studied back on the east coast. I had always wanted a decent pair of hiking boots and found some rugged Raichle imports for about $125, which was a lot at the time. Judy thought that I was too casual in my Maine clothes so she insisted that I be presentable for my interview in Juneau the next day. Although I knew from my previous visit that Alaska was even more informal than Maine, she convinced me that I must look presentable. I went along with it, next visiting a clothing store where I bought a nice tweed jacket.

Our next leg of the trip was a flight on Alaska Air, which turned out to be a true adventure, at least for me. Night began early as it does in the north in November with shortened days. As we approached the Juneau Airport the pilot gave a little speech, which I'm sure was well known by the regulars aboard on this run. He asked us to be sure our seat belts were good and tight. The only way into Juneau at that time involved a somewhat dramatic maneuver in which our 727 put its wings straight up and down as it threaded its way in a narrow opening between two mountains. I loved it but I could see Judy was, to say the least, a bit alarmed. A moment later we leveled out and swooped into the airport, a neat trick. They've since modified the approach; a less exciting but safer route into Juneau.

The next day we made our way to the office of the Center for Natural Areas (CNA), located in an old ramshackle house on the edge of town. As I suspected, I was overdressed and felt like a city slicker, not the best way to start. The man in charge was quite young and dressed in jeans and old boots. He quickly informed me that the job involved taking whatever environmental data were available and massaging it to suit the customer who was looking for a permit to build or develop. This immediately put me off as I was not a so-called "data bender." I had encountered a similar situation years before at Texas A&M. We had been collecting river flow data on the Mississippi River and our customer had asked us to change the survey dates by several months to coincide with grant funding period, a gross violation of our integrity. We scientists refused to submit the data and I wasn't happy with the prospect of this sort of manipulative science again.

Judy and I were given a room to stay in at the office, a small attic loft reached by a ladder. From the single window we could look out over the snow-covered town below us. It was certainly picturesque, but I was distinctly unsettled about the prospect of this job, as well as my new relationship. As I lay there gazing at the town, I was suddenly overwhelmed that it was all wrong and that I couldn't go through with the job, the unfamiliar location, and my new life and partner. I said, "I've got to go back home, it's no good!" We apologized to our hosts and left the next day.

And so, in one brief period, we came and went. Maybe it was just as well, I thought, and not meant to be. We flew back to Portland, and, unsure what to do next, I spent a few days back at Southport with Karyl and Amy.

A number of start-overs followed, and it finally became clear to me that the rift between Karyl and me was irreconcilable. I was still captivated by Judy, as much as I knew I should be returning to my family. Just before Thanksgiving, Judy convinced me to dash off on another wild trip. We were staying with Marcia and Mique again in Boston and decided to take a "drive-away" car to the west coast. We had seven days to deliver a not-so-fancy older car to San Francisco. Given $75 for food and gas, we set upon a marathon cross country trip as winter approached. Near the end of the drive, we stopped in Palm Springs on Thanksgiving Day, rode up the tram to the mountain-top restaurant and walked up San Jacinto Mountain, my old California haunt. We arrived in San Francisco late in the evening on time, then climbed aboard the bus for another long ride home.

This time, returning home was far less fun. Karyl and I attempted to restart our relationship with a trip to Quebec over the New Year's holiday. We had reservations at a small, inexpensive hotel in the old city fittingly blanketed in snow. Karyl tried in every way to get our marriage back on track to no avail. I simply couldn't see fitting myself back into my former life. And I was still infatuated with Judy and an exciting new life.

Some weeks later, Judy and I took a third and final West Coast trip in our last attempt to escape to a different place. We drove my weary, old white 1996 Saab 96 to San Diego in the hope of finding work and a place in the West that I had so liked years before. I had bought the car when Karyl and I first arrived in Maine and by now, it had logged more than 250,000 miles and was becoming somewhat unreliable. The interminable driving on my part was offset by Judy, who sat quietly, knitting a heavy green sweater for me, one that I still have.

In San Diego I looked up my old friend, Bob Brown, whom I'd worked for in 1972 at Plessey. Like most of us, he'd changed jobs several times. We had a pleasant luncheon visit but he was vague at best about any promising job opportunities. We stayed several days but soon grew discouraged and, a little like the Alaskan trip of the previous fall, we quickly cut and ran. On the return trip the car's starter quit entirely and, not wanting to stop and find one of the few places that repaired Saabs, we made sure to park on a hill whenever we stopped to eat or sleep so we could coast down and start. This trick became a bit of a feat in some of the flat Midwest towns.

During this period there was yet one more relocation attempt. Somehow, we thought we could make a start in Eastport, Maine, an improbable place due to location and its repressed economic state. In the dead of winter, with her father's blessing, we loaded his old, blue 1966 Chevy truck with furniture and headed to Eastport where we had seen an ad for a cheap house to rent. Unfortunately, the house was cold, old, and in need of considerable repair, a daunting venture at this time of year. While we considered the size of the job ahead, we rented a room at a boarding house on the water. After several days of evaluating the house we were to rent, we decided it was more than we wanted to tackle.

In January 1975 Judy, John, and I rented the second and third floor of a house in Augusta.

For a few weeks, Judy had gone back and forth with Ernie, her ex, and I had also been living off and on back in Southport, as well as staying with Peter Larson, who was also separated from his wife. Now, in the middle of winter, Judy and I decided to live in Augusta. I had resigned my job in Portland at TRIGOM when Judy and I first left for Alaska, but I found some temporary consulting work with the Natural

Resources Council and the state Planning Office. We found a two floor apartment across the river on a quiet street just off Route 17. These were stressful times for everyone involved.

In the meantime, Karyl had decided to begin divorce proceedings, a process I didn't look forward to. Suddenly, I felt like the bad guy on the wrong side of the law. She picked a local Boothbay lawyer, Stan Tupper, who was a former US Congressman. Interestingly, Pete Welles had been an aide to him in Washington some years back.

During all these wild excursions, Judy's son was being lovingly cared for and looked after by his grandparents, John and Jan Ellery, in Dover-Foxcroft, the small mill town north of Bangor where Judy had grown up. Poor fellow, he had been yanked around from one place to another ending up in five different schools during his fifth grade year. When we settled down in Augusta, John came to live with us. Amazingly, he survived it all and seemed unaffected by all the moves.

That spring, we rented a small house in South Harpswell, about ten miles south of Brunswick, almost at the end of the peninsula on the water. The two-story house sat on a windy point of land with a spectacular view down the bay toward Portland. In fall, John began school at Harpswell Elementary.

It was always ten degrees cooler in South Harpswell than in Gardner where I was now working. We had a large grass yard with a dock at the end and boats could only dock at high tide. It was heaven with the constant seagull cries when we awoke in the morning.

In the spring of 1975 Judy, John, and I moved to a rented house in South Harpswell on a windy point by the sea.

That fall, I convinced Judy's father to loan us the 12-foot sailing dinghy he used at Sebec Lake. Built by Grumman, it was known as a Widgeon, and had a sloop rig. I set it out on a mooring off the dock and sailed as often as I could. One day, John, Judy and I sailed out to nearby Haskell Island. We landed on the large island, walked a ways, and found a farm, vacant and beautiful, the sort of place Judy had always dreamed of.

That fall also brought us a particularly stormy night with strong southwesterly winds and seas. I stood on the dock trying to see if our little sailboat was still out there, but couldn't see anything in the rain, wind, and dark. I worried all night. When I awoke the next morning, the borrowed boat was gone! The storm had cleared out and it was a crystal clear day with a northwesterly breeze. I wandered to the end of the cove, and amazingly there was the Widgeon, floating upside down in a mass of flotsam and seaweed, mast broken away from the step. Luckily I found all the parts, from tiller to rudder. I promised John Ellery that I would have it fixed soon. I learned my lesson: borrowing things is always risky.

Around this time in 1977, I heard that my old friend, Colby roommate of two years, and sailing colleague, Pete Welles, had died at the very early age of 46. I attended the reception in Boothbay at the family home of his wife, Peggy Luke. Pete was one of the first of my many friends to "shuffle off" in an untimely fashion. In a way, it was not a surprise. Pete had always felt he would die young, like his father; Big Pete had died from a heart condition. Over the years, Pete had become a sort of recluse. Even though he and Peggy only lived a short drive away, I rarely saw him. When he came home at night from his job in Augusta, he turned off his phone and was incommunicado.

John, age 11, Judy 33, and Amy 13 at the South Harpswell house.

Amy came to visit us in South Harpswell, although somewhat against her mother's better judgment. Karyl wouldn't let her stay overnight since Judy and I weren't married. Amy and John began an important sibling relationship that has lasted over the years. As both are only children, each filled a need for the other.

I continued to work at the Natural Resources Center, but I had also started my own consulting group which we called NECOG again, with an office in Brunswick right on Route 1. My partner in this venture was Garret Clough, a small-mammal biologist who specialized in island fauna. He and I and many others had taken on a large contract with the US Fish and Wildlife Service that involved some twenty scientists and a Cambridge consulting company. Stuart Fefer, the project leader, became a good friend and later moved nearby when we moved east to Cutler years later. Similar to the TRIGOM contract for the Bureau of Land Management, the project was called "An Ecological Characterization of the Coast of Maine" and later became a long report of six large volumes.

My job at NRC was winding down. In May, my work friend, Terry DeWan, mentioned that a house and a large lot of land was up for sale in Bowdoin, a half mile from where he and his wife lived. He said the house was still occupied by a large family in the stages of being evicted, and if I were interested I should contact a realtor in Lewiston. He drew me a sketch of the long narrow lot that had a house and barn near the road. At $13,500, the house was quite cheap but in need of major work.

It wasn't until sometime in October, that Judy, and I were able visit the place. The farm was at the end of a long, paved road in the town of Bowdoin but closer to Lisbon Falls. From the end of the paved road, a dirt path continued up a steep rocky hill that had once gone all the way through to the other part of the town. After the fire of 1947, a major fire which burned vast parts of the state, the road was abandoned. This dead end became one of the many that I lived on throughout my life. With the house came ninety-one acres complete with a pasture and a thin, sparse cedar growth that ended at a pretty beaver pond.

The house, a barely recognizable Cape-style building, was run down and in serious need of roof repair, paint, siding, and as we were to find out, much more.

It had a central chimney and, based on our first view, appeared to have been built between 1780 and 1810. On the side of the house, the current occupants had created their own personal dump, piled high with trash, used vinyl siding, and appliances. The barn was a nondescript small structure with several stalls. In the pasture behind the barn, lay an amazing collection of nine junk cars, mostly worthless, except for the 1955 Nash Metropolitan, a collectible English mini convertible. As I saw it, the house had real restoration possibilities, but the rest of the farm was a disaster.

Our next project was the dilapidated old house in Bowdoin with 91 acres. It needed serious repairs when we bought it in the fall of 1975.

As we discovered, Mockler, the former tenant had rented from his father-in-law but became delinquent in his payments. He had a horde of children from babies to near-adults; we counted as many as nine mattresses on the second floor in pretty squalid conditions. Mockler was in the vinyl siding business and at the end of each day, dragged home a truckload of scraps and dumped them in swale beside the house, amidst the old stoves, refrigerators, and other junk in what appeared to be a bottomless pit.

By mid-1976, Karyl and I had reached an amicable divorce settlement. I had readily agreed to pay child support for Amy and to let Karyl keep the house and its stable environment rather than try to split or sell the house. Out of the guilt I felt from my abrupt departure, I gave her everything in the house except my personal belongings. Luckily for Amy there had been very little contention between Karyl and me.

Karyl had met an attractive man at this time who worked at *The Times Record* in Brunswick where she had her cooking newsletter "Cook and Tell" printed. Bob Bannister came along just when Karyl needed a mate and helper. She and Bob hit it off perfectly and soon after were married. Bob, a tall, trim man, and former Marine, was more mild-mannered than tough, and seventeen years older than Karyl. He was also a big help in raising Amy, who had now begun to spell her name "Amie." I was most happy for Karyl.

Over the years I became good friends with both Karyl and Bob on my occasional visits to Southport. When I was working in Brunswick, one of the locals commented that Bob Bannister might be a bit older but "he still had a spring in his step."

262

By the fall of 1976, both Judy and I had jobs. She was working at General Electric in South Portland as a secretary and I was coordinating the scientists on the Fish and Wildlife contract out of my office in Brunswick. With both of us working we were able to get a bank mortgage for the Bowdoin house and paid the asking amount of $13,500. Mockler was finally evicted in November. We never met him nor wanted to. I still have his hard hat with his name crudely carved in the metal. From what we'd heard, he was a borderline criminal.

The house and environs were a mess with rooms full of old clothes, trash, and broken furniture. What's more, Mockler was a lousy engineer. He had cut the ridge pole of the roof to put in a large dust-pan dormer so the roof sagged badly and, of course, it leaked. Nor was Mockler a good plumber because the sewage drained into the cellar through a broken pipe; whether by design or accident, we'll never know. The well, not far from the house, was contaminated, which meant we had to drill a new one.

To say the least, we had our work cut out for us that winter. We spent considerable time commuting from South Harpswell to Bowdoin on weekends. During this time, we lost an old friend, but gained a new relationship. One snowy Sunday afternoon, we were driving Amie back to her mother's in my old trusty blue 1950 Chevy pickup truck, all four of us crowded in the front seat. The road was snowy but not overly slippery. As we entered a sharp turn, a car coming the other way side swiped us. Luckily, none of us was injured, just shaken, but the truck was totaled. It was clearly the other driver's fault, but as we found out, he was uninsured and we were told it was not worth trying to take him to court.

It was a sad day; the truck had been a good and faithful friend for several years. It was towed to The Airport Garage in Brunswick, the same junkyard where I had bought my second Maine car in 1952, the 1941 blue Ford convertible. The next day I returned to collect a check for $25, all it was worth as junk. The Airport Garage, just across the road from the now decommissioned Naval Air Station, is still in business today as a used car lot.

Around this time, Judy and I got married. I remember sitting in church in early December when Judy smiled at me and said quietly that we should get married. We engaged a justice of the peace on Bailey Island, and while John and Amie stood by as our witnesses, we were married that evening. We invited Peter Larsen and a friend to join us for a celebratory dinner, and met them at a restaurant in Lewiston with a salad bar in an old vegetable truck. Now that we were "official," Amie could stay with us overnight.

That winter, George Cabot, who worked with Judy at GE, asked us to help unload a tractor trailer that was to deliver the lumber for a house he was building. We showed up on a chilly morning and worked most of the day, unloading heavy timbers off the 45-foot trailer. That day, we became acquainted with the driver, a friendly man named Dave Sycamore, and we decided to all go to dinner. Realizing that I was intrigued with his truck, he let me drive the ten miles or so to the restaurant. It was a big thrill and something I'd always wanted to do, shifting through all the gears in a big rig. Dave returned to our home with us and spent the night. We had a long discussion on eccentric things like the hollow earth theory, and he left me a book by L. Ron Hubbard, the founder of Scientology. When he left the next day, he said he'd take me on a long distance drive out west, but I never followed up with him.

The extensive renovation continued regardless of the season. As soon as spring arrived, one of our friends in Brunswick, Zandy Clarke, a fine carpenter, rebuilt the roof rafters on the house. He also installed two Velux rotating skylights that gave the upstairs more light and fresh air and a few bugs, since screens were lacking. Judy and I spent a number of days nailing the Grade A cedar shingles on the roof.

With a whole new roof structure, there was now room for insulation. Through her GE connection, Judy obtained surplus boiler insulation in heavy bats of asbestos. Back in those days, before the disclosure of asbestos and its danger of lung cancer, we nonchalantly hung the bats, amid coughing and wheezing.

Judy usually carpooled with George, and he helpfully volunteered to do all the wiring for free. He was going through a divorce and had lots of time to help us. He even took time to make me a large wooden tool box which, I'm happy to say, I still own and use.

I inspect the roof afters after the hideous dormer is removed.

After the roof, we replaced all the siding with high-grade cedar clapboards. Next came the drywall and mud, which we also did ourselves. We took great pleasure documenting the renovation in numerous photo albums.

A few times during the reconstruction, we wondered if we had taken on too much. On one day in particular, before the roof was complete, we arrived to see the entire roof open to the rain and looking like a war disaster site. Mercifully, it all began to come together in late spring. Even Judy's parents, who visited one day when things were still a mess shook their heads and said they were glad it wasn't their problem. Later, when things had vastly improved, they admitted we had done a good job.

We spared no detail in keeping the building specifications as authentic as possible. When we nailed the clapboards, we were careful to space them exactly as was done in seventeenth and eighteenth century houses, and as I had done in Amesbury. This craftsmanship also provided better protection from the snow in winter. On our weekend travels, we found an ancient, eighteenth-century paneled door with its original latch, which we used for the front door.

Inside, we decided to modernize the kitchen and bathroom. Since there was no septic system and quite a mess outside, we chose to go with an Ecolet composting toilet similar to one our South Harpswell landlord had installed. For heat, we had installed a Jotul box stove in green enamel which was amply capable of heating the whole house, but there was no backup heat if we wanted to leave the house for a length of time.

Our new home now complete in spring of 1976.

By the following June, our project in Bowdoin began to look like a proper house, stained dark brown with a barn red front door and window trim and we moved in full-time once John's school was out for summer. The last major item was the mess in the backyard the open dump left to us by the Mockler bunch. Unable to find anyone to excavate the mass of garbage, we hired a local Bowdoin contractor to fill the swale with some 300 cubic yards of sand and gravel. Some twenty-fifth century archeologist will undoubtedly have a field day exhuming the Mockler trash pile.

On the other side of the house to the west, we started a large vegetable garden which Judy and I had looked forward to after having none in our other places. Now, all we needed with our barn was a few animals, which currently consisted of Tasha, the Samoyed dog and Wiggy, our orange Maine coon cat. Tasha immediately loved the farm and unlimited space to roam outside.

In search of additional farm animals, we went to the Common Ground Fair in September. That fair was still in the original location, in nearby Litchfield and sponsored by Maine Organic Farmers and Growers Association. The fair, in its third year, was also still small and very much a genuine country event featuring animals and all aspects of farm life in Maine, right down to the chicken throwing contest that John and Amie had decided to enter.

In hindsight, it seems a bit cruel, especially for the chicken. The goal was to see who could throw a live chicken the farthest distance. Naturally, the kids won, and the prize was you guessed it the poor traumatized chicken, who came home with us. Unfortunately, the chicken didn't last a day. Somehow our dog, Tasha, got hold of it, leaving behind only pile of feathers and a mangled carcass. Believing that once Tasha got the taste of fowl, she could become a menace to our farm neighborhood, we felt she would do better elsewhere. We were lucky to find a woman from Lewiston who had been looking for a Samoyed. Although Tasha was a friendly and loveable dog, she wasn't easy to train. The woman immediately decided to take her anyway.

Life in Bowdoin was good; we had a small and interesting community. Our neighbors included the Obertausch family next door, with kids John and Amie's age. They all played together with Olivia, a girl who lived on the farm across the road. A little further along the road was a lawyer, Mike and his wife, Mary Beth who operated a large cattle farm. Their property was one of the original houses on the road, dating from 1750, and was in good condition. Terry and Nancy DeWan, who had been responsible for getting us there in the first place, lived across the road. Terry and I had decided to leave the rat race of the Center for Natural Areas and about the same time. Terry had begun his own landscape design business which became quite successful, sometime later involving me on a couple of collaborative jobs. Nancy, a weaver who raised goats and llamas for the wool sold her goods at her shop in Freeport. Beyond our place to the east, up the rough, dirt track that once was a road, another couple were just starting to build a small shed roofed cabin where the navigable road ended. And not far from Terry there was a dairy farm where we went buy delicious raw milk, a treat not readily available in supermarkets.

By the winter of 1976-77, the house was complete and warm and livable. Rather than hire someone to plow the driveway snow, I opted to buy an old plow truck specifically for that job. I'd always wanted one. I found the perfect truck listed in the statewide *Uncle Henry's Swap or Sell It* weekly publication, a 1953 GMC one-ton stake bed with a plow. I paid $700 for it, and I didn't care that it was old and tired or that it had dual wheels with split rims and probably needed a lot of maintenance. It did the job with snow and, as it turned out, provided endless trips for our next move. My other joy, and must-have toy, was the Farmall tractor with a cutter bar. I didn't do much grass or hay mowing but used the power takeoff to run a large saw for all the cord wood for our Jotul stove.

The first winter I found a very used GMC one-ton stake bed truck with dual wheels and a plow. It was worth all of the $700 because it made more than 20 trips when we moved to Cutler the next year.

During winter school vacation while John visited his grandparents, Judy and I decided to take a trip to Prince Edward Island. I found the idea of seeing this island in the middle of winter intriguing. We drove bravely in the old Saab 96, and left the house on its own, unheated. The most memorable part of the journey was the ferry ride to PEI. Normally a 20-minute ride, on this occasion the ice was thick and the ferry had a slow go of it. With a great amount of grinding and crunching, the ferry worked its way backing and then running forward until it stopped. After two and half hours, we finally made it.

The snow on the island was about four feet deep, much like central Maine. We stayed in one of the only motels open, a jolly but bitterly cold adventure. As we drove out in the country, we noticed the extremely long driveways to most farms. Some were a quarter to a half mile long. Some plowed, some not. Our four days were fun and satisfied my winter craving.

267

That spring, we tried our hand at making maple syrup from the trees right out in front of the house. As usual, we learned the hard way that one doesn't attempt to boil the sap indoors on the stove. The house became sodden with excess moisture in no time, so we moved the operation out front boiling down many gallons of sap to make quarts of syrup. It was an extremely labor intensive process, but yielded good results.

It was around this time that my mother became increasingly ill with cancer. She had become interested in Christian Science through Karyl, and was receiving help from a local practitioner. During this time my mother made several trips and visits to Maine Medical Center and later to the Christian Science Benevolent Association in Chestnut Hill, near Boston; on a few occasions, Judy and I drove her there. Her absence was understandably hard on my father; he depended heavily on her and didn't do well by himself.

We visited their house on Road's End as much as we could, often finding my father on cold winter mornings sitting on the side porch, bundled up in his down jacket reading or just looking at the frozen harbor. When it seemed unlikely that mother would be able to return home, and realizing he needed more care that we could give, we took him to several different nursing homes, finally settling on one in Freeport. I soon learned what deplorably depressing places they are, mostly full of near dead and dying old women. I felt so guilty leaving dad there. Two or three days later he called, with a desperate plea: "Get me out of here!" Soon after, we discovered that because he was a veteran of World War I, he was fully covered at the local Veterans Hospital in Togus, about fifteen miles east of Augusta. He seemed to actually enjoy being there and was certainly well cared for.

During the spring of 1977, I visited my mother in Chestnut Hill and dad in Togus. My father at this time had also shown an interest in Christian Science and had been attending the Society in Boothbay Harbor for some time before going to the VA Hospital. Physically, he appeared fine, but he felt he had little to live for and missed my mother terribly, as I later found in the bittersweet and sad letters they wrote one another.

With spring came the planting of a large garden to the west of the Bowdoin house. To save money, I had disconnected our telephone and for several weeks we had lived comfortably without a phone. On June 7, in the midst of gardening tasks, Terry DeWan drove up in a rush to tell me that my mother was on the phone at his house half a mile up the road. I vividly recall taking the call at his house; mom sounded very distant and somewhat faint-voiced. She said that in so many words she felt she was ready to "depart." We spoke briefly, in a surreal way. About two or three hours later the Benevolent Association informed me that she had passed on. It was not a surprise, but a gentle parting with no grief.

The harder part was what to tell my father, who by this time was barely communicating with us when we visited the VA Hospital; he was mostly asleep. It seemed best to say nothing because I was sure he knew somehow she had died. He hung on for less than two weeks. I went to Chestnut Hill to retrieve my mother's belongings but found that her rather beautiful wedding band, a gold octagonal ring, had disappeared. I never knew if she had died with it; I would have loved to have had it to remember her by.

About a month later, her friends from Boothbay, mostly Christian Scientists, held a lovely memorial service in their house at Roads End with appropriate readings. At the end someone read from her book *The Color of The Country*, the Chapter "The Best is Yet To Be." As she wrote in 1947, "I'll live, no doubt, like all my family, to an outrageously advanced old age." Yet, at 77 years, she didn't. Still, the thoughts she expressed in that last chapter were a fitting epitaph.

Mother and dad were both cremated. Judy and I spread the ashes in a little private ceremony in the side yard at the house in Bowdoin on the recently planted blueberry bushes.

We kept their memory alive in our house with some of their furniture, antiques and artwork that I had grown up with and valued. The remainder of their estate was sold, with some of the proceeds going toward a new Saab 99. Since I was the sole heir the estate was quickly settled.

My mother left an inspiring legacy of her writings and artwork She had written and published ten books, a number of articles, and several hundred columns that appeared in the *Philadelphia Evening Bulletin* and other various newspapers. She left me untold manuscripts and pieces in her inscrutable handwriting, and a number of oil paintings starting with those from the Academy to the years at Sugarbridge. She had started a more personal biography in her last year but it only began with her St. Louis childhood. Her later works, all about country living, should be republished; much of it is still fresh and relevant. In 2013, I wrote a biography of her life as a companion booklet to the one I had written on my father in 2010. Her story was part of a talk I later gave to the Friends of Gladys Taber Society in West Chester, Pennsylvania.

My father left even a greater legacy of his illustrations and writings, the collection of which I have curated and exhibited in various libraries, museums and schools. I truly regret spending so little time with my parents in their last days. I wish I had been able to ask them all the questions that I failed to ask. I had hoped to eventually tape record interviews with each of them but time escaped us.

Now, with the house complete, it was time for the next chapter. I began to see that Judy became restless at times; she was driven by having a goal or mission, while I was content where we were. I called it the "spring nesting urge" and knew only too well that soon she would start looking at places where we could move next. On weekends we loved to take long car rides through the countryside exploring new places, usually with John along. He, of course, like any youngster was extremely bored sitting in the back seat. He continued to be most capable of entertaining himself, reading books during our drives. On several of these trips, Judy commented that we needed more space in a bigger house for all the new furniture and artwork, foreshadowing our next move.

Chapter Fifteen

We're Off to Cutler

In the summer of 1977, Judy and I decided to roam through eastern Maine toward The County, as Aroostook County, the largest of Maine's sixteen counties is known. As we drove north from Calais, leaving the wooded and unpopulated area of Washington County and entered Aroostook County, the land opened onto an enormous plain of rolling hills mostly designated for potato crops. Trees were scarce. We spent an entire day there, overwhelmed by its vastness. Returning south the following day, Judy suggested we visit Cutler Harbor, an idyllic coastal town in eastern Washington County, where the sun first rises in the natiion. Her uncle, Richard Ellery, an artist and half-brother of her father, John, spent his summers there in a cottage by the water. A visit to meet Uncle Dick sounded like fun and as it turned out, most propitious. We headed south for the cool air of the coast.

Dick lived along a narrow and rocky dirt road that climbed over a steep hill down to a house where he had added a large studio. With high ceilings and a spectacular north-facing window directly overlooking the harbor, it was the sort of setting artists crave for both perfect light and view. A somewhat successful painter, Dick was a flamboyant and entertaining person with a succession of wives, all of whom he had managed to outlive. His current wife was from Switzerland, where they spent most of their time.

From our vantage viewpoint, Dick pointed out an inn across the bay in Cutler Harbor and casually mentioned it was for sale. That was all it took. Judy's eyes lit up and I could see she was off on her next adventure, and I was going along for the exciting ride.

Before we left Cutler that day, we walked around the two and a half acres of the vacant Little River Lodge, as it was known, peering in the dirty windows of the house and barn. At the top of the hill behind the huge house, we encountered a spectacular view of the harbor and small village. From that high rock promontory, we could also see out to Grand Manan, the disputed American-Canadian island with a history going back to my ancestor, Daniel Webster, and the Treaty of 1842.

The Lodge, although larger in earlier years, could still accommodate two dozen guests on its three floors. Although it hadn't been lived in year-round for more than two decades, there had been a succession of owners, all of whom had strange stories about their time there, as we later learned. The asking price of $65,000 seemed steep for the little town of Cutler, but was probably worth it, we reasoned. Good buy or not, we were hooked and made an offer soon after. It was some time before the owner, John Fairbanks, a state judge from New Hampshire, accepted our offer of $63,000 late in the winter. Judy was beside herself during this time, convinced someone else would come along and outbid us. Yet no one was crazy enough to take on such a white elephant as the Lodge. Certainly, the townspeople of Cutler couldn't imagine such a price for a somewhat run down, old hotel, a full seven-hour drive from Boston.

The house in Bowdoin, although complete, needed some last-minute items before we could sell it. We were in that unenviable position of having two houses; luckily, the housing market was strong, and by early spring we got a lone offer for the asking price of $41,000, which included the Farmall tractor I had bought for the farm. The buyer was a quiet, single guy from Portland named Kimball. We were delighted at how well it had worked out.

While waiting for the property closings, we had made several trips to Cutler to find out more about the Lodge. Along with the three-story main building, there was a long carriage shed which was attached to a large barn. Later we found old pictures of additions to the main building that stretched back up the hillside, giving the hotel a capacity of sixty-five people.

Hotel Cutler later became Little River Lodge. Here it is in original glory
1888 with its impressive turret.

The house had a noteworthy history, as we discovered from the local townspeople. Built in the latter part of the nineteenth century, it was first known as Hotel Cutler, and until about 1920, the property belonged to the Pejepscot Paper Company, a division of the Hearst Empire. The surrounding property consisted of several thousand acres of timber for pulp wood that lay mostly inland. The barn had been a rough dormitory where the wood cutters had roomed. The second-floor rooms were plaster walled and many were inscribed with names, dates and the cords of wood the workers had cut.

The barn, unique in its construction, was known as a "hung barn," its framework hung with long vertical steel rods attached to the roof trusses. Later, the property became Little River Lodge, a tribute to an earlier time when the town of Cutler was known as Little River. Our new place was steeped in history, as we excitedly learned from the townspeople's stories of growing up in and around the Lodge.

It seemed as if everyone had a personal connection of some sort with the Lodge. Cynthia Cates Rowden, one of the first Cutler residents we met, recalled that sometime during the end of World War II, the then-owner of the Lodge, a German man named Eric Zwinkle, was a clever and enterprising person who invented a device he called the Zwipper. He observed how the local lobstermen used wooden pegs inserted in the lobster claws to keep lobsters from tearing each other apart in holding tanks. Lobstermen later began using rubber bands. Zwinkle's invention, still in use today, was a hand-operated plier that quickly and efficiently spread the rubber band around the claw, greatly reducing time required for pegs. Zwinkle also started a local bus service in the region. However, Cynthia told us, he was always suspected of being a German spy for the Nazis. When he sold the Lodge in the 1950s, it was rumored that a number of dead goats were found in the cellar.

The way we first saw Little River Lodge in 1978 now a single-family residence with many rooms.

Closing day came in April of 1978. We met John Fairbanks and his sons that spring before we moved in. He asked to stay at the Lodge while they cleared a piece of beautiful wild land they still owned on the Head out past Dick Ellery. Fairbanks seemed like a regular guy, not your typical judge. Some years later, in 1989, Judy sent me a clipping depicting an abandoned pickup truck and a mystery involving the upstanding Judge Fairbanks, who had absconded with ten million dollars of client's money and disappeared into Canada. He was finally tracked down in a hotel room in Las Vegas in 1994, having committed suicide. No trace of the money was ever found. If asked, I would have said of Fairbanks, "He seemed like such a nice person."

We gradually moved Downeast using the old GMC 1-ton truck; I shudder to think of the number of trips that old truck made from Bowdoin to Cutler and the gas it used. Townsfolk were glad to see that a family would be living in the Lodge year round. In late June when Judy, John, and I arrived with the last load from Bowdoin, we were immediately given a warm welcome by several of town neighbors.

Cynthia Rowden, who rode up our driveway on a motorcycle. She was a native of Cutler from the Cates family, one of the older and more prominent families. A cheerful mother of two young girls, she was involved in town affairs and politics as were many of the Cates. Her husband, Terry, was originally from Detroit and had been in the US Coast Guard assigned to Cutler and stationed at Little River Light House in 1970, shortly before it was decommissioned. He had gotten out of the Coast Guard but decided he liked Cutler and married the local Cates girl. He had transferred to the Naval Communications Station just up the road where he was a civil servant and worked as a painter.

Little River Lighthouse as I sketched it in 1979. It now rents rooms in the restored keeper's quarters for $175 to $225 per night.
Drawing by Ned.

Terry and Cynthia both rode Honda motorcycles and showed us all the back roads as well as the important aspects of town politics — who were the good guys and who were not. Cynthia's mother, Isabel, was the postmaster and her father, Jasper, known to us all as "Junior," had recently been elected Head Selectman. Most of

274

his time was spent as a lobster and scallop fisherman. In a Maine town of about 500 people, as Cutler was, it's important to take part in town government and even more so to know who is related to whom. And, since nearly everybody was in some way was related, you had to be careful what you said about local people.

Cynthia and Terry lived about a quarter mile up the road toward Machias in an older house that Terry spent lots of time improving. They visited us frequently usually late every afternoon after they had finished supper. We found the townsfolk were on a different schedule than we were. Most of the men either worked in the woods or as fishermen hauling traps in the early hours of morning and were ready to eat an early supper. We city folks didn't start to think of dinner until seven o'clock Our other nearby neighbors were Maxine Porter in the house just behind us and her mother, Arlene Dennison, right next to us. Maxine was the town clerk and married to Verlan Porter, a carpenter who went by the nickname of "Hunky." They had two boys, Michael in high school and Cary, who was John's age. Arlene was a master craftsperson and made beautiful and very expensive quilts. She was commissioned by people from all over Maine and beyond to make specially designed quilts.

Upon moving in, we had acquired two shoats from a local farm. These little piggies were about a month or two old and still pink and nearly hairless. The farmer handed them over both in a feed bag the proverbial "two shoats in a tote sack," an old southern phrase used to describe a young shapely, gal walking down the street Needless to say, they did wiggle and wriggle.

Our piggies, Harley and Norton, grew from shoats to full grown in the fall.

275

We built a pen for them under the barn on the south side. They seemed happy and at this time assumed the names of "Harley" and "Norton," after the American and British motorcycles, respectively. Somewhere along the way, I had heard that a farmer got better hog efficiency if he raised two hogs together since they competed fiercely trying to see who could eat more. The scheme was to poke as much food as you could to them toward that fateful and dreaded day of slaughter in the fall. It seems a bit cruel now to think of the untimely end of those two cute pigs, but be it ever thus, their fate was sealed.

Between the pigpen by the barn and the boundary fence was a sloping field measuring about 100 by 150 feet that was to become the garden. It was far more than we needed but fun to think of all the vegetables we could grow. We bought a rear-tined Ariens tiller that made ground preparation and planting easy. Judy was in her own heaven with perfect space for potatoes, squash, corn, peas, beans, tomatoes, and more. Alas, the garden required much of our time and not the results we had hoped for. Cutler was, we found, too much of a cool maritime climate for crops like tomatoes and corn that wanted warmth and longer time to mature. The day-after-day of cool fog and little sun produced stunted crops. On the other hand, peas, beans, and potatoes thrived. We knew that with pork and beans, we couldn't starve.

Cutler was one of the most satisfying and happy experiences of my life. The friendliness of the townspeople to us as outsiders made us feel like part of the town from the beginning, something we had not experienced in the other communities where we had lived.

I continued to work as a consultant and ran my environmental contracts from Cutler, although it meant there was a lot of traveling to Augusta and Portland. I operated using the company name of as I had before. I also conducted studies for the Town of Cutler and planning work for Machias, Belfast, and other Maine towns receiving federal or state money at the time. Stuart Fefer, my colleague and project leader for the Fish & Wildlife Service contract, and his wife, Peggy, had moved to Cutler shortly after we did and exchanged wedding vows in a memorable ceremony by the shore near their home. Afterward, we all walked back to the Lodge for the reception. They had found a secret hiding place away from the bustle of the real world as we had.

Perhaps the best part of the Cutler years was that Amie decided she wanted to come and live with us. Although it was hard for Karyl to let her go, it was an important part of Amie's growing up and being on her own. As Amie tells the story, she had gotten fed up with her mother's house rules and on a summer day in 1979, impulsively hopped on a Greyhound bus to Machias without telling Karyl. When Amie arrived, she called me for a ride. As soon as we got to Cutler, I made her call Karyl so she wouldn't worry. A few weeks afterward Karyl and Bob drove to Cutler with Amie's requested belongings. Suddenly, John had a sister.

That fall, Amie entered her sophomore year at Washington Academy (WA) in East Machias. Like ten or so other academies throughout the state, WA was a public high school for about eight nearby towns. The school drew some three hundred students from a twenty-five-mile radius. John was still in the Cutler school system in the eighth grade.

It was fun to have my daughter living with us, but it was also a bit trying. One of the reasons she left was clearly to avoid her mother's strict rules. We had a few rules, too, but she was fairly free to do much of what she wanted…and she did. Amie enjoyed her new freedom and became well integrated into WA over the next year. She and a group of five other girls, called themselves "The Buds," and spent all year together. We suspected they might be into drinking and drugs on occasion, but had no evidence. I had even met with the principal and expressed our concern; he said he had been keeping an eye on them. He knew, he said, it was easy to tell by watching their grades. We felt better. But there were times when I despaired of having a daughter. Like the night I recall so well as I kept waking, listening for the boyfriend's car. Finally, at four-thirty the next morning, as it was getting light, they drove up. There was some long story about a car window being bashed in, so on. I was just terribly relieved to have her home in one piece.

Or the time that Judy and I got a call from the Machias Hospital. Amie, now fifteen, had recently gotten her Maine driver's license. Because Maine was a rural farming state where many kids needed to drive farm vehicles around their homes, they were allowed this privilege at the young age of fifteen. I had taught her to drive my old white Saab when she was around thirteen, not long after my leaving home, and I felt she was quite good at it. We were assured she and her young friends were all right, but we rushed into town to find four somewhat shaken looking girls standing in the hospital waiting room.

Amie told us at that night that she and her three friends were driving on a slightly windy and hilly narrow roads when a car coming toward them moving at a fast pace came over the hill. She swerved to the side to avoid it, and running into soft sand, rolled into a ditch with her car landing upside down. All four girls had their seat belts fastened and all climbed out with barely a scratch. It was a real tribute to the Saab design which has always featured built-in, reinforced door posts, much like a roll bar. Otherwise the roof would have likely collapsed. So, like father, like daughter, she had her brushes with death at an early age.

By this time Judy had found a job as a secretary in Machias and then soon after, went to work for the US Air Force in Columbia Falls at the Over The Horizon Radar station. She always was able to land good secretarial jobs even though she really didn't like the work.

In late 1978, I received a membership invitation from The Explorers Club in New York. The invitation letter was quite flattering, mentioning my accomplishments and books. I decided to become a member. I've always wondered how they had found me; possibly it was a recommendation of my old friend Ken Drummond, already a member.

In the fall of 1979, Judy, John, Amie, and I went to Pennsylvania for a memorial show of my parent's art work. It opened during Chester County Week, the annual celebration put on by the Historical Society. It was always on the first weekend of October and included a tour of historic houses, fall foliage, food, and antique shops. My father had written a poem or an essay for the special edition newspaper produced for the occasion. For this issue, the entire back page was dedicated to pieces by and about my parents.

With the initial work of Dr. Robert E. at West Chester State College, I had printed a bibliography of nearly all of both Ed and Barbara's writings. And with very great help of Evelyn Spence, who was a student with my father at the Pennsylvania Academy of Fine Arts, we put on a show of his drawings at the Chester County Art Association. Evelyn, who was easily in her mid-80s, made mats and titles for dozens of his originals, many on loan by local friends. It was a wonderful show and a great tribute to both of my parents.

During this event, we stayed with my mother's dear friend, Jane Carter, who lived near Westtown and kindly put us up. Her latest book, *Edgemont, The Story of a Township* was the last book that dad illustrated in 1976.

On our return to Cutler, in my then fairly elderly '69 Saab, we got caught in an early fall snowstorm, about eight or ten inches. We fought our way along Route 9, better known as the Airline Road, that runs from Bangor to Calais. This was before they had improved and straightened its winding, twisty path along glacial eskers and up steep hills. I look back on the trip as great fun. Driving in the snow has always been a delight to me.

This was also the year I had expanded my horizons by becoming interested in energy conservation. After working at TRIGOM on the offshore oil development problem and having gone through the first and second energy crises, it was clear to me that there was going to be a large market for home energy conservation. Judy and I both thought this might be the right time to jump in early.

We formed our company, Home Works, with a letterhead designed by Terry DeWan and rented a small storefront in Machias on Main Street, where we sold energy-saving products. Energy stores were popping up all over the state; one in Belfast and another in Hallowell where Jay, the owner, was one of the first Window Quilt dealers. He set us up as a dealer in December of 1979. Frank Raftery, who ran an energy store in Belfast got us interested in an innovative, passive solar hot

We install solar hot water collectors on our roof.

water collector system that used Freon to heat water. Becoming a dealer for this product meant learning how to assemble a system, including silver soldering all the connections. I later took a four-hour exam to be licensed by the State of Maine as a solar installer. My first job was assisting a crew from Belfast with installing a solar hot water system on the roof of the Cutler house. We managed to place an 80-gallon tank in the attic space above the third-floor ceiling, well braced for the weight of that much water. The collectors were mounted on a frame attached to the roof which faced due south. The whole works cost $4,000 which was about a third of the cost for same unit sold in Massachusetts, where the government tax refund was 80% instead of Maine's 20%. People in Massachusetts didn't seem to care if they paid a lot more, as long as they got a large amount in tax savings; the heck with the savings in the cost of hot water. Our house was eventually to become an energy efficient demonstration home.

I got all the books I could find on alternative energy and efficient housing design and in the fall of 1980, I found there was an opportunity to teach a night course at the high school in Machias. A good number of local people signed up. The books I had were a great help and I learned enough to stay ahead of the class.

Our demo home in Cutler didn't start off as it should have. We didn't have a lot of time to get ready that first winter so we decided to buy a wood furnace for hot air since there was already duct work in place. The real mistake was trying to heat the house without any insulation, so we wound up burning enormous amounts of wood and not being very warm. During late summer, I had bought a truck load of tree length green wood amounting to about twenty cords. It was dumped in the field near the garden, about forty feet from the house. I was faced with sawing a giant pile into two-foot lengths and then splitting with a rented splitter. That fall I moved the split logs up to the house by wheelbarrow and loaded it through a small cellar window for the hungry furnace below. It makes me weary just thinking of all that effort! I had bought a Jonsred chain saw imported from Sweden, which all the local woodsmen teased me about. They all used the true American McCullogh. I thought my saw was as good as theirs and I still have it. Once the wood was in the wet and damp cellar I stacked it all on pallets. While the furnace put out a lot of heat, we were by no means warm… we were living in a sieve. At the end of the winter I realized that there had to be a better way to heat that house.

Our first step in the right direction was to have an insulation contractor blow in cellulose for the whole house for about $5,000. The payback was rapid, perhaps as short as two years. We also took advantage of being a Window Quilt dealer and installed them throughout the house. Finally, through a friend I gotten to know at various meetings, Albie Barden, I found the perfect heating system for us. Albie and wife Cheryl, lived in an old farm house in the country near Norridgewock. Their company, Maine Wood Heat, specialized in various European designs such as Russian or Finnish fireplaces. Albie also was a distributor for the Tirolla cookstove/ heater from Austria. It was a wood-fired cook stove with a boiler jacket that provided hot water to radiators.

After I found four enormous old cast iron radiators being sold from a building in Machias, I then had the job of plumbing them to the stove with copper pipe. My experience in soldering with John Stark in Southport and, more recently, with silver solder for the Freon solar collectors came in handy. The four radiators were placed in the four major rooms in the first floor. Boy, were they ever heavy to lug into the house! But in the end, we had very efficient wood cook stove that heated the whole insulated part of the house with about five cords of wood. The stove was also hooked into the domestic hot water system with a storage tank directly above in the bathroom. The only drawback, like the Bowdoin house, was we had no back up heating system which meant if we had to be away for over a day, someone had to stoke the fire. But we rarely left Cutler in the winter.

The following summer, the old sailing bug began to nibble away at me. I saw an ad for an unusual type of sailboat in Winterport, just down the river from Bangor. Judy and I went to see it and soon after, I bought it for around $5,000. The boat was called an Amphibicon 25 and had the character of *Ocarina* in that she had reverse sheer and very light construction using one inch square strips glued together. Her designer was Cy Hamlin, and her builder, E. Farnham Butler, from Mt. Desert Island. The cabin top could be raised about five inches on four folding legs when in harbor, allowing more headroom and ventilation. And it had to be a centerboard boat, as many of my boats were to be.

Rather than hauling my new prize, now named *Osprey* to its future home in Cutler via the road, I opted to sail her downeast. I got two old friends from my days at Bill Reed's to join me on a cruise. We left Winterport, floating leisurely down the Penobscot River in July. The next day, we ran along Eggemoggin Reach in light winds and a dense, low fog. We had no modern devices for navigation; GPS was many years in the future. We just did dead reckoning with a compass and not even a log line to measure distance. Most times if it was quiet enough, we could hear waves breaking on nearby islands and rocks and we steered clear. We finally made our way south of Mt Desert, and wound up at Cape Split on the fourth day. By then, both of my crew had to get back to their jobs. I left *Osprey* on a mooring until the next weekend.

An Amphibicon 25 like our Osprey. *We bought it in Winterport and sailed it home to Cutler.*

Judy and I, with Denny, our Shetland sheepdog in tow, returned to our moored *Osprey* and had a pleasant and gentle sail along the coast to Cutler with Denny truly enjoying the day. The pup had had quite a summer, with a recent near death experience. He was about a year old and still a very playful and, as was typical of Shelties, eager to chase small kids and unfortunately, large trucks. One afternoon he ran alongside a large dump truck across the road from the Lodge, one of his favorite pastimes. Somehow he miscalculated, got too close, and was run over. It was several hours before we found him in the grass as he struggled to try and return home. His

Denny, left, our dear Sheltie, that we raised from a puppy had a near-death experience with a dump truck but survived a broken back and lived to age 14.

back had been broken. The veterinarian told us there was no way to save him. Judy, on the other hand, decided we would try to heal him and with some ingenuity and rigged up a sling that held him just off the floor in the kitchen. In a rather amazingly short time, his backbone fused together and being so young and limber, he began to mend. I really didn't do as much sailing out of Cutler as I had expected, for the tides and currents were strong and it always seemed the winds were light. That first winter I followed the suggestions of the local fishermen: I built a simple wooden cradle for her and they helped me to steer her on a ramp where they hauled boats. Then, as was the custom, they dragged her up the street using a logging skidder, the all-important and ubiquitous woods vehicle. I used the driveway of a neighbor who was only in town during the summer to store the sailboat. In an odd coincidence, this neighbor was the mother of Bill Clements from the Haverford class of 1949. A few years later, she purchased one of my Andrew Wyeth originals, something I regret.

The next year for the winter haulout someone had recommended a boatyard that might be better for storage, some thirty miles away. I sailed *Osprey* there in the fall and the yard hauled her out and, as was the custom, left the mast in her. All would have been well except for a nasty, lurking winter's storm in February with very high winds. Not surprisingly, the 100-mph wind dismasted her with severe damage. It was unfortunately a repeat of the *Ocarina* disaster and again almost a total loss. Someone with more ability and time than I bought the remains. My luck with boats was not good.

282

It seemed as though we had achieved the perfect state of equilibrium, but Judy was becoming restless again. She thought our energy business would be more successful in her hometown of Dover-Foxcroft, a town more lively than Machias and Cutler.

Her wanting to move may also have resulted from her experiences working with the local fishermen. She had started to work as a sternman, hauling lobster traps on various locals' boats. It was tough and hard work but she did well at it until some of the wives began resent her presence aboard their husbands' boats.

Our move to Dover-Foxcroft seemed a proper next step. It was only temporary, so we left most of our belongings in Cutler. My father-in-law, John Ellery, found us a nice house to rent that belonged to the woman who ran one of the hardware stores in town. I was delighted to find that our new house was heated by hot water, as it meant I could install the Tirolla in the kitchen and heat the whole house with wood, which in Dover-Foxcroft was really cheap.

In addition to a change of place, we discovered that Dover-Foxcroft was a center of alternative energy and conservation the perfect location to move our business. An entrepreneurial energy guru named Charles McArthur had recently moved from Connecticut with a collection of electric cars and an equal number of innovative ideas on energy conservation. He had found that the town would lease him a 200,000-square-foot mill on the river being used as a warehouse. Better still, the mill had a working water-powered electric generator that brought him a check from Central Maine Power Co for $10,000 each month, a bit of a of golden goose.

He rented four of the five floors to a local fabric mill needing storage space and on the top floor, he had started a small business "hatchery." In a small ten foot by fifteen foot space with a window looking out on the river, Home Works set up shop for a very low rent, less than $100 a month. I certainly couldn't have found a place in the town as cheap. It was here I met a group of characters all with similar interests. When we started in 1980, there were probably eight or ten booths rented. Among them were Maine Wood Products, representing wood lot owners; Kathleen Irish, who sold books and gift items; and Sidney Marshall, a general fix-it guy who repaired broken appliances. Sidney and Kathleen turned out to be long-term friends of mine over the years. There was also a small museum in the mill basement, showcasing strange alternative vehicles Charlie had collected.

Charlie and wife Annie lived in what had been the mill manager's home alongside the mill race. The race, a separate narrow channel, went directly to the generator turbine house below, while the dam handled the main flow of the river. It was a lovely spot to sit and watch the water go by. At the end of the day several of us would usually be invited to Charlie's house for cocktails, where he served wicked martinis and entertained us with his latest energy scheme. Formerly successful in the printing business, he was now out to promote alternative energy and his mill.

He drove around town in an electric car that normally held two passengers, but with some effort three could squeeze in.

The mill was truly a wonderful environment. The entire space was heated in this very cold climate in central Maine by an enormous wood fired boiler Charlie had converted from oil. He had very luckily inherited the plant engineer from the former mill operation, an elderly local man named Hermie, whom Charlie had saved from being laid off and now was the heart of the mill, keeping the fire stoked. He also knew all the mill's operating secrets. Where Hermie was a lot like Walt on the *Earle of Desmond*, Charlie could be likened to the "Pied Piper" of the mill.

Our "hatchery" neighbor, Sidney, had been evicted from his land by the US government over an eminent domain issue. He was so bitter over this heavy-handed move that he decided to drop out of regular life and become a non-person without an identity. This type of dropping out was much easier back then. Sidney could fix anything electrical or mechanical. As word spread locally of his services, people brought in broken toasters, radios, record players, and other slightly antiquated appliances. He had managed to get them going again usually for ridiculously cheap prices. He also worked part time at the local radio station, WDME, or "W dummy" as he called it. He was a wonderful study of the underground culture that existed (and probably still does) in our country. He hated the US government and paid no taxes, although I doubt he had enough income to pay taxes anyway.

Sidney was a firm proponent of alternative energy. He brought with him a small wind generator, lots of batteries, and solar photovoltaic panels. He had rented a tiny cement block house on the road to the dump where all of these were installed. In his impecunious way, he didn't use power from Central Maine Power and lived from his alternate energy sources. And just down the road was the town dump still at that time open to the public. Sidney would frequent the dump where he found all sorts of routinely abandoned household electronics. He knew when they would burn the dump so he would show up shortly before and claim prizes, some of value and some not. Then he would tote them back to his house. These he would fix to sell or have for future use. He coined the phrase for the dump the "free mall."

My space at the mill turned out to be a good location as it was easily accessible. After a few ads in the local paper, Home Works got a good start. Of all the products that Judy and I picked for the store, the one that shone the brightest was Window Quilt. At that time the company name was Appropriate Technology Coporation (ATC). Over the subsequent years it is the only product that has survived in my business. My first job in 1979 while we were still in Cutler for a dozen or so windows on a new house in Eastport had been a near disaster. Like any normal American male, I bypassed the instructions on how to measure and put in my order for this new product. As dealers, we were supposed to add fourteen inches to the measured height of the window. So, of course, I missed this important point and consequently, all twelve of the shades were too short. Luckily for me, the folks at ATC were most forgiving in these early days and they made the order over for free which saved me from financial ruin. Not long after this, the company computer included the addition of the extra fourteen inch allowance for the roll-up of the fabric which should have been done in the first place. This rocky beginning was a sign of things to come as the Window Quilt company was dedicated to high standards and made an excellent product. I went on to sell a lot in my local area the over the years.

At the time of its development, around 1978, the Window Quilt was a marvel of high technology involving five layers of cotton polyester bonded together by high frequency ultra sound. The middle layer, made of Mylar, melts to seal all five layers together. This makes an air tight shade unlike sewn shades with needle holes. The shade runs in a track on the sides and seals on top and bottom reducing any air flow. It has an R-value of about 5.0 which is equal to having five layers of glass for a window. Although it started with only one color and pattern it later evolved into in 48 colors and three patterns.

The rising price of oil for heating that fall of 1980 had made everyone aware of the value of window insulation. I recall one of my larger jobs just west of Dover-Foxcroft where I installed a number of Window Quilts. A problem developed shortly after installation which I couldn't solve, so I called for help from ATC in Vermont. Instead of a technician, the company sent Aaron Bogosian, one of the company's vice presidents to fix the problem. It was an indication of their commitment to supporting dealers something we were to see less and less of in years to come.

The freon solar hot water system, the other product that should have done well, didn't catch on. Perhaps the overall cost was beyond most people in the area. I recall selling one system in Guilford. I wasn't about to tackle it by myself and borrowed an experienced crew from a Bangor dealer. It was a one-day job of mostly tedious silver soldering the copper pipes and collectors. While we were on the roof it began to snow quite hard and we waited a while until the sun came out. Remarkably, the date was May 22, some sort of record for late snow. The job was a success but was probably my last for this product.

We were all settled now in Dover-Foxcroft, with Amie and John happily in school at Foxcroft Academy (FA) and Judy, who in her usual capable way, had found a secretarial job with the US Agricultural Department on Main Street close to home. We even tried our hand at raising pigs again. We started with small shoats as we had in Cutler and built a pen in a vacant space near the mill not far from the river. But sometime over the summer we were away for a day or two when it was very hot. Although we had someone feed them, when we returned we found them both dead. It was most sad and I felt terrible about it. Either they didn't have enough water or as

Charlie suspected maybe there had been toxic chemicals in the ground from the mill. It was my last attempt at pig farming.

Our Christmas that year was idyllic. We got a real shot of bitter winter cold along with lots of snow and everything looked like a typical New England Christmas card with church spires and smoking chimneys. On Christmas Day, I walked over to the mill in 35 degrees below zero; with ample sun and no wind it was bearable. Judy, John, Amie, and I were joined at our house by Charlie and Annie for dinner. We splurged on a large crown roast of pork with all the trimmings. This took the place of the usual Ellery over-the-top Christmas with present opening that usually went on for hours. John and Jan had left earlier for Sedona, Arizona and a winter stay in the warmer Southwest.

It wasn't too long before Judy began to hate her job for being dull and underpaid. Realizing she would be much better paid if she worked in a large urban area like Boston, she began to make plans to move down there. At the end of the holidays, she left for Boston, hoping to find that better paying job. She stayed with her sister, Marcia, in Needham and was quite happy in the new situation, at least for a while.

Amie, John, and I were left to hold down the fort. Amie did the shopping and cooking and I remember her saying she thought that all three of us could get by on $15 a week! It was hardly elegant fare but we did make that goal some weeks. We spent a lot of time in the kitchen near the fire in the wood stove. We just hunkered down and enjoyed the rest of a Maine winter.

As spring finally crawled up from the south and the Easter bunny was hopping along just down the road, I drove down to Needham to spend a weekend with Judy at Marcia's house. It was nice being re-united after three months or so but I didn't feel she had really missed me. A few weeks later, she quit her job and came back to Maine. It was great to have the family back together but some time in that spring period I could feel her unrest coming on.

Instead of looking for a new place to move, it seemed as if she was ready for us to part ways. After she had moved out briefly, at her suggestion, I decided to go out on a date a while later. The first one was with Kathy Carnaveri who worked at the local deli, owned and run by Jane and John Periboni. Jane had started up a New York style deli in a former restaurant on Main Street in Dover-Foxcroft. John Periboni had left Jane that spring to return to academic life in New Jersey giving up on Maine, winter, and Jane. My mill shop mate, Sidney, used to hang around the deli a bit and soon he and Jane became a pair. So one night Sidney, Jane, Kathy, and I went on an old fashioned double date at a drive-in movie near Bangor. At first it seemed a bit strange to be dating. I knew little about Kathy other than she came from New Hampshire but I knew nothing of her former marital background. She was attractive with a quick winning smile, curly dark hair and dark skin but I had little interest in dating at this stage of my life. I was still in love with Judy.

By this point, Judy had returned and was ready to move back to Cutler. Our sojourn in her old home town (Dover Foxcroft) hadn't been as magical as she had hoped and her eternal restlessness continued. This news of a move back didn't sit well with Amie, who had firmly planted herself in the town and at FA where she was about to enter her senior year. She refused to accompany us back to the coast. Amie had a group of friends at school that she really liked and was dating the son of a local hardware store owner. I saw no reason to force her to go with us. She had a friend, whose mother agreed to let Amie rent a room in her home for the final year.

Karyl wasn't too keen on the arrangement, but at some point, she acquiesced. Still, there was a hitch because the school required that there be a responsible parent in town since Amie was seventeen and still a minor. Karyl and I met that spring with the principal and legally declared her to be an "emancipated minor" and signed a document to this effect. What it meant was that if Amie didn't show up for school some morning, the school office wouldn't have to notify either of us as parents; she alone was responsible for her attendance. She graduated with high honors among the top ten students of her class, making all of us proud.

With Amie rooted in Dover, Judy, John, and I packed up all our belongings in the truck and headed back for Cutler the summer of 1981 and the hulking, three story Little River Lodge. We had brought back the Tirolla stove with us and now re-installed in its place in the kitchen. We had a relatively energy efficient house and I felt it was time for me to return to my science and environmental interests.

Having been a big fan of the Common Ground Fair from its inception, I decided to have a Window Quilt display that fall and shared a booth with Peter Talmage and his alternative energy equipment, wind mills, and solar panels. Lots of fairgoers stopped by and business was brisk. The fair lasted all weekend so some booth keepers slept in tents or if they could afford it, in motels. Among people I met was a group of students from College of the Atlantic (COA) in Bar Harbor. When the fair closed that evening I was invited to share a spot in large tent with about fifteen students where we spoke about alternative energy.

The job situation in Cutler was not as dismal as I'd thought it might be. I had been able to get two contracts through the Maine State Planning Office for small study projects on coastal revitalization using my company NECOG. The most rewarding projects were the waterfront designs for Machias and Belfast, Maine. Both attempted to open the eyes of the townspeople to the somewhat abandoned waterfront areas. Both required having land use and planning expertise. I teamed up with my former neighbor and friend, Terry DeWan, who had been involved in many similar jobs.

In Machias, the aim was to revitalize the river space behind the buildings on Main Street by finding access routes, cleaning up the banks, and emphasizing the beautiful waterfall, thus instilling a pride in the history of the riverfront. At one time the river area had thrived in commerce, ship building, and trade. But in subsequent years as this sort of activity disappeared the river became a waste conduit and dumping ground as local citizens turned their backs on it. Much of our report was done by Terry with plans and drawings for a walking bridge across the river near the waterfall and lovely paths on both sides. It was a several months job that laid the groundwork and made some broad estimates for phases of development and associated costs. Some years later and long after I had left Cutler for greener pastures, I received notice that there was to be a grand opening of the Machias Waterfront Park. I rode my BMW motorcycle from Portland to Machias to be there for the opening. It was certainly gratifying to attend and see that the town had realized what a gem of a spot they had and had carried out our plan. I was proud to have been part of it.

*My 1978 BMW R-80 with only 22,000 miles on it. Ellie and
I rode many backroads here in Maine.*

The job that followed Machias was quite similar, as it also was about waterfront improvement for the town of Belfast. Terry and I combined our efforts to help Belfast re-design their harbor and waterfront. They had a federal grant to examine various ways the harbor could both be more practical and more appealing as a recreational facility. Although the Waterfront Committee selected NECOG for the job, we got a bit of a boost from the mayor who turned out to be none other than my old friend, Mike Hall, from the days in Annapolis, and Karyl's former boss at *Skipper*

288

Magazine. When I caught up with Mike for lunch we had a good visit but sadly his wife Kathy had developed a brain tumor that sounded terminal.

The waterfront in Belfast had become commercially developed over the years for railroad use and especially for the chicken industry, not for waterfront activities. The raising of chickens for broilers and eggs had gotten a firm start in Maine in the 1950s. Broilers were raised in large, cheaply constructed barns. The feed for these chicks was brought in by rail, and in the case of Belfast, was stored in several large grain elevators located on what should have been prime waterfront land, once very cheap, but now potentially valuable. From here, the feed was transferred to the chicken barns on land as much as thirty miles inland. This model worked well until the price of feed rose in the early 1970s and suddenly the industry collapsed overnight. The margin was so close that even these small changes killed it.

Belfast was left with railroad tracks with no business that ran along a nice harbor, ugly and useless grain towers, and a lack of proper access for pleasure and commercial boats and the local public. There was a small and barely usable dock by the parking lot. This all took place about 1978 at the time of the second oil crisis. Our job was to re-design the waterfront for a possible marina and better public access. We did this with a series of sketches and plans for the new waterfront in a report to the City.

Today, Belfast has implemented all our recommendations and expanded their dock and access. There are several restaurants right on the water, a public boat ramp, and a large number of docks. The grain elevators are gone and the railroad has moved slightly north and become a summer and fall tourist attraction. A town that was once chickens, fish and low income employment is now a gem that attracts tourists to the Maine coast. I return every summer to see how the town is prospering with their spectacular view of the water.

I saw Terry DeWan some years after our Belfast project. He has been as successful with his own company, TJD&A, based in Yarmouth with eleven employees and some 300 jobs to his credit. Nice to see young fellas succeed!

Amie continued in her senior year at FA. Sometime in the late winter they got a wild idea of dropping out of school and going to Florida with another young couple. I told Karyl, and we knew right away it was a bad idea. We quickly called her boyfriend's parents and convinced them to do all they could to dissuade this move. A month or two of missed school when they were so close to graduating wasn't a smart thing to do. We couldn't prevent them from going; we could only appeal to their common sense; something that seventeen-year-olds have little of. After a week of great uncertainty, we prevailed and they gave up the idea. Cabin fever in a northern climate? Not long after

Amie was graduated and all of the extended family attended the ceremony at FA with pride.

That summer, one of the College of the Atlantic students I had met the year before at the Common Ground Fair called to ask if I would be interested in teaching a course in alternative energy. I gave her an enthusiastic "yes!" even before finding out details; I rarely turn down new and different offers.

In fall of 1982, I signed up to teach a one-semester course that was part of the normal curriculum usually taught by an engineer currently on sabbatical. The pay for sixteen weeks of a class per week was $1,500, a rather paltry amount, with no travel allowance or other benefits. And the distance from Cutler was ninety miles each way. But it was a wonderful opportunity to be in an exciting college that was very different from most others and to be able to fashion my course any way I wanted. I knew it would take lot of preparation.

In September, I attended a two-day orientation gathering for all the faculty, both old and new. We all met at a wonderful rustic and remote camp northeast of Bangor called Nicatous Lodge on a beautiful lake. The lodge, started in 1928, was without commercial electrical power but had a generator and all of the features of a real camp. About twenty-five faculty members gathered here for two days each year to discuss the direction and future of the college. At ten-thirty each night, the generator was shut down and we all went to bed by lanterns. It was a grand introduction to COA and to be able to meet and talk with all the faculty. My class that fall had about fifteen students ranging in age from early twenties to mid-thirties. They were eager and interested in most aspects of alternative energy. The final exam was to design a house that used the various principles we had discussed. I remember several good submissions. Teaching the class was a rewarding experience for me.

The next event in the Cutler saga was the realization that it was time to move on. We saw that the house needed an enormous and increasing amount of maintenance, not to mention the barn was beginning to self-destruct and collapse. Neither Judy nor I had much in the way of income. And with spring, came Judy's restlessness and desire to find a better, cheaper place to live. I, too felt this way, but hadn't wanted to face it. So, with reluctance we put the Lodge on the market. We listed the property with an asking price of $79,000 with Marge Ahlin, our friend from Machias, an excellent local realtor. But the very size of the house and its hotel history wasn't too inviting for most prospective buyers. We had to appeal to someone from away, to whom the charm and history would be a plus, someone with enough money to take it on. Certainly, there had been significant growth in real estate value over about five years but it took the better part of a year before we sold Little River Lodge.

At this time, Judy was working as a teller in the Machias Savings Bank and happened to hear of two houses on adjoining lots on Water Street that were true fixer-uppers. Judy was always looking for new opportunities; a good part of our lives together had been spent on this sort of home improvement. We figured why not try it as a business deal? The houses were small and in fairly good repair but in need of facelifts. They were priced at an incredible $5,000 and $10,000, respectively. Early- to mid-nineteenth century with no particular appeal, we bought them and found we had our work cut out for us. We got part way through foundation and floor work, new Velux roof windows, and other things over the next year. It may have been our move from Cutler but along the way we lost interest or hadn't time and we decided to sell the houses at a small but acceptable profit.

Our fixer-upper houses that Judy and I bought on Water St in Machias. We made enough money to cover our materials.

Meanwhile, with all the energy efficient improvements we made, we just about broke even in selling the Lodge. We had gotten one offer and felt lucky at that taking somewhat less than asking price. It turned out that 1983 was right in an economic downturn and we were even luckier to sell it at all. The new owners, Carl and Nancy Sundberg from New York, turned out to be good caretakers for the lodge. Carl was a VP at a bank who had been pushed out with an early retirement and a good settlement package. He was probably in his late fifties. Nancy was a nurse and found it easy to get a job at the local hospital in Machias. Carl blended in surprisingly well the local fishermen and thus with the community.

Sometime during this transition period, before we left Cutler, Amie and her boyfriend drove up to the lodge one morning and announced, somewhat casually, that they had just gotten married. In a way, it was no surprise. It was part of her impetuousness and being eighteen years old. She never told us about the decision, it just happened. Neither of us was particularly enamored with our new son-in-law, but what the heck? Give the kid a chance.

Judy and I had found another house to buy near Cutler. We knew we wanted something much smaller and more manageable and somehow found just the right spot in the neighboring town of Whiting. The property was located at a corner of Route 191, just off Route 1, heading toward Eastport and the Canadian border. Route 191 went another seven miles into Lubec, also a border town, with the island of Campobello across the bridge. The house, built around 1875, faced south on the road and stretched back with a long kitchen and woodshed, and joined a good-sized barn complete with a two hole outhouse. One and a half acres came with it and part of the land was on a tidal river that eventually flowed into Passamaquoddy Bay. We paid somewhere around $28,000 for the house — a pretty neat deal. The best part was the large kitchen where we put a Jotul wood stove. The long wood shed was fully stocked — what a joy and bonus! John didn't have to split wood right away. There were no working fireplaces or large central chimney. It had few notable architectural details and was hardly as inspiring as the Amesbury house had been. Still it was nice to live in.

As we began packing up to move fourteen or so miles, I began to feel more and more like a gypsy. The International half-ton stake bed truck was again pressed into service. I hate to think of the miles that poor truck covered moving our earthly belongings around the state of Maine. John tagged along as he always had, from one place to another, without a complaint. Fortunately, he would see most of his Cutler friends and other schoolmates at Washington Academy, where Whiting, like Cutler, sent its students.

Like the present day greeting, "please listen carefully, our menu has changed," I felt my life with Judy was also changing. In her continual and eternal search for herself and for her right place, Judy had decided we should both enroll in the Marine Trade School at Eastport. She had been a fisherman in the lobster and scallop industry and now wanted to take the additional fishing courses offered. She also thought there was a great opportunity for me to specialize in boat painting, another course offered at the Washington County Vocational Techncal Institute. I went to the school to observe the painting operation and in reading the course literature determined that it seemed to be a good way to learn a trade. The emphasis was on high-tech paints and finishes, like Awl Grip, a two-part epoxy. These finishes were popular for both boats and airplanes. Because of the volatile nature of the paints, special breathing apparatus was required. I was intrigued with the high-tech part and then best of all we found out that we could both qualify for Pell Grants which would nearly pay for the tuition.

I was fairly excited over the thought of a new career, especially one that was supposed to pay well without much apprenticing. But, as many times is the case, my bubble was again burst when I found that only one member of a family could receive the tuition grant of $2,500. The remaining tuition was far more than we were able to pay, so Judy decided she would be the one to go school.

In September, Judy began school in Eastport, carpooling each day with another student who lived nearby. Actually, it worked out better for me. Since we had left our beloved Tirolla stove in Cutler, I had gone in search for another woodstove that summer at the nearest dealer I could find was in Brewer, a two-hour ride from Whiting. The store was a new branch of the Black Stove Shop that had originated just north of Augusta. It was here in Brewer that I met Wayne Leite, the manager and at the time, the only full-time employee there. After buying my Jotul box stove, Wayne had asked if I would be interested in working at the shop selling and installing stoves. I said I'd keep it in mind. So, a short while later as the boat painting door closed, the stove door opened. I was, in fact, about to go off in a new direction one I already knew something about, but was eager to learn more.

The only problem was the distance from home in Whiting to the job in Brewer. Certainly a four-hour daily commute was out of the question, even though fuel was still cheap. But to the rescue came my daughter Amie. She and her new husband had moved to Bangor and had a nice second floor apartment with an extra bedroom. They were pleased to let me stay there during the week. Problem solved. Since I was working in retail sales, it was a forgone conclusion that I would work Saturdays, something I had rarely, if ever, done in my life. But it was not as bad as I thought, because I had Sunday and Monday to return to Whiting. It might have been more acceptable if the pay was better. My base was barely above the minimum wage with a sales commission as an incentive. I learned all too soon that the owner was a bit stingy and only offered us a measly one percent, paid each month. Many sales jobs I found usually paid between five and sometimes ten percent. But there were not many other jobs available then.

As it turned out, I found I enjoyed the work, learned all about stoves and heating and became a good friend with Wayne. The store was in the first floor of an old house on the main street in Brewer across the Penobscot River from its sister city of Bangor. In this part of Maine, the wood stove culture thrived and had made a comeback due the energy crisis. The Black Stove Shop was the only major stove shop in either town. Our parent shop in Augusta ran ads frequently throughout the state so those early cool fall weekends kept us very busy.

Wayne was probably ten years younger than I and, like many Mainers, had held a variety of jobs, mostly in sales. He had grown up in New Bedford, Massachusetts as a member of the Portuguese fishing community, later coming to Maine to attend Unity College and then stayed. We both had been accustomed to burning wood in our home.

293

Our Jotul 118 box stove was very efficient and kept our houses in Bowdoin and Whiting toasty warm.

so we felt comfortable when we sold stoves to our customers. There was nothing more convincing than to be able to tell someone, "I have one just like this and it does it great job heating the whole house."

A while before the fall sales season, we got a visit from the company owner and our overall boss, Ray Mannochio. Originally from Massachusetts, he had lived some time in Maine. In his other life, he had been a salesman and rep for Van Waters and Rogers (VWR) a science supply house in Massachusetts. And like lots of us in the 1970s, he had escaped the rat race and come to Maine where he and his wife bought a farm north of Augusta where property was still cheap. The first energy crisis was the perfect time to start in the wood stove business. He was built like a bull and was a dynamo of a worker, always wrestling and lifting heavy stoves to prove how strong he was. Except for an occasional visit to Brewer, Ray mostly left us alone to run the store.

At this time, Amie was working at grocery store in Bangor but later moved across the river to a better job with a beverage company that bottled and distributed Pepsi and Miller Beer products. She was also attending the University of Maine at Orono part-time, taking courses toward an English degree. My mother had very wisely left her a small stipend of $5,000 for her education. Her husband was a warehouseman at Dennis Paper Company.

Mostly, I remember the good times at the apartment in Bangor, when Amie and I would have early morning breakfast meetings before her husband was awake, engaging in thought-provoking discussions on books and politics. She and I had not had the occasion to have these times together when she was growing up at home. We would share what we'd been reading in an informal type of book club. I recall telling her of two books in particular I'd read about the nation: *Blue Highways* by William Least Heat Moon, a tale of a road trip to all forty-eight states but only on secondary roads and *Nine Nations of North America*, a view of nine very different regions of our country.

In the deep of a Bangor winter, where overnight temperatures were regularly in the negative numbers, I had recently purchased an Isuzu diesel truck that Wayne had recommended from experience as a car salesman. It proved to be a great vehicle for my long-distance commutes to Whiting, getting 38 miles per gallon. Its one nemesis was, however, the 14-to-1 compression ratio of a diesel engine, making it extremely hard to start in those cold mornings. Yet, somehow the truck managed to start every time with its glow plugs and without a plug-in engine heater.

So went my year, cycling between Bangor and Whiting every week, making a skimpy salary/commission, and beginning to see signs of Judy's next period of unrest. This time it was the director of the boat school in Eastport, a tall, somewhat handsome older man, balding, and perhaps a father figure to Judy. Junior Miller had been involved in boat building for a good thirty years and was an avid sport fisherman and one of the local good old boys. He had reportedly been one of the vigilantes and leader of a group that went around stealthily blowing up old and now unused dams up a river that had formerly been used for power generation. Their purpose was to remove part of the dams to allow fish such as salmon to freely pass up the river to spawn. Newer dams all had correct passages or ladders for the fish to move up freely.

I wasn't home most of the time but it was clear that they were becoming especially close friends. On nights when I was home, they talked on the phone for long periods. I would usually choose to leave the room, feeling better not hearing whatever went on. Since I didn't like confrontations I never spoke up or demanded that this behavior stop. This was the beginning of the end of our marriage, although it was to take another year to completely dissolve.

It turned out soon after that he had a very swift-moving form of lung cancer. It had come from the lifetime of working with fiberglass and the insidious needle-like particles so easily inhaled. Few people in the early days realized the dangers associated with the fiberglass industry. He died a month or so later.

Chapter Sixteen

Back Down South

The summer of 1984, Judy finished the fishing course and, in an attempt start over after her affair, we decided to sell the Whiting house. We certainly weren't in an ideal location no town to speak of, only a small grocery store at the corner, and miles from even the small towns of Lubec and Machias. I had decided to quit my job at the Black Stove Shop, affectionately called the White Slave Shop by its employees. It was time for a change and this job had no future.

We had fixed up, painted, and renovated the house and it sold in less than two weeks for around $32,000, giving us a small profit. We knew we didn't want to live in the city, opting instead for Peaks Island, the perfect mix of a small town with the city of Portland just a half-hour ferry ride away. Judy had lived on the island from age two to six and her mother, Janice Randall and aunt, Nancy, had grown up there. Judy and I had also visited the island several times after we first met in 1976.

So, in a little over a year, we were back in the moving mode. While looking for a place on Peaks Island, we were lucky to be able to live temporarily with her grandparents, Walter and Marjorie Randall, in South Portland. They had also lived on Peaks Island from the 1920s to the early 1950s. Grampa Walter had run the gas station. Several generations of Randalls came from Peaks, along with Trefethens and Sterlings, two of the four founding families on Marjorie's side. Cliff Randall was well remembered as the captain of the one the Casco Bay Lines boats. Judy's childhood memories of the enchanting island spirited us forward.

To help us in our house search, we met up with Margaret Randall, a cousin in her nineties who knew the history and various available properties. Margaret met us at the ferry one foggy morning in her ancient VW and proceeded to tour us around some houses she thought we might like. One of these was on Upper A Street at the reasonable price of $24,000. It backed up to one of the island cemeteries on one side but was very close to another house on the other side. The only problem, she warned us as we bumped along the rough dirt road, was that there had been a fire recently at night before the mostly-volunteer fire brigade could be rallied to put the fire out. Although we had tackled a variety of older house restorations, when we saw it we realized this was way beyond our abilities. We needed something we could move into immediately and get our belongings out of the Randall's garage in South Portland where we'd been for nearly a month.

On a second visit to Peaks, we were introduced to Roland Dorais at the restaurant by the dock. Bearded, heavy-set, attired in shorts and a most casual Hawaiian shirt, Roland was recommended as the island's best real estate agent. He told us that, although there were few properties available, he had some in mind for us. He showed us one on Elizabeth Street several blocks from the water, heavily shaded and lacking appeal. We passed on that and the next. The only other property available was hardly our dream house, but we felt pressed to make a decision. Like so many I had bought before, this house was another compromise. After having taught classes about finding a well-sited property, it was hardly ideal, on a north slope with the direction of south at an angle off the back corner.

Our last three houses in Whiting, Cutler, and Bowdoin had all been squarely facing south. But Peaks Island offered no other choices. The present owners, Tom and Cassie Murphy, had already moved out. Tom, who had become an island building contractor, had begun by practicing on his own house. It had a relatively new roof and chimney, but the shed roof had no overhang for a gutter. And while it was partially winterized, more was needed. Yet the remaining work to be done didn't stop us from moving in right away, and we paid the asking price of $37,000 that day. That price seems a bargain in today's market, even considering that similar summer cottages on the island had sold for a quarter of that amount as recently as the early seventies.

In early September, we rolled our fully loaded U-Haul truck aboard the *Abenaki*, the island car ferry, and then drove to our new home. The standard fare for a car then was $7.50 each way, although a truck was a bit more. This was long before Casco Bay Lines got the idea of charging for a round trip. Moving to an island was an exciting experience for us.

Our new house had been built around the turn of the twentieth century as one of three cottages for the three daughters of the Jordan family. Initially on one parcel of land, the properties were later separated into three lots, which made for no set-back lines and very close-together homes. Two of the daughters, although rather elderly, were still living in the house alongside of us when we moved in.

The house was rather poorly posted and not very sturdy. The west side of the porch, made of old window sashes, had been used as a repair shop for bicycles. The opposite side was an open-ended mud room and entrance to the house. The former owner had installed a Petit Godin coal burning stove in the center of the main room. As with most cottages, there was no basement, just a crawl space partly open to the sea breezes. We later heard tales of how the whole house shook and vibrated when the washing machine went into spin; and one tenant in a nightgown, according to the story, was seen crawling beneath the half open cellar on a bitter freezing morning with a gas torch to thaw frozen pipes before taking her shower.

The cellar was unfinished and partially open to the coming winter winds and possible frozen pipes.

That fall we dove into making major improvements. We hired Bradford J. Brown, known as "Jay," a young island contractor who eagerly tackled our project. He began by converting the bike shop into part of the living room. This included new support beams, sheetrock for walls and ceilings, and two new windows. I managed to install two sets of book cases for all my books now moved for the umpteenth time. The shelves of wide clear pine came from a sawmill up country. Upstairs, Jay removed a small stained glass window, likely original, and in its place put a large five-foot window in the master bedroom, giving us a spectacular view of the bay, which unfortunately over the years, has been nearly obscured by tree growth.

As always, Judy quickly found work, this time as a secretary for Allied Construction in Portland. For several weeks, I worked for Jenny Yasi in the Harbor Deli, scooping ice cream and making sandwiches alongside Cynthia Cole, whom I discovered later was the former wife of John Cole, founder and editor of the weekly newspaper, *The Maine Times*. I also worked one day a week at Hillside Lumberyard on the island. Later, I found fairly steady work as a Window Quilt installer with Ken Bixby who ran All Season Comfort, a window treatment company in Portland. He kept me busy three or four days a week. Between Ken and the Hillside Lumber, I managed to eke out a living.

Working for Ken was, at times, difficult, as he was very set in his ways. Yet to his credit he taught me a lot about Window Quilt that I didn't know from my previous experience in my own business. Ken was the ultimate perfectionist and required exacting detail. For each job, he did the measuring and would write precise notes on an index card, telling me exactly how to do each job. Sometimes I felt as though I was back in high school. The pay, around $8.50 an hour, was meager by today's standards, but far better than the Black Stove Shop. On most jobs, I went out alone, which I preferred as I found him nearly impossible to work with on jobs that required the two of us. I wound up installing around fifty quilts a week and got fairly good at it.

By Thanksgiving, the house was done and comfortable to live in. I had managed to buy a Kent wood stove imported from New Zealand from the Black Stove Shop for a good discount as a former employee. With that and an ancient propane floor furnace we managed to keep warm, although we really weren't into winter yet. I had also talked Ken into giving me a discount on Window Quilts for the house, which made an enormous difference on old leaky windows. Jay had tightened most of them with plastic channels, removing the sash weights, and filling the void with insulation. However, when the wind howled across the bay that first winter it was hard to stay warm. The cellar was partly open and the cold blew up through the cracks in the floor. On these nights, we couldn't keep the house above sixty degrees. Over the years, I made major improvements that allowed us to be comfortable at well below zero.

And we still had our dog, dear old Denny. Judy and I would stoke the fire, take the 7:15 boat each morning leaving Denny inside. We came home on the 5:30 evening boat and Denny had to hold it all day, which he did without mishap. We also had Wiggy, the beautiful orange Maine coon cat, who had been with us for a number of years. John had graduated from Washington Academy and was living in Florida, with a job at Disney World.

Wiggy, short for Wee Wiggles, named by the kids. He was a beautiful orange, striped Maine cooncat. We had had Wiggy since Harpswell.

I was beginning to get used to island living that fall and winter even though there was always the constant struggle to finish my window installations in time to the truck —usually blocks away — catch a boat, let Denny out and get the last embers of the fire to start up again. My one day a week job at the lumber yard was a nice break to the commute and also a chance to get to know people to whom we made deliveries. My work mates were the manager, Frank Davis, and Philip Daigle who had grown up on the island and was recently out of high school. Tall and lanky, with a western-style swagger, Frank was a man of few words. He often made jokes such as, "You know why you can't keep Jews in jail? They eat locks." Philip entertained us with tales of how he and other kids eluded the island police in an old car or a snowmobile racing past the police station.

Our other regular yard employee was Charlie Day, another long time islander in his seventies who smoked a pipe. He knew a little about everything, especially lumber. Charlie and his wife lived in the apartment building around the corner from us. In the familiar Maine accent, he often grumbled to us how he had to take his wife uptown but it could only be at half-tide. She wouldn't or couldn't navigate a sloping gang plank.

Many Maine towns used enormous, heavy horse drawn rollers like this one in a painting by Rockwell Kent dated 1909.

300

Charlie vividly remembered winter days when he lived in Damariscotta, where, rather than plowing, the town had used a giant horse-drawn roller to pack the snow hard enough to drive on. Charlie and his wife are now long gone. They left the island shortly after I quit the lumber yard that fall. It was fun while it lasted.

My difficulties with Ken Bixby soon became apparent. He was the Maine rep for Window Quilt, as well as being a dealer. But he didn't trust me and thought I might steal customers so he took my dealership away from me. The most memorable and unpleasant episode with Ken occurred as we neared Christmas of 1984. I had installed several quilts for a woman in Falmouth. I handed her the invoice that Ken had prepared and she went to get what I expected to be a check. It was, in fact, an envelope with $425 in cash. This was the first time on a job for Ken that I had received cash. I didn't count it but simply took it on good faith that it was right. When I got back to the shop I handed Ken the envelope. Several weeks later, just before Christmas, he called me in and told me that normally, he would have given me a bonus for the year. But unfortunately, on the Falmouth job, he had no record of payment even though the invoice was marked "cash." He was implying I had kept some of the money for myself. The whole incident was bizarre and I felt especially stupid for not having made him count it and sign for it. This was the end of whatever friendship had existed with Ken. Although I continued to work for him for several months more, it wasn't a pleasant time.

My relationship with Judy was also on its way out. She complained frequently of not having enough money or, more specifically, that I wasn't making enough. Change was on the horizon, although I couldn't quite see that far. And it came in the form of a co-worker of hers at Allied Construction in Portland.

His name was Gene Hayes and he came from Ohio, was a union worker, crane operator, was recently divorced and made good money. He also drove a shiny new sports car. I met him at a dive bar on Commercial Street on a Sunday afternoon in the spring of 1985 after Judy and I had returned from a trip. Gene was tall, a bit overweight, gray to white hair, with a small goatee. He treated us to a drink and with some flourish hauled out an enormous roll of twenty-dollar bills. A man of means, clearly; I could see that Judy was quite impressed. After her concerns with money and, as we were at the moment, particularly strapped, this did it. What followed was quite predictable. Each evening Judy would come home, excited and talking openly about her new friend Gene. I knew the end was at hand.

In March, Judy announced that she and I were going to Cincinnati to an all expenses paid company party put on by Allied Construction for its employees. We stayed in a hotel downtown and on Saturday night, there was a big dinner and dancing. While I enjoyed the treat, I knew that Judy was moving on to her next chapter. When we got back to Maine, she rather casually announced that she and Gene would be living together in Portland. It was so simple, but also terribly painful. And I knew deep down, that no matter what, I still loved her. I couldn't just turn it off like a light switch. She tried to convince me that change was always for the better, yet still, it was hard to take. And I told myself that I must have got what was coming to me.

To add to my feeling of gloom, I had decided to have a medical procedure for a double hernia that I had been unable to overcome through Christian Science. Judy had insisted on the operation while I was still covered by her medical insurance, since I had never had any insurance. Shortly after Judy moved off the island, I went into Maine Medical Center for a few days.

I returned to an empty house sometime in April, forbidden to work for several weeks: no heavy lifting, not even my tool box. I was still working for Ken Bixby, and by May, when I went back to work, it was only for a few days a week. I found myself having trouble concentrating on what I was doing, idly thinking about the last ten years being a sort of waste. I'd thrown away a good life, a wife and child, for what? For a woman who hopped and skipped in and out of my life leaving me devastated. Then I realized feeling sorry for myself wouldn't solve anything. Soon after, I quit working for Ken. I didn't need another toxic relationship at this point in my life.

While I was taking it easy I found time to again respond to a personal ads in the *Maine Times*. I met Pat Foley through an ad toward the end of May. She came over to Peaks one day and we sat on the couch and talked. I was attracted to her but maybe I was on a sort of rebound. She had short curly hair, a nice cheerful smile, was about my height and about ten years younger. After one more visit she suggested that I come over to live at her place in Portland. I don't recall what had become of her husband but she lived in a large old house in a nice part of town with a barn out back where her twenty-five-year-old son, Happy, lived. After all my depression, mild as it was, I decided to move in with her in June.

After a week or two I began to realize that Pat was a bit difficult to live with. She insisted that I pay for my groceries which was okay but as I had no income it began to cut into my savings. Toward the end of June, it was clear that she and I were not that compatible. I left and was happy to return to the island.

During the summer, I experimented with several other relationships which were all very tentative and vague. I had found out about a singles club in Portland that had weekly dances and other functions. It was easy to meet a number of women, some of them fairly interesting, but I exercised caution with all of them. Close relationships weren't in the cards as I soon realized they had all had bad experiences and were not ready to get serious with anyone. After my failed time with Pat, this sort of "keep your distance" attitude was probably just as well. For the rest of the summer, I went with the "gang" on hikes, bike trips, boat rides, and singles dances.

In August, Judy and I made our divorce final. It was actually quite simple and since nothing was contested and there were only a couple of pages of lawyer talk, the total cost was $145. During this sort of withdrawal time, Judy keep coming back into my life feeling sorry for what she had done in leaving me. She even suggested that she might move back in with me, an offer I firmly rejected.

Chapter Seventeen

I Embark on My Next Adventure

Autumn progressed and I decided to go back to work for Ken Bixby – "better the devil you know, than the devil you don't," as the saying goes. Every so often I would drive down to Needham, Massachusetts to visit Judy's sister, Marcia and her husband Lowell. On one such occasion Marcia thought I might be interested in meeting a friend of hers. This friend, a schoolteacher, had been single for a while and lived in Newton. "Nothing romantic," Marcia said.

A few days later, I called Ellie Palais as Marcia suggested, Ellie said that she had a date for Friday and Saturday nights but she was available the following Saturday afternoon, so we set up a date for Saturday, November 2, 1985.

Meantime, I had been thinking of selling the island house and embarking on a grand adventure, as inspired by my reading of William Least Heat Moon's book *Blue Highways*. After he had fought "the Indian wars" and lost, with his wife, also a Native American, he customized an old van and drove across the country on the back roads or "blue highways." I had the fantasy of doing the same with my old island 1970 green Ford Econoline.

My plans were roughly sketched out. My first move was to list my house with an island realtor. I signed a contract sometime in October that I would sell the house for $70, 000 — the price had doubled in one year! Things were in motion but hardly well planned. My vague thoughts were if the house were to sell, I'd put all my belongings in storage and head west, eventually arriving on the west coast where, naturally, I'd buy a boat to sail across the Pacific Ocean. Yet, my plans didn't include meeting a partner. It's interesting how the road turns and how various choices affect our lives; I like to think that I've made the right ones, like Robert Frost and his "Road Not Taken": "and that has made all the difference."

I drove from Maine to Massachusetts to meet Ellie on that November morning, and arrived mid-morning at her home on Ferncroft Road in Waban, one of Newton's thirteen villages. Ellie liked to remind me over the years that I showed up at her house in my clattering pickup truck, in my slightly torn North Face down jacket with a patch over a burn hole, your typical "man from Maine." We sat in her living room exchanging stories from our very different backgrounds. It turned out that we knew many of the same people, namely my former boss, Carl Tillinghast, the

Assistant Director of Smithsonian Astrophysical Observatory. Although we came from different environments my country roots set in eastern Pennsylvania and her Manhattan childhood we were roughly the same age and our parents were both from Pennsylvania. We immediately hit it off.

We took a road trip that day, driving out to pick up bird food at the Audubon Center in Lincoln. On the way back, we decided to stop at Walden Pond for a brisk walk, my first visit there. All the time we chattered away; I'm sure I dominated the conversation bragging and name dropping. She told me later that she couldn't believe I was for real: why was I single and unattached? We returned to Newton and said goodbye. Although she had a date that evening, she asked if we could meet again. Sometime later she confessed her "date story" was made up; she didn't want to appear eager or "dateless." I agreed to call her later. I left feeling very positive about my first date with Ellie Palais.

I spoke to her sometime during the next week but we didn't make a date until the second weekend. I came back to Newton and we had a movie date where we went to Chestnut Hill to see *The Kiss of the Spider Woman* with William Hurt. Afterwards we went back to her house. It had begun to snow and we lay on the floor in front of the fire and watched the snow in the back yard. And the rest is history as they say. Soon after Ellie came to visit me on Peaks Island, around the end of November. I well remember her bringing a suitcase which she dragged down the street on its wheels, the sign of someone from away. She soon graduated to a small back pack, much more in keeping with island custom. By December, it was clear that we had each found our ideal partner. Every Friday, after working for Ken, I would head for Newton and spend the weekend with her.

To my utter surprise, in early December the real estate agent called with the happy news that a woman from away had made an offer at full price! At this point I did not want to sell the house as I was to embark on a more exciting adventure. I awkwardly backed out of the deal, much to the displeasure of the realtor. I was saved from sure disaster by Ellie Palais. I'm sure I would have disappeared into the depths of the Pacific Ocean.

As we approached the Christmas holidays, Ellie told me she was renting a house in North Conway, New Hampshire as had been her custom in the past. Here, all her three grown up children and her then eighty-year-old mother would spend about a week. I was invited to join the gang and arrived a day or two before Christmas. There was plenty of snow, skiing, and a real old fashioned New England type celebration. Neither the children or her mother made any comments about Ellie and me sleeping together – it just seemed natural.

This was my first chance to meet her kids: Julie, twenty-eight, a graduate of University of New Hampshire, and a recent PhD in glaciology from Ohio State working at University of Rhode Island; Robert, twenty-six, a Harvard graduate with a PhD in math from UC Berkeley; and David, twenty-two, from UNH and on to graduate school at Arizona State in geology. What an academic family! And Ellie's mother Madeleine, who'd arrived from New York City, a math teacher and still teaching at a private school in Manhattan.

We spent the rest of our five days in North Conway enjoying the snow and the holiday atmosphere. But there were, I found, small family tensions. I knew this was common in many families, in my experience as an only child, I didn't have these conflicts. After the week, we found it was time to go our separate ways and we parted with hugs and cheers for the New Year.

I returned to my dull job for Ken Bixby, but was happy that to have found a perfect and compatible partner in Ellie. Not long after the holidays, I decided to move in with her in Newton. I was still working part time for Ken and spent weekends in Newton, and it seemed perfectly normal to live with Ellie. By this time Judy and Gene had moved from Portland to Old Orchard Beach and soon after, to Saco, Maine. Judy continued to write me letters as if I were family.

Ellie and I visited them in once in Saco. I had agreed to keep Wiggy, the cat, while Judy took Denny, which was a good arrangement since I wasn't on the island much. Sometime that spring we took Wiggy to live with Amie who was now living at Lake Lucerne, near Bangor. I missed the animals, but not their care. After her divorce, Amie and her new boyfriend had moved into a cabin on the lake. Ellie and I went to visit later in the spring. By this time, the cat had gone wild because they weren't home a lot. He was an old cat and I felt bad that he had been abandoned. I secretly hoped some good neighbor had taken him in.

Also abandoned in Amie's move was my parents' four post, bell and ball antique bed with a hard, lumpy horse-hair mattress that I had given her when I left Cutler. Not having room for it while she was living with her Bangor friends, the Saindons, she had stored it in a friend's empty house. For several years, I had half-heartedly attempted to rescue it. I never did find it, though. I hope someone put it to good use. I, like lots of my contemporary vagabond colleagues, have left a scattered trail of shed belongings like a snake sheds its skin from Texas to Florida to California and back. The bed would probably bring a pretty price these days. My remaining memory of the bed is a cherished pastel drawing by my father from when they lived at The Philadelphian.

I have a cherished pastel drawing my father made of the bed in their bedroom when they lived at The Philadelphian. It brings back pleasant memories.

Antique beds had been part of my life for decades. Karyl and I bought the first of many from Clarkie Bailey in Newbury, Massachusetts while we were living in Amesbury. Like most eighteenth century beds, it was about three feet high at mattress level and had very delicate shaped thin pencil-like posts and the original rust red color. Its distinction was that it was a roped bed; the rails, head and foot boards were held together with a network of rope. Somewhere we found the proper tools to assemble and string the bed. These tools were a wooden mallet, a twisting device that had a slot that fit over the rope and had a handle; finally, two fids or wooden spikes. It was best put together with two persons, at least until the first rows of rope where in place to hold the rails together.

I was slowly slipping away from my antique past into the modern day present. Sometime during the spring of 1986, I also slipped away from my not so pleasant job with Ken Bixby and found my way to Cambridge Alternative Power Company, better known as CAPCO in Cambridge, Massachusetts. This was to be my niche for the next three to four years and, for the most part, a very pleasant and educational experience or at least until the bitter end.

I first found CAPCO by noticing the store as I drove by. It was hard to miss if you drove west on Concord Avenue in Cambridge as there was a large old style, windmill out front on a forty-three-foot tower, the kind that was used for pumping water on farms. The remodeled building, once an Amoco gas station, was the most appropriate symbol imaginable new energy overtaking the old. The business had been started in November of 1978, following the second energy crisis of 1977, by three men with quite different backgrounds: Nelson "Buck" Robinson, bookstore proprietor and a prime mover in the Sierra Club; Bert Johansson, owner of a twenty-five-year-old passive solar home and retired journalist from *The Christian Science Monitor*; and Dr. Alfred , a "no-nukes" former dentist.

These three had combined their talents, realizing there was an opportunity to start a business based on the available alternatives to conventional energy. The symbol of the defunct gas station was perfect and an article in *The New Yorker* of January 14, 1980 captured it in the "Talk of the Town" section. A moneyman, a newspaper writer, and an entrepreneur hit the market at just the right time. They did in grand style what I had unsuccessfully tried some time too early in Machias, start an energy store. Of course, there was no location better than Cambridge, with its multitudes of academics and wealthy, tweedy liberals eager for the energy revolution. The store featured a variety of woodstoves, a myriad of energy saving appliances, and of course, my trade, Window Quilt. At the time of my arrival there CAPCO was the largest and most active dealer of Window Quilt in the United States. Interestingly they never attempted to promote or sell wind energy generation, but the tower with the multi-bladed mill on top became their logo and attraction on the corner of Concord and Walden for at least ten years.

By the time I arrived on the scene, the original three founders had sold out and moved on to different things and the new owners, Norm Coburn and Peter Lavenson, were a completely different pair. They also owned New England Hot Tubs in Natick and were aiming at the wealthy, upscale crowd in Cambridge. They were more interested in making money than serving the alternative energy followers. I started off in sales, as well as installation, mostly of window treatments. Around the fall of 1986, both Window Quilt and woodstoves became much in demand. I would be given three or four leads and appointments a day to measure and close the sale. Between the sales and installations, I was quite busy and happily making money again.

Norm and Peter may have been an odd couple, but they seemed to get along well as business partners. Norm, a portly man in his early forties, had grown up in Newton, gone Newton North High School, and as the story goes, was chased home after school by the big kids. He was always pleasant and polite to me. I would bring him an invoice for my installation work and he would exclaim "that seems like a lot… but if you're making money, we must be too." Peter Lavenson was completly the opposite. He often wore an inscrutable smile — almost like the Cheshire cat. I always felt uncomfortable with Peter but never knew just why. I believe Peter came from a background of money. His father had a fancy sailboat and cruised the Maine coast summers.

Peter had a large modern house in Wayland where he usually would give the company Christmas party. I recall a cold evening there when some of us enjoyed his steaming hot tub outside on the deck. Although it was fun to try out the hot tub I never felt I would want one. Of course, hot tubs were the specialty of CAPCO and the eventual escape route for the business when the energy fad began to fade. During the CAPCO years, I was happy with the job I had. And at that time, they were making plenty of sales and money, riding the energy conservation bubble just before the tax credits departed and the energy business began to slide downhill.

That first year or so living with Ellie involved lots of outdoor activities, trips, and fun. That first spring after we met we decided to try Blacks Woods at Acadia National in mid-April during her spring vacation from Belmont High. It was even for me a bit on the chilly side, sleeping out in a tent at the park, and it is fun to look back on. Also, Acadia doesn't have the luxury of most other campgrounds and only has cold water bath/shower facilities — a bit Spartan.

Our further travels took us to Newfoundland for a few weeks that summer. We had read about two islands lying off Newfoundland, St Pierre and Miquelon. These islands belonged to France and were actual French territory, but only six miles from the Canadian coast. They had been settled near the sixteenth century and had an interesting history. No one I knew had been there or even heard of them. A worthy goal indeed.

We gathered our camping gear, including a new Sierra Design two-man dome tent, cooking supplies, and two of Ellie's sleeping bags, and put them in the back of my truck. We drove most of the day from Peaks Island along the coast past Cutler, then past Whiting to Lubec and across the Canadian border to Campobello Island. It was a review of my previous life, place by place. We had decided to stay on Campobello at a provincial park. As I had found out when Judy and I camped previously, the provincial parks were usually uncrowded and cleaner than most to the US state parks and sometimes even the federal parks.

Campobello Island is about nine miles long by three miles wide, and lies on the narrow entrance to Passamaquoddy Bay and Eastport. Strong, deep water currents of up to five knots flow by it. It is joined to the Uniited States by a modern bridge. It looks as though it should be part of Maine but has always been firmly under Canadian ownership.

We set up our campsite right near the shore. After cooking our favorite corned beef hash, we sat around the fire, and turned in early. We had just drifted off into what we expected to be quiet slumber when a group of teenagers in a nearby tent erupted into loud hollering, well past eleven o'clock. I, being a light sleeper, was not able to get back to sleep. Suddenly, Ellie, usually a quiet person, sat up and leaning out of the tent, shouted in a commanding voice, "It's time to be quiet — shut up!"

President Franklin Roosevelt's summer "cottage" on Campobello Island, New Brunswick. It is now operated by the Roosevelt Campobello International Park.

I was impressed. I'm sure I would have grinned and borne it, so to speak. But Ellie being a longtime school teacher knew how to command respect and quiet. That was the end of the loud kids.

The next morning, we decided to play tourist and went to visit the "cottage." The term cottage was popular in the late nineteenth century for the enormous mansions used as summer retreats for the very rich in wealthy towns like Camden and Bar Harbor. The Roosevelt cottage, we were informed, had thirty-four rooms and rambled on and on. Most of the rooms commanded impressive views of the Head Harbor Passage, between small islands into the Bay. This narrow stricture with surging currents was one reason Eastport, Maine was rejected as a possible oil terminal in 1973.

Around noon, after looking for the ferry to Deer Island, Ellie and I found our way to the small and poorly marked dirt ramp on the north side of Campobello, where a wooden barge just big enough for two cars was beached. A rather hefty lobster boat was tied alongside. We drove on, realizing the barge was double ended so we could drive off. The trip to Deer Island, New Brunswick was about ten minutes across the bay waters that swirled between the islands. This was probably the shortest ferry crossing I'd ever experienced, except possibly one across a river in Virginia where the barge took only one car, was attached to a cable, and pulled over by hand.

We drove onto Deer Island where there was no customs or immigration, just a road across the island marked as a Canadian Highway. After about a ten minute ride, we came to "real" ferry dock where more cars stood in line, having arrived from Eastport on a similar ferry. Presently we drove onto a much larger ferry, part of the free highway system. In about twenty minutes, we ended up in St. Andrews, saving several hours of driving up the whole west side of Passamaquoddy Bay on US Route 1. It was Ellie's first time here, but I was familiar with the town from earlier business trips and vacations. We continued on, since our goal was Fundy National Park some miles away. We passed through St. John, the largest city in New Brunswick, with some 70,000 residents. It seemed to be mostly an industrial and commercial port city. We pushed on to the park.

We finally arrived near dark and pitched our tent at Fundy National Park, located at the head of the Bay of Fundy. The heavily-wooded park was one of the most beautiful we were to see. Our campsite was close to the shore on a high steep cliff, looking over the bay and its remarkable thirty-foot tidal range. The next day we pushed on to Nova Scotia, arriving late in the afternoon in North Sidney, where we were to board a ferry for Port au Basques on the southwest tip of Newfoundland. The ferry didn't leave until nearly midnight, so we had time to kill. Not knowing when our next meal might be, we found a cheery restaurant that served reasonably good food.

Our boat was referred to as the "slow boat," as it took six hours to make the crossing. We sat in line in the truck at the terminal, a bit like our Peaks experience but on a much larger scale. The ship was probably several hundred feet long. Once we drove into the mammoth hold and parked we went up a level with several lounges, private cabins, and dining facilities. We soon saw that the Newfies grabbed carpeted floor space to bed down for the trip overnight to Port au Basques.

Ellie and I had read up a bit on the history of Newfoundland before we left. This large island, first discovered by the Vikings around 1000 AD with a semi-permanent settlement on its northern tip called L'Anse aux Meadows, was later visited by various British explorers among them John Cabot in 1497 at Bonavista in the northeastern tip. Here also about this time were small groups mainly of Irish fishermen. The island was later claimed for England in 1583 by Sir Humphrey Gilbert. It was then the first English colony in the New World and remained more or less under British control until after World War II. At this point and with some debate, the territory of Newfoundland and Labrador voted to become part of Canada in 1949. As the tenth province of Canada, it was the poorest, relying on its forests and fisheries with a bare subsistence economy and virtually no major agriculture.

As we toured, we discovered a deep distrust of the new government that had developed in the 1960s as part of consolidation and government streamlining. Most of the small fishing outports that lined the island's periphery were closed and the residents moved to newly created and more centralized towns. This heavy-handed move on the part of the government alienated most of the old-time residents.

Our first night was spent at a provincial park at the town of Blow Me Down an hour or two north of Port aux Basques. The area lived up to its name. A strong wind blew mist and at times light rain as we set up our tent. We were impressed, as with other Canadian parks, with the cleanliness and overall quality of the campsites compared with the state parks we had been at in the US

Next we headed north along valleys and deep cuts through great bare, ice carved rocks and spectacular views. Soon after we came to Cornerbrook, the largest town on the west side of the island with a population of about 20,000. All I remember was the enormous paper and pulp mill that produced sheetrock and smoke and was entirely too industrial for our liking. It intruded on the beautiful and stark countryside.

Our next destination was the Gros Morne National Park, the main attraction on the west coast, and the entrance to the western peninsula on the way to Labrador. As we drove up especially steep inclines, we noticed our diesel truck began to have problems making the steep grades until we were barely crawling at 15 or 20 mph. I figured it was due to different type of fuel in Canada. Just south of the park we came to the small village of Rocky Harbor, a coastal fishing town with a store and restaurant several miles from the park. The area had once been inhabited by the Mikmaq tribe, then later became a French fishing site. The village had grown to a population of nearly a thousand after the opening of the National Park in 1973.

The National Park lay at the foot of Gros Morne, which rose about 2,000 feet. It had outstanding facilities as we had seen at other Canadian parks with spotless wash rooms with running hot and cold water and indoor cooking spaces. We would have liked to stay more than one night but felt we should be pushing on toward the other side of this 600-mile-long island. However, we did take time to make a side excursion because I had wanted to look at the northwest tip that almost touched Labrador.

The weather was cool and misty as we drove along the coastal secondary road to St. Anthony, a port town made famous by Dr. Wilfred Grenfell and his Christian Mission. With nearly 2,500 residents, it was located only twenty-six miles across the Straits of Belle Isle to Labrador, the other part of Newfoundland Province. Here in St. Anthony, Grenfell had started his Mission to help local fishermen in the early part of the twentieth century, but it later reached across the straits to help native inhabitants. There wasn't much to see on this less than summery day so we headed south to continue across the northern stretches of the island. On our way home that night on the small narrow secondary road we saw at least one moose, eyes shining by the side of the road.

The next day we packed up our gear and headed across the northern part of the island. We stopped south of Lewisport for the evening and, not being able to find any kind of suitable campground, slept in the back of the truck where it was hot and the mosquitoes fiercely buzzed outside our screens. The scenery was especially dull, flat and treeless.

We soon missed the spectacular west coastal scenes as we moved on past Gander. This had been an airport, first built in 1936 as a refueling stop for transatlantic aircraft, and later became an important part of getting aircraft ferried across the ocean during World War II. At one point over 13,000 planes stopped there annually. I recall landing there to refuel as I flew on a Pan Am four- engine Constellation from England in 1960, hardly an exciting stopover. With the advent of the jet plane, the airport's need declined. We didn't stop to inspect or take a "gander."

We'd read about the northeast corner of Bonavista, a small peninsula on the Atlantic coast; the freelance Venetian explorer, Giovanni Cabotto, aka John Cabot, had been one of the first here. Cabot was hired by England's King Henry VIII to find a route to the Orient. But instead, Cabot, in 1497 fetched up on this point saying "O Buon Vista!" ("Oh happy sight") And it was. We drove down a winding narrow road out to a point with a lighthouse; on both sides, there were marvelous fences made of woven tree branches. Later, we had lunch at a simple house in the village of about 4,500 people, recommended by someone we'd spoken to. We almost turned up our noses at the unimpressive building housing the restaurant but we were pleasantly surprised to find quite a good place to eat. Over our meal, we talked to two women who described the wonderful experience of a three-week adventure by steamer along the entire Labrador coast and all the stops at the various outposts.

That afternoon, we were directed to a hike nearby up a nearly overgrown dirt path that led to a field and cliffs overlooking the sea. There were remains of old frame buildings and houses from an abandoned village. Most of the walls had caved in and were rotting away. This was one of the hundreds of abandoned outposts that the new government closed in the 1960s, in an effort to move inhabitants to centralized towns. Soon the grass and trees would take over. Nearby, a group of what appeared to be wild horses grazed, evidence of the tragedy of the displaced families. It was very moving to see firsthand.

That night we camped at Terra Nova National Park on the way to St. John's, the major city of the island with a population of more than 100,000. We had noticed the increasing number of tourists and the park was crowded, hot, dusty and overrun with noisy families, just what we had wanted to get away from. We were coming back into an urban setting which had no appeal. The best part of Newfoundland, we suddenly realized, was behind us on the west coast so we turned around and giving up our goal of St. Pierre and Miquelon and hightailed it back to Gros Morne.

We were happy to be back there the next night; it felt like home. In the remaining week of our vacation we took some short side trips, the most memorable being our day trip to Western Brook. Western Brook is actually more of a pond and is according to advertising, the only true fjord in North America. The pond has been cut off from the ocean by a glacial moraine and is about a half mile walk and a hundred foot climb along a path in scrub growth. Our trip leader spoke at length of the adventure of dragging the 55-foot motor boat up this grade in the winter over ice and snow. Luckily I had my first video camera along and have captured much of this trip up the fjord. Perhaps they did it with a team of oxen as was done years ago in Maine with houses from the mainland to islands over frozen harbors.

About twenty-five of us clambered aboard the land-locked ocean vessel. As we cruised slowly along the quarter mile-wide vertical ice-carved walls, the skipper recited the history of the glacier and the region. Some of the walls were easily one thousand feet high. This two to three-hour trip took us through what was probably the most spectacular canyon views on the east coast of North America.

During the rest of our time we took a several other side trips. One was a two-hour hike to the Tablelands in another part of the park. The attraction here was the barren landscape and its various geologic features. The guide pointed as we walked along a boundary feature of the continental margin with mantle and crust sequences occurring. Its long gradual slopes on wide open stretches of red-brown rock were more like our western states and far less interesting than the fjord. For these and other reasons the park was designated a UNESCO World Heritage Site.

There were several things that stood out in Newfoundland that we noticed when we arrived. Similar to my time in Alaska, the vegetation grew amazingly large during the short growing season but with extra long days. Queen Anne's lace was two or three times larger than what you might see in Maine. The same went for pitcher plants. It was like being in a science fiction drama. One night while traveling in the misty fog, a giant moose wandered right in front of us, hardly afraid. And near the same spot one sauntered across at noon. All the tales we had heard were right: avoid running into a moose. And as we were getting close to departure time we came on a treasure trove of ancient wooden lobster traps made of bent branches on a road side beach. We took what we could stow aboard our truck. Other treasures were two tape recordings of local groups with their quaint Newfie accents.

My last recollection of that visit to Newfoundland is as we were about to drive on the ferry at Port aux Basque. We were directed through what appeared to be a car wash. Our truck was thoroughly washed and rinsed, making sure that no plants or agricultural products from this island was transported to the US Our visit was a great success; even if we missed getting to those little French islands, we knew we would return. Which in fact we did the next summer. Our visit had lasted about three weeks, during which we had nearly perfect weather, although we'd heard that we could expect but a few nice days. Yes, there were a number of foggy times but very little rain and chilly days. Newfoundland had been one of our best vacations.

Over the next two or three years we were drawn back to this *Wonderful, Terrible Island*, the title of a picture book we picked up. Two of my fondest memories were our excursion to Burgeo and the visit to L'Anse aux Meadows.

Burgeo lay about seventy-five miles east of Port Aux Basques, which, up until 1990, had only been reached by fast commuter boat, but it had now a road in from the north. The road, more than a hundred miles of dirt and gravel cut straight through rather uninteresting scrubby country, was totally uninhabited. The village, a well-protected harbor and steep surrounding hills, was a typical pretty fishing town of about 2,000 inhabitants. We had dinner at a small restaurant and then drove out of town to a local park right on the ocean where we got a camping permit from the resident game warden and spent the night.

Ellie and I had both read the book *A Whale for the Killing* by Canadian author Farley Mowat, about the area. When he first moved to this remote and isolated coastal fishing village in the late 1960s, he was overwhelmed by the friendly reception he got from the all the villagers, even though he was an outsider from Ontario. These people were uncorrupted by modern technology. He had, he thought, found a small part of heaven. In fact, he found he could leave his door unlocked and neighbors would borrow tools return them or he could do the same. But over the course of the eight years there he became disillusioned as he found the dark side of this idyllic community. During a storm an errant 80-ton Fin whale became trapped by falling tide in a lagoon — and worse yet in a monthly tidal cycle where the water height recedes. For twenty-five days, the whale was completely trapped. Then, as Mowat watched dismayed, his neighbors he had so liked, began to taunt the whale by shooting at it for target practice. With the death of the whale, Mowat was so disgusted that he left the village and moved to another province.

Had we not known about the whale episode, there were no clues that Burgeo and its citizens were as Mowat had portrayed and somehow, I dared not ask anyone about it. As we headed north out of town that morning, we were happy we'd seen a bit off the beaten path.

On a subsequent visit we returned to the northern area of Newfoundland to visit the impressive L'Anse aux Meadows, another UNESCO World Heritage Site. The area was carefully documented by Dr. Helge Ingstad, a Norwegian explorer, who along with his wife, Ann Stine, proved conclusively that a group of Vikings had wintered in several earth-bermed dwellings. There was a museum displaying many artifacts. We then walked through the reconstructed earth houses nearby. It was a bit of a thrill to stand inside of one of these huts and imagine living in this dark, gloomy space nearly a thousand years ago. We stayed at a B & B just outside the park. From our room's porch, we had a spectacular view of the water, where we saw our first ever icebergs gleaming a brilliant silver-blue in the late evening sun on their slow journey south from the west coast of Greenland.

Our camping and tenting experiences continued, with one of the favorite local spots was Balsam Cove campground in East Orland, Maine. We found this was probably the best we'd come across in all our camping trips. It was nicely situated on Toddy Pond just off Route 1 halfway between Bucksport and Ellsworth with about forty sites all close to the pond. It was run by Sandy and Dwight Gates from

Whispering Pines camp ground in East Orland on Toddy Pond between Bucksport and Ellsworth.

Danvers, Massachusetts who'd been there for almost as many years. We usually stayed three or four nights and tried to reserve the same site, B10. There was something serene and well-mannered about the grounds, never loud or noisy. Dwight kept the grounds and bathrooms neat and clean. It was such a pleasure to visit. I can remember how exciting the day was that we all saw the eagle fledgling fly from the top of a pine tree. And nearly every evening as we sat around the campfire in the still of the lake, we would hear the loons cry. We made recordings of them, as well as lots of video shots of the camp. We must have gone there for more than a decade. Sadly, in 2010, the Gates told us they had decided to sell the camp, that it was time to retire.

My relationship with CAPCO continued in good stead and I stayed busy with window treatments. But by 1988, Norm and Peter concluded that the alternative energy business was on the point of tanking, as all of the energy tax credits had been wiped out by the Reagan administration and the public had lost interest in the energy conservation movement. Instead, the folks at CAPCO expanded the hot tub business which had started in Cambridge and now also included an elegant line of sunrooms. The business was called New England Hot Tubs and Sunrooms, located in Natick on Route 9.

The product shift was an indication in a broader sense how much the nation had given up on saving energy and now slipped back to their old habits of consumption. The promising start that President Carter had brought about was all but abandoned. It's interesting to note that in the late 1970s the White House had installed a bank of solar collectors for heating hot water as a national symbol of using the renewable fuel of the sun. And shortly thereafter, President Reagan ordered them removed. Thirty-some years later, the Obama administration authorized the return of solar hot water collectors on top of the White House. One step ahead, two back, one ahead; solar collectors went up and down like a toilet seat.

For Christmas of 1988, Ellie and I flew to Los Angeles to be with her sister Margy, and brother-in-law, Danny Kivelson in Pacific Palisades. Joining us were David, Robert, and Amie who was now living in Southern California, and Ellie's mother from New York. It was a fun family event with all of us together except for Julie, who was in Antarctica and John, who was in Florida. With my recently purchased 8mm video camera, I shot several hours of footage as we all walked along the beach and boardwalk on Venice Beach. Later, in early January, Ellie, David, and drove up to San Francisco via Big Sur to attend Steven Kivelson's wedding. When we returned, Los Angeles was cold and un-California-like with snow down to one thousand feet, and chilly, wintry walks on the beach. When we flew home to Boston, I found myself in a changed job.

In January 1989, CAPCO was leased to David Giller, reportedly a slum landlord with questionable political connections. At first, David seemed to be genuinely committed to continuing to run the business in the spirit of the former owners through conservation and energy efficiency. But all too soon as time went on, began to realize Giller, like many other businesspeople, was really only in it for the money; in fact, the entire sales team began to see writing on the wall, especially when it came to collecting their sales commissions, with my closest sales colleague leaving the company over the struggle to collect paychecks.

Most of my time was spent installing Window Quilts and less in sales. During the winter, David found a lucrative opportunity with the city of Leominster Housing Authority for several of their public apartment buildings which amounted to about six hundred Window Quilts. I wrote the proposal and we won the bid in March. The project amounted to $88,000 and was funded by money that came back to the state from overcharges by Exxon Oil at no cost for the Housing Authority. Unfortunately, since David had made the sale, I got no commission.

My job was to measure the windows and when ready, install all the shades. spent a couple of weeks measuring in Leominster and managed to talk David into

317

letting me hire a couple of helpers. As the quilts came in, we worked four days a week with a daily goal of twenty-five shades a day. Each day, we commuted the eighty mile round trip to Leominster. My helpers prepped the shades, while I hung them. I moved along as fast as I could but it was exhausting work; we progressed through the spring into June. On days with no problems and things going smoothly, however, it was satisfying. And, because the project was well funded, I was able to collect each week from David.

The project was not without difficulties. Due to an oversight by both my helpers and myself, a number of Window Quilts in one of our orders had been measured incorrectly, with width and height dimensions reversed. When the Quilts came in several weeks later, they were all wrong and worthless. I drove to the factory in Brattleboro, Vermont and pleaded with one of the VPs to give us a break but to no avail. By this time, CAPCO's sales were sharply declining and the company wound up eating about $5,000 to have all of the shades remade. This was the beginning of my problems with David Giller.

Sometime in late July, I took a trip to visit Amie in Southern California. I spent four or five days staying with her and her two roommates whom she had first met and lived with in Bangor. Amie was working for a PR agency and she traveled a lot to Idaho on a project. One day, we all bicycled along the harbor and beach; on another, we all went deep sea fishing. These few days were a nice break to see Amie and to get myself straightened out.

Although there was plenty of work when I returned to CAPCO, it was clear the business was not doing as well as it had under the previous direction of Norm and Peter. By this time, David Giller decided to close up shop. And, he was refusing to pay me back invoices, mostly because of the money lost on the Leominster job. He owed me around $2,200. My only recourse was to take him to court, which meant I had to serve him with a summons to appear.

This was an interesting process. I had to climb a narrow outside stairway in an old building off Lechmere Square in Cambridge, plunk down $45 in cash to a sheriff who I was told would take David to the Cambridge District Court nearby. I appeared in Judge McDonald's court in mid-September, and stated my case: that I had performed work for which I was not paid. Ellie and I spent several hours sitting in the back of the courtroom listening to the complaints of housewives claiming shoddy workmanship. There was no murder or mayhem as I had listened to in Machias years before.

We went through at least one no show of David, which apparently is a normal tactic. Some of the other CAPCO employees also brought similar claims. Finally, David appeared a month later and called me out in the hall where he offered to pay out of court for the lesser amount of $1,350. I weighed the various possibilities and decided it was better than being out-maneuvered in some unsuspecting way. But with one of my other colleagues, he showed a reluctance to pay and the judge, perturbed by his manner, ordered the bailiff to take Giller away to a detention room. All of us cheered at this event. That was the last I ever saw of him. I read a small clip in the *Boston Globe* sometime later that he and his crony lawyer who was also a local politician, had been indicted for some scam or crime. He had been employing illegal immigrants from Ireland and renting his slum apartments to them.

And so ended a perfectly good business run into the ground. Norm and Peter sold the building; its new tenants were a group of accountants who made few changes. The sloping glass sunroom facing south remained with its awning. The windmill tower, long a familiar land mark on Concord Avenue survived for a while. Gradually the old Amoco gas station look disappeared. The final funeral for CAPCO was held sometime later that Christmas at a party thrown by Buck Robinson, one of the founders. A good number of the old timers showed up as Buck presented Norm and Peter with one of the gas nozzles from the original station nicely mounted on a display board and engraved with some mention of gas and solar energy.

With the end of the CAPCO era I was on my own. I had struck up a friendship with Jan Henshaw, a Window Quilt dealer in Bedford. She was primarily involved in decorative window treatments but also sold quite a few Window Quilts. She had been lucky to have been handed an enormous list of existing customers from another dealer who quit the business. She got a lot of orders and was able to give me installation jobs just when I needed some work. She had located her shop in a small office rented from Ben Sears, a local realtor and business man. As with so many serendipitous encounters it turned out that Ben was a Colby College graduate from the class of 1952. And, Ben's classmate Joe Lovegren was a Portland architect living on Peaks Island. Strange connections.

Not long after meeting Jan she announced she would be leaving the area because her husband, an architect, had found a better position in Vermont. She tried her best to interest me in buying her business. It might have been a good move but I felt her asking price was too much. I had received a similar offer from Norm and Peter who had a list of 6,000 names for which they wanted ten cents apiece. This too, seemed a large unknown since many names were old and people were moving frequently at that time. So, I did nothing which turned out to be the best move.

What I did do though, was to take over the office space that Jan had occupied in Bedford and set up shop for my business, HomeWorks, which later became Mainely HomeWorks. My rent for the space was $425 per month and Ben Sears included some basement storage area for parts and pieces of the Window Quilt business. It turned out to be a good location on a major route through town although I didn't get much walk-in traffic. Ben and I exchanged Colby news and through him I discovered my old girlfriend Carolyn English was working just down the road in Bedford at Milipore Corporation. She and Ben had become active in Colby alumni affairs.

I called Carolyn and met her for lunch at Milipore shortly after. I hadn't heard from her since our times together at Colby in 1953, nearly forty years before. Over lunch, she brought me up to date in her life. She had married her high school sweetheart; they had five children, now grown. After a divorce, she remarried a retired Navy chief. It was fun to catch up with her and relive my Colby days and her friends' various adventures or in some cases misadventures.

My shop, HomeWorks, in Bedford, Mass where I sold energy efficient products.

Over the years of the early and mid-1990s, Ellie and I continued our close and happy relationship. We talked openly of our thoughts and positions on the subject of marriage, but we couldn't bring the subject to any resolution. Luckily, we didn't have any children or former spouse problems to pressure us in any direction. We both still kept in touch with former spouses, planning family visits with her former husband, Dick Palais and his wife, Chuu Lian, when Ellie's kids came to visit. On my side of this equation, Ellie and I became good friends with Bob and Karyl, visiting them in Southport and although invited, they never came to Peaks Island.

I thought it was time to try my hand at boats again as we were surrounded by water and many of the Peaks Island residents had boats. I found that one had to have a mooring permit from the City of Portland. Past experience from other coastal towns had shown that there would soon be a limit on permits, so Ellie suggested that I apply even if I didn't have a boat. So, in 1992 I got a permit which required the name of the boat. I had already picked *Aurora*, a name popular among polar explorers; Dr. Frederick Cook's vessel was also called *Aurora*.

In spring of the following year, I noticed an ad in the *New York Times* for a twenty-four-foot Dolphin sloop that caught my interest. It was designed by Olin Stephens and built in 1965 by Marsco in Boston as hull #76. Ellie and I drove to Bridgeport, Connecticut to see it. At first, I was bit put off as I had somehow expected a white hull. She was black and had an outboard well and a 9 hp motor. Even though everything seemed in good shape, I decided to have her surveyed. I found a well-known surveyor and small boat expert named Hewitt Schlereth, who had written eleven books on marine and navigation topics. Satisfied, I paid the advertised price of $4,400 which included a small dinghy. I made a number of trips to Bridgeport to work on her and finally in late June I contracted with a boat transporter to take her to Southport Marine in South Portland.

One of the first things I did when she arrived was to have a sign painter make a quality name board for her stern. Now, I was back in business upon the water. Although *Aurora* had a fiberglass hull, the trim and mast were wood, which meant lots of maintenance but looked so nice. A year or two later, I took the mast down to bare wood and put on nine coats of varnish. Jay Brown made me up a cement block for a mooring which was cheap but I found out later was not nearly heavy enough; the ice that year dragged the mooring down the bay where I later found it. On our first sail down the bay, Ellie came along to be a good sport. As we passed the end of Peaks, the breeze piped up and we bowled along at what was probably maximum hull speed. I was thrilled. I later found out that Ellie was not used to sailing in a stiff breeze especially when the leeward rail was under water, and was a bit frightened. She hadn't complained but I could see she didn't enjoy this kind of sailing. While I launched into six wonderful summer seasons sailing with friends as far east as Boothbay and Damariscove, Ellie remained happier ashore.

Aurora, my twenty-four-foot Dolphin sloop that we cruised along the coast.

My window-shading business made mild progress in the early 1990s, still under the name HomeWorks. Now that I was operating in a more upscale environment. Ellie had suggested putting the word Mainely in front so instantly we became Mainely HomeWorks. We had also learned there was a company in Wellesley with the name Homeworks. I advertised in the local papers with only modest success and also joined the Bedford Chamber of Commerce, at the invitation of Ben Sears, where I got to known many of the businesspeople in town. During our monthly meetings, we exchanged business cards and socialized. I also exhibited at the New England Home Show in the fall and built a display booth. The eleven-day show generated quite a lot of good leads and subsequent business over the next two years.

In May of 1990, I was offered the opportunity I'd always wanted. Ellie's daughter, Julie, asked if I would take part of her job on the Greenland Ice Sheet Project 2 (GISP 2). This was to be an exciting new turn of events for me. I asked Stuart Moss, my old friend and colleague from CAPCO, to take over sales that summer while I was away. Since it was the slow time for my business I could install what he sold when I returned.

Chapter Eighteen

Greenland Ice Sheet Project 2
(GISP2)

During the late 1980s, I wanted to become involved in some aspect of what was then called global warming, now a somewhat controversial term in these divisive political times, and later replaced by the term climate change. My early geology courses, as well as subsequent graduate work in meteorology related to world and local climate change, had planted the seed. It seemed like a bright new field with an increasing number of scientific papers documenting rising temperatures and the connection to man-made contributions.

While working for the Maine Department of Marine Resources in Boothbay Harbor during the mid-seventies, I took measurements in bottom sediments on the Sheepscot River that had shown a gradual temperature rise over a number of years. One of the old timers there, Bob Dow, had shown lobster population data versus temperature over long periods. Although he was scoffed at back then, recent data from southern New England were showing significant declines in lobster populations, almost certainly due to sharply rising water temperatures. Clearly something was going on. I wanted to be part of this new field however possible.

My step-daughter, Julie Palais, had been working for a number of years in the Antarctic and Arctic, starting with her PhD work at Ohio State. In 1990, she was scheduled to work in Greenland, when she got an offer to join the Office of Polar Programs of the National Science Foundation (NSF) in Washington, DC. The assignment meant she needed someone to fill in for her for the remaining three weeks in the Arctic that summer. By May of 1990, I had landed a three-week job with the University of New Hampshire (UNH) team in Greenland, who were working on the Greenland project called GISP 2. For me it was a dream come true, just where I had always wanted to be in snow up to my neck or maybe like Br'er Rabbit in the Briar Patch.

The history of GISP 2 goes back to 1956 when Per Scholander at the University of Oslo first noticed that the gases trapped in tiny bubbles in ice cores taken from depths might yield accurate data on paleoclimates. Gases trapped over many centuries and even millennia were exact proxies of earlier climates. Following the initial sampling of ice cores at Camp Century, a US Army base in northern Greenland in the 1960s, a serious scientific project was begun at an abandoned radar site, Dye 3, in southern Greenland from 1979 to 1984 and was later called GISP 1.

There were problems introduced by the site location being too far south where errors were introduced by the ice cores melting. This later brought GISP 2 into existence with increased funding, improved protocols for data collection, and most importantly a better sampling site. The National Scienced Foundation invested $25 million to ensure success. In 1989, several scientists from UNH, led by Dr. Paul A Mayewski, surveyed and picked a site at the main ice divide called "Summit" . Here in the following season, construction of a permanent camp and a sheltered drilling dome began. Initial drilling started on what was to become a multi-year project to drill into bedrock more than three thousand feet below the surface. In three years the goal was accomplished. A parallel effort, which gave supporting and verifying data of the ice cores, was mounted about sixteen miles away by a European funded group, called GRIP.

After receiving a thorough physical exam which assured NSF and UNH that I was fit for work at higher altitudes, I was scheduled to leave for Greenland on August 11, 1990. Ellie and I decided to forgo our annual summer trip back to New-foundland and instead spent a week in Nova Scotia prior to my departure. It was okay, but we realized how much we missed camping at our favorite spots. August 11 was Ellie's birthday, but instead of celebrating, she and I waited at the rest stop on Route 95 until around ten o'clock that night, when the UNH vehicle came to pick me up.

In preparation for the worst-case scenario, I had purchased all sorts of cold weather clothing: expedition weight long johns, warm jacket, an expensive Marmot shell, gloves, hats, a neck gaiter, boots, and a very warm down sleeping bag. All this was packed carefully into two large cargo bags. Paul Mayewski was driving the University van with mostly graduate students and other helpers. I rode up front with him as we headed west to Scotia, New York where our transportation to Greenland, the 109th Air National Guard (ANG), was stationed, .

Paul told me of his plans for renting a summer estate in Blue Hill, Maine, for scientific meetings. To my surprise he had been negotiating with Anne Nevin Chamberlin, Berto's older sister, on her palatial house, "Arcady," originally built for Berto's grandfather, the famous American composer, Ethelbert Nevin. What a coincidence! I hadn't seen Anne or heard much about her since my days at Berto's in 1949-50. This made for good talking and stories I told for the rest of the night's trip.

The next morning we all rallied at the ANG airport, got a briefing from some Air Force officers about the trip which would be made on their Hercules C-130 cargo planes equipped with skis. It was very exciting for an airplane buff like me. We were to dress in cold weather gear since the plane wasn't heated and in case we went down somewhere in the Arctic — a cheerful thought. Many of the people on the trip had been there before and took all this routine as very ordinary. But I was having

We boarded an Air National Guard C-130 equipped with skis at Scotia, NY on August 12.

fun and took it seriously. All our gear was packed and loaded through the enormous tail door ramp. However, we all had to squeeze through a small hatch forward and emerged into the giant hangar-like inside of the C-130.

We sat on benches along the side of the aircraft with plastic webbing for seats. Behind us were small portholes from which we could look out. We had been issued small, yellow foam ear plugs because the engine noise was incredibly loud and made it hard to talk except by shouting in someone's ear. For the next five or six hours, we slept, read, or listened to tape players. When there were no clouds we could see barren, unexciting bits of the ground as we got into snow-covered country and then mountains, narrow ice covered bays, and finally the approaches to western Greenland and Sondrestrom Air Base. We could see out as the plane came in over the runway and with a rather harsh bang touched down on a long, paved surface noisily putting full reverse pitch on its four, large propeller engines. It was a sound that we all got know over the many landings of the C-130s we were to experience.

We sat on plastic webbing in the cargo area along the sides of the aircraft.

The airport at Sondrestrom was a modern building with a European flavor and daily commercial flights to and from Denmark. By 1990, Greenland was just beginning to become a tourist destination with about 5,000 visitors per year. The airport had been the site of what was called "Bluie West 8" during World War II, an important stopover for aircraft being ferried to Europe. It was an American base leased from the Danish government until 1992, when the United States left and the name was changed back to the original Innuit language, Kangerlussuaq, for a nearby fiord. The base had quite a history under the command of Col. Bernt Balchen, a famous Norwegian polar pilot and explorer, who joined the US Air Force for this assignment. Balchen had been one of the first to fly over the South Pole with Admiral Byrd in 1929. I wasn't aware of his involvement and all the history of the area until I came to Greenland.

Our group was housed at the local hotel, which had been US barracks during the war but now were nicely renovated. There was a more upscale hotel on the other side of the base for tourists. GISP had a building where we all congregated. We were issued any winter gear we wanted, and received briefings on our next leg of the trip to Summit at the top of the glacier, scheduled several days hence. We ate at the base chow hall where the food was pretty good and most everyone there was military personnel. There was a small store for food and tourist gifts. All the facilities were run by either Danes or Inuit. There was no village of natives and apparently never had been. The population in 1990 was about 450, dropped by half when the Americans left and has remained close to that figure over the decades.

Greenland (*Kalaalit Nunaat*), the "Land of the Greenlanders," is the largest island in the world. The island has been inhabited by Inuit intermittently for 4,000 years. Nordic settlements began in 986 AD, led by Eric the Red but were abandoned around the fifteenth century, due partly to lack of European support and more to the sudden colder temperatures. Then in 1721, a Danish-Norwegian priest named Hans Egede started a settlement at Godthab — presently called "Nuuk." This town is the largest of the island with a population of roughly 16,000. The present population of Greenland is about 56,000, mostly Danes and Inuit mix and twelve percent European. Greenland is an autonomous country, obtaining home rule in 1979, whereas the Danish Kingdom gives financial per capita support of $11,300 per year. Most of the economic value is in minerals and fisheries, but not enough to be self-sustaining. Shortly after World War II, the US offered to purchase the island for $100 million, but then as now Denmark still holds on firmly onto Greenland, refusing any offers.

After spending a couple of days exploring the hills and regions near the glacier which lay about twelve miles away, we were herded back aboard our C-130 and took off for the camp at Summit, which sits at 10,500 feet above sea level. The

Greenland is the largest island in the world but still part of the North American tectonic plate.

temprature at Sondrestrom had been in the 50° to 60° F range, as it was late summer. Now in the aircraft we were back in our winter gear looking out at mostly snow-covered, flat scenery with occasional bright blue melt pools, the drone of the engines putting us to sleep.

And then without warning we dropped slightly with a solid bang onto the packed snow-runway as the plane landed on its skis — wheels retracted — and slid for what seemed forever to a final stop with great clouds of snow blown by the reversed-pitch props. We had arrived! The rear door dropped and we all clambered down the ramp into brilliant sunshine and the bracing, zero-degree air atop the glacier. As far as the eye could see and beyond, the white expanse was completely flat, no hills, no trees, no nothing. With the sun overhead both day and night, it was difficult to orient yourself and equally hard to tell direction with no sunrise or sunset.

We were welcomed by the camp work force and others of the scientific team, mostly because we brought freshies — fresh fruit and vegetables — and other things that were missed from the civilized world, including mail from home. The departing crew climbed aboard along with the ice core samples to be analyzed and archived. The plane made a quick turnaround and took off. We would not see another aircraft here for three weeks. We were, to steal a phrase from the GISP language, "trapped like rats in a blinding white hell."

Our first meeting there on the ice sheet was held in what was known as the Big House. It would be our central home for these next three weeks. This prefab structure had recently been assembled in about three days on steel legs twenty feet above the flat, hard snow and ice surface so blowing snow wouldn't drift over it. I noted with interest that the building was manufactured in Brattleboro, Vermont, the same town where Window Quilt was made. Here we ate, lived, listened to music, had group meetings, and on Saturday nights, we danced.

The group consisted of fifty or so people, mostly men, with enough women to make a nice mix. The average age was mid-thirties, but with some undergraduate students and professors, and a few older folks like me. At fifty-eight, I was probably the second or third oldest, but as we worked equally hard, we were all one big family.

The "Big House" was a central gathering place for meals and recreation.

Chief Scientist Paul Mayewski laid out the operating procedures for the participants, who were referred to as "beakers." Jay Klink, Camp Manager, told us all the other rules, most of which I've forgotten. I was part of the camp work force and was a GFA, general field assistant, a grunt in Army terms and was on the UNH payroll. Then there were the drillers, a slightly elite bunch who worked for PICO, the Polar Ice Core Office, part the University of Alaska at Fairbanks. There really was little class separation, but occasionally we got into squabbles over who did what or worked for whom.

As new arrivals, our first decision was to choose where to sleep. There were two major options: inside or outside. There was room for nearly sixty inside, which was known as the "weather port," a bright red half-tube like structure with a vinyl/canvas cover over an aluminum frame. The ports had plywood floors and somewhat smelly oil heaters with up to fifteen people in each unit. Those of us who disliked crowding and preferred a bit of privacy slept outside, but it meant colder temperatures and a move to a city of one-man tents. These ranged from lightweight back pack type to the heavier and totally opaque "Scott tent," which made for better sleeping in the 24-hour daylight conditions. As you might suspect, I chose outside and the Scott tent.

Several times the temperature dropped to -15° or -20° inside the tent. Upon awakening, I would find long icicles hanging down over my head from my breath. Over my total of four summers in camp, I tried both types of tents. I was told by an old-time ice camper that I would need more than just a foam pad under my sleeping bag; two or three layers of a cardboard boxes were essential. I found some in a storage port and it did help. Actually, I started out in one the of the weather ports but after two nights found it too warm and smelling of kerosene from the stove and much too noisy. Reminiscent of my sleeping quarters at the DKE house at Colby, I quickly adjusted to leaping into a freezing sack. And we all lived in our long johns. The Big House was our island of safety out of the sometimes bitter cold and blowing snow.

Beside Paul the only other person I knew was Julie. I only saw her briefly as she was leaving camp the day I arrived to her new position in Washington. But it took no time at all to make friends with many of my fellow workers and most of the scientists. My place of duty was in the core processing line (CPL). It consisted of a hundred-foot long trench, thirteen feet wide, and about fifteen feet below the ice surface. It was initially dug by snow blowers and chain saws but each year more snow accumulated on the surface making it deeper, so more steps had to be added at the top.

Entering a small room next to the drill dome, you would descend into a really deep and very cold cellar lit by a string of lights stretching down a long, dim corridor. The temperature here started off around -22° in the beginning of the season, and had warmed to -4° when we left in September. The cold temperature ensured that none of the ice properties would be affected or changed. Here, each core five inches in diameter and about eighteen feet long was sawn in half lengthwise, examined on a light table, partially analyzed in various side labs, and placed in a tube, ready for return to the States. Although it was cold, we kept moving, carrying cores, and other general labor, so I found I was comfortable in long johns and jeans, sweater, and Marmot uninsulated shell.

Those "beakers" who had to stand doing analysis in the line or a lab usually wore heavily insulated freezer suits. Feet were the most vulnerable. The Japanese-made "Bunny Boots," insulated with a layer of antifreeze liquid, were the best for this task. These had been issued to us and made life quite bearable. If I were working outside and moving around, I found my cheap, knock-off Uggs were fairly effective. We worked with the scientists and usually put in a ten-hour day with an hour for lunch. The drillers, as I was to find out the next year when I joined them, worked twelve-hour shifts since the drill ran twenty-four hours a day for six days a week. The whole process is fully presented and described by Paul Mayewski in his book, *Ice Chronicles*, (2002).

One of my favorite stations to hang out at when there wasn't a job for me was at the light table where Dr. Tony Gow and Deb Meese worked. They were from the Army Cold Regions Research and Engineering Lab (CREL) in Henniker, New Hampshire. On the light table they logged and carefully scanned down each core as it rolled down the processing line. I can remember Tony pointing to the light and dark bands visible with a bright back light, saying "summer, winter, summer, winter." These distinct layers of dust or higher density particles were like tree rings: each pair was a year. So events like volcanic eruptions, the date of Hiroshima, the "Little Ice Age," and on back in time became daily happenings seen in the cores. The core was like a giant, long history book.

The drill rig was the heart of the project and was housed in a geodesic dome fifty-two feet in diameter and about a hundred feet high. This whole area was kept cold to preserve the ice samples. The drill hole was filled with a special drill fluid, N-butyl acetate, to keep the ice from closing in on the hole. Among earlier drill fluids used were diesel,or Jet A-1 and others but we were the first to use N-butyl acetate, which had a low freezing point and was safer than diesel. Each drill run took several hours getting longer as we got deeper.

The Drill Dome housed the drill and accessories which measure 52 feet in diameter and 110 feet high.

I had never had a chance to drive a snowmobile until my time at GISP. We used them to pull sleds loaded with cores or supplies or just for getting around camp, and we had two other camps to visit. One was about twenty miles away called "Fresh Air," where three or four guys roughed it, with none of the luxuries we had at Summit, like the Big House, flush toilets and hot showers. Their mission was to take surface samples of snow for analysis of airborne trace elements of various contaminates like those from automobile exhausts from the US and beyond.

The other camp was the European core facility called GRIP, nearly twenty miles to the east. They were drilling a core of 4-inch diameter that paralleled ours. We made visits back and forth to observe each other's activities and to have parties. Mayewski points out in his book that our core of 5.2 inches produced twice the volume of ice as the 4-inch European core that had been developed sometime earlier and thus more ice for PIs (principle investigators) to analyze.

We all learned how to drive snowmobiles for getting around and hauling things.

We were served some of the best food you could ever wish to have, similar to being aboard a research vessel. A good cook and great meals were as vital to the morale of a ship as they were here at the camp. We had two cooks who turned out excellent meals, making sure we got about 5,000 calories a day. Since we were all working very hard in extremely cold conditions, we needed extra amounts of calories. Even when we worked late shifts as the drillers did, there was always food left for us outside the galley. We had plenty of meat, lots of hearty stews, good salads as long as fresh produce lasted, and fresh bakery items every day.

The other luxury was the bath house located about twenty yards from the Big House. It was a one-story building with a wash room, three toilet stalls, and several showers, with the snow supplying all our water. The generator room, where enormous loads of snow were melted for water, was attached to the bath house and supplied electric power to camp. Hot water was used to flush the air-assisted toilets and all waste was put down a hole in the glacier.

The diesel fuel for the generators was brought in by C-130s in large plastic bags that were dumped out the stern ramp as the planes landed and taxied, looking like giant animals popping out babies. Our whole operation was entirely dependent on the services of the 109th ANG and its eight, ski-equipped planes to bring us supplies.

In our spare time, most of us hung out in the Big House after meals reading, writing letters, listening to music or, on Saturday nights, dancing. After dinner, the camp manager treated some of us to shots of his favorite, Gammel Dansk, a Norwegian bitters liquor, definitely an acquired taste. Sundays were a day off when the drill stopped and some of us went skiing or snowmobiling, or just walking away from camp into the most amazing quiet I've ever experienced. I remember lying on my back on a sled that I pulled behind a snowmobile on a perfectly clear, cold day, staring at the sky and hearing absolutely nothing. I watched the contrails of one plane after another at 35,000 feet without a sound on their way to Europe and wondered whether the passengers on those planes knew we were there.

In my three weeks there we saw no people except fellow GISP employees; no animals, no birds or polar bears. An errant sea gull had been found dead and very frozen years ago, and had been mounted outside on a pole as a weathervane. It had finally disintegrated and someone carved and painted a wooden replica. At one time, we may have seen some snow buntings. It was a long way from the coast and with absolutely nothing to eat, not a likely place for wildlife.

The last days of my tour at GISP 2 were memorable. Now the first week in September, the sun was finally sinking lower in the sky after the days of total and continuous light. And this meant it was getting colder. One evening after dinner another one of the GFAs, Mark, who was still an undergrad at UNH, and I went for a brisk walk near the runway. The sun was already down and there was a frosty mist. I had on my warm, long LL Bean parka with coyote fur around the hood all zipped up. Taking deep breaths was a sort burning sensation. We checked the temperature; it read forty below zero. It didn't matter whether it was Fahrenheit or Celcius, as they are the same at this point. I could truly say it was cold; the fur around my hood was covered in frost. My picture from this walk appeared later in the *Colby Alumni News* that year.

As we got ready to pack up and leave, there was some anxiety whether there were to be any C-130s available as all aircraft had been pressed into service for Desert Storm, which was in full battle process. This was likely nothing but a camp rumor; our rides home showed up on time. There were jokes about sweeping out the sand out of the planes, but I don't believe any of our ski equipped C-130s were involved in Desert Storm.

My three weeks on the ice was such a thrill, I wanted to return the next season. Some time later I remember hearing the adage, "the first year it's for the experience, the second it's for the money, and then it's all you know how to do." Meanwhile, I boarded the waiting C-130 with most of the science crew and a large load of cores going to the freezer for future analysis. Many of us climbed up on the pile of duffle bags and slept on our way home. We made a brief stopover in Sondrestrom, where there was already a dusting of snow covering the hillside of bright orange fall colors. When we landed in Scotia, New York, it was still the last of summer and felt like a forgotten other world. No more all-white everything and endless days — cars, traffic, people, and keys; nothing had ever been locked or needed a key at GISP. But it was wonderful to be reunited with Ellie and all my home friends. She had arranged for tickets to hear the Boston Symphony at Tanglewood with an overnight stay at a hotel. It was a memorable homecoming.

As I settled into life as usual with my Window Quilt business and visions of snow and cold receding, I worked to catch up to waiting customers. Thanks to Stu Moss, I had a backlog of customers for a while. In November, I was invited to bid on a sole-source shading project for Hanscom Air Force Base at the Officers Club. It was a result of the earlier business card exchanges at the Bedford Chamber of Commerce. The Club had added a large sunroom on the south side, built by my old friends Norm and Peter from New England Hot Tubs and Sunrooms. It was the largest sunroom I had ever seen.

The base commander had requested a shading system, not for energy savings as I first suspected, but simply because when he wanted to make slide or movie presentations during the day and he needed darkness. And because I had met him at one of our Chamber gatherings, he arranged for the contract to be administered by a non-government on-base entity called Rest and Relaxation, avoiding all the regular government contract stipulations. The job came to more than $18,000 the biggest project I ever had.

The installation took quite bit of time and required the assistance of Bob Spencer, from CAPCO days. During this time, Desert Storm had resulted in a higher state of security at Hanscom and all military bases. The MPs at the base gate were always more curious about my entry, probably because I had Maine license plates. And because I was working there I could eat any time I wanted at the Officers Club, which had very good food. The commander was happy and I got paid immediately instead of waiting for weeks or months for regular government procedures.

Around this time, I got a free trip to NORAD, the North American Air Defense Command in Colorado, compliments of the local Chambers of Commerce. Two of us from Bedford and around thirty others from various Chambers in the region were invited on a two-day trip. We all assembled at Hanscom Air Force Base and got aboard a chartered 727. Somehow I got lucky and was offered a seat on the flight deck for the takeoff. What a thrill to be right up front looking down the runway! With a giant whoosh we were off. It was perhaps the only time I'd get to really feel what jets are like up front.

We were fed and treated to everything except motel rooms. The next day we were bused out to Cheyenne Mountain where NORAD is buried deep inside an impenetrable fortress, as seen in the movie *War Games*. The flashing lights, giant doors, and *Dr. Strangelove*-like insides with the "big board" were spectacular. Our group was just like the one in the movie. At the time, the Soviet threat had diminished but NORAD remained on alert stance. Now it seems most of their effort is spent on tracking Santa and his sleigh.

During the winter of 1990, I got a phone call from Terry Gaecke at the PICO office at the University of Alaska, in Fairbanks. He wanted to know if I would be interested in joining the drill team at GISP for the upcoming season. I jumped at the chance and said "yes." Being invited back meant I would join an elite group who I knew worked extremely hard but enjoyed their job. The team consisted of eight drillers who worked in two shifts of twelve hours each, so the drill would run continuously unless, of course, it broke down. Terry told me that I would probably be there for four months starting in May and leaving in early September.

All winter I planned out what I might need for a longer stay based on what I learned from the first season. I again had to undergo another thorough physical exam for PICO who were now to be my employer. I again also turned my business over to Stuart Moss, but it was the slow time so I didn't lose much. During the first trip, I had taken my 8mm video camera and begun to capture lots of footage of camp activities. This year, I bought a new Hi8 camera with a far better resolution that approached broadcast quality. I purchased the camera and a portable playback unit with a small three-inch viewing screen and twenty tapes. At the suggestion of the camera store representative, I filled each one with a favorite movie we could all watch, then planned to record over as necessary, a great idea.

Since I had started recording events with my regular 8mm format, I started planning for taking footage and making documentary of GISP 2 with the support of Paul Mayewski and UNH. He worked at getting some funding from one of his grants for the effort. I had also received training from the local access cable station in Bedford so I knew some of the finer points of shooting and doing interviews. That spring I worked as a volunteer at that station and learned to edit video tapes.

As the time of our departure grew near I became excited about my return to the ice. With all the extra hours we would be working, I figured I would making around $1,200 per week, much better than the year before. Ellie was most supportive.

In early 1991, I got a call from Marge Hieser, a producer at the local Newton cable TV access station. She also hosted a weekly show there and was desperate for someone to shoot an interview at the upcoming Republican state convention in Boston. I agreed, as long as I could use my own camera. Several days later, I showed up at a downtown Boston hotel where the convention was being held. I set up my camera, tripod, light, and microphone in one of small rooms off the main hall. Marge had said the interview was to be with the Secretary of Defense, Dick Cheney, the featured speaker for the Republican state convention. I couldn't help but feel slightly like a plant for the opposition, spying on the enemy.

As Marge and I waited for Mr. Cheney, he blustered into the room, slightly irritated with the interview being televised on a local access station instead of a major network. We shook hands and I put the microphone on his jacket. I didn't even have a wireless mike so there was a wire running to the camera. Marge was most professional with her questions and through the entire process.

I was working the camera and concentrating on the shot when something went wrong with sound. I had to stop him and adjust things. He became even more irritated and growled at me which was, we all found out later when he became Vice President, very much in character. I still have the footage from that shoot and most of it aired soon after. A few days later I was about to fly off to Greenland and Secretary Cheney was about to embark on a visit to Saudi Arabia in the lead up to Desert Storm.

In late April, 1991, I — and two large cargo bags of gear — began my journey and return to Greenland. I flew out of Philadelphia and sometime later was aboard a commercial chartered 727 filled with contract workers and our GISP drillers. We then flew out of Resolute, a small hamlet of roughly two hundred residents in Nunavut, Canada after midnight. Resolute — *Qausuittuq* in Inuktitut — means "place with no dawn," which seemed fitting. We stopped at Thule AFB, then flew on to Sondrestrom. We drillers stopped over there for several days and I bunked in with Harm De Bow, an older man from Alaska, where most of the PICO drillers were from. He was a newcomer, so I filled him in on the GISP camp. He and I got along all right at this point. His background was engineering which usually means dull and he was. Nonetheless, it was wonderful to be back in Greenland. I had time to do some exploring and climbing in the hills away from the base. It was now May and still quite chilly but hardly the cold we would be having up on the ice.

We were all eager to get to camp and get started on the task ahead drilling to the bottom of the ice sheet and into bedrock. Some of the GISP regulars had preceded us and were in camp when we got there. The temperature was hovering around thirty-five below zero or so, but the sun was strong and, most importantly, by the first week in May it was light for twenty-four hours.

I spent the next several weeks getting to know the drill procedure and what my job was to be. There were at least ten on the team at this point. The head driller, Mark Wumkes from Fairbanks, had a long experience with PICO starting in Nebraska where they had formerly been located. He was an easy going, very bright and handy jack-of-all-trades type. His job was running the drill and the overall operation. Most of his time was spent in the drill booth two floors above the main floor where he could oversee all and control the drill.

Those of us who worked either on the drill floor or up on the platform where we made the connection of drill strings all wore butyl rubber suites over our many layers of insulated clothing. These suits protected us from the drill fluid, that constantly rained down and covered us. N-butyl acetate (N-BA) was chosen as the best fluid for drilling as it was inert chemically, wouldn't freeze, etc. It had a strange, sweet smell like apples. But it was easily absorbed through the skin, was not to be inhaled, and was thought to attack the liver and do harmful things to the lungs. In addition to the rubber suits, we wore breathing masks with high tech filters that totally shielded us from the effects of the N-BA. We felt like we were in space suits except not so glamorous — ours were a dull olive drab. And, once suited up, it was hard to tell who was who because of the full-face masks and respirators. Most of us had our names scribbled on tape on the suit. We all wore microphones to talk but sometimes yelling was just as good. All in all, I felt very clumsy. Somehow the cold didn't bother me.

We took turns everyday either on the floor, up on the platform where a team of two did the hookup and disconnect using a very clever rotary rig that held a half-dozen six-meter core barrels. This contraption sped up the process of quick turnaround the removal of the ice core and placement of an empty barrel ready to go back down. It was strenuous work. One of the tasks for those working on the platform was to beat the core barrels with heavy hammers to remove ice and debris. I found it particularly hard on my shoulders; one of the workers developed a rotator cuff injury from this motion. Later in the season, I began to have very painful problems with my shoulder muscles and tendons and had to be excused from this torture. I wasn't eager to try the surgical operation for this problem.

We were to start drilling this year at about 1650 feet. Our goal was to reach bedrock somewhere around 11,000 feet, as indicated by radar measurements. As drillers, we had a fair amount of time waiting as the drill descended deeper and deeper. We would sit in a small room under the control room in a heated space which was a luxury only for drillers. This included afternoon popcorn from the microwave. Or there were always chores such as salvaging the drill fluid from the ice cuttings by spinning it in a large centrifuge. Like all our supplies, the fluid arrived by plane in 55-gallon drums, estimated to cost about $10,000 per drum by the time it got to the ice, so we did our best to save and recycle it.

There were eight of us on the drill team. We worked round the clock four on a twelve-hour shift. We felt we were an elite bunch.

We drillers were an elite and tight group, a sort of family. Many of the support group worked at their jobs year-round, migrating to Antarctica after Greenland. This included drillers, GFAs, and the cook staff. I'm not sure I would have liked this pole-to-pole life. For a while, I thought it would be a great experience to have a chance to work in Antarctica, but as the summer wore on and my four months dragged heavy, going home seemed just fine.

We didn't have any live communication from the camp but we did have snail mail every three weeks or so when the supply planes came in. Ellie wrote frequently, which was welcomed. For my sixtieth birthday, she had asked all my friends from college, high school, and beyond to send me greetings, letters, photos and such since I wasn't around. My old gang from West Chester had a major reunion that summer. I received lots of cheers and pictures from them and others. I kept a diary during my first two years on the ice, faithfully transcribed by Ellie in 2013 after being lost amid all my mess of papers.

Our drilling progressed well through 1991 and 1992, but with occasional hitches such as problems with the drill cable, or when the drill stuck down the hole. There were times when it seemed we might all be sent home but we got through it. One of the dullest jobs I had for a while was being a "human level wind." Our drill cable was about an inch in diameter and wound on and off an enormous hydraulic winch and drum. As the core came back we had to manually spread the cable evenly on the drum and prevent overwraps. So, I stupidly stood, sometimes for hours, on cable wind duty. I think I used to count the number of dots and marks on the cable cover out of sheer boredom.

As a reminder, I have a piece of the cable with the dots and dashes on a small display on the corner cabinet at the house at Peaks Island. I have placed my blue driller's safety helmet and rebreather mask on the sculpted "head of Ned" at fourteen years old. Behind is a marker from one of the core trays saying 3,250M, the depth where we hit bedrock. My camp name "Grateful Ned" is on the back of the helmet as well as the insulated bunny boots, which I managed to sneak away from camp.

In the summer of 1992, on our return to Sondrestrom waiting to fly to the ice, we met and talked with men from the Greenland Expedition Society. This group from Atlanta had been working since the 1980s to find and recover a squadron of World War II aircraft forced down on the ice cap by bad weather on July 15, 1942. After some forty years, the two B-17s and six P-38s were located buried under 260 feet of ice near the coast of southeast Greenland. A large amount of money and manpower, funded mostly by R. J. Reynolds Company, had been spent on the recovery of one P-38. The men we spoke with told of the enormous amount of labor involved in drilling with a specially designed hot water drill. It sounded like more fun than our ice core drilling. Details of this adventure are fully described in *Lost Squadron* by David Hayes (1994).

Of note is the fact that Donald Kent, son of Arctic artist and explorer and one of my heroes, Rockwell Kent, was a member of the rescue team in 1942 that brought the airmen to safety eleven days later. And in another strange coincidence of intersecting lives, Norman Vaughn, then a major in Army Air Corps, led another team to recover the secret Norden bomb sights from the B-17s. I had met Vaughn at the Explorers Club in New York in 1989 and videotaped an interview with him, Brad Washburn, and my mother-in-law Madeleine Galland. Vaughn was on his way, at age eighty-four, to climb Mt. Vaughn in Antarctica, a mountain of 10,000 feet named by Admiral Richard Byrd in his honor, and then live on to be a hundred. The final result of nearly a decade and a million dollars was the recovery of one P-38, *Glacier Girl*, now reconstructed to fly again.

In 1993, our final year, we were getting close to the bedrock. Everyone was excited, as this would be the deepest and longest ice core ever recovered. I continued to film most events with my Hi-8 camera. Paul Mayewski and I had worked on a script for a 30-minute video and I had made several interim versions using the editing equipment at the Bedford access station. On July 1, the drill approached a depth of 10,600 feet. All the scientists gathered to look at little pebbles and sand in the ice core as it was extruded. Finally, at 10,670 feet, we hit bedrock and then took a short rock core — the grand finale. We all celebrated in the core area of the dome with lots champagne and cheers. I got it all on my camera, as well as one of our scientists, Mike Savage, in his tent sending a ham radio broadcast to the world of our accomplishment. I had carried an Explorers Club flag to make note of the event. The video footage amounted to over fifty hours and gave me a major project to make it into a 30-minute show.

And now it was time to go home. Before departing, I took one last small side trip on July 13. Our friends with the 109th Air National Guard invited Dr. Candace Kohl and me to take a day flight with them to East Greenland. Candace was a scientist from California, who specialized in capturing extraterrestrial particles in the snow and ice mostly in Antarctica, but also in Africa and South America. We had become good friends.

We were invited to sit up on the flight deck, which is always fun. We sat right behind the pilots and as we revved up, I began filming while we made the slow, lumbering takeoff of the C-130. Our mission was to pick up two generator sets in the village of Kulusuk in East Greenland. The ANG always flew two C-130s together as back up for each other; we were the lead plane. Once up, we were over nothing but glaciers and mountains for a fifty-minute duration.

The first town we flew over was Angmasalik, on an interior bay. It is the largest town in East Greenland with a population of nearly two thousand. In the distance, we could see lots of icebergs lining the shore as we made a wide turn and flew up a narrow valley of rugged mountains. We let down on a short dirt strip by a hangar, kicking up clouds of dust. All of this and what followed are on video which I've never edited. We were met by a beat up, old pickup truck. Eight of us plus the flight crew rode in back. Here it was mid-summer yet the narrow dirt road was lined by snowbanks ten or fifteen feet high. We passed a small cabin built on a large rock with thick cables anchoring it against the strong winds. The temperature was in the sixties and pleasant in the sun. We soon arrived in the village of houses all painted in wonderfully brilliant blues and reds.

The Kulusuk settlement was started in 1909 and has a population of around three hundred. The village is quite isolated and even has its own language. It has one of the only two airports on the east coast of Greenland, with many visitors from Iceland. As we approached the village, local children ran alongside the truck, shouting a welcome. Each house had multiple dogs chained outside, hides and skins hung to dry, sleds in front yards, and the usual unkempt look of Arctic villages. We got out and went into the store. The shelves were mostly bare and had nothing of interest to us as tourists. We walked down to the town harbor which was still mostly frozen in; fishing must have been a really short season.

Upon returning, the local kids besieged us to buy native art. Candace and I knew that all of the native crafts using ivory and fur were banned as imports to the US but we bought some anyway. I got Ellie an ivory pin and a seal fur bracelet hoping I could somehow smuggle them in. As we returned to the airstrip another flight was coming in. It was a small two-engine plane arriving from Reykjavik, Iceland not far to the east. It brought several dozen ubiquitous Japanese tourists each with a fancy camera. It was time for us to leave along with the two gen sets and we roared out in the clouds of dust.

One afternoon, Harm and I were told to clean up storage yard out back. We lifted and tugged scrap metal and junk. But there was this fifteen-foot length of heavy pipe. With each of us on an end we struggled to lift it and carry it a short distance. Somehow we discovered it weighed 400 lbs.! Not wise for me. Harm was well over six feet tall and strong. I'm sure this lifting contributed to another hernia operation, which was prompted by lifting dozens of heavy boxes of books when we moved from Newton to Lexington.

My four summers on the ice are filled with more memories of the fun, cold and pleasant events, and less of the hard work of drilling and the science trench. One such memory is the day spent out at "Fresh Air," the clean camp eighteen miles from us at the Big House. We went out to bring back some equipment and had a tour of the camp and the measuring stations and procedures they used to avoid any contamination of samples. It was a cold, cloudy day probably around zero degrees. One of the researchers, a French scientist from University of Pittsburg, seemed totally at ease as he went about his sampling. I realized how soft we were at GISP, always having a place to come in out of the cold. This camp was freezing and I hadn't dressed warmly. By the end of the day I was quite chilled. On the return ride, I rode on top of the pile of equipment on a towed sled, shivering in the breeze as it grew colder and I wondered if I'd make it back. It was the coldest I've ever been, except the time I was diving in Lake Travis in Texas in 1955.

The one type of entertainment that had been missing at camp was movies. Instead, Saturday nights were always a gathering in the Big House with music and fun. Scientists would all dance, act, or do something different. One of the favorites was the music from *Rocky Horror Picture Show*, and luckily, I had the twenty or so movies on my 8mm tapes. Each weekend, a select group would sneak away to someone's tent and watch whatever I chose to show on my tiny 3-inch screen. At one time, we had thirteen of us all crowded together both to watch and to keep warm. Once we had viewed a film, I could erase it and use the tape to record the camp video project.

And so ended one of the most exciting phases of my scientific life. Over the next several years hundreds of papers were produced, touting the importance of our ice cores and the many revelations these data made toward a better understanding of climate change. Although we drilled to a depth of almost 11,000 feet, the lower portion of the core was quite disturbed and fractured so only the upper portion dating back about 125,000 years was worth analyzing.

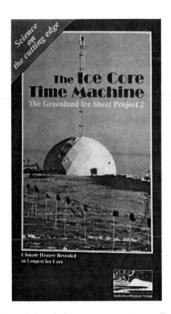

I made a 30-minute video of the whole ice core operation called the Ice Core Time Machine. It was partially funded by NSF. I later sold several hundred of them.

Upon my return, I realized my days as a sailor in the sun were beginning to take a toll on my skin. It had started when I was kid sitting out at the quarry or the beach with my friends, getting sunburned and thinking nothing of it. Those days were more about getting a good deep tan than protecting us from the evil rays. In fact, my grandmother rubbed me with olive oil when I was three or four years old at Stone Harbor, New Jersey. By the time I was working on ships in the Gulf of Mexico in the 1950s, I would spend all day on deck or while in port scrubbing the top sides with no shirt or sun protection. Then, we didn't know about the cancer-causing effects and, of course, we thought we were all immortal.

Ellie prevailed on me to consult a dermatologist. In 1994, I first visited Dr. Valorie Treloar in Wellesley, Massachusetts, who began treatment of my many areas of sun damage. She assured me that most of these areas had resulted from heavy sun, years before and were simply treated with liquid nitrogen. She said she "was delighted to have sailors as patients because they would help put her children through college." For spots on my face she referred me to a surgeon, Dr. Don Grande, who used what was known as Mohs treatment of basal cell cancer removal. I've gone to visit Dr. Grande for nearly twenty years in which time we have become good friends, occasionally exchanging books about the sea.

I resumed my activities in my window treatment business, catching up on a backlog of business from the summer. But after only a year or so I realized that the business was coasting at best and certainly not increasing. For a season, I tried small display ads in local papers but little came of them, so I began to look around for other types of work. At age sixty-two, I found it hard to find anything close to what I would like to do. I sent many letters in response to ads but with no interest. Someone suggested trying temp jobs. I went to an agency in Waltham that sent me to various companies. I spent about three days at Thermo Fisher Scientific in Waltham not doing any science but as an office boy sorting and running mail around to various labs and offices. This was the pits. Not only dull but at $6 an hour, just not worth it.

Next, I was told to report to a small company in Watertown. Two other men and I met one morning in a large factory room full of machine tool equipment that was being sold as the shop had closed. This was likely the beginning of American factory work being sent overseas. Our job was to spend the morning cleaning and wiping down each piece of equipment. We weren't told why, but to "just do it and make sure they're all sparkling clean." We completed the task, and at noon on our lunch break, I still wondered why?

The answer came right after lunch as a professional, high class photographer walked in having been flown in from Detroit for this one-day job. He told us he would be photographing each machine separately. There were drill presses, giant lathes, and planers. Each would go into a catalog for a special sale at auction. I couldn't help wondering why send a guy all the way from Detroit? We were to learn this guy was a real pro. He asked each of us to climb twelve-foot stepladders and had us hold a white drop cloth behind each machine to block the view from other machines all crammed in close together. "Now," said the photographer, "shake the cloth vigorously." He began to take pictures with his ancient camera on a tripod. We did what we were told, still curious. No flash, just a long exposure. He finally explained that the drop cloth with its motion became a fuzzy background where the folds and lines in the cloth would not be seen. Each machine would be separate in the catalog. Very clever. I've always remembered this trick. It made the low pay worth it.

My next — and last — temp job turned out to be of some interest and a better match for me. I was told to report to an office in a large, modern building along Route 128 near Lexington. It was called Electronic Data Corporation (EDC) a company started by Ross Perot, one-time candidate for President and a wealthy entrepreneur. The company had branches all over the country and was most successful. Perot was not at this location nor did he ever show up.

I was one of three temp guys that had been assigned to a large office of engineers sitting in typical little cubicles. It reminded me of my days at Westinghouse in Annapolis thirty years earlier. The group was composed of men, all in white shirts and ties; the only women were secretaries who typed and got the men coffee — very déjà vu. I vaguely remember my two office mates; one, a former engineer, retired and the other, a hardware salesman who missed calling on his dealers all over northern

New England. We I were given the task of contacting representatives from a large list of companies all over New England and inviting them to attend a series of free workshops featuring demonstration of some EDC products. spent many hours over the next month on the phone each day, recruiting potential attendees. It was a professional atmosphere and surely better than polishing machines, but still not what I was hoping to do with my life. I had at least one day off a week to keep up with my Window Quilt business, such as it was. The pay, around $200 a week, was hardly enough to live on, but still better than the previous jobs. Thank goodness for Ellie and her good paying teaching job. On my day off I kept searching for a real job since this one would expire soon. My daily phone calls were occasionally of interest and more importantly gave me a feeling of belonging to a company. I must have made several hundred calls and may have signed up fifteen or twenty workshop attendees.

The most satisfying accomplishment upon my return from the ice was the completion of the video about Greenland and GISP 2. Over the span of the next year, I assembled and produced the 30-minute video piece *The Ice Core Time Machine* which told the story of the GISP 2 cores. It was done with the helpful guidance and funding from Paul Mayewski, then still at UNH. Although it took a lot of time and work at the local TV access station, it was very satisfying to complete. By this time, the station had moved to Lexington, where there was better equipment and instruction and with the help of the station operators I learned how to put my piece together. I later sold nearly three hundred copies at $20 apiece, many to schools and universities as well as many of the GISP crew.

Chapter Nineteen

On to Window Quilt

On my next day off from EDC, just after the Christmas holidays, I paid a visit to the Window Quilt factory in Brattleboro, Vermont. On other visits, I had made friends with the sales and marketing manager, Deborah Reynolds. I had prepared a proposal to produce a newsletter patterned along lines of several previous ones published by the company under former owners. As I made my pitch, she responded in her usual enthusiastic manner, "What we really need right now is a sales rep to visit all our dealers." I didn't need any more of an invitation and I was hired on the spot, becoming the new rep for Southern New England. I immediately resigned my temp job with EDC and began on my new career—a traveling salesman.

Before I started the new career in early February 1996, Ellie and I attended a family reunion in Washington, DC We took the train from Boston; driving at that time of year could be problematic with snow, ice, and resulting traffic problems. Even though I love to drive, it was good we had made this choice because shortly after we arrived at Julie and Rick's the area received one of its most memorable snow storms. Walking along an unplowed sidewalk near the Capitol Mall reminded me of my days in Greenland. With a foot and a half of snow on the ground, the city was immobilized, usually shutting down even with six inches.

We all gathered in a hotel room with Ellie's relatives Margy and Danny Kivelson, his sister Nina Auerbach, Steven and Pam Kivelson, Val and Tim Hoefer along with daughter Rebecca, and, of course, the matriarch, Madeleine Galland. She was still quite able to get around with a walker. Later some of us met at the Smithsonian Museum for lunch.

At the end of the visit Ellie and I boarded the return train to Boston. The storm had blanketed New England and was followed by typical bitter cold with clearing weather, as usual. Somewhere north of New York the conductor announced apologetically that they were having problems with the heat in the cars. Then without an announcement the train just stopped around Providence for nearly half an hour. It was quite cold but no one complained as by this point we were presumably all hardy New Englanders. We arrived at the station around one thirty in the bitter cold morning. As a special treat, the train shifted over to the south-bound track, saving us the long walk up the steps and over the bridge to the car garage.

A day later, I reported to the Window Quilt factory now known as Northern Cross Industries in Brattleboro, Vermont. I was starting off on a new part of my career at age sixty-four, which meant going back to work full time with a reputable national corporation, something I hadn't done since TRIGOM, more than two decades ago. I was quite excited; I had a title, calling cards, a desk in Brattleboro, and an expense account. Yet I was still driving my somewhat elderly truck, the 1983 Isuzu diesel pickup. I decided even on my meager $17,000 salary, I should have a proper car.

Having been a fan of Saabs in the past, I started looking in that direction and wound up at Saab Nashua North outside of Nashua, New Hampshire. The salesman told me that he had a clean, low mileage 1992 Saab 9000. Although it was four years old it only had 12,000 miles! The sales manager, Curt O'Donnell, explained he had found the car on Long Island where he had lived. Here he said many people, especially little old ladies, don't ever drive off the island into the horrible city traffic of New York, resulting in very little mileage. The car turned out to be barely broken in and served me well for over 180,000 miles in my sales job around New England.

My job description as sales rep included as task number one, to contact and visit every dealer in the states of Massachusetts, Connecticut, and Rhode Island. The list of three hundred-plus was in definite need of updating; many were no longer in existence. The weekly paycheck, while modest, was steady, and allowed me to pursue my own sales and installation as long as it didn't take business away from my dealers.

Although my immediate boss was Deborah Reynolds, I found I was also taking orders from Bill Hoag, the owner and CEO of the company. He lived in Hampton Beach, New Hampshire and drove up once a week to Brattleboro for the day. Bill was one of the most unique businessmen I've ever encountered.

Quick witted, extremely intelligent and intense, Bill had managed to become quite wealthy over the years. As the story was told at Northern Cross, he and several college buddies had stumbled on a piece of land with oil potential in Texas. Each was to put up $10,000. Bill had pleaded insolvency and said he would pay later, although it was unclear whether this had actually occurred. Needless to say, they all became rich when oil came in. Thus began a series of income-generating acquisitions: a division of General Electric that later become a major player in painting locomotives; land purchases; and various struggling, near-bankrupt, companies.

In 1990, he purchased Appropriate Technology (ATC), which later became Window Quilt. During the nation's leap into energy conservation at the height of the energy crisis and just before the Reagan administration took over 1985, ATC was running three shifts with more than one hundred employees, and grossing five or six million or more a year. But by 1990 with no tax credits and less demand for energy conservation, things began to change. The now-deflated company had thirty or less year-round employees with a dozen or so seasonal workers during fall rush. Bill had bought the company for slightly more than one million dollars which included a modern building of 200,000 square feet, and expensive machinery specifically designed for this high-tech product.

By the time I arrived in 1996, the company was on a slow downward spiral, doing $1.5 million in business annually. Most employees in production, marketing and engineering had been let go; only four remained in Customer Service. I had been hired to rebuild the dealer network and was eager to get out on the road and revitalize the Window Quilt product.

I spent my first weeks planning trips to various dealers and setting up appointments over the phone. To get a feel for the upcoming meetings, I visited a few local dealers. It had been quite a while since they had seen a rep, and many of them were unfamiliar with the product and its installation. Many were afraid to sell the shade or felt it was too hard to install. Gone were the days of eager enthusiasm for Window Quilt; newer shades were cheaper and faster to install. Clearly, I had an uphill battle to convince dealers to get out and sell the product.

My first road trip came in mid-April during school vacation so Ellie was able to join me. It was a bit like being on vacation as we headed to western Massachusetts. I had a list of visits which would last up to an hour each in the towns of Northampton, Amherst, West Springfield, and Holyoke. Most of these were small shops that sold a variety of different shades. We spent three or four days on these visits and afterwards I submitted a written report on each visit with recommendations for ways to help the dealer.

Over my several years at the company, Ellie and I traveled all over New England for my sales calls. One of our favorites was staying at the Howard Johnson motel just south of New Haven, Connecticut and having dinner at the inexpensive but good restaurant across the street. Business travel like this was one of the perks of the job.

Over the summer I chipped away at visiting each dealer in my territory. My boss seemed pleased with my progress. And Bill Hoag agreed, expanding my territory to include Maine, New Hampshire, and Vermont another several hundred dealers. I successfully negotiated a raise, bringing my salary to $20,000. Unlike most sales jobs, this position offered no commission or bonus, but at the time, I felt lucky to have a job.

The best part of my territory was, of course, Maine. Here was an excuse to travel to all my old favorite places, sometimes with Ellie but mostly on my own while she was teaching. I saw Houlton, Presque Isle, Caribou, and Mount Katahdin in all the glory of fall colors. Dealers in these small towns had never had a representative call on them, and, as in many small towns, the dealers worked out of their homes. I also worked with The Curtain Shop, a dealer with four branches in Bangor, Lewiston, Augusta, and Portland. Their account was by far the largest in Maine.

In late 1996, my boss told me she was quitting. Her suggestions to improve sales involved investing time and money up front, and fell upon deaf ears. A series of sales and marketing managers were hired, with none lasting long. Although not staffed at full capacity, we did hire another sales rep.

Part of my job responsibility was training the new rep, Catlin McNally. I took her on sales trips and taught her how to install. Later we produced a training video for our dealers, detailing the measuring and installing of Window Quilts. I wrote the script and shot the video, using Catlin's house in Brookline for the studio. She demonstrated the installation technique while I narrated. With Bill's approval, the video was then professionally edited and produced, and part of it is still used by the present company.

It's hard to say whether my dealer meetings helped the company's overall sales figures. Many of the weaker dealers I trained became more confident and able to sell Window Quilt but it was difficult to tie my visit to increased sales, since many other factors were involved. We had done virtually no national advertising and only sporadic local newspaper ads; other products such the cellular, "honeycomb" shade made by Hunter Douglas and Comfortex were becoming much more popular. With the advent of toll-free phone numbers and the Internet, suppliers could deliver their shades in three to four days from as far away as Texas; yet our delivery time had slumped to four weeks.

For a while we had a general manager who oversaw our daily operations. But neither he nor any of the remaining employees were given any incentive to improve our sagging delivery times. Morale was at an all-time low. And Window Quilt was seasonal, booming in the fall and early winter then slacking into spring and almost inactive in summer. Most of the employees in the factory were laid off in the summer and collected unemployment. The factory only operated three days a week.

Sometime in 1998, Bill realized this cyclic aspect of the business needed to be addressed. He was always shopping for bargains, and was even known to buy a dozen McDonald burgers at a time when there was a sale and freeze them for future meals. This time he found a small company for sale in Malden, Massachusetts that had manufactured futon covers for the past forty five years. The owner had recently died and the widow was selling everything for a mere $1 million. With almost no research into the market for futon covers, Bill jumped at the chance and bought Malden Products feeling sure this move would fill in the other half of the year for Window Quilt. The sale included all the sewing machines and related pieces including the availability of several of the key employees. Everything was to be moved to Brattleboro including any employees who wished to go.

Although Bill never discussed it with any of us, we heard the story soon enough. On his way to the closing of the purchase of Malden Products, Bill got the shock of his life when he went to the bank. He had thought he had plenty of cash in the account only to find it nearly empty. It turned out, so the story went, that the financial manager at his Chelsea-based paint company, Glyptal, had embezzled nearly $4 million from the company to feed his gambling habit. Consequently, the money to purchase and operate Malden Products had to be stripped out of what was left of Window Quilt. Spending on much needed items such supplies, repairs, and machine maintenance was drastically curtailed.

I remained the only sales representative and my duties expanded to sales calls on existing futon cover dealers, mainly in Massachusetts. I had no interest in the fine points of futon covers and didn't receive additional pay. Futons had been a big fad in the 1980s and '90s but were a bit passé when we started manufacturing them and were mostly purchased by college students in the Boston area.

On the brighter side, I participated in a national interior decorating show in New Orleans, which included futons and fabrics. I took along a Window Quilt exhibit. Bill came along to learn about his new product and see the competition. We were there in July, a terrible time to visit New Orleans with its sweltering heat and choking humidity. Because expenses were tight, I shared a hotel room with Bill, an experience not to be missed. Hearing the stories of his childhood and youth made me realize what a unique person he was.

I spent some time exploring the city. It had been more than forty years since I had been there to deliver my professional paper to the Gulf Coast Geological Societies, and a few years later Karyl and I spent part of our honeymoon there. The city now was mobbed with tourists, the food was expensive and the quality poor, and I was lucky to have seen it in its glory in the 1950s when the French Quarter was still seductive. Not long after we left New Orleans, Hurricane Katrina came along, devastating the city and surrounding areas.

Another of Bill's ideas was to manufacture hammocks, since we were already in the fabric and sewing business. Unfortunately, his vision of a new and unique hammock shaped like a person's back never got fully off the ground. Although he spent much time and money on the advertising and promotional materials and had purchased the canvas quite inexpensively, he later learned the fabric was the wrong type and couldn't be used for the hammocks. We produced a few demo models with better canvas for Relax the Back-type stores, but none showed an interest in taking on the line.

And then there was the toothpaste. Some smooth sales person must have gotten to Bill; for several months, it was all he could talk about. The product, called Denti-Thin, claimed it was "the only weight-reducing toothpaste on the market. Bill bought four large pallets with cartons of Denti-Thin and was in the process of lining up a sales force when he discovered the product which was supposed to help you lose weight by controlling hunger had never been tested or approved by the Food and Drug Administration.

Sadly, the much-needed money to resuscitate Window Quilt had been squandered. For the next year or two the four pallets of Denti-Thin were abandoned in a far corner of the factory. Every time I went back there, I smelled the peppermint toothpaste and to this day, I still have a tube of it.

Bill was also briefly enthusiastic about one of my ideas: setting up dealers to assemble Window Quilt shades the way Comfortex did, with its dealers whom they called "Composers," in keeping with their musical product names. In the Comfortex model, which had many fewer parts than we did, the dealer made a healthy payment of $7,500 to $10,000 for which he would receive training at the factory along with parts and six colors of fabric. These composer/dealers could turn out a basic shade cheaper and faster than the factory, and for a lower selling price. I had envisioned a similar sort of arrangement for Window Quilt.

We explored the type of license contracts, parts we would supply, and how we controlled the fabric under our patents. Unfortunately, like most of his schemes, Bill lost interest and the project never got off the ground. However, he did raise the prices on all the parts about thirty percent, after I pointed out he was losing money on most parts, as the list had not been updated for a number of years.

My hope that Window Quilt would turn a corner came in the form of a new marketing and sales manager, Cynthia. For the most part I was pleased. She seemed willing to learn about the product, which previous managers hadn't. I fed her lots of ideas which she got Bill to accept, including my pet project to produce and distribute a newsletter. She and I wrote several over the next few months. I hosted a technical column in which I spun out some of my tricks for installers, many of which I had learned from Ken Bixby in Portland.

Suddenly the job was fun again. We dusted off our displays and Bill seemed willing to spend a little money. Cynthia and I went to a couple of trade shows with mild success and it begin to feel like old times where I was of value. Unfortunately, Cynthia's tenure was as brief as her predecessors. She lasted about a year and decided to move on, discouraged I'm sure, by the lack of support or commitment for any serious money for advertising which we all knew was vital to staying in the game.

Our gradual but sure slide downwards continued in spite of all my efforts to turn the business around through dealer contact and training. It seemed almost as if Bill wanted the company to fail.

Near the anniversary of my four years with Northern Cross, Bill called me shortly after noon at home. I had just come back from a promising visit to a dealer in Nashua, New Hampshire, who had a large condo account. She had installed Window Quilt in more than two hundred units fifteen years earlier and now wanted our help in ordering new ones. I was eager to tell Bill but my elation crashed when in a very matter-of-fact and unemotional manner said, "Ned, I think we've come a point where my goals and yours have to part. We don't need a rep anymore."

That was it. No thanks a lot or anything or even a penny of severance pay. In fact, my salary was terminated at noon on that Thursday. This was a long way from the employee friendly termination I'd gotten at Smithsonian, and more like more like the "Valentine's Day Massacre" in Annapolis.

My first inclination was to throw out everything related to Window Quilt in a fit of anger, but I didn't. And because it had become such a routine I kept going to Brattleboro out of habit and volunteering my time for no pay. I became, in a strange way, a "ghost" rep. Because there was no one who knew many of the technical answers, I stepped in. I avoided contact with Bill as best I could, later billing him for my consulting time on a special design for a sunroom shading system. He paid me, but made it clear that the payment was a one-time occurrence.

During this phase, I came upon the brilliant idea of reverse charging my account with Window Quilt, somewhat like a reverse mortgage. Jean Turner, the current sales manager, had been with company since 1983 and was the most knowledgeable employee in the manufacturing process of Window Quilt. On occasion, she called on me for technical assistance. In those days I, as a number of dealers, were allowed to have company accounts for the products we had ordered. In my case I had a $5,000 limit which I paid on each month but was always a bit behind.

I convinced Jean to approve a monthly invoice of $750, billed as a credit on my account; this went on for several years. Bill may have known about it but did nothing. It was tacit approval, I thought. I certainly spent lots of my time working in behalf of the company-designing, looking for parts, and being available to answer dealer questions, even in late evenings for those on the west coast. I used my own phone and traveled to Vermont on my gas. Little did I know that my generous and kind efforts would haul me into a court case with my former boss.

Chapter Twenty

Our New Home in Lexington

At the beginning of 1998, Ellie and I began to explore the idea of a move. Ellie had bought our current house in Newton before we met. Ideally shaded and cool during summer, it had a grand backyard but in the winter, due to its orientation, it lacked any sun exposure. And its eternally damp and sometimes flooded basement, along with overall required maintenance, was becoming costly. A few of our friends had recently been looking at condos, so we visited several converted school buildings in Newton Highlands and Newton Center, but none were appealing.

That spring we experienced an especially wet time. We knew we were in a flood plain where a small stream ran past, and suffered in times of heavy rain like many neighboring houses. I rented storage space in Allston and moved the majority of the basement belongings, partly to avoid the dampness and also to begin to ready our house for sale. By May, we had listed with a local broker. We cleaned, picked up, and removed all the clutter and knick-knacks from the living room. The house was shown a few times but yielded nary an interested party. In spite of no action, we vowed to keep it clutter-free through fall and continued our search, touring nearby condo complexes. Our goal was to stay close to Belmont and Ellie's school. These all seemed like dull apartment buildings and didn't grab us at all.

Ellie's sister-in-law, a commercial property broker, suggested a realtor colleague, C.J. Snow, from Lexington. C.J. called us soon after and we met at Potter Pond in south Lexington. On a hot day in July, we made our way to this rural setting of houses clustered around a pond. Number 13 was in the middle of three other houses in an "L" shape. With their wooden shake roofs and varying shades of paint, the houses were both distinctive and attractive. As we walked through the living room, I noticed some small photos on a table. Recognizing one of the people in the scene, I showed it to Ellie. To our amazement it was Carol Stix, Ellie's cousin. Her son Alan and his wife had owned this house for some time, but were now ready to move. Was this some sort of a sign? The house was adequate but not quite for us, so we didn't make an offer. We liked the location, the type of home, and setting and told C.J. to keep us in mind if another Potter Pond property came on the market. Priced around $400,000, it was a bit more than we had hoped to spend.

One Sunday afternoon in September, after we had stopped our active search, our realtor called to tell us of an open house at Potter Pond. We were on our way back from a weekend on Peaks, and toured the property late that afternoon. It was a brisk fall day with leaves beginning to turn. The house was empty and unfurnished. The realtor, a tall, imposing woman stood in front of the fireplace and told us this was one of only a few free-standing units of Potter Pond's one hundred-plus condos, with a shared garage between it and the other unit.

Ellie and I immediately liked it. Although there were no current offers on the table, the realtor expected more soon because so few Potter Pond properties were for sale. This fact made it all the more appealing; it was by far the best place we had seen. That night we decided it was worth proceeding, yet Ellie remained cautious. We were about to enter into a contract on a new property without having even an offer on our present house. I was completely confident that we could sell the Newton house, even with the housing market's mid-October cooling off period. I had done this once before; I knew it would work out although I understood Ellie's apprehension. Luckily there was no mortgage on the Ferncroft Road house.

We sweated our way through the fall, simultaneously waiting for a buyer to come forward and going through the necessary steps of purchasing the new house. Our realtor found us several possible buyers, with one low-ball bid of $425,000 which we flatly turned down.

Finally, in November, at the point of mild desperation, we got a bona fide offer of $458,000. Far from what we might have gotten had we waited for six months into spring, we accepted the offer. We closed on our Potter Pond house in December, 1998 for $375,000, purchased from its original owners who had bought it for around $175,000 in 1984. Not only did the property double over a decade and a half, but we would later see it double again in half the time.

We had decided to spend some of the money from the sale on the new house, as it definitely needed a face lift. The entire first floor was covered with worn and dismal carpet. A pipe had burst flooding the linoleum floor of the kitchen which required replacement. Recalling the Newton house, we installed hardwood floors for kitchen, living room, the stairway to the second floor, and in the den, formerly a bedroom. We knew we would enjoy this significant improvement, and that it would add to the value of the property.

Our planned moving day was to be December 15, usually a snowy and cold time of year, but by a wonderful stroke of good fortune it turned out to be unseasonably warm and sunny with temperatures in the 60s. We had been frantically packing and throwing away the junk that had accumulated over the years. I had put all my books in heavy duty plastic storage boxes, many of which had been moved from Amesbury to Annapolis to Miami to La Jolla to Southport not to mention Dover-Foxcroft, Cutler, Whiting and so on. And some still resided on Peaks Island. Still there were sixty boxes in all. I transported all of them, several at a time, in my car to Potter Pond. In my usual impetuous way, I carried too many of these extreme ly heavy boxes, which strained my old hernia condition.

We had figured out where all the furniture was going except for the ten-foot couch that Ellie had owned for a long time. It was most comfortable but badly sagged where too many people had sat over the years. We lugged it out to the curb for the trash truck and watched from the living room window on the morning of our departure as two Newton garbage men fed it into the jaws of the dumpster. The once wonderful couch was crunched into small pieces.

That afternoon, as the movers finished bringing everything into our new home at Potter Pond, we sat on the still-green lawn out front and had a marvelous picnic that Ellen Flatley, Ellie's colleague from Belmont High, had brought over for us such a treat on an unusually warm afternoon in mid-December.

All the improvements we planned had been completed by the time we moved in including inside painting, floors, new closet on the second floor, and carpet in the bedroom just in time before the new heavy furniture came. Only the kitchen remained unfinished.

We had decided to gut the original outdated kitchen and splurged on stained wood cabinets. The centerpiece was the gas/electric stove. Ellie's sister had strongly advised us to pick a top-quality stove saying we wouldn't regret spending the extra money on such an item. We took our time searching for the perfect stove and finally settled on a Thermador at the whopping price of $2,200. It was, at the time, exorbitant but very satisfying, and a thing of beauty. What's more it was great to cook on, in spite of a few control panel flaws. As always, Margy was right.

95 Potter Pond, our new home in Lexington, 1998.

We were all moved in and settled by the end of January 1999. The location of Potter Pond was perfect for Ellie, about a seven-minute commute to her school, just up over Belmont Hill. And for me, it was equally good being three minutes from Routes 2 and 128/95. Although the location was good, we also realized that in ways we missed Newton. I had never liked Newton and its city feel but I found Lexington less pleasing. Gradually, we grew to enjoy being in the country, with no bright lights at night, no street noise but faint traffic sounds in the far distance, and an overall feeling of being hidden away. We were closer to the town of Belmont, where we did most of our shopping. Lexington village was a small, retro town with few attractions for us, at best, a couple of restaurants we liked. Most of our friends were still in Newton.

Dolphin 24, an Olin Stephen's design built in 1966. The first Aurora.

That winter, I decided to sell my boat *Aurora* and look for something a bit larger. I had received an insurance settlement for $3,600 because another boat owner had moved my boat at the dock where it was badly gouged. After searching various boat yards and ads, I found what sounded just what I was looking for, in the *Want Advertiser*: a 1967 Tartan 27. Olin Stephens, the designer of my 24-foot Dolphin, had also designed the Tartan 27 in 1961.

The boat was located in Kittery in the owner's backyard; it hadn't been in the water for several years. Don Tibeau, the owner, had first kept it up the Piscataqua River but, wanting it closer to the ocean, found he was on a long waiting list for

Tartan 27, also a Stephen's design built in 1967 named Aurora II *Purchased in 1999.*

a local mooring and decided to sell it. He had put in a brand new Yanmar 2GM Diesel in 1995, which appeared to be in good shape. I came back at least once more and then decided to make an offer.

Don showed me all the invoices for the engine and necessary modifications amounting to $10,600. He was asking $10,500 but gladly took an even $10,000. In May I hired a boat mover to transport it to Portland. It was an exciting day — and just the beginning of much fun and considerable expense over the next few years. My new craft became *Aurora II* and the focus of my attention for the next decade and beyond.

Chapter Twenty-One
Life After Window Quilt

A year after Bill Hoag fired me, he decided to sell the company and the building. He made this decision over the holidays, at the end of the tax year, a difficult time for the few remaining employees. The owner of the adjoining property, a large auto dealership, purchased the building from Bill for a million dollars, nearly what he had paid for the entire business a decade ago.

Around the same time, Keith Denner from the largest Window Quilt dealer in the country asked if I was interested in buying Bill's business. Intrigued to play a part in this proposed new company, I spent several days with Keith in Brattleboro exploring possibilities. Keith had purchased the company from Bill for $50,000 with the idea of quickly selling it to someone who could properly finance the operation. Keith and his brother also operated a large number of energy efficient apartment buildings, all requiring Window Quilts for optimum performance, so they couldn't allow Brattleboro to go out of business.

Within a few days Keith found a fabric and manufacturing company in Seattle, known as The Warm Company, with plants in several locations around the country. At first, it sounded like the perfect setup with enough money, engineers and sales force to thrive. But running the business from a distance proved to be more problematic than the new owners realized.

For several months, production was at a halt, as machinery was moved to a new location. I attempted to fill in as a technical and sales consultant but with little success. The word was out that the company had failed or was moribund; things looked grim. Bryan Whittler, a sales and technical associate at a local energy products dealer, was brought in to run the show. He was completely familiar with Window Quilt and picked up quickly on the manufacturing process.

I continued to be a Window Quilt dealer as production was resumed. Eventually The Warm Company decided to move once again back to the still vacant previous building after a few renovations. The company was still largely run from the west coast by someone who spent part of his time in Brattleboro and the rest in Seattle. The Warm Company did not seem to fully understand the Window Quilt product or how to work with the dealer network. They made their own energy efficient shade, a do-it-yourself sewing project and most of their business was in production and sales of fabrics. My focus became to fulfill requests for Window Quilt orders and parts from all over the country. I stocked up on lots of parts and stayed busy with that task.

The "Green Machine," custom-designed to produce Window Quilt shades, on its way to the town dump as the factory is dismantled and closed.

Things didn't go well for Window Quilt. When The Warm Company finally decided to pull the plug and call it quits, it was rather sudden. I recall going up to the factory one morning and seeing a large truck taking almost everything to do with sunroom shading to the dump. It was very sad and appeared to be the bitter end. The company was for sale that winter of 2006-7 with several potential buyers. Bryan and I pursued these for a few months, flirting with a couple of New England-based energy companies. We also looked for a better home for the factory that wasn't so expensive as the old factory.

After all the negotiations, Larry Digney of Princeton, Massachusetts became the new owner and put in $500,000 of his own money to get things going again. He had very definite ideas of how to proceed and we discussed my possible role. In the end, I was not included in any way, although I had hoped to continue as part of the company. I'm just as glad; he and I didn't hit it off. Bryan, who was absolutely essential to re-establishing production, remained an employee. They moved what was left of the machinery to a very small but adequate space in a much larger building, the former Book Bindery.

Bryan proceeded to design and build a better "green machine," that stitched the shade. He and two employees turned out an excellent product over time, far better than the previous two decades. Larry's direction for the company was to put more into Internet sales and less into the dealer network. At first, I was somewhat skeptical but it seemed to be working. This way the company gets the full price where in the past the dealers got a 40 percent discount. The company had modest success over the years, and after the rough economic period of 2012 coupled with an unseasonably warm winter, Larry Digney decided to sell the business to Bryan.

With Window Quilt mostly behind me, I kept busy with a number of projects during my semi-retirement years.

On behalf of a group called Friends of Gladys Taber, Alta Hoffman asked me to be the group's featured speaker in June in West Chester. I compiled a slide show about Sugarbridge and my memories of growing up there. Gladys had been a colleague of my mother; the two had written *Stillmeadow and Sugarbridge* (1953) together. Ellie and I drove down to Pennsylvania and were treated royally to meals and a room. The group consisted of older women from the fifties or earlier and I kept up a correspondence with Alta for a while.

In early September 2001, my neighbor, Avner Eisenberg, and I departed Peaks Island for a week's cruise we had planned for some time on *Aurora II*. We followed the same route we had in previous years, stopping the first night at the Basin, a nearly land-locked pond with a narrow entrance off the New Meadows River a few miles south of Route 1. It was considered one of the safest hurricane holes on the Maine coast, better described in Curtis Rindlaub's, *A Cruising Guide to the Maine Coast* (1996).

After a restful night with water still as a mill pond, we left this idyllic spot the next morning and crossed the river to Cundy's Harbor on the west side. We asked the young fellow at the dock to fill our fuel tank. He seemed quite excited about the news event of an airplane crashing into a building in New York, and said we should go up the dock to Watson's General Store. Started by the family of the same name in 1819, it was the oldest family operated store in Maine. Inside we found a group of solemn old geezers gathered around an ancient wood stove in the center of a large, dark, smoky room and a prominent black and white TV. The store featured "all the necessities of life right next to each other — shackles and candy bars, pot warp and newspapers, rubber boots and lobsters."

No one said a word as we stood around the television, watching as the unbelievable drama of 9/11 unfolded. We returned to *Aurora II*, cast off and proceeded up river speculating on what had happened without hearing any newscast. In about an hour our water depth began to shoal to four feet so we turned around and went down river. Not really knowing what was going on in the outside world we decided it was best to head home. It was too late to make it to Peaks Island so we headed up into Quahog Bay to another idyllic anchorage just east of Snow Island, arriving late in the afternoon. We called our spouses who were equally uncertain of the future at that point. The memory that still stands out to me was the utter silence in the skies. All aircraft had been grounded. There were no contrails so common, with flights going into Portland, and no small plane or jet noise. It had been a day of a surreal experience woven into the ancient background of Watson's General Store. Little did we realize we had witnessed the beginning of the era of world insecurity.

That year, my colleague from the Explorers Club, Eric Takakjian, asked me to give a presentation to the Boston Sea Rovers forty eighth annual meeting in 2002. The Sea Rovers is a small but very prestigious group of divers that put on a large show every year. He suggested that I could speak about the history of small manned submersibles and my involvement. I felt it was an honor to be invited and went ahead to prepare about a 30-minute slide show. It was like old times to be assembling the history of all the diving vehicles and my adventures with some of them.

The evening before the presentation in early March of 2002, Ellie and I attended a large cocktail party in a downtown Boston hotel filled with old time divers and marine tech people. Early the next morning, she and I were on hand and I was the first speaker to address an audience of nearly seventy-five people. The talk went well with a number of questions. Later, we toured the exhibit hall highlighting the latest diving equipment.

I spoke with a few of the remaining Cousteau family and exchanged stories of working with the team in California in 1965. Ellie made me a gift of two caps embroidered with the name "Aurora" and a sailboat embellishment, which I still have. It was fun to be guests there and watch their film festival with the large crowd that evening. The best film was the one of an octopus climbing out of a tank at night to rob another across the room and then returnng to his tank. Soon after I received a nice note from the Sea Rovers with a certificate thanking me for the talk.

USS Thresher *SSBN 593 lost April 10, 1963 with all 129 hands,*
220 miles south of Boston while on sea trials.

In April of 2003, Ellie and I attended the fortieth anniversary memorial service of the sinking and loss of the USS *Thresher* SSN 593, held at the Portsmouth Naval Shipyard, in Kittery, Maine. I had become very interested in the history of this disaster that occurred on April 10, 1963 some 240 miles southeast of Boston and had been researching all I could find out about it. The construction and subsequent testing raised questions about what some at the time thought were inadequate and possibly deficient test results. The disaster took the lives of 129 men — there were no survivors. The official hearings over many months proved little except that the Navy protected its own; no charges were brought against any persons involved. It simply was an accident. However, as a result, many changes were made to correct the design faults and the certification process. I thought it would be a great story to tell.

The service we attended was very moving with many from the families of the lost sailors. I got the feeling that rather than the possible indignation at the Navy's faults, these people believed the deaths had been a noble and patriotic cause.

Facts, such as only 13 percent of the 3,000 silver-brazed pipe joints had been hydrostatically tested, didn't seem to matter. It only had taken one to fail at the test depth of 1,000 feet. There had been urgent need to get SSN 593 into service by Navy high command. Admiral Hymen Rickover had been a skeptic of silver solder all along and insisted on welding all joints in his reactor compartment, but he wasn't listened to for all those through-hulls joints in the rest of the boat. He was right, it turned out. Soon after the sinking, the Navy required all through-hull piping to be welded. I believed this background should be made known.

I found a literary agent named Harmsworth through a friend and gave him a draft proposal. He politely pointed out a number of problems with my approach. Further, I realized that there were very few people I could still interview as most had died over the years since 1963. I also realized things had changed since my book days with W.W. Norton where all you had to do was dash off three chapters and an outline to get an advance. Now my agent admitted I'd need to finish the book first. By this time, my interest had cooled off. I didn't have the luxury of research and writing without pay. Although that was technically the end of the story, it still intrigues me.

That year, Ellie and I decided it was time to take action on our long held dreams of improving the back of the house at Peaks, specifically to take advantage of the ample sunshine there. For years, I had been complaining that the best exposure for winter sun was wasted on the bathroom. Moving things around a bit would let the sunshine into the rest of the house. Little by little, our desires took shape in sketches and finally in discussions with Harvey Johnson, of Thompson-Johnson Woodworkers, a fairly new contractor on the island.

Harvey had set up his shop in the old hardware/telephone building on the corner of Central and Island Avenues, right next to the house where Judy Ellery lived until age six. Rachel, his designer, turned our ideas into a pleasing set of drawings — certainly enough to get started. We planned to renovate the kitchen, with the real goal of a sunroom with plenty of windows to grab that winter sun. The first problem we ran into was that because of the extremely small lot size of about an one eighth of an acre, the City of Portland forbid us from expanding the footprint of the house by even an inch. We had hoped to extend the back a few feet at least.

On the east side, behind the dining room there was a small room that had been my tool room with a work bench, table saw, hanging racks, and storage. Here we planned to put the the laundry and bathroom. The next step was for the engineer/ builder to provide a final estimated price. As the spring of 2003 passed, we began to see that Harvey and Co. might be a problem. We had no assurance of cost control and although we had applied for a building loan we were uneasy that the project might have runaway costs or become something we really wouldn't be happy with. We paid for the plans and said we would find our own contractor/builder. Harvey wasn't pleased but understood our concerns.

We immediately liked our new builder, David Lang. He was originally from New Zealand, was a sailor, and reputed to be a fine craftsman. After looking at the house and the plans, he told us although he wasn't accustomed to taking on a whole job like ours, he'd give it a try. He had never dealt with subcontractors but we felt we had better chance in controlling the costs with him than with Harvey. The project began that summer.

We had realized the back yard had to be graded and made usable as it sloped toward the house. For this we turned to Donnie Groeger who was best known on the island for his remarkable stone walls. Donnie was a true local. Although not originally from Maine, he'd been on the island a long time. He put in two beautiful low walls that created separate levels with flower beds in back and on the west side. He also put in a French drain, along the back of the house to prevent drainage through the cellar

It was no surprise that soon after David Lang started he found the entire rear shed, an add-on to the original house built around 1900, was rotted and needed complete replacement. This added to the cost and certainly to the time involved. The project lasted a year and a half, giving us only partial use of the house. All the furniture was gathered in the living room.

One of the major improvements we decided upon was the inclusion a forced hot water baseboard heating system. This added $10,000, a large cost, but one we have been most pleased with over the years since. This, too, didn't happen easily. Being on an island, we had only two contractors. One was too busy. After waiting for several months with winter approaching and no action from the other we, went off island, enlisting Pine State Oil of South Portland, who completed everything in just two days. At last we had heat and the final work could go on. Despite the numerous glitches and problems, in the end Ellie and I were so pleased with the final results we quickly forgot the agonies of building.

The low retaining wall built by Donnie Groeger in front of the house.

Pine State Oil of South Portland installed our forced-hot water heating system in two days.

Every time I sit in the sunroom on a bitter cold winter morning, taking in the swirling snowdrifts in the backyard and luxuriating in the sun's warmth, I realize it was definitely worth it. The final cost came out around $70,000, twice what I had paid in 1984 for the whole house.

Not long after this project, I took on another. Amie had commented how much she would like to hear more about our family history since she and I were, we thought, the only living relatives. For my birthday, she'd given me a book called *Legacy, A Step-By-Step Guide to Writing A Personal History* to get me started in writing a family history or memoir. I read parts of it but put it aside and decided to start on my own. Recently, I found the book in the cellar and paged through it. The author, Linda Spence, suggested using a bound blank paged book. I chose to tell my tale on the ubiquitous yellow legal pad. By the time Amie and I were together in Alaska in 2007, I had filled several of these 50-page pads and then typed up the notes. Amie had also launched a similar effort of her adventures. She read the initial part of mine and we shared a lot of our memories both funny and sad. My part continued sporadically.

Over the years, writing had always been a part of my life. When I first began going to Peet's Coffee in Lexington for a morning cup of tea, I would sit at the counter in front by the window and write. Then as my Window Quilt work got busy in the fall and winter seasons I found I might not write for many months. I kept notes scribbled in little pocket pads as ideas and old names popped up: people of some fame I had met or seen or heard, old girl friends, cars, boats or funny incidents. Although Ellie often commented that I was spending too much time looking backwards and living in the past, the project invigorated me for more than a decade.

While writing in the early mornings at Peet's I began to notice a boisterous group of coffee drinkers who sat every day at the same table. They all seemed to know each other; most were in their fifties or beyond. Every so often there would be a birthday celebration with a cake with candles, then singing, and cheers all around. After watching this for some time I finally walked over from my lone post by the window. They asked me to join them if I wished; and I did. Joanne, the official organizer, had started the group in 1986 down the street at the Coffee Connection. Then, sometime later they were asked to leave because of their loud noise. The group moved to Peets just up the street and Coffee Connection became Starbucks. Pete Peet's became our daily meeting place.

There were about thirty in the group but usually only about a dozen at a time. I was one of the first to show up around six thirty each morning with others wandering in on their way to work for the next couple of hours. There was quite a mix of academics, computer savvy types, and literary sorts, some self-employed, as I was, and some retired. The group was decidedly on the liberal side but there were a couple moderate conservatives. We had numerous debates on political issues, generally in friendly terms. For me, it took the place of working in an office or shop, which I had missed as I had worked by myself for quite a few years. I thought at times of writing a small piece on the diverse bunch or maybe even filming a series of video interviews for our local TV access station. At the time, I had just read Larry McMurtry's *Walter Benjamin at the Dairy Queen* where a similar group in a small West Texas town find the only place to gather for coffee and discussion was the local Dairy Queen. I'm sure I passed this book around as I did with others to those who cared. Perhaps there were many such groups around the area but I like to think ours was unique. My essay still sits on a back burner, simmering.

We met every morning at Peet's Coffee Shop in Lexington. It was here that I began this memoir in 2004, hand written on 10 yellow pads.

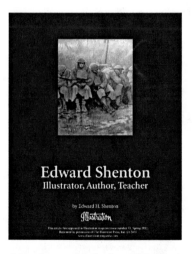

Illustration Magazine *produced a beautiful collection of my father's illustrations drawn over his lifetime in their Spring 2011 issue.*

My next project was assembling all I could find about my father's life. Years earlier, I had produced a bibliography of all his illustrated books and other written publications collected over time. Robert Carlson, a professor at West Chester State College, had prepared the first edition of this bibliography for the memorial exhibit at the Chester County Art Association in October 1979, which I used as the starting point for my project.

I was most fortunate to have the talented help of a colleague from the Explorer Club. Rex Passion was very capable with computers and soon after we met, produced a web site, edwardshenton.com, showcasing much of my father's artwork. In 2010 with Rex's help, I wrote, printed and later sold a 6,600-word booklet about my father, complete with color illustrations. Through a suggestion from Doug Smith, an artist on Peaks Island, I submitted an article to *Illustration Magazine* which was published in spring, 2011. The editor used more than thirty of my father's best illustrations, nearly all in color, many full page, and produced a tribute article, "Edward Shenton, Illustrator, Author, Teacher."

Most recently, after three years of attempts, I placed a small exhibit at the Owls Head Transportation Museum in Maine which ran from June to October, 2012. It featured a number of wooden, hand-carved racing cars my father made as a boy along with ten full size posters of book dust jackets. My ultimate goal continues to be generating more awareness of my father and his unique style.

Ellie and Julie celebrate Ellie's birthday in Iceland in 2006.

In 2006 Ellie and Julie decided to celebrate Ellie's seventy-fifth birthday with a trip to Iceland. Much of their week there is nicely told in all the pictures they took as they made their way around the island staying at farms and hostels. The day they left they bathed in the hot springs near the airport.

Not to be outdone, Amie and I began planning for my seventy-fifth birthday in the spring of 2007. We considered possible foreign countries but they all seemed too expensive. After researching various California spots, we settled on Alaska; Amie hadn't been there and knew I had enjoyed it in the past. She found through an Internet search that a little town, Moose Pass, south of Anchorage was having a big blast celebrating the Summer Solstice. It seemed different and worth a try. She found us a cabin, the Cranberry Creek Guest House, to rent for a week and for her running interests there was to be a half marathon in Anchorage the day after we arrived. It sounded like an adventure, especially with a name like Moose Pass.

Amie began sending me background info on Moose Pass and the Solstice Festival. The town was founded in 1909 by two men who built a small log cabin on the original Iditarod Trail, supplying gold miners up north. Now it had a population of 220, mostly men. I was amazed to read that median income in 2000 was $87,200, almost twice the per capita income in Maine towns. We found out later "oil" was the magic word.

Cranberry Creek Guest House in Moose Pass, Alaska where Amie and I spent a week celebrating my 75ᵗʰ birthday in 2007.

On June 16, I flew from Boston to Anchorage, stopping briefly to pick up Amie in Phoenix. We arrived at midnight, rented our car, ate at a diner, and snoozed in the car. Amie would be running in the Mayor's Marathon in the morning.

When I was last in Anchorage in the early 1970s, I had been on my way to Fairbanks to visit Don Hood, my old Texas A&M professor, at the University of Alaska. Then, it was a small city but now its population of nearly 300,000 — half the entire state — seemed incongruous, surrounded by so much wilderness. We found a Starbucks, had a snack before the race and arrived at the start where everyone was milling about. It was cloudy and cool, perfect for a run. Once she finished, we headed south to Moose Pass, about a hundred miles down the Kenai Peninsula. The countryside was mostly flat and reminded me of Maine and Newfoundland.

Amie ran in the Mayor's ½ marathon while we were in Anchorage.

In Moose Pass, we were greeted by our host, Heather Lindquist. She and her husband, Tom built an elegant small and very modern cabin near their home which rented for $120 a night. Amie had the loft and I the downstairs. We made our way to the town center where the solstice fair was in progress. It was quite small and had two rows of tents with usual sort of country fair events. It reminded me our Common Ground Fair in Maine without the animals. The best part was the people in attendance. Most were good ol' boys with large bellies and thick beards and many with heavy Texas accents — the oil guys most probably out of work as the boom had gone bust. I couldn't find much worth buying and settled on a t-shirt.

367

Later Amie and I decided to take a flight over the countryside. We chose the ever-popular sea plane common to Alaska. I sat in front next to the pilot with Amie in back, recording our trip on videotape. It was great fun for both of us. We splurged on the twenty-minute trip for $300; what the heck, it was my birthday celebration. I filmed spectacular views of the mountains and lakes. Unfortunately, most of the time we were there it was cool, drizzly or foggy with only a few peeks of the sun. We spent the rainiest time in the cabin reading and writing. I worked on my never-ending memoir and Amie worked on a bit of her own. We talked at length of our days in Cutler and her growing up experiences, many which I'd never heard. It was a true father-daughter bonding opportunity.

The next day we joined a charter whale watch boat we had scheduled earlier. It left from Seward about thirty miles south, where nearly all the tourists arrived via cruise ships. Our whale watch was another part of the vacation I memorialized on videotape. Although we saw a few whales they were quite a distance away and not as spectacular we'd hoped for. An hour or so later, as we got farther out of the bay, we began to roll in the large waves of the open ocean; I have some footage of Amie drowsily sitting by the window. No one got seasick but I'm sure some thought about it. At lunchtime, we headed up a rugged fiord and stopped to watch a small glacier approaching the sea with large chunks calving off and making enormous splashes.

We hired a pretty yellow sea plane and took a half hour tour of the beautiful mountainous scenery of Moose Pass.

A typical glacier calved large blocks of ice while we were on a
whale watch in a fjord.

In our remaining time on the Kenai Peninsula, Amie ran the Mount Marathon in Seward while I relaxed out at the base of the trail. We also hiked a trail near Cranberry Creek in the Chugach National Forest. At the trailhead, signs cautioned us about bears and possible avalanches. The steep trail rolled onto a flat meadow at 2,000 feet, with a small lake lined with a few traces of snow. We saw no bears, only bear scat. Once near the cabin we thought we heard a bear in the underbrush, leaving us both wishing we'd seen one.

Our final day was spent on the west side of the peninsula in Homer, a busy tourist port known as the Halibut Capital of the World. The pier was lined with halibut drying, for sale, and show. From Homer, we headed to the Anchorage airport and home. The plane took off around three o'clock in the morning, just as the sun was rising through the clouds. The trip was a great success and one of my best visits with Amie.

We spent the day in Homer, Alaska, the Halibut capital of the world.

Once home, I resumed working on my many projects. A few years after Rex had launched the website for my father, I began to receive a number of inquiries. In particular, Mike Snyder from Pottstown, Pennsylvania, related his genealogical work and details of the Thomas and Shenton families in Pottstown. He showed me 1870 and 1880 census data about my great grandfather, Henry Shenton, who, according to the census, had eleven children by two wives. Henry had immigrated from England in 1852 with his uncle Frank, and joined the Union Army a decade later. This information prompted me to dig further into my family's history.

I had also been contacted by Mark Ritts in Los Angeles who informed me his mother was a cousin of my father. I had known Paul and Mary Ritts in the past, and I thought they were merely friends of the family. Mark described visiting Sugarbridge as a youngster, probably while I was in Texas. The Ritts were Philadelphia television personalities with a puppet show. My father was never much interested in our family tree and was reluctant to mention the Ritts.

I was excited to learn of my new cousin and we exchanged several messages. We made plans to meet the following year when Ellie and I made our annual visit to her sister's in California. When I contacted him right before the trip in 2009, I found to my dismay that he died at age sixty-three. His obituary in the *New York Times* described him as TV personality and actor of some fame in which he appeared in costume as *Lester the Lab Rat*, a popular CBS show that played in ninety countries. Another one snuck away, this time before I ever met him.

Lester the Lab Rat, *starring my cousin Mark Ritts. He appeared on the CBS national children's program for a number of years.*
Sadly Mark died at the young age of 63 before I ever got to meet him.

Ellie and I occasionally visited Karyl and Bob in early July for a joint celebration of Bob's and my birthdays. Bob's birthday fell on the fourth of July and, in true patriotic spirit he and Karyl liked to say his initials of "RWB" also stood for the "red white, and blue." In 2005, I called Karyl several days before our birthdays to ask her and Bob to join us for a birthday lunch on the dock at Robinson's Wharf, as we had on several other occasions. Karyl calmly told me that Bob had passed away the day before, at age eighty-six. He was a great guy.

Around this time, I received an email from Shane Murphy, the son of Robert "Bob" Murphy, the *Saturday Evening Post* editor and a dear friend of my parents. Shane wanted to know anything I could tell him about his father, who had died in 1971. I wrote up all I could recall. Shane told me about his eight trips to the Antarctic as a boat driver and his visit to Greenland. Even more of interest, he told me that Bob had been a member of the Explorers Club for his work with peregrine falcons on Ellesmere Island. He also mentioned having some of my father's original drawings. He now lives in Rim Rock, Arizona not too far from Scottsdale.

Swedish Car Day. Every September the Lars Andersen Museum in Brookline, Massachusetts invites owners of SAAB and Volvo to display their cars.

In mid-2009, General Motors decided to dump Saab along with Oldsmobile, Saturn, and Hummer. GM was in deep trouble due to the financial recession. At the very end of 2009 GM announced that Saab would close. Many of us didn't believe it would happen. Although Spyker Cars had made an offer, the future looked grim. On December 18, *The New York Times* ran an article called "Saab Stories 2009," in which they invited loyal present and former Saab owners to submit their experience with this Swedish marvel. There was an enormous outpouring of stories from all over the world.

I submitted my story of the fourteen Saabs I had owned, and it was posted on the Internet along with many other stories. Despite heroic efforts, by 2015 the company ceased manufacturing Saabs entirely.

Each fall for a number years, I attended the Swedish Car Day event at Lars Anderson Museum in Brookline where there were many Saabs and a handful of Volvos on display from all over New England and mid-Atlantic states. It was quite a spectacle heand a tribute to a nearly dead marquee (Chinese owned Volvo thrives in the market). I admire and covet the older Saab Sonnets, seven of which were showcased at the 2012 event.

Ellie and I had been talking for a couple of years about traveling west to explore Yosemite National Park. She had been several times and felt I too should have the experience. She began making reservations during the winter of 2009 for the following year, as hotels there fill up early. We decided to spend four or five days in the park at the park-run Yosemite Valley Lodge toward the end of June. We both bought new backpacks for day hiking and spent all spring excitedly planning and reading up on Yosemite events.

Toward the end of June, 2010, we flew to San Francisco and spent our first night in a grand hotel. Ellie's son, David, and his wife, Brenda, drove down from Redding to join us for the evening and dinner. The next day Brenda had to return north, but Dave stayed with us as we drove out to Yosemite. By the time we got out in the desert, it was blazing hot the usual change from cool coastal to scorching inland. We spent that night at a motel with a refreshing pool. Dave left the next morning while we headed south to Yosemite, about thirty miles away. The road to the park was a narrow, winding two lanes up through the hills to the entrance.

Our room at the lodge was on the first floor and on the end where we could just see the falls and certainly hear them. The falls were running more than usual since there had been lots of snow that winter. So much snow, in fact, we found the road to the Tuolumne Meadows wasn't even open yet. Over the following days we took part in lots of events, walks, and lectures. Ellie was right. The trip was worthwhile.

The following year, 2011, began a series of eightieth birthday celebrations. First it was Dick Palais's turn. He invited us to join a three-day party at his home in Irvine, California. It was a fine family reunion with Ellie's kids; Julie, Robert, and David and many of Dick's colleagues in the math world, some of whom I knew, and many I didn't. Dick hosted several extravagant dinners, giving us a chance to visit with many people we hadn't seen in years.

In August, we staged a grand celebration of Ellie's eightieth on Peaks Island by renting a house where Dick and his wife, Julie, Margy, David and Brenda stayed; Robert and his friend, Micah, slept at our house. It was great to be all together on the island rather than traipsing back and forth to hotels across the bay in Portland.

We had a big dinner gathering at Di Millo's and a second one the next night at the Muddy Rudder in Freeport. Both were memorable even though a bit expensive. We figured we only do this once.

Our retirement travel continued with another trip to California the following year. Instead of the usual one week school vacation spent with Margy in California, now that Ellie had retired we decided we should take a longer stay. In mid-January of 2012 we spent an entire month at Margy's house in Pacific Palisades. We thought it would be a real break from the worst of our New England winter only to find out in our absence it was one of warmest winters on record. However, southern California was still warmer and we basked in the 70s with lots of sun. Margy took us to the orchestra and a play of *Our Town* at a theater in Santa Monica.

As spring arrived, Ellie and I made plans for my eightieth birthday celebration, inviting my side of the family to Peaks for four days which included both of my birthdays, July 5 and 7. Although it was smaller than the other festivities, John, Tari, Maddie, Kate, Rollie and Amie all had fun being together with us. Our granddaughters had grown so much since we'd seen them two years earlier.

In July of 2012 it's my turn for an 80th and my side of the family comes to Peaks Island.

My summer sailing continued but as my crew, Avner, became more involved with his acting and its required overseas travel, we found less time for our long cruises and shifted to shorter trips. Our favorite run was to Damariscove, an island lying about eight miles south of Boothbay Harbor, where we would spend the night and then sometimes go on toward Pemaquid Point and around through South Bristol. Going through the narrow passage there was fun as you had to blow the horn for the swing bridge and sometimes circle several times until it opened. Then we would head for We started with a dinner at the Inn On Peaks Island sponsored by the family. Ellie organized another of her famous treasure hunts which the girls loved and remembered from a previous visit. Amie and I did our kayak tour over to the Diamond Islands. I had hoped for a short sail in *Aurora II* but time didn't allow it. We went to a planned dinner at the Muddy Rudder where we also included our neighbor, Carole Eisenberg, at a perfectly-located table overlooking the river. It was topped off with a delicious chocolate cake, custom made by Carole's friend, a baker who owns Katy Made Cakes. Whew! Welcome to the eighties! Boothbay, spending a day or so there, and then through another bridge at Southport. The Lewis twins, Dwayne and Dwight, had been the bridge keepers since Karyl and I had first moved to the island in the 1970s.

Each time we went through the bridge, one of the brothers would holler down from their station atop the bridge for our boat's name and name of the master, which was kept in a log. On some of our trips, Avner and I would put into Love's Cove and pay a short visit to Karyl, where he gave her juggling lessons and she served afternoon tea. Across the Sheepscot River we usually stopped at supper time for fresh lobsters at the wharf.

Our most memorable trip in that area turned out to be a bit alarming. It was mid-September and there had been a storm out at sea. The remains of the storm amounted to rather large waves off the mouth of the Kennebec River on our way back to Peaks. The wind had dropped and we were running in the trough. The waves had risen to nearly twenty feet. Had our engine quit, we would have been in real trouble. Fortunately it didn't, but we both realized we shouldn't have come out in these conditions.

The last years of the decade were pretty much spent closer to home. Avner couldn't join me so I did a few day sails and overnights at Diamond Cove, just twenty minutes from my mooring. These overnights are most pleasant; I can enjoy all the delights of a small, glittering harbor with several cruising boats on their way to or from somewhere. And it's also protected from the local southwest swells, allowing for a good night's sleep. The Casco Bay ferries come in every hour or so.

Most times I tow my eight-foot sailing dinghy, *Fatty Knees*, along and rig it for a sail around the harbor and occasionally outside. Then I motor home to my mooring at the club, back to our safe harbor, as if I'd been on a long ocean voyage. In 2012, I wrote a piece about the cove which was published by *Points East Magazine*, "One More Cruise to Diamond Cove," October /November 2013.

Fatty Knees *my 8 ½ ft. sailing dinghy which I keep at TEIA club for fun sailing and rowing.*

Around mid-October of 2012, Ellie began to have trouble reading emails on her iPhone. I paid little attention until two days later when she spoke to her doctor's nurse, Brenda Moissette. Brenda correctly suspected it might have been a stroke and told us to go immediately to the ER at Massachusetts General Hospital (MGH). Ellie had, in fact, suffered a mild stroke but without any physical impairments; but there was some memory and peripheral sight loss. After a long night in the ER, she was admitted to the neurological section for four days, with a subsequent re-admission for tests soon following. Near the end of October, she had a fall at home wounding her already fragile legs.

At the time, I was out on a Window Quilt job. An ambulance was called in which the operators insisted on strapping her to a back board. It was most uncomfortable for her. Nevertheless, she rallied and by November 6, was able, upon discharge, to vote in the Obama election at her polling place in Lexington. Sometime in here she had both a CAT scan and an MRI which were not interpreted for her at the time. At a meeting with her neurologist, Dr. Scott Silverman, in March of 2013, he felt things were going well but gave us few details. While she made a remarkable recovery in her reading, it was a bit slow going. I took on the job of caregiver, cook, and many of her usual tasks and chores. We finished the year quietly at home with near daily visits from home health nurses and therapists. During the fall Julie, Amie, David, and Robert all came to spend a few days in helping. Amie had been scheduled to run in the New York Marathon but it was canceled at the last moment by Hurricane Sandy so she diverted and came from New York to help out. We ended the year with a quiet Christmas and a positive outlook for 2013.

Also toward the end of 2012, I received an email from Nancy Sixsmith. I immediately recognized the last name as that of my cousin Jack. She introduced herself as the great niece of Edward Shenton and daughter of Jack and granddaughter of my Aunt Betty Shenton Sixsmith. We began a flurry of messages, shared photos and discovered previously-unknown relatives. This inspired me to read through and organize the numerous boxes of my parents' letters, manuscripts, sketches, notes, and journals.

Around this time, Alta Hoffman contacted me again, and, as in 2004, asked if I would be the featured speaker for the annual meeting in 2013 of Friends of Gladys Taber (FOGT). Although I wasn't sure Ellie would be up to the trip, I accepted and Alta was delighted. I realized this might be a good chance to gather together all the extraneous bits about my mother for the talk. The general subject was to be built around Sugarbridge. One of the FOGT members had previously suggested that I write a booklet about my mother as a companion to the one I had produced about my father earlier.

In early 2013, I began digging through all the papers, letters, scribbled notes that my mother had left behind. It wasn't long before I realized there was a lot available, in fact, it turned out there was too much to read and digest in a short time.

I had until June to write, edit, and print a booklet of about fifty pages and produce an hour powerpoint show. With the help of Ellie as editor and Rex Passion as production manager we got both tasks done just in time. Luckily, I had very little window shade work and could devote nearly full time to the booklet.

We drove to the Inn in Mendenhall, Pennsylvania on a Thursday, an eight hour drive that went smoothly, with only one brief rest stop in New York. About forty people showed up from all over the country. The following day, we visited the new home of the mural my father had painted in 1956 in the old courthouse. It was now transferred to a brand-new courthouse building and Judge Thomas Gavin gave us fine presentation on the history of the move and how the mural was peeled off the wall and restored at great cost.

The mural my father painted in the new courthouse in West Chester, PA.

Saturday, we took a bus trip to see Sugarbridge, now for sale just shy of $ million. The owner, Tom Schindler, was no longer living there but was on hand t let us wander through the house and barn. It was sad to see the almost complet destruction of the studio as it no longer belonged to the farm and had been aban doned since 1968. The pool also was empty with the dam breached. The hillsid behind the house was hard to recognize as it was totally grown over with large tree The wonderful beech that had stood some 250 years at the top of the hill had fallen Things change.

During the summer of 2013, Ellie had wisely prodded me to have a patio buil in the back of the 95 Potter Pond house. Since we were spending nearly all our sum mers in Maine, I felt we wouldn't use the backyard and further, it was always jus too darn hot. But I agreed and we contracted our condo maintenance supervisor t install it. As usual, Ellie's foresight was accurate. The patio has been a great additio especially since our travel was limited after her stroke. We found it a wonderfu extension for entertaining and relaxing.

In August of 2013, Ellie experienced a mild seizure and spent some time i MGH. Again, we were fortunate there were no physical effects, although her read ing ability suffered another blow. A second lesser seizure occurred in January but sh made good recovery. The following year, she unwisely attempted a rearrangemen of a top shelf of linens. Balancing on a small step stool, she fell and broke her le hip. We returned again to MGH, where they immediately operated and placed titanium pin to hold the broken bone together. By mid-July she was starting t walk with a cane which she named "Able." Her physical therapist, was great help i getting her walking.

With this major change in our lives, we spent much less time at Peaks. Eve before Ellie's first stroke, the furnace quit during a very cold spell, freezing pipe dishwasher and washing machine, and allowing water to pour over the electric box on the cellar. It was a classic meltdown which in the end wound up costing over $3,000. We decided to completely shut down the island house for the winter.

Around this time, I also learned another of my oldest friends had departed. I had been trying to visit my pal, Berto Nevin for some time but our travel limitations made it difficult. Finally, Ellie and I had decided to visit him and his wife, Jennifer, in Blue Hill. The morning I called she said that Berto had died the night before. I knew he wasn't well and had been battling cancer. He had lead such an interesting life. There were so many things I wished I had a chance to talk to him about.

Shortly following Berto's departure in late 2013, I found out that I had severe arthritis of my left hip. It had come on rather rapidly, making walking uncomfortable. One more trip to MGH in April for surgery: a replacement ball and socket of titanium in a smooth operation lasting a little over an hour. I was even able to watch it on a TV above my head as I had spinal anesthesia. My goal was to attend my 60th Colby Reunion in June.

Amie came east just before the operation to help Ellie with appointments and housework while I recovered at MGH. Ellie later joined me at the Meadow Green rehab facility just up the road from Potter Pond, where we spent eleven days, me on Medicare and she paying full price. On Easter morning, Amie surprised us with a beautiful basket. She stayed with us after we returned home helping with meals and errands since I couldn't drive for three weeks and Ellie hadn't been able to drive since her stroke in 2012. So, with the help of a good physical therapist, I drove myself to Colby two months after my surgery and joined about forty classmates and spouses for a weekend of festivities. Ellie wasn't up to the trip and Robert stayed with her in my absence.

Meantime, my Window Quilt business coasted along, with a few jobs and help from my neighbor, Dennis Healey. The fall months brought more work.

Amie had planned to retire from her insurance career at the end of 2014, and was able to take some more time in the east, spending six weeks with us and with her mother. In June, she ran the Lubec-Campobello International Marathon and visited friends in Bangor. She returned when John, Tari, Maddy, and Kate came from Memphis on their vacation. Instead of their usual visit to Peaks they came to the Boston area for several days. The girls had grown so much since we saw them two years before. We all took a trip to the New England Aquarium and around Lexington's historic spots, and celebrated their time here by eating at Cabots in Newton. Later Amie joined them at the camp at Sebec Lake for a week of fun, water skiing, and swimming. For Ellie and me it was a real family gathering and a treat to see our grandchildren.

Then in late July Julie Palais called to ask if I would be interested to go to the August premier showing of James Cameron's new film *Deep Sea Challenge* in New

York. Of course, I said yes and we met at the Museum of Natural History. As a special treatment, Cameron had arranged for Woods Hole Oceanographic Institution to display his submersible Deep Sea Challenger on the street out front. After his historic dive in 2012 to 35,000 feet, he had donated his $7 million sub to WHOI. The event was sponsored by Rolex and The National Geographic and was attended by many important New York people. The 90-minute, 3D movie was entertaining and afterward Julie and I had a chance to talk to Cameron. I mentioned my working with the Cousteau Soucoupe and said I would send him a copy of my book, *Exploring the Ocean Depths*. Julie invited him to come to speak to her NSF group in Washington. Cameron, I found later, had produced the two highest grossing films of all times at nearly $5 billion.

James Cameron, famous for movie productions Titanic *and* Avatar, *displays his one-man submersible* DeepSea Challenge *which he dived to 35,800 ft. in the Marianas Trench in 2012.*

I sent Cameron an inscribed copy of my book and had nearly forgotten it when I later received a letter from the legal department of 20th Century Fox advising that Mr. Cameron could not receive unsolicited materials and my book was being returned unread. The "unread" got me. What a slam! But not to be defeated I contacted Colette Bennett, wife a former Explorers Club president and also a friend of Julie's, to see if she could help. She kindly said she would forward the book to Jim Cameron avoiding the 20th Century Fox blockade. She later told me the book was delivered by FedEx to wherever Cameron has his secret quarters. And so ended my brief brush with the very rich and famous. His movie was worth seeing, especially as it was connected to the 1960 descent in *Trieste* by Walsh and Piccard.

Chapter Twenty-Two

Reflections

In reflecting on the propitious events in my moderately long life — and it's not over yet — several people were key to steering me on my career path. I'd like to say that my parents played a major role, but they didn't. They gave me the right tools by sending me to good schools; started me reading at an early age; and provided a nurturing home. They never scolded me for mediocre grades and had no rigid expectations of what I should become when I grew up. Unlike N. C. Wyeth, who home schooled and rigorously trained his son Andrew to become one of the outstanding artists of the twentieth century, my father, an accomplished and successful illustrator, refrained from suggesting I follow in his footsteps or pen strokes, although he did send me, at age fifteen, to Saturday art classes at the Museum School in Philadelphia. Perhaps he soon realized that I wasn't interested or didn't show much talent. I didn't pursue art any further, although I can draw and still enjoy sketching marine scenes. And my mother, who was such a talented writer, never pushed me down the writer's path. I'm extremely grateful I was allowed to find my own way.

Some young people at an early age seem to know exactly what they want to be. The British documentary, The *Up* series shows examples of children at age seven beginning to have ideas of their future careers. The made-for-British-television film was based on the Jesuit premise, "Give me the child until he is seven and I will give you the man." This captivating film series interviewed children who already knew what they wanted to be: an astronaut, a jockey, a scientist, an explorer. Not me! I hadn't a clue what I wanted to be or become at age seven and well beyond.

In keeping with the point I've made about the importance of "who you know" are several who I call Key Guys (and one Key Gal). While they have all been described previously, they are acknowledged separately here.

Charlie Dethier

I first met Charlie Dethier when I entered Haverford School in 1945.
He was the floor master on the third floor in the Oaks Dormitory.

The first "Key Guy," Charles Dethier (pronounced De-chair), who I met in 1945 at the Haverford School, was the floor master on the third floor of the Oaks, our dormitory. Tall, lean, and athletic, he taught math in the lower school and coached squash and tennis in the upper school.

He had a quick mind, was a bit sarcastic, and had the amazing ability to speed read by quickly scanning a page diagonally and then tell you anything appearing on that page, a true photographic memory. By the end of my fifth form year I had a serious math deficiency due to a poor foundation in public school and subsequent mistakes at Haverford. I thought I would be sentenced to dreaded summer school to make up for my Algebra II failure. Knowing about this, Charlie recommended his cousin Bernie as good math tutor and, if I could get myself to Blue Hill, Maine, I could have summer learning sessions for what I needed in math and perhaps get in a little sailing too. I took him up on the offer and I had a wonderful summer experience. Without Charlie's help, I doubt I would have found my way to Maine and all the friends I made starting in 1949. That's not to say I became a whiz at math, but I did get by and passed the exam to graduate.

In 2012, Ellie and I went to visit Charlie, who has lived in Blue Hill year-round for a decade or so. Charlie, then ninety-five, looked well and much the same as I recall him fifty years ago. He was still driving to the supermarket up the road a few miles. He passed away in 2016, and I'm not sure he realized how important his tutoring offer was to introducing me to Maine and all the events that followed.

Chet Harrington

In that same summer of 1949, I met Chet Harrington, who worked for Charlie at the Kollegewidgewok Yacht Club. Chet and his buddy, George Wales, were the dock boys and race assistants during the summer and would be juniors at Colby College, in Waterville, Maine. They double-teamed me to think seriously about coming to Colby the next year. The seed was planted at that moment. That fall and winter I dragged my feet in applying to colleges, (the beginning of my habit of procrastination) and finally submitted an application to Stanford and Swarthmore. I had rather poor grades and I have no idea why I would have chosen those colleges; I was quickly refused by both.

In May of 1950, I remembered Chet's invitation and submitted my last-ditch hope to Colby. I remember visiting Colby about that time with my parents and being interviewed by George Nickerson, Dean of Men. To my great amazement, I was accepted a few weeks later. I knew by then that Maine was the place for me. Had it not been for Chet Harrington, I doubt that I would have come to Colby. During my freshman year there, Chet, a big football star playing quarterback, took me under his wing like an older brother. He even helped forge my draft card so I could be served beer downtown. Not long ago, I wrote Chet to thank him for his help and guidance and to tell him what I'd been up to for these last sixty years.

Ken Drummond

Ken Drummond `was a friend when we were at Texas A&M and later hired me into the Satellite Tracking Program at Smithsonian Astrophysical Observatory in Cambridge, Mass. in 195

Toward the end of the summer of 1958, while working at a summer job as GS-3 fishery aide in Woods Hole, I received a phone call from my next Key Guy Ken Drummond. "Ol Drum" had been a close friend and part time boss at Texas A&M from 1954 to 1956. Originally from La Jolla, California, Ken had gone to Bates College in Maine, then was in the Navy in World War II and wound up in marine operations at A&M. He was a tall, easy-going westerner with a lovely smile and pleasant personality.

In 1958, Ken joined the Satellite Tracking Program at the Smithsonian Astrophysical Observatory as part of the International Geophysical Year. He had moved to Cambridge, Massachusetts where SAO headquarters were. Ken called me to ask me to join him in the newly-formed program with twelve worldwide stations. I had been searching for my next job and here it was, dumped right in my lap. Of course I eagerly said yes and by early September I was working in Cambridge. Again, it was another of the "who you know" situations.

I started as a GS-9 observer after training in New Mexico, then had operational duty in South Africa. After several years, "Ol Drum" decided to promote me to Chief of the Stations as a GS-12 in 1960, a sizable amount of responsibility. I was only twenty-eight years old and in charge of seventy-two men at nine of our twelve stations. Shortly after this I made visits to Spain, Curacao, Argentina, Peru, Florida and Iran. Without Ken's presence, I doubt I would have risen in the ranks as easily

Ken left the tracking program about the same time as I did, in 1962, to work for his old friend, Roger Revelle, at Scripps Institution of Oceanography. I didn't hear much from Ken until in 1978, when he nominated me for membership in the Explorers Club. We spoke several times by phone but by this time he was living in Seattle and not traveling east. He died at at eighty-seven. I had always wished we could have had another visit.

David Scott

David Scott and me. David was a student of my father at the
Pennsylvania Academy of Fine Arts who helped me get a job in
Annapolis as an oceanographer in 1962.

The next in line, David Scott, didn't come along for a while although I had known David since I was fourteen. My family and I went cruising with him on the schooner *Heron* in 1946. David, as captain, was offering his father's forty-six-foot vessel for charter. He was nineteen at the time and a very competent sailor. He was also a student of my father at the Academy of Fine Arts. He entered my life again in 1962, now as Art Director at The US Naval Institute in Annapolis, Maryland. My father had kept in touch with David over the years and at this point had been doing some drawings for the monthly publication, *The Proceedings*. As dad's drawing jobs for books began to diminish, David sent many good drawing opportunities his way.

About this time, I had been at the Smithsonian Astrophysical Observatory for four years and was getting ready to move back into my field of marine science. But there were no openings. I had tried the federal agencies, major companies, and employment agencies with no response. Karyl and I were living in Amesbury, Massachusetts and one day who should call me but David Scott. "There's a small company here in Annapolis looking for an oceanographer, he said. If you're interested I can put in a good word for you because I work for them." I immediately jumped at the offer and was hired shortly thereafter. It was again the case of not what you know, but who you know that won the job.

The small company was called The Geraldines Ltd., a most unusual group of characters. David's little favor would become an important part of my multi-faceted career. He also became a good friend while we lived in Annapolis as he and I had such fun "simply messing about in boats" while working for the new company. A large part of his life was built around boats as his wife Joanne so beautifully describes in her reflections, *Legacy* (1999). Right after our arrival, David also helped Karyl get a job as Art Director at *Skipper Magazine* where he did free-lance art for them.

By this time, it was becoming apparent that each of my new and different jobs were to form stepping stones to the next opportunity. This boost by David Scott led me to the next step, even though it ended two years later in the demise of The Geraldines and the loss of my job. If I hadn't spent my time at The Geraldines, where I worked closely with one of the first small submersibles, the Perry Cubmarine, I probably wouldn't have been offered my next job with Westinghouse Underseas Division and the Cousteau Diving Saucer. After being out of work for several months, the Westinghouse offer was most timely and welcome. Among the many good things that came with this job was the chance to write my first book, published by W.W. Norton & Co.

Just before the Saucer team was scheduled to leave for the California coast, my parents arranged for a visit for all of us with Bob Farlow, Senior VP at Norton. On hearing my expected future with the Cousteau group, he was eager to give me a contract. This was 1965 and Cousteau was barely known to most people. By the time my story had been told and published in 1968, Cousteau was nearly a household name; the book sold well for a first attempt.

Julie Palais

Julie Palais, Ellie's daughter, who hired me to go to Greenland in the summer of 1990 to be a general field assistant on the Greenland Ice Sheet Project till 1993.

Finally, on my list of Key Guys is a Key Gal. When I met my wife, Ellie, her daughter, Julie worked as a glaciologist in the Antarctic for the National Science Foundation (NSF). In July of 1990, Julie needed someone to take over her job in Greenland where NSF was drilling an ice core. I had been trying to find a way to get involved with the new science of climate change, then called global warming. That August, I was on my way to the top of the Greenland Ice Sheet and Project GISP 2. This adventure led me to a very timely and exciting position on the cutting edge of climate science. My job as a general field assistant and ice core driller lasted over four summers. With it came the opportunity to make a video film, *Ice Core Time Machine*, describing the NSF project. I managed to sell several hundred copies to schools, as well as offer it on Amazon.

To all the Key Guys and Gal I extend my deepest gratitude and many thanks for the help you've given me to get started in so many different directions. It's been real fun.

More Reflections

Looking back, I believe I inherited some of my minimalist character from my mother. She taught me how to do the most with the least. Although she hardly grew up in any kind of want or lack of material goods she always was driven to save even the smallest amount. Ahead of her times in the 1940s and 50s, she was the prototype environmentalist, saving odd bits of string, paper bags and old food in the fridge to be recycled into tomorrow's lunch. Much like me, she would have completely ignored the "best if used before" phrase found in supermarkets.

And of course, she loved her vegetable garden with strange variants such as oyster plant, eggplant, kohlrabi, swiss chard, so on; mostly nonstandard types. Her "less is more" efficiency inspired me, and I implemented it throughout my life.

As I became a home owner, I was careful to recognize the importance of house siting as our first home was properly oriented with long axis perpendicular to the south for maximum sun exposure. The eighteenth century designers got it right with lots of windows on the south and few or none on the north, with caution on the east and west against overheating. Of the eleven houses I've owned (not including those rented), only four — Amesbury, Cutler, Bowdoin, and Whiting were correctly oriented; the others were off-axis, making it harder to heat or cool. These four were also eighteenth and nineteenth century buildings, where orientation was an important requisite.

The Cutler house was, perhaps, the best example of putting into practice many energy efficient principles. Over several years, we spent a good deal of the time and money with improvements in the entire house: blown-in insulation, Window Quilts on all the windows, a high efficiency wood cook stove with hot water jacket to run radiators, solar hot water, and a south-facing greenhouse attached to the front porch. Unfortunately, we didn't stay long enough to reap the savings and comfort.

I wistfully look back with a longing to have had the opportunity to have designed and built the "perfect" energy efficient house. But my life as an oceanographer never allowed me to find the perfect site, or have time and money for such a venture — maybe in my next existence. Today, I remain committed to using less more efficiently.

We live in an era of ever increasing power use, which reminds me of President Eisenhower's belief that the newly-created generation of nuclear power would be "too cheap to meter." As we have seen, it was a hope never achieved, as nuclear electricity has been neither cheap nor safe. Some people believe that nukes will be our savior. I still favor using less and that we can't continue to use more without paying with some unpleasant consequences. Others are convinced that we can get ourselves out of the impending dilemma by our recently discovered development of hydro fracking for enormous amounts of oil and gas; their argument is that new technologies will prevail and provide. Perhaps the use of solar and wind will increase in various parts of the country, especially offshore. I wish I could be around in the next decade or two to see the outcome of our divergent courses. Or maybe I shouldn't wish. It's for the grandchildren to deal with. I hope they do better than our generation has.

Chapter Twenty-Three

Things Change

Looking back, I was perhaps too close to everyday events to see clearly that things were changing with Ellie's medical condition. In the fall of 2014 she began having problems with dehydration and her chemical balance, which meant more frequent visits to Mass General, usually for several days at a time. On these visits, she would get a dose of fluids and be fine...or so I thought. She was her old chipper self; she was never in pain and her thinking was fine. She had to get around with a walker and was having difficulties getting in and out of the car. I took her to her book group meetings in Newton where she enjoyed being with her longtime friends. I spent a large part of every day being a caregiver but I never resented it.

I recall her primary care physician, Dr. Michael Bierer, telling me as we stood outside her hospital room in mid-December, that her kidney function was below 10% and that the end could come at any time and would be quite swift, but I paid little attention to his comments seeing how strong she seemed.

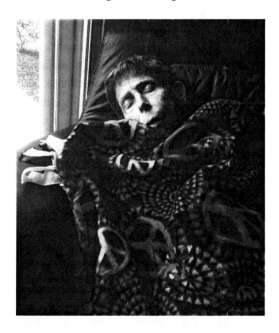

Ellie asleep with her Christmas blanket, 2014

Earlier, she and I had decided to take the train and spend Christmas with Julie and, although it would have been a grueling trip for her, we had even made reservations. Then Julie called in December to say she and Rick and the dogs would like to come for Christmas. It turned out to be a wonderful solution. Julie and Rick arrived along with Robert who came from Utah and David from California a day later. We had one of those perfect holiday gatherings in Lexington with a grand dinner .We all spent hours cooking in our small, crowded kitchen. Ellie was in great shape and it was like a story book Christmas. The "kids" left the next day. It was so good that I, as the eternal optimist, had no inkling as to how little time was left.

Around New Year's, at the loving urge of several relatives, Ellie agreed to try hospice care. Dr. Bierer had suggested this earlier but she had strongly refused. In early January we began receiving frequent visits from Karla from the Wellesley hospice office. At this point we understood that the goal was to keep Ellie comfortable even though she wasn't in pain. The previous weeks had become rather difficult as she got slower and slower. Her three-times-daily medications, and frequent bathroom trips brought me to the point of exhaustion. I felt like I was being dragged over a cliff.

It was on Monday, January 12 that her kidneys finally failed. She objected violently to everything we tried but luckily, Karla and her helper, Michelle had just come along and they took over. They managed to calm her down, and she rested peacefully in her bed. From this point we had round the clock help from Michelle and another caregiver, Paula who spent lots of time with her.

On Wednesday, she looked at me with her cute little smile and said "I'm fine"! It wasn't till much later that I understood what she meant. She realized, before I did, that she was transitioning and all was well. Then at about five forty five that evening she sat up in bed, throwing off the covers, and said to Paula "I want to go to work." Paula replied, "But Ellie, it's quarter to six in the evening, you're not going to school." She was, I thought, referring to her spiritual work. These may have been her last words. All that evening I kept whispering to her "I love you." They said she probably heard but could make no reply. I quietly crawled into bed with her at about mid-night. Michelle came in at about twelve thirty just to check up. We were both sound asleep. At one fifteen in the morning of January 15, I woke suddenly to realize she was no longer breathing. And that was it. At about two thirty, the hospice nurse came over to do the paper work. Ellie was off to better things no longer having to drag her little body around.

The next several months was a seemingly never-ending course of meeting with lawyers and financial advisors, going over wills and trusts, closing joint bank accounts, and reducing the number of credit cards that we had shared over the years. It was, in fact, a simplification of my new life. I had no idea how complicated the departure of a loved one could be.

The memorial service, with family and friends from all over the country, was on July 29 in Portland aboard the Casco Bay Lines Ferry, *Bay Mist*. About 85 people showed up to share their memories of Ellie. We had a catered lobster bake aboard as we tied up to the dock in Diamond Cove near Peaks Island. It was a most memorable event and a great send off. We had been married for nearly 30 years. My pal, best friend, and dear wife were, and are, terribly missed.

The rest of the year whizzed by as Amie helped me put the Potter Pond house on the market. With the skilled help of a "stager", it sold in several weeks. I put most things in storage and took my books and small items to Peaks Island in my new Subaru Outback, a real work horse.

My house on Peaks Island where I moved full time in winter the of 2015

Although OK for a while, I find living alone is not for me. I have a group of women friends that I dine out or have coffee with from time to time, but nothing romantic. I still have little flashes when waking from a nap, of Ellie's lying as usual on her couch. Roger Angell says it took him a year to get over the same sensation after his wife died.

Winter arrived very late in 2015, with six to eight inches of snow and cold and I am slowly getting accustomed to my cozy little house. I eargerly look forward to planning for the installation of solar panels on my roof and working toward energy independence. As Mrs. Eddy says in the beginning of *Science and Health,* "To those leaning on the sustaining infinite, today is big with blessings," or as my mother writes at the end of her book, *The Color of the Country,* "The best is yet to be."

So How Does the Future of the Earth End?

T.S. Eliot in "The Hollow Men" (1925) says in the final stanza, may be the most quoted of all of Eliot's poetry

This is the way the world ends
This is the way the world ends
This is the way the world ends
Not with a bang but a whimper

Or more aptly Robert Frost wrote in "Fire and Ice"

Some say the world will end in fire,
Some say in ice.
From what I've tasted of desire
I hold with those who favor fire.
But if it had to perish twice,
I think I know enough of hate
To say that for destruction ice
Is also great
And would suffice.

Finally, my favorite closing poem as a sailor and explorer is from last of "Ulysses" by Alfred Lord Tennyson

'Tis not too late to seek a newer world.
Push off, and sitting well in order smite
The sounding furrows; for my purpose holds
To sail beyond the sunset, and the baths
Of all the western stars, until I die.
It may be that the gulfs will wash us down:
It maybe we shall touch the Happy Isles,
And see the great Achilles, whom we knew.
Tho' much is taken, much abides; and tho'
We are not now that strength which in old days
Moved earth and heaven, that which we are, we are;
One equal temper of heroic hearts,
Made weak by time and fate, but stong in will
To strive, to seek, to find, and not to yield.

But I couldn't end the poems without Eliot's Prufrock's lament:

I should have been a pair of ragged claws scuttling across the
floors of silent seas...

My Life with Cars

The first car I can remember is my father's 1935 Ford Phaeton, a four-door convertible with a V-8 engine and a three-speed manual floor shift. We were living in Paoli, Pennsylvania.

No. 1: 1940 Plymouth "woody" station wagon.
It had a 6-cylinder in line 84 hp engine with a three-speed manual shift on the column. When I was eleven years old my father taught me to drive it from the house to the barn close by where it was kept every night. What a great first job to bring it up the lane to the house. This car lasted us all through World War II to 1946.

No. 2: 1946 Willys Jeep CJ 2A
It was one of the first vehicles available after the War. It had four-wheel drive high and low range gears. It could double as a light tractor on a farm. It had an eight-speed manual transmission floor mounted with two and four-wheel drive. I used to drive it on back roads in early mornings at age fifteen with no license. The Jeep became mine at age sixteen when I got my license and drove some thirty miles each day to school in Haverford in 1948. Shortly after my sixteenth birthday I was involved in the serious accident with an eighteen-wheel truck. Although hospitalized for six days, I survived. The Jeep was repaired and I continued driving it through 1950 when I graduated from Haverford School.

No. 3: 1949 Studebaker two-door coupe, green.
My father helped me pick my next car which turned out to be a good choice for the many trips it made from home to Colby College in Waterville, Maine. It got good gas mileage because it had overdrive, a new addition like a fifth gear although it was electronically switched. I took many of my classmates back and forth at vacations from Colby. At the end of my sophomore year I sold the Stupidbaker and began with Fords.

No. 4: 1937 Ford two-door, black, $175
I was now ready to buy my own car with my own money and advice from Pete Welles who later became my best college friend. He had a family summer house on Southport Island near Boothbay. The town clerk was selling her car for $175. I was eager to buy it in spite of its burning a little oil. Too late, I

discovered my naïve mistake driving it on a vacation. I had to stop and add oil every 100 miles. Good old dad came to the rescue treating me to a rebuilt 100 hp V-8 engine to replace the original 85 hp. But the car's days were numbered by rust, treacherous mechanical brakes, and fourteen brutal Maine winters. Pete and I went looking for a newer body for the 100 hp engine. After searching dooryards and back rows of dealer's lots we found the perfect match in the Airport Garage in Brunswick.

No. 5: 1941 Ford V-8 Deluxe convertible, pale blue, $100
On a bitter cold February day, Pete drove the '37 Ford and I steered the '41 in tow for an hour and a half ride to Waterville with the top down; brrr! We found someone to do the engine transplant and I had a great car for several years even making a summer round trip to Casper, Wyoming where roommate Derek Tatlock and I worked in the oil fields. That car lasted me up till my final year at Colby and was one of my best cars, certainly for the cost.

No. 6: 1948 Mercury V-8, four-door black, $600
This was probably one of the worst cars I owned with serious electrical problems and other winter ills. I was glad to get rid of it and go back to Fords.

No. 7: 1939 Ford V-8 beach wagon, $35
Another Woody but in bad shape. The wood had been painted a light gray and only the front seat was covered. The local dealer in Waterville was asking $50 but we got him down to $35. We were both near broke and couldn't afford registration. I had found a Wyoming plate the year before and decided to use it and made a fake inspection sticker out of a chewing gum wrapper. We somehow made several trips to Southport that spring without incident. College kids get away with a lot.

No. 8: 1949 Ford V-8, four-door green, $500
During the summer of 1954 instead of getting s job related to my upcoming graduate work in oceanography, I decided to work at the local A & P market so I could also race sail boats with Pete on Saturdays. I had Wednesdays off and I would drive cars back from Peabody, Mass. for Honest John the local car dealer. I realized my old '41 Ford probably wouldn't make it to Texas and grad school, so John let me pick a real nice car at the auction for a wholesale price. Another winner-Ford that made 18 round trips from Texas to my home in Pennsylvania and lasted over two years.

No. 9: 1950 Jaguar XK-120 roadster, white, $995
I met Pete in Fort Lauderdale, Florida during spring break. By this time, he had inherited a large amount of money from his parents, and was driving a fancy Jaguar XK 140MC. He said it was time to pay me back for the $35 I loaned him for the beach wagon. We went shopping and wound up with the XK-120 plus a lot of repairs. In my usual renegade manner, I just switched plates from the 49 Ford and drove without insurance. I had to return to my graduate work and on the way north, we stopped at the Daytona Beach race. Great fun with all the international drivers. Of course, I got stopped for a headlight violation and managed to talk my way out of an illegal registration. Those college kids! The Jag saw me through two more years in Texas and my MS in Oceanography. I finally sold it to an Electrical Engineering professor.

No. 10: 1948 Oldsmobile 98 straight-8 convertible, gift from Karyl's father
Karyl Mader, my sweetheart from Boothbay days, and I were married in 1957 in Needham, Mass. Her father gave us his 1948 Oldsmobile convertible for our trip back to Texas, Although it was hardly my type of car it got us through the next year with only the $150 expense of repairing the electric windows. By June I had an offer of a job in Woods Hole, Mass. And the Olds was not the car for the moving trip.

No. 11: 1949 Dodge ½ ton pick up. blue, $300
The Agriculture Department was selling a freshly painted truck that seemed right for the trip. We added a fourteen-foot trailer with all our stuff and made it without a problem. But I couldn't be content with an old truck and went looking for something more sporty for my job at US Fish and Wildlife Service.

No. 12: 1956 MG-A roadster, bright green, $2500
The "A" was an inexpensive British sports car with two seats, wire wheels. and a four-speed shift. Great for a young married couple but with minimal trunk space. It got us through the winter, but when we heard strange engine noises on a trip to Pennsulvania, it was time again to find a dependable means of commuting from our new home in Amesbury to Cambridge. A brand-new Volvo was the answer.

No. 13: 1959 Volvo P 544 two-door, blue, $2495
It was the ideal commuter for our forty-mile trip to Boston. I dropped Karyl in the city and went to my new job at Smithsonian Astrophysical Observatory on the Harvard campus. Over the year or so we drove the 544 for 175,000 miles. It was one of the best cars for the cheap price of $2495 and few repairs.

No. 14: 1948 Chevy four-door, black, $750
I found this classic American beauty appealing; it was used lightly by Karyl and was one of several American antique cars I dabbled with.

No. 15: 1964 SAAB 850 GT Monte Carlo two-door, bright red $3500
I decided it was time to try the other Swedish car. The 850 was a two-cycle, three-cylinder, 57 hp engine. Instead of adding oil to the fuel, the 850 had a gear driven mixer, a real advantage. Our family now with child -- Amy age one -- set off on a trip to take a new job in California. In the open roads of the west we cruised in great comfort in aircraft style seats at 75 to 80 mph. Later, back on the east coast, we found that it was prone to drowning in heavy rain. Karyl decided it was time for a more conventional American car.

No. 16: 1963 Ford Fairlane V-8 Station wagon $1500
What's to say but it was big, squashy and totally dependable. It served us well as a tow car for No. 17.

No. 17: 1957 SAAB 93B two-door, two-cycle 38hp, , blue, $35
I found this faded blue, forlorn car under a drift of snow in the back row of Gasto Andre's Used Cars in Framingham, Mass. It had belonged to a Vietnam vet and was one of the first SAABs in the US, with front opening "suicide" doors, and free-wheeling transmission. It could cruise at 65 mph. The salesman Carl Hard was happy to move it for $35. We towed it to Annapolis behind the Ford; it lasted 20,000 miles until it rusted away.

No. 18: 1964 Volvo 544, two-door, black, $2000
I have no memory of any details on this one but it's on the list.

No. 19: 1964 SAAB 93F two-door, two-cycle, black, $2500
This replaced the worn out 93B and like all SAABs, except 850, required a quart of oil with every eight gallons of gas. Sometime that year I loaned it to a friend who didn't believe you had to add oil. That was the end of the engine but not our friendship.

No. 20: 1967 Volvo P1800 four-cylinder Sports Coupe, gray, $5000
I was intrigued by the Italian design and sleek look and thought it was time to try a Volvo again. After a year of sporty driving we realized it was too small for three of us.

No. 21: 1965 SAAB two-cycle station wagon, blue, $2000
SAAB had just come out with its first wagon, which seemed right for us with a hatchback door. It was 1969; Amy was now five and Neil Armstrong was walking on the moon.

No. 22: 1968 Volvo 544 wagon, white, $4500
This was one of the few brand-new cars I bought. At this point I had a job in Miami so the air-conditioned car sounded perfect. When our small startup company, Oceans General, failed and I found employment quickly in La Jolla, but I found that the high compression Volvo engine wouldn't run on the low-grade California gas and annoyingly knocked and pinged.

No. 23: 1948 Plymouth two-door antique sedan, $750
For the year we were in Florida, I couldn't resist another oldie and used the '48 to go to work and once to the Sebring International Races. It was not for California and was sold.

No. 24: 1961 Mercedes 190 four-door sedan, black, $950
What cars did the people in La Jolla drive? Mercedes of course! We found ours at a repair/dealer who was very German, Heinz Geitz. The car was in perfect condition and we were pleased with it.

No. 25: Mercedes 180 diesel four-door, blue, $700
Now that Karyl was a free-lance, artist she needed a car to get around the San Diego region; we found this one in the newspaper. The 180 was small and cute and for $700, how could we go wrong? Later, when the water pump failed, we realized that Mercedes parts were expensive; the only one available came from Florida at $700!

No 26: 1939 Plymouth four-door, $700
I kept my interest in antique cars with this oldie although I didn't drive it a lot. It braved the hills of La Jolla.

No. 27: 1962 Mercedes 220S four-door, six-cylinder. grey, $2000
This was one of Heinz's cream puffs, so we went on a coastal road trip through Big Sur but on a slight grade at a modest 50 mph, a large dog bolted across the road. The car ahead was able to stop but we weren't. The lovely 220S was badly crumpled as designed; no one was hurt but No. 27 was totaled.

No. 28: 1968 VW Type 2, Kombi van, tan, $2500

Replacing the 220S, we took a sharp turn and chose a VW Camper. We had taken to the hills of California and car camping. Also, every September Karyl went to a church meeting in Boston so this seemed the perfect way to do it. It had bunks and a galley just like a home; Amy and Karyl loved it but I thought it a bit slow especially in a head wind.

No. 29: 1957 Mercedes 220S, four-door, six-cylinder, beige, $950

I decided to go back to the older Mercedes that were hand assembled and found one that had been rebuilt by a Navy chief. Inside was the classic wood and red leather that was so desirable. We had decided that we should return to the east coast and live closer to the family and the old car made the 2500-mile trip as if new. For the next three years, I put the car away in the garage to protect it from the road salt and ice. In 1975 I put it up for sale at $2200 and it went immediately. It was the best of my antique cars.

No. 30: 1972 SAAB 96 V-4, two-door, white, $2500

I needed a good car to commute from Southport to Portland every day and the SAAB was the car for the rugged Maine climate. By now, realizing that the two-cycle engine, with the oil and gas mix was a liability, SAAB put a four-cylinder Ford Taurus engine in the 96 model body. For several years, our 96 went for over 250,000 miles including a cross country trip to California. It finally met its fate when Amie and her friends rolled it over due to an oncoming car just south of Machias. No one hurt but car was totaled. My friend John Dandy managed to transplant the engine to another SAAB.

No 31: 1950 Chevy ½ ton pick-up with stake bed, blue $250

This would be Karyl's car to continue her freelance artist jobs. It ran okay, but lacked a heater for those bitter winter days. She braved them with heavy boots and her mom's raccoon coat. Its fate came some years later when Judy, Amie, John, and I were side swiped on an icy road to South Harpswell; we were all in the front seat. The poor old truck was junked at the famous Airport Garage for $25.

No. 32: 1978 SAAB 99 EMS four-door, red $2500

By this time, we had moved to Cutler in eastern Maine and I thought I should try out the latest SAAB 99. It had an all-new 1.8 liter, four-cylinder 110 hp engine and new body style, but it wasn't made the rough eastern Maine roads and in a year the front end disintegrated. For a nearly-new car it was a disappointment.

No. 33: GMC 1 ton stake bed with plow, black and ugly, $700
At this point we were living in Bowdoin in the house Judy and I had rebuilt. We knew we would need plow come winter, so I found a rugged-looking truck with one. It was fun and practical and when spring came we were on the move again to Cutler and the old truck made over 29 trips back and forth with all our stuff.

No. 34: 1969 SAAB 96 V-4 two-door, blue, $2200
In spite of the bum 99, I was still a big SAAB fan so, on Valentine's day I bought another 96 from Clyde Billing in Augusta. It became our number one vehicle while in Cutler and we finally sold it in 1982 for $650 at our moving yard sale.

No. 35: 1972 International ½ ton stake bed pick up, green, $1500.
I found it at a dealer near Cook's Corner. Perfect for our now established nomadic life. From Cutler and the Little River Lodge days, we moved to Whiting with the truck. Then a year later to Dover-Foxcroft, where I started my Window Quilt business.

No. 36: Isuzu Diesel ½-ton pick-up, tan, $8500
My first diesel, it got 38 mpg and ran wonderfully in Maine winters. At the time, I was working in Brewer at the Black Stove Shop and staying at Amie's apartment in Bangor during the week and home to Whiting on the weekends. Again a good commuter. The truck served us well to our final home on Peaks Island although we left it on the main land where I used it in my business and we had to buy an "island car."

No. 37: 1970 Ford V-8 van, green, $500
For nearly seven years it became our "island car" with no problems and no body rust. Another good investment, but it finally gave out, so I brought the Isuzu to the island and looked for a better mainland car.

No. 38: 1987 Isuzu ½-ton gas pick up, two-tone grey, $11,000
It was new and very comfortable for a truck, and it had never been registered. It served me well in my business for nine years. In 1996, when I became a salesman for Window Quilt in Brattleboro, Vermont, I decided that I should move up into a respectable vehicle, not a truck. So back to SAABs I went.

No. 39: 1992 SAAB 9000 hatchback, five-speed, citron beige, $15,000
For seven years, I drove all over New England as a sales rep putting on 192,000 miles by 2003. The hatchback would take materials up to one hundred inches long; as good as a truck for my shades.

No. 40: 1994 SAAB 9000 CS, five-speed, citron Biege, $17,000
This was to be Ellie's going-to-school car as well as mine at times. By 2007, it had developed a starting problem as well as the typical body rust around the door. Village SAAB was uninterested in our problems so we turned to another car.

No. 41: 1984 SAAB 900, five-speed, blue, $1350.
We had to assign our 1997 Isuzu to the rust graveyard and this became our new "island car." I found it in Reading, Mass and it survived several hard years on Peaks but had serious body rust, too. Repair was not the answer, so John's SAAB in South Portland took it for junk at no cost to me.

No. 42: 1993 SAAB 900S, five-speed, red, $3500
I found it in Acton, Mass from a private owner, who had bought it new from Village SAAB. It was too nice to be an "island car" as it was in almost-perfect condition with only 101,000 miles. The red finish was beautiful; I was so proud of it, then disaster struck. When left the island each week I would park it on Welch Street by the VFW. Some drunk decided to damage the car by "keying" it with long gouges. From there on it was downhill for the beautiful car. Although it lasted till 2016, the power steering went out, the brakes were bad and it was hard to start. Time for another burial. I sold it to John Kamp for $65; sad.

No. 43: 1999 SAAB 9-5, five-door, five-speed, citron beige, $17,000
We found this one at Cold Spring SAAB in Skowhegan, Maine; a four-year-old leased car, with only 20,000 miles on it. It had special features such air flow seat for summer use, marine band radio, and a 100,000-mile warranty. Like its predecessors, it began to make strange, loud engine noises right around that magic 100,000-mile mark; time yet for another replacement.

No. 44: 2003 SAAB 9-5, five-door, five-speed wagon, smoke gray, $20,000
I decided I needed the extra space the wagon had, so I asked my dealer friend, Joey to find me one with low mileage and in good shape. After three months, he produced the perfect one with only 28,000 miles and three years old. In ten years of my window business I got to 195,000 miles and it became an "island car" in 2016.

No. 45: 2008 SAAB 9-3 Aero Sport, four-door, peach grey, $20,000
This was the replacement for Ellie's aging 9000. The Aero was the top of the line with a 285 hp, six-cylinder engine and the amazing acceleration that she wanted; and 32-34 mpg highway mileage. Also, as part of GM, it had rain sensitive automatic windshield wipers and it beeped when she backed up. But by 2015 when Ellie passed on, I had no need for the car and sold it before leaving Lexington to move to Peaks Island.

No. 46: 2015 Subaru Outback, five-door, automatic, tungsten metallic, $33,000
Knowing that my 2003 SAAB was terminal, and the SAAB brand no longer existed, I turned to Subaru, like many of my friends had. My local dealer in South Portland had new 2015 Outback with every possible accessory that seemed just right; otherwise there would be a three-month wait to order one so, I took it in March of 2015. Now two and a half years and 40,000 miles later, I have to admit it's probably the best car I've owned. With the safety features and alarms it's the next step to the self-driving car; just around the corner.

No. 47: 2004 SAAB 9-5, four-door, midnight blue $1995
To end on a SAAB note, the old trusty 2003 SAAB 9-5 "island car," not wanting to face another winter, finally packed, up so I found a gem of a car at Portland Motor Sales. It had belonged to the daughter of the owner, John Gove, a former Peaks Island resident. With 195,000 miles, it was inspected and in good-running order; it's just what I needed. Let's hope SAABs live forever!

Index

N

R

S

U

V

W

Y

Z

GRATEFUL

My camp nickname at the Greenland Ice Core Project was "Grateful Ned" and in looking back over my past years, I do have a lot to be grateful for.

I am grateful for my childhood with two unusually-caring parents, both artist and writers who early on inspired me to find and follow my own path. I was raised on a ninety-acre farm in rural Pennsylvania surrounded by a huge library of books. As an only child, I spent much of my time around grown-ups.

I was always forgiven, never scolded, even when I wrecked the family car. Only now, in retrospect, can I appreciate my parents love.

Throughout my professional life I have been grateful for my many colleagues who helped me succeed in my diverse choice of careers.

And for my daughter Amie who got me started on this project.

So here I am, a truly GRATEFUL NED.

I wish thank those who helped bring all the pieces of the book together in this fifteen year project:

Suzanne Fox who suggested my camp name, Grateful Ned, for the book title.

Rex Passion who assembled and edited my text and photos.

David Vincent who solved our computer problems and helped with promotional materials.

Mira Ptacin for her literary insights and inspiration.

And finally, my daughter, Amie, who got this project underway in 2004 asking me to tell her some things about the family as we had few living relatives. Thanks Amie.

Ned Shenton
Peaks Island, Manie, 2018

CPSIA information can be obtained
at www.ICGtesting.com
Printed in the USA
FFOW03n1148180618
47147892-49731FF